# PROTECT THE LIVING WORLD ON OUR MOTHER EARTH

(Food & Water Security, Environment Protection, and Adaptation to Climate Change – Imminent Needs of the Living World)

VIDYANAND RANADE

**BLUEROSE PUBLISHERS**
India | U.K.

Copyright © Vidyanand Ranade 2025

All rights reserved by author. No part of this publication may be reproduced, stored in a retrieval system or transmitted in any form or by any means, electronic, mechanical, photocopying, recording or otherwise, without the prior permission of the author. Although every precaution has been taken to verify the accuracy of the information contained herein, the publisher assumes no responsibility for any errors or omissions. No liability is assumed for damages that may result from the use of information contained within.

BlueRose Publishers takes no responsibility for any damages, losses, or liabilities that may arise from the use or misuse of the information, products, or services provided in this publication.

For permissions requests or inquiries regarding this publication,
please contact:

BLUEROSE PUBLISHERS
www.BlueRoseONE.com
info@bluerosepublishers.com
+91 8882 898 898
+4407342408967

ISBN: 978-93-6783-002-4

Cover Design: Sadhna
Typesetting: Pooja Sharma

First Edition: January 2025

# Dedication

Dedicated to those Scientists, Engineers, Environmentalists and Social Activists who have relentlessly contributed for protection of the Environment and the Natural Ecosystems, to make our Living World more habitable for the Plant kingdom and Animal kingdom, including humans, on Our Mother Earth.

# Author's Note About the Book

Solar energy, Air, Water and Land, are the four life support systems for the 'Living World' on our earth. All these resources are freely available for the terrestrial and aquatic ecosystems, which evolved, developed, and modified, always remaining compatible to the availability of these resources at any place and time on the earth. Spark of life kindled on the 4,600-million-year-old earth about 3,650 million years before. Plants and animals evolved since then by the process of natural selection. Very recently the primates gradually evolved into *'homo sapiens'* – wise man – around 0.3 million years ago and later entered on the scene as 'modern man' around 12,000 years ago. With the entry of modern man on the scene, composition of the living world started to change very rapidly. He firstly encroached on the land resource i.e., terrestrial ecosystems – forests – to grow pastures for domesticated cattle and to grow food grain crops to meet his food needs. It was the start of destruction of forests, which has continued unabated even at present. Out of the above four natural resources, only water is a renewable resource and more importantly is amenable for its development, management, and use, to meet various needs of the humans. Land resource has been a medium for producing food for his survival and for meeting his other developmental needs.

Food needs and various competing demands of water for his rising population have been continuously increasing rapidly during the last more than 2 centuries, inevitably at the cost of corresponding reduction in the availability of water for the terrestrial & aquatic ecosystems and causing their destruction and degradation. It was the start of qualitative degeneration of most of the riverine ecosystems due to unplanned water use for the urban growth centres & for the industries. 'Slash and burn' technique adopted in the past to bring forest land under cultivation had resulted in carbon emissions and had stopped the carbon sequestration that was automatically taking place continuously through trunks and branches of the growing trees. Some agricultural operations (ponded paddy crop) and tending of domestic flatulent animals by the humans have increased emission of methane gas, which is more potent than the carbon dioxide - one of the greenhouse gases. Use of fossil fuels for thermal power generation and for the industries has resulted in phenomenal increase in carbon emissions during last two centuries. Use of mineral oil and natural gas by the transport sector has also increased the carbon emissions very rapidly during the last century. Emission of all these greenhouse gases in the atmosphere has obstructed reflection of solar energy back into space, to cause increase in the temperature of the globe, which has resulted in 'Global Warming'. Such rise in temperature of the atmosphere around the earth has imposed adverse impacts on the climate, which is called as the 'Climate Change'. These effects are detrimental to some developmental sectors of which water sector and agriculture sector are the prominent ones.

Having worked in the water sector in the Maharashtra state (India) for 34 years, I gained field experience about all aspects of the development, management, use and governance of water resource to meet various competing and conflicting needs of the people. I had worked as a Consulting Engineer in in the Philippines for one year and in Ethiopia, Kenya, Uganda, Zambia etc. in the African continent. I had also worked as Consulting Engineer for more than 20 years in Micro Irrigation Systems for a world-famous company in the Maharashtra state. While presenting papers & posters and participating in the deliberations of more than 30 National and International conferences in India and abroad, I became aware about the latest trends in the water sector and about severity of various water related problems faced by many countries of the world. First challenging problem was about lack of sustainable food & water security to the underdeveloped countries of the world and the second one was about severe pollution of rivers in most of the developing and underdeveloped countries of the world.

In the year 1992, I wrote a book in English titled as 'Reservoirs and Environment', based on comprehensive study of two major dam-canal projects in the Maharashtra state. It highlighted benefits of such projects for irrigation and other purposes, but also emphasised the need to minimise their inevitable adverse impacts on the environment during their planning stage itself. I have suggested some measures to mitigate them and planted about 1 million trees in the project area, out of which about 0.7 million had survived. In the year 2004, I had written a book in 'Marathi' – my mother tongue and language of the Maharashtra state – on 'Watershed Development technology and technique', a subject which was important for the water related development of small and marginal farmers in the upper reaches of the river basins where no other irrigation facilities were available. Between 2004 and 2009 I had written 50 articles in 'Marathi' covering various aspects of the subject 'Water' in a magazine.

In the year 2021, my 345-page book covering all aspects of integrated water resource development, use and management, written in 'Marathi' and titled as 'पाण्या तुझा रंग कसा?' was published by 'Rajhans Prakashan' - the publishers. It covered all technical details of the subject 'Water Resource' for the benefit of in-service engineers, administrators, policy makers, social workers, and Non-Govt Organisations working in the water sector. It highlighted the serious issues before all states in India such as uncontrolled river pollution, need for involvement of water users in the management of water, improvement in the water-use efficiency in all its uses, adoption of modern irrigation systems, preparedness to adapt to the adverse effects of climate change in the future etc. Because these issues could be resolved in the state only by the initiative of policy makers, copies of the book were given to Hon. Ministers, elected representatives of the State Assembly & the Parliament - National Assembly. Copies of the book were given to the administrative heads of all the departments which were involved in the development, use and management of the water resource in the Maharashtra state. Copies of the Book were also issued for libraries in the offices of all engineers, administrators and organisations looking after water sector in the state Govt. It was expected that this action would create awareness about water-related issues amongst policy makers and implementers and positive action would be taken to improve the present grave but restorable situation. With a view to achieving 'Sustainable Development' – *'Meeting needs of the present generation without sacrificing needs of the future generations'*, necessary enabling Acts would be passed, and rules would be framed to improve the degrading situation. In accordance with them, it was hoped that the executing agencies would carry out implementation of those policies to resolve these problems on a sustainable basis.

For presenting papers in various International Conferences starting from nineties of the last century, I had studied various issues related to the integrated development and management of water resource. I had carried out exhaustive study of one representative river basin (14,700 square kilometres catchment area) in the Maharashtra state, in the Peninsular India and prepared a document in the year 2002 titled as *'Vision for the development of upper Bhima basin by 2025'*. Same was presented and discussed in the first South Asia Water Forum held in Kathmandu, Nepal in the year 2002. Important issue of 'Interlinking of Rivers in India' was studied by me, and a paper was presented in the Yellow River Forum in China in 2005. Vital issue of Climate Change was studied, and paper titled as *"Adaptation of Water Sector to Global Warming and Climate Change"* was accepted for national conference held in Ahmedabad, India in 2013. From the field experience in the water sector gained by me as above during my service, and later during participation and exposure during the several International Conferences during last 2-3 decades, I became aware about some vital issues faced by many countries of the world. Further study indicated that, at the global level in all there were following three issues wherein all countries of the world would have to contribute in one way or the other, to resolve them.

First emerging problem before the underdeveloped countries was about the urgent need to achieve food and water security on a sustainable basis to their rapidly increasing population and simultaneously to take measures to reduce the present rate of rise of their population. Population of some developed countries is decidedly showing declining trends. Population of China has recently stabilised and that of India is likely to stabilise before 2050. But population of all the sub-Saharan countries in Africa and underdeveloped countries in Asia is rising at a fast rate and as per present trends it is likely to stabilise by 2100. It is absolutely essential for these countries to take strict measures to drastically slow down rate of rise of their population. Aim should be to plan in such a manner as to stabilise their population latest by 2075. All these underdeveloped countries at present have very poor infrastructure for water resource development and hence much less area is presently under irrigation. With the result, they have very low average productivity per hectare of land which is being cultivated mainly as rain-fed agriculture. Any severe drought in these countries in the near future, would certainly result in acute food grain shortage resulting in heavy casualties due to starvation.

Developed and developing countries having some surplus stock of food grains would then have to export it to enable them to face the grave drought situation to avoid deaths of people due to starvation. But it cannot be a permanent solution, and supportive actions as suggested below would have to be taken right earnestly by the developed countries of the world. Gravity of the problem is likely to increase further because frequency of severe droughts would certainly increase in the future due to adverse effects of the climate change. Due to implementation of well-planned actions to increase food grain production, India and China had achieved sustainable food and water security to their rising population during the third quarter of the twentieth century. Land productivity per hectare was appreciably increased by them due to substantial increase in the irrigation facilities created by construction of water resource development infrastructure on a large scale and by supplementing it with the 'green revolution' technology effectively introduced in the agriculture sector. It is essential for the underdeveloped countries to take similar actions to achieve sustainable food and water security.

Unfortunately, not much is discussed at the world level about the serious problem of lack of food and water security, which is imminent before the underdeveloped countries, and perhaps they may also not be aware of it. Only by providing assured irrigation to the rain-fed land, productivity per hectare can be increased by 2.5 to 3 times. However, they need financial support and technical assistance to create the capital-intensive infrastructure for water resource development on a large scale. Simultaneously, it is necessary to introduce latest technology in the agriculture sector to bring 'green revolution' and further increase their food grain productivity per hectare. Such actions would also reduce the rate of destruction of forest land to bring it under cultivation to increase total food grain production of the country as is being practiced at present. If such supportive actions are taken by the World Bank and other International Financing Agencies, there is possibility that these countries can achieve sustainable food and water security within the next two decades. United Nations Organisation should now take a lead role in bringing this issue before the developed countries and countries with emerging economies right earnestly, by organising special International Conferences. It is also necessary to monitor implementation of supportive actions by the donor countries as suggested above.

Second problem before the developing and underdeveloped countries, is about degradation of most of the rivers due to release of untreated or partially treated urban sewage and industrial effluent in the rivers. Most of the developed countries have gone through that phase during last century and had taken necessary actions to treat urban and industrial effluent fully prior to its release in the rivers. Special attention should hence be given in the world level conferences to this issue hereafter by reviewing present situation in all the above countries and by monitoring the activity of taking remedial measures to improve the situation. This action would have to be taken by the developing and underdeveloped countries, and they would certainly be benefitted by it. However, financial assistance may also have to be provided to some developing and underdeveloped countries to enable them to take suitable actions to treat the effluent prior to its release in rivers for restoring the polluted rivers to their natural state.

The third problem is a global problem about adverse impacts of the 'Climate Change' which is presently faced by all countries of the world. To limit these adverse impacts within safe limits, time bound actions are expected primarily by the developed countries and the countries with emerging economies. It is necessary to drastically reduce their 'greenhouse gas emissions' i.e., 'carbon and Methane emissions' to limit adverse impacts of climate change within the pre-decided acceptable safe limits of rise in the global temperature. Because reduction in carbon emissions by the underdeveloped countries would stall their development, financial assistance would have to be given to them by the developed countries to tide over the situation. United Nations Organisation has taken a lead role in bringing all countries on a common platform to deliberate on this vital issue. All out efforts are being taken to ensure that all the developed countries and countries with emerging economies commit themselves to the implementation of a time bound programme of reduction in their carbon emissions.

In the first issue of food & water security, development of 'Water Resource' plays the most crucial role. The second issue of river pollution has given rise to degradation of most of the aquatic ecosystems, and their restoration to natural state is essential. Water sector and the agriculture sector are vulnerable to the adverse effects of the third issue of 'Climate Change'. **Hence, I thought that all aspects of these three intimidating problems before to world should be covered in the book in full detail.** Since the element water is central to all the three problems, for the benefit of the reader, I thought it essential to elucidate about unique characteristics of 'Water' which have contributed significantly to the evolution of life on the earth. Same are covered in detail in the first chapter. Very interesting history of 3650 million years of evolution of life on the earth has been covered in detail in the second chapter. Evolution of life on the earth was an extremely slow process, but it was based on natural and logical principles. However, in the distant past the natural evolution process was subjected to some catastrophic interruptions because of the 'mass extinctions' and 'ice ages.' But after occurrence of all such calamities, every time the living world restored to a 'new normal' though very slowly, by following the same principles of natural selection. Evolution in the animal kingdom culminating to the species 'Homo Sapiens' – Wise Man, about 0.3 million years ago was a game changer. Perhaps the 'Mother Nature' was tired of monitoring the evolution during last 3,650 million years and decided to hand over the charge of regulating evolution thereafter to the intelligent species which she thought would be capable to take the decision-making process of evolution in its hand, for the good of the living world.

At the end of the last ice age about 12,000 years ago, the *Homo sapiens*, took the reins of the living world in his hand. Entry of the wise man on the earth was the start of emergence of changes in the natural process of evolution. Having the background and full knowledge about the extremely slow and principled process of natural evolution, one should read all the next chapters. **These chapters would elaborate how the man brought about revolution on the earth just within few thousand years to benefit him alone, with total disregard to the life of plants and animals in the terrestrial and aquatic ecosystems on the earth.** It took all the remaining chapters of the book (chapters 3 to 17) to cover activities of the 'Modern man' who entered on the scene very recently. Compared with long history of 3650 million years of the 'Living World', he has made significant undesirable impacts in many ways during this very short time. To begin with, he commenced destruction of forests i.e., the terrestrial ecosystems which is continuing even at present in many underdeveloped and some developing countries. He then started practicing irrigated agriculture to increase food productivity per hectare to meet needs of the rising population. Due to inadequacies in planning and implementing such measures to increase food grain production, there were millions of casualties due to food grain shortage during many severe droughts in the recent past in India and China.

On that background, creation of adequate infrastructure for water resource development on a large scale to increase area under irrigation was the first step which these countries had undertaken. As the technology advanced and necessary machinery & equipment for construction of the infrastructure was available, size of the water storage dams increased appreciably. It was essential to meet ever rising needs of water by the humans. Adoption of latest technology in the agriculture sector to bring the 'green revolution' into a reality was the second step. Full details of both these measures taken by India and China to achieve sustainable food and water security have been covered in full detail. Details of surface water and ground water resource development, use, and its management for different competing and conflicting uses of water for the humans have been extensively covered in the subsequent chapter No. 6 to 10. They cover in detail all aspects of development, use, management, and regulation of water resource. **This information would provide good guidance to the underdeveloped countries who are facing the problem of food and water security at present. They can increase the area under irrigated agriculture by constructing infrastructure for the development of water resource and concurrently bring 'Green Revolution' to achieve food and water security on a sustainable basis.**

During the last century, development and use of water resource has increased phenomenally in many developed and developing countries, which had affected most of the lotic and lentic ecosystems quantitatively and qualitatively. The issue of degradation of most of the rivers in the developing and underdeveloped countries due to release of partially treated or untreated urban and industrial effluent into the rivers has come to the forefront now. Details of extent and gravity of degradation of most of the aquatic ecosystems and remedial measures to resolve this problem are covered in the relevant chapters. To ensure optimum and equitable development of the water resource, necessity of imposing some governance and regulation has also been emphasised. Droughts and floods are the two extreme climatic events, and their intensity and frequency are certainly expected to increase because of the adverse impacts of the climate change. Measures to ameliorate their ill effects are elaborated in chapter No. 11. Concept of global warming and climate change has been explained in detail and the need to act by all countries of the world to limit its adverse impacts in the future is also highlighted. **History of evolution of life on the earth extending over 3,650 million years has been covered in the first two chapters, but to elaborate the complex dynamic relationship between man, water, environment, and the climate during the last 12,000 years, it has taken all the remaining chapters of the book to cover it.**

During the last 50 years, all aspects related to the water sector & human development and the climate change, have been discussed and deliberated at the world level in several international conferences initiated by the United Nations Organisation. Details of deliberations in such conferences and various activities carried out at the world level have certainly increased awareness about the problems and some actions were taken by the countries as committed by them in these conferences. It is felt that contents of the book would now draw attention of the developed countries to the dire need of providing financial assistance and technical guidance to the underdeveloped countries of the world to enable them to achieve sustainable food and water security during the years to come. International Financing Agencies are expected to take proactive role in providing them necessary financial assistance and technical guidance. India has the firsthand experience in this field and hence India can and should provide technical guidance and possibly some financial assistance to these countries. **The book would also act as a guide for these underdeveloped countries to initiate all actions necessary to ensure optimum & equitable development of water resource to increase area under irrigation and bring the green revolution into a reality.** It is essential to discuss at the world level, the issue of achieving food security by the least developed countries and to motivate the developed and the countries with emerging economies to take necessary supportive actions. Reduction in carbon emissions by the underdeveloped countries would affect their progress towards development. Assistance should hence be given to them by way of extending carbon credits. To confine ill effects of the climate change within pre-decided safe limits, drastic reduction in carbon emissions by the developed countries and countries with emerging economies does not appear to have any alternative at present. They would have to switch over to non-conventional sources of energy generation such as solar power, wind power, atomic energy etc. It is necessary on their part to commit to the time bound plans and to monitor their performance in the world level conferences periodically.

World famous thinker and philosopher 'Henry David Thoreau' had said *"If a man does not keep pace with his companions, perhaps it is because he hears a different drummer. Let him step to the music he hears, however measured or far away."* Majority of the people, thinkers and even some policy makers appear to be unaware of gravity of the serious problems as explained above which are being faced at present by our world. They do not appear to be aware about the necessity to act immediately on all fronts to confine their adverse effects within safe limits before they cross the 'threshold of irreversible stage'. It is essential on their part to listen to the *'Distant drums'*, and act before it is too late.

All countries of the world should now act like a 'World Family'. As per the Indian culture, it is the 'वसुधैव कुटुम्बकम'- *'Wasudhaiv Kutumbakam'* (i.e. World is one Family). Hence all countries of the world are part of that family and should behave like that to resolve all problems before the 'Living World'. It would then be the responsibility of the two elder brothers – developed countries and countries with emerging economies – to fulfil their primary responsibility to proactively act to resolve all the three issues amicably. First one would be to limit the adverse effects of the climate change within the pre-decided safe limits. Simultaneously it is also their responsibility to provide financial assistance and technical guidance to their weak younger brothers - the developing and underdeveloped countries - to enable them to achieve sustainable food & water security, environmental restoration of rivers and adapting to the adverse impacts of the climate change.

*'The standing boy of Nagasaki'* has become a symbol of unity in Japan. Motto of family of the Living World should hence be - *'He is my brother ... She is my sister. If they fall help them to rise. If they are weak support them to become strong'.*

**Vidyanand Ranade.**

# Acknowledgements

During my service of 34 years in the Irrigation Department of the Government of Maharashtra, India, I gained lot of field experience about the development, use and management of water resource in the state. It was very useful to me while writing some chapters of the book, and I am grateful to all my senior engineers for their valuable guidance during my career. I am grateful to Shri. P.R. Gandhi, retired engineer-Secretary who had been my guide and mentor during my service. My wife Seema looked after all household activities during this period, nurtured and guided our two sons during their formative age and till they graduated, married & well settled in their lives. I am grateful to her for taking on this responsibility, and only because of that I could concentrate in all the technical activities during my entire professional career.

Dr. M.A. Chitale, retired Secretary Water Resource, Govt. of India, who belonged to the Maharashtra cadre, had been my guide, motivator, well-wisher, and inspirator during last 30-35 years. Due to his encouragement & guidance, based on my field experience, I could prepare technical papers on various subjects about water resources and the environment. The same were accepted by the organisers, and I was invited to participate in more than ten international conferences held abroad between 1992 to 2006. I am very grateful and would remain indebted to him forever for the same. Participation and deliberations in these international conferences and many National conferences enabled me to learn about the latest issues in the water and the environment sector at the Global level. Based on this varied experience in the water sector, I had written a 345-page book in 'Marathi', my mother tongue and language of the state, about the multifaceted natural resource – Water. The book received an Award from the Govt. of Maharashtra in 2022, for contribution in the 'Environment sector,'. The Book also received two more awards by other institutions. This knowledge about water resources, food security, protection of the environment and climate change motivated me to write the present book which primarily deals with some imminent problems which are being faced by our living world. It is expected and hoped that necessary actions to mitigate their growing adverse impacts on the living world would be taken by all countries of the world.

While drafting some chapters of the book, some civil engineers, agriculture experts, and technical personnel had furnished very useful information to me. Dr. D.R. Bapat, Ex Director Research MPKV (Agri. University) and Dr. R.M. Patil, Scientist Agharkar Research Institute Pune, had furnished very useful information about the 'Green Revolution' in India. Mr. Franklin L. Khobung, Jt. Secy Ministry of Agriculture, GoI, and Mr. Somnath Jadhav from JISL Jalgaon, India had provided information about the trends of development and use of Micro Irrigation Systems in India and other countries of the world. I am thankful to Jain Irrigation Systems Ltd. Jalgaon, Maharashtra, India, because my association with them for more than 20 years, I learnt about scope of Micro Irrigation Systems in the future. Very exhaustive information about Water Resource Development in India and Maharashtra state has been compiled in the Book 'Integrated

Water Resource Management' Volume I & II – 1330 pages, (Year 2022) written by the Lead Author Dr. S.V. Dahasahastra, and four engineer co-authors. I am thankful to them for making available some information from the same for inclusion in this book. Prof. Dr. Sameer Shastri from Sinhagad Engineering College Pune furnished useful information about Sewage Treatment infrastructure. Mr. Shashank Deshpande, retired Sr. Geologist GSDA, Pune, provided useful information about groundwater development and use in the Maharashtra state. Mr. Sharad Chandorkar, Retd. Engineer from Water Resource Deptt. of GoM had reviewed the draft chapters and made some useful suggestions. I am grateful to all of them for their contribution which has added value to the contents of the book. All sketches in the chapters are drawn by the author. I am thankful to 'Rajhans Prakashan' Pune – publishers of my above 345-page book, for giving consent to include some sketches and some maps from that book for inclusion in this book.

I had forwarded text of draft chapters to Dr. M.A. Chitale, Retired Secretary Water Resources, Govt. of India and Retired Secretary General International Commission on Irrigation and Drainage, New Delhi, and to Dr. C.D. Thatte, Retired Secretary Water Resources, Govt. of India and Retired Secretary General International Commission on Irrigation and Drainage, New Delhi, for review and suggestions. I am grateful for his Observations by Dr. Chitale and for the Preface by Dr. Thatte. Dr. S.M. Seth, Ex Vice Chancellor Poornima University, Jaipur, India, had made some useful suggestions about contents of the Book. There are several websites such as Wikipedia, Britannica, Vedantu, Drishti, etc. which have taken lot of efforts to compile exhaustive information on various subjects and made it available free of cost for the benefit of the readers and researchers. Several such websites were accessed, and the information collected on the topics included in some chapters of the book was screened and corroborated prior to its inclusion in the final draft of each chapter. It was a time-taking & complex job and if there are any shortcomings in the text, the same is due to my inability to interpret and present the information properly. I desire to give full credit to the compilers of all these web sites, for the spread of information and knowledge they have acquired for the good of society.

Our younger son Abhijit and his wife Swati, both had read draft chapters of the book critically and made very useful suggestions in the text, from the viewpoint of a third-party non-technical reader. Both of them also helped in various issues about computer graphics and other things related to the presentation of the book. I am thankful to Mr. Nitin Kandhare, our driver, who has carried out all miscellaneous work such as xeroxing of draft chapters, making hard copies of the draft of the book & doing all other related work about the book.

If mention of any person who has contributed to drafting text of chapters of the book has remained, it is through oversight, and I may please be excused for the same.

**Vidyanand Ranade.**

# Observations

One way to look at the future is to treat it as a linear extrapolation of the current situations. With the rapid and sustained growth experienced by Europe in the past 3-4 centuries, that type of extrapolation is normally ingrained in the pattern of thinking. But civilisations with long history and culture as in India, social and economic changes are considered as a part of a wider cyclic phenomenon that takes place on the globe.

With new strides in science and technology, the time stream has shrunk. New style of human existence that took thousands of years to take shape in the past are not getting formulated within the life span of one generation. To cope with this rapidity is the current challenge before humans.

Evaporation patterns have a deep impact on the life cycles of the living beings on the earth. That aspect of the climatic behaviour will require more comprehensive detailed studies about what happens on the earth, as also about the changing patterns of solar radiations if any! Colourful rings exhibited in the cross-section of a tree are indicative of the alternating wet and dry periods of the climate experienced by the living beings on the earth. Width and frequency i.e. density of the rings per centimetre in the cross section of the tree trunk can give some clue to the range of the alternating changes in the climatic situation on the earth.

There is a risk of temptation to extrapolate over a longer time span the information gathered from the few centuries recent data. That information needs to be corroborated with indications from other sources and historical literature including *'Puranas'* (Ancient Indian culture) literature. Apparently, they were compiled to provide a glimpse of the long past, socially as well as climatically. How much hazy that may appear, they need to be studied and analysed in a scientific manner with academic rigour to understand the true story of human history over the long period.

This type of accumulated traditional wisdom in the civilisations with long history is now required to be checked with the recent new data available about the atmosphere on the earth. The longest time series about the climatic data is said to be developed by Hungary in the Eastern Europe and the river flow data for thousands of years by Egypt on the Nile. Written evidence about such type of evidence of information about Indian rivers is not yet forthcoming from the historical Indian literature or from the books in the Indian religious centre.

To formulate any definitive proposition in this respect, statistically we need information for about twenty such cycles at least; i.e. for over one thousand years. That much data is presently not available in a scientific manner. Compilation of data on these lines commenced in the recent history only four-five centuries ago. We will have to wait for many more years, continue to collect, compile, and analyse information about human activities in an organised manner on a long-term basis before anything definitive can be stated in this context.

Apart from the Indian concept of 'sixty years of climatic cycle', the descriptions of Indian history in terms of 'Yuga' (aeon/epoch) e.g. Treta yuga, Dwapar yuga etc., need to be critically analysed in depth in the context of climatic changes on this globe. Such descriptions about the transformations in the climate and the society are randomly spread through the *'Puranic'* (Ancient Indian culture) literature, e.g. *'Waman Purana'*. Their scientific and historical significance needs to be properly deciphered to understand more about the India's past in a more accurate manner.

In addition to the recorded human history about the past centuries, transformation from fossils is now being collected and analysed to understand the cycles of climatic changes. The indications are that changes on the globe are not linear and tangential. They appear to follow a cyclic pattern in nature.

As far as the climate on the earth is concerned, it is going through cyclic changes somewhat on similar lines as suggested by the rotational pattern of 'sixty years' in the Indian traditional science about the atmosphere on the earth. Specific names have been given to each year of this sixty years of cyclic exposition of the atmosphere on the earth like a *'A furious year'* or *'A year of plenty'*.

Food habits and references are quite different in the different parts of the world. They are influenced by the nature's productivity in the agricultural terms, grass lands, trees, water bodies and wetlands. Trees, creepers, grasses, each has a different role to play in the productivity, development, and its sustainability in the geographical area. There is no single pattern of 'green' land as such. An integrated pattern of these together gets evolved over many years of experience. Technology greatly influences the choices made by the society in the different parts of the world. An appropriate integrated package of varieties of green cover gets evolved over many years of experience. Irrigation of the farmlands in the early morning hours before sun's rays strike the land gets encouraged in areas faced with hot arid climate.

Proper understanding of the environmental set up on the earth is very much necessary to get ready for the future in an enlightened manner. It is seen that there is some resilience in the climatic behaviour of the earth. That aspect needs to be properly deciphered from the direct or indirect historical information. Human societies would be able to appreciate the events of the past in the light of such information in more clear terms. That will help to march in the future as an enlightened society and face the future with a more confident and bolder attitude.

Studies presented in the book in a well-reasoned manner is a very useful step in that direction. Shri. Vidyanand Ranade deserves our hearty congratulations for helping us in our march on this path. Taking an inspiration from this work, it is hoped that more such studies will continue to be undertaken. They will progressively give us a better and clearer understanding about the environmental developments in the future. Let us also hope that more such well researched treatise on this important subject will emerge in the near future.


**Dr. M.A. Chitale**.


(Dr. M.A. Chitale - After working for about two & half decades in WR Deptt. of Maharashtra State, he worked as Secretary WR in Mumbai for 2 years. He then moved to Central Water Commission New Delhi in 1984 rising to be its chairman. Then was selected as Secretary WR (GoI) New Delhi, worked for more than 3 years and retired in 1992. He started celebrating 'Water

Resource Day' in India for the first time. He is a 'Stockholm Water Award Laureate – 1993. After retirement, he worked as Secretary General, International Commission on Irrigation and Drainage, New Delhi for six years and then as Chairman South Asia Technical Advisory Committee, Aurangabad for five years. His contribution in the development and management of the WR sector at the world level is note-worthy.)

# Preface

The Author Shri V. M. Ranade, an eminent Civil Engineer of India has to his credit a series of books in Marathi and English, depicting his all-round experience of the last 6 decades, in the 'Water Resources (WR)' sector. His last book of 2021 in 'Marathi' (his mother tongue and the official language of the Maharashtra state), described the entire range of "Facets of Water". It covered the development, use and management of WR to meet various needs of people, and of the entire terrestrial and aquatic ecosystems. The book received an Award in 'Environment Sector' from the Govt. of Maharashtra in the year 2022. It served as a 'guideline' to the in-service engineers in the Maharashtra State and to the State policy makers in improving the related Acts and policies to ameliorate adverse impacts on 'Environment'. In the present book in 'English', to start with he covers our solar system, with 'Earth' as its focus and elaborates evolution of life on earth through use of its natural resources: air, solar energy, land, & water. He conveys the unique role of 'WR' emanating from clouds, snow-rain, glaciers, springs, streams, rivers, wells, lakes, estuaries and oceans, while emerging as 'lifeline' for the plant and the animal kingdom on our earth. Plants produce food by making use of air, solar energy, with the help of nutrients & minerals from the soil, absorbed through the medium of water. While describing contribution of all these elements - macroscopic to microscopic; he explains how it supports inhabitation of earth by all life forms: vegetation, animals, birds and humans … their presence, growth, and variety.

He thus covers the earth's inanimate & animate world with 'WR' as the central theme. The centrality of development of WR by mankind and in its judicious management round the year is then brought out describing its availability in the form of snow – rain – vapour. Its quantity is dictated by its varying availability from year to year and from place to place around the earth surface, as dictated by its geography, atmosphere and the periodic climate cycle while providing food/energy for the subsistence/ sustenance of all the life forms. Ingenuity of human mind and his resourcefulness was extended beyond problems of water shortages at some places and times. He introduced a variety of "infrastructure" to ensure year-round WR availability and even attempted 'artificial' rain at needy places by cloud-seeding of existing moisture stock in the sky.

Water is essential for humanity to provide for food, drinking & domestic needs, industrial use, for generating hydropower, and indeed for providing security for all life forms on the earth. But yes – desirable, only if environment (both terrestrial and aquatic ecosystems), making this possible, is protected securely. All the developmental (human & economic) activities by and for the humans, profoundly impact the environment and the climate, consciously or unconsciously, unless they make conscious efforts to minimise adverse Impacts and take measures to adapt to the emanating climate change (CC). While availing WR (both surface and sub-surface), humanity has modified its availability along its entire course. With ever growing needs of competing and conflicting demands for water, they had to overcome year-long variable availability of natural surface/sub-surface WR, by building storages behind dam-structures and/or by diversion of some of it, to the needy area. Environment being the key to WR, was likely to be over-exploited and its protection became a cornerstone of success, while harnessing WR.

History of WRD in India must be seen into two clear periods: prior to and post-independence period. Even the 1st period gets divided into two parts: prior to and post British regime. The Author shows that during this 1st period (up-to 1947), the country had encountered several severe droughts. In each of such drought people died for want of sufficient food grain. With that background after 1947, Indian Central and State Governments accorded priority for construction of large dams to store water and to supply it by canal system to increase area under irrigation. Irrigated agriculture together with the introduction of 'Green Revolution' in the form of improved/hybrid seeds and use of chemical fertilisers & insecticides, per - hectare land productivity increased many folds. Hence the country became self-sufficient in food grains by the end of seventh decade of the twentieth century. Like India, China also had a long history of severe famines and floods in the 19th and 20th centuries, causing loss of lives in each such catastrophic event. By following similar measures: construction of dams (more than 20,000 large dams in later half of the 20th century) and resorting to Green Revolution practice, China also became self-sufficient in food grains.

Unfortunately, some underdeveloped countries in the sub-Saharan Africa and Asia lack in adequate irrigation facilities, resulting in poor land productivity and starvation deaths. A severe future drought in these countries could result in continuation of such distress. Even if food grains are transported and provided by grain surplus countries to tide over the situation, it cannot be a permanent solution. The book could serve as a good guide for these countries to make optimum use of WR by introducing necessary infrastructure; and by practicing modern irrigated agriculture supported by latest technology. Many International Financing Agencies are capable to support such effort and have to be motivated by them.

In case of rain-fed agriculture, crops are grown to suit the yearly average rainfall pattern. The crop productivity drops during drought. But irrigation through canals from storages or river diversions, as per crop needs, wherever carried out, appreciably increases crop productivity per hectare. Variety of crops grown due to assured supply of irrigation water boosts the rural economy. With the increased agriculture produce, food processing industries can be also set up in neighbouring semi-urban areas. Basic human needs of food such as grains, pulses, vegetables, oil, sugar, fruit etc. could then be easily met with due to growth of irrigated agriculture. Along-with food-crops, it can provide fodder for farm and dairy animals where needed.

With increase in industrialisation in India, new industries and industrial estates have been set up near many cities. Because of increasing employment in industries and better education facilities there for their children, families from rural areas are eventually migrating to these semi-urban and new urban areas causing growth of urban population. Earlier, water stored in reservoirs was used mainly for irrigation. With growth of industries and urbanisation, more and more of it was used there, causing curtailment of supply for irrigation, leading to urban-rural conflicts. Such conflicts need to be settled quickly & amicably. Secondly, release of treated (fully/partially/little) urban sewage/and – or industrial effluent in streams, has caused their heavy pollution calling for treatment before use. But such re-use had created new problems.

Availability of water depended on the rainfall pattern in the river basin, which is spread across geographical–political entities: countries, states, provinces, districts, down to villages. With WR getting intricately woven with economy, politics, laws, Governments - et al, get into an amalgam of lives & people of each basin area. Transfer of WR from surplus to deficit sub basins within a basin, was indeed an 'intra-basin transfer' and from one basin to other was 'inter-basin transfer'. Interlinking of rivers within the country was planned to utilise WR from water-surplus rivers by transfer to water-short river basins. During the latter part of the 20th century, actual use of river water from large part of Indian sub-continent was done as per Awards of River Water Dispute Tribunals. Disputes did arise between Award parties that were resolved as per relevant laws/awards. For instance, a demand for renegotiating and modifying the oldest and so far, successfully operated 'Indus Water Treaty' (IWT) between India and Pakistan has recently started.

Reservoirs created by large size dams submerged forest land in some cases, and villages & cultivated land in some cases. They often became centres of conflicts & or controversies, associated with opposition by environmentalists and social activists, requiring careful handling. All such WRD was approved as per law of the land only after assessing and minimising its adverse impact on environment while attempting maximisation of a boost for local economic investment, employment generation, and well-being of the impacted population. India is the cradle of riverine area adjoining Himalayas which is a birthplace of some of the world's major rivers: Ganga, Brahmaputra, Sindhu (Indus) and Meghana, supporting large populations of adjoining countries: India, Pakistan, Nepal, Bhutan, Bangladesh and China.

The Author clearly brings out how our living world needs global actions in WRD, on the following three prime issues for survival & sustenance. They are: i) achieving sustainable food & water security, ii) restoration of air/water quality, and iii) adapting to & limiting adverse effects of CC. The book provides detailed technical guidelines to the needy underdeveloped countries, for adopting large scale WRD and to introduce 'Green Revolution' technique, to increase land productivity to achieve sustained food & water security. It also provides detailed measures to ensure treatment of urban sewage & industrial effluent to improve water quality of riverine aquatic eco-systems. Indian sub-continent presently provides a good lead with positive intelligent action in development, use, management and regulation of WR. At the same time, he covers the status of actions at the global level by some selected major developed countries of the world in limiting their carbon emissions and stresses the necessity, to follow strictly the time bound programmes agreed to by them.

To conclude, developed countries of the world ought to provide necessary financial assistance along-with technical guidance to the under-developed countries, in achieving i) sustainable food & water security, and ii) restore the polluted riverine ecosystems. Simultaneously, both together should prepare time bound plans to reduce carbon emissions at the global level, to confine adverse impacts of climate change within the predetermined safe limits and then strictly follow them. They should also extend the facility of providing 'carbon credits' to the underdeveloped countries so that their developmental activities do not get affected while adapting to the climate change.

**Dr. C.D. Thatte.**

(Dr. C.D. Thatte - After working for 4 decades in WR projects of India's States of Bombay (Maharashtra) & Gujarat, notable being Sardar Sarovar (Narmada) Project, he moved to Central Water Commission, New Delhi, rising to be its chairman. Selected as Secretary WR (GoI) New Delhi and retired after a 2-year stint. Later, appointed as Secretary General International Commission of Irrigation and Drainage, when his work around the globe for 6 years is well-known. His work in R&D and in strengthening of WRD is note-worthy.)

# Contents

Chapter 1: Unique Properties of Water. .................................................................................. 1

Chapter 2: History of Evolution of Life on the Earth and role of Water in the Evolution .......... 12

Chapter 3: Characteristics of Surface Water Resource and its Assessment to meet needs of Nature and Man. ................................................................................................. 23

Chapter 4: Water Resource Development Infrastructure Constructed in India Prior To Independence In 1947. ......................................................................................... 36

Chapter 5: Achieving Food Security to The Country After Independence by Green Revolution and Meeting the Challenge of Droughts in India. ................................ 49

Chapter 6: Water Resource Development Infrastructure Evolved in India After Independence. 67

Chapter 7: Use and Management of the Water Resource for Irrigated Agriculture .................... 82

Chapter 8: Integrated Management of Water Resource to Meet All Its Competing Uses. ......... 99

Chapter 9: Development, Augmentation, Use and Management of Ground Water Resource .. 112

Chapter 10: Governance and Regulation on the Development, Use and Management of the Water Resource .............................................................................................. 129

Chapter 11: Droughts and Floods – Two Extreme Events of the Climate ................................ 143

Chapter 12: Artificial Rain ..................................................................................................... 157

Chapter 13: Virtual Water ...................................................................................................... 164

Chapter 14: If the River Could Speak – Autobiography of a River .......................................... 170

Chapter 15: How the Water Sector can Adapt to the Adverse Effects of Global Warming and Climate Change ............................................................................................ 177

Chapter 16: Actions at the World level on Water, Environment and Climate Change .............. 189

Chapter 17: Way Forward ...................................................................................................... 205

**Note – The Book has been printed in Black and White, including all Maps in the different chapters. However, it is felt that the 'Reader' would appreciate the contents of the maps better if they were in colour. Please send email to the author at the email-id <vranade2003@yahoo.com>, to get soft copies of the maps in colour.**

# Chapter 1
# Unique Properties of Water.

*We are all familiar with 'Water' because of the role it plays in our day-to-day life. However, such familiarity usually leads us to take it for granted and to underestimate its vital importance in our life. We might have learnt something about the subject water from the textbooks during our school or college days, but in all probability most of us have forgotten about it by now. Water has many unique inherent properties which have facilitated in initiating kindling the spark of life, its evolution to the present stage, and its sustenance on our Earth. How many of us are aware of the incredible role water has played in all these natural processes of evolution spread over the last many millions of years is a point to ponder on. Text of the chapter throws light on all these unequalled properties of water and the vital role it has played which has enabled the earth to make it habitable to transform it into the 'Living World'.*

Even when science of physics and chemistry was not developed, the subject 'Water' had challenged the imaginative faculty of many thinkers and philosophers from all over the World. Greek Scientific Philosopher Thales (Engineer by occupation) from Miletus, Turkey (624 to 546 BC) promulgated that 'Water was origin of all things in Nature and all things on the earth have originated from that basic element' (it was seen to be untrue later). Aristotle observed later about Thales' hypothesis that the originating principle of nature and the nature of matter was a single material substance; water. 'Water was the origin of things, that is, out of which everything arises, and into which everything resolves itself'. Thales observed that water was important in everyday life and was needed for nourishment. As per the Indian culture, Earth, Water, Light, Air and Sky are considered as five basic elements essential for existence of life on the Earth. To the earlier presumption of four basic elements viz. Earth, Water, Air and Fire, Aristotle added the fifth element 'Aether', the divine substance of the heavenly spheres, stars and planets.

As the science based on conclusive inferences drawn from actual observations in the field and in the laboratories advanced during last 4-5 centuries, more and more scientific information about various properties of water came to light and were known to us. It could then be inferred that the water has many astounding properties, making it unique in the evolution of life on the earth. Experiments revealed that all materials on the earth can exist in solid, liquid, and gaseous condition depending on the temperature and the pressure imposed on it. Oxygen gas becomes solid at (-) 218.4° C but melts into liquid form at (-) 183° C. Iron melts into liquid form at 1535° C and starts boiling at 3000° C. By changing the temperature and pressure for all materials, one can change their state from solid to liquid to gas. But surprisingly, water exists on the earth naturally in all the three forms simultaneously. It means that actions of freezing, melting and its evaporation are taking place simultaneously at different locations on the earth. However, by balancing temperature and pressure, scientists can reach the point of thermodynamic equilibrium, where matter exists in liquid, solid, and gaseous state at the same time. This state is known as the triple point or the triple boil. Water reaches the triple point at 0.1 degrees Celsius and the pressure of 0.006 atm.

Another unequalled property of water is that its density in its solid form (ice) is lesser than in its liquid form, which causes the ice to float on water. For all other materials when their temperature is reduced, their volume reduces, and the density increases. But water is an extraordinary exception to it. Volume of water is least when its temperature is $4°C$, but it starts increasing as the temperature reduces and its volume increases by about 9 percent at $0°C$, which causes the ice to float on water. Hence when atmospheric temperature reduces well below $0°C$, a layer of floating ice gets formed on waterbodies (lake or sea), which prevents the contact of water below with the atmosphere. It then remains in a liquid state which allows many forms of aquatic life to remain active and survive in the water below the ice layer. If the ice were to be heavier than water it would have subsided below, thereby exposing water near the surface to low temperatures and causing its transformation into ice incessantly. It would then have resulted in complete freezing of water bodies in many parts on the earth and would have confined sustenance of aquatic life only in tropical climatic conditions on the earth.

One more extraordinary property of water is in its very high capacity to store heat (thermal energy). Energy required to increase temperature of 1 gram of water from $14.5°C$ to $15.5°C$ is the unit of thermal energy and is called as one 'Calorie'. Energy required to increase temperature of any liquid by one degree Celsius is called as 'Specific heat' of that liquid. Even if specific heat of water is 1, it lies only between 0.27 to 0.54 for liquids such as Acetone, Alcohol, Sulphuric acid and Benzene. Specific heat of sand is 0.2 and that of iron is 0.1. Because of the high specific heat of water, even if it absorbs a lot of solar energy during daytime, its temperature does not increase much. During night-time when the atmosphere is cool, water releases the stored heat energy back into the atmosphere, which reduces the difference between the daytime and night-time temperatures. In the deserts, since there is not much moisture in the dry atmosphere and the specific heat of sand is only 0.2, daytime temperatures are very high, and night-time temperatures are very low. That is why there is temperate climate in coastal areas and even near shorelines of large lakes. Thanks to the high specific heat of water due to which, atmospheric conditions in many parts of the earth have become favourable for the living world.

If heat is applied to ice which is having temperature below zero degrees Celsius, its temperature starts increasing. When it reaches to $0°C$, the temperature remains at $0°C$ and the applied heat causes the ice in the solid state to melt and transform into liquid state, without any increase in the temperature. This heat is called as 'Latent heat of melting' which is about 80 calories for water. Similarly, when we continue to apply heat further, temperature gradually rises to $100°C$ and then the water starts boiling. If we continue to apply heat further, temperature does not increase but water in the liquid form gets transformed into vapour in the gaseous form. About 538 calories are required for the conversion of water from its liquid form to gaseous form and it is known as 'Latent heat of Evaporation'. In that comparison, Latent heat of Evaporation of Acetone, Alcohol, Sulphuric acid and Benzene is much less and lies between 94 to 203.

Other peculiarity of water is that its evaporation takes place continuously from all water bodies and even from land at normal atmospheric temperatures. Due to high latent heat of evaporation of water, appreciable amount of solar energy gets consumed in such transformation, which keeps the atmospheric temperature low. Role played by water in storing sizeable solar energy due to its high specific heat & in its transformation by evaporation, keeps the day temperatures low. During night-time when atmospheric temperatures are low, water cools down due to release of heat energy. This action reduces variations in day and night temperatures. Third peculiarity of water is that when it evaporates, all types of salts and minerals dissolved in the water bodies (sea and lakes) are left behind and then it is pure water vapour. Evaporation takes place continuously from the soil, rivers, water bodies and the oceans. Evapotranspiration takes place continuously on the earth from leaves of all plants and trees. Another property of water vapour is that it is lighter than the air. Because of this property the vapour rises to higher elevations in the atmosphere to initiate the start of water cycle as explained below.

As the atmospheric temperature reduces at higher elevations, condensation of vapour takes place in the form of minute water particles, thereby releasing latent heat of evaporation back into atmosphere which is very cool. As the vapour travelled further upwards in the sky and the air temperature cools down sufficiently, fine water particles are formed which later get condensed around particulate matter as nucleus to form water drops, which is known as clouds. These particles then combine to form large size water drops which drip on the earth as rainfall. When atmosphere at still higher levels is cooler, water drops get converted into ice particles by absorbing energy from atmosphere. These ice drops then fall on the earth as snowfall in temperate climate zone and on high mountains even in tropical climate zone. In the tropical zone, when water particles move further upwards with the wind, they freeze and condense to form large size ice clusters and then fall on the Earth as hailstorm. This entire process of evaporation of water, its upward journey resulting in formation of clouds at higher elevations, condensation of vapour in water drops or ice drops and its release back to the earth in the form of rainfall or snowfall is called as 'Water Cycle'.

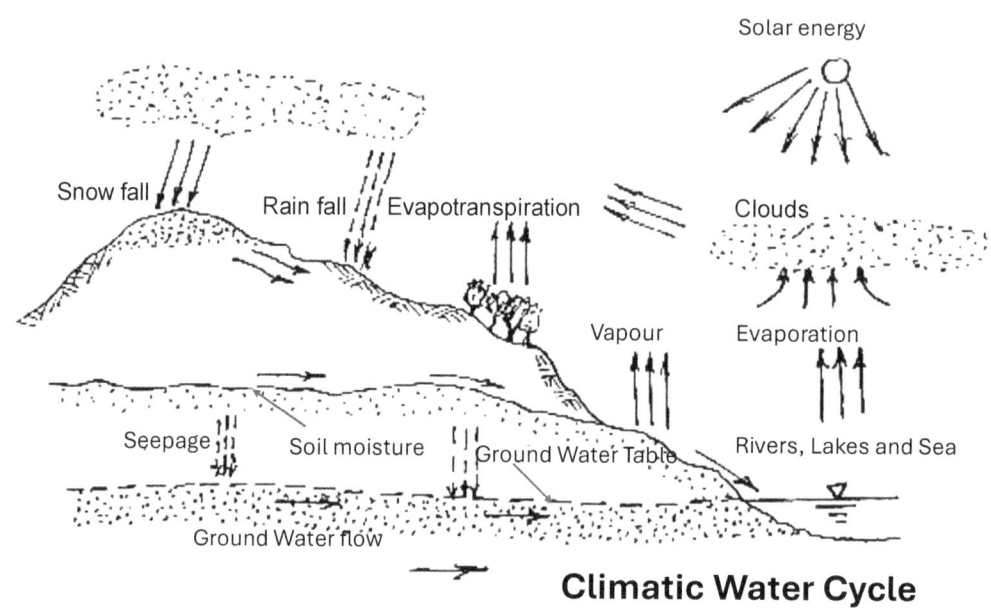

**Climatic Water Cycle**

When snowfall occurs in temperate zones or at very high peaks in the tropical zone, snow gets stored there during the entire winter season. Snow thus stored above the 'Snowline' - which is an imaginary line above which atmospheric temperature remains below $0°C$ - would not melt and would accumulate there in the entire winter season. When the atmospheric temperature starts rising above snowline in the summer season, snow starts melting from the surface. Then the snow melting would have continued only from its surface, but the snow layer would have remained adhered to the land below due to friction. In that case, snow layer would not slide to lower levels along the land slope to accelerate its melting due to increase in temperatures at lower levels. But in reality, as thickness of the ice layer and so its pressure at its bottom increases, it starts melting at the contact of ice layer with the earth even at temperatures below $0°C$. Melting of the snow layer at its bottom then acts as a lubricant and the entire layer of the ice slides along the slope due to reduction in friction, which is caused because of this incredible property of ice. The resulting very slow sliding of ice layer along the valley in the mountainous regions is actually a river of snow and is called 'Glacier'. When the glacier very slowly slides towards lower levels, it scraps and erodes a lot of material from its bottom and even parent rock from the rock layer, to transport it downstream. As the glacier slides further very slowly to lower levels, atmospheric temperature increases, thus accelerating the rate of melting of snow layer even from its surface. At lower levels where the glacier melts completely, the transported solid material at its bottom gets deposited as unconsolidated debris at that location and is known as glacial till or 'Moraine'. In this way, even the glacier causes erosion of rock, transportation of scoured material from upper levels and its deposition at some other place downstream at lower levels. The melted water then carries scoured finer material with it and flows through valley to meet some river downstream. It then feeds the rivers during summer season to sustain life in that aquatic ecosystem and could also be used to meet human needs in the summer season. As the snow accumulated at higher levels slides to lower levels as glacier, it makes space for the snow fall to accumulate there next year and the cycle continues. If the melting point of ice had not been reduced with the increased pressure, the snow layer would have remained stationary at that place. With every winter season then, the height of snow layer would have continued to increase indefinitely. The snow accumulated in major part of the temperate zone and on the mountains above the snowline in the tropical zone on the earth would have been of no use for sustenance of life on the earth.

It is well known that a molecule of water is formed by the combination of two hydrogen atoms and one atom of Oxygen ($H_2 + O = H_2O$). Hydrogen gas is inflammable, and oxygen is essential in the process of burning, but it is surprising that the water formed after combination of these two elements helps in extinguishing fire. Another property of water is that, of all the liquids known to science, many types of salts, minerals, and chemicals in solid form dissolve in water and hence it is known as 'Universal solvent'. Even if many of these salts, minerals, and some chemicals are dissolved in water, there is no chemical reaction between them, and they remain in water in a dissolved form. Some of these salts and chemicals remain mixed in the soil which is formed during the very slow process (extending over millions of years) of disintegration and decomposition of the parent rock. It takes place due to sustained action of variations in daily atmospheric temperature and its decomposition due to reaction with some chemicals in water seeping through cracks and crevices in the rock layers. Some of these minerals and salts in the soil formed due to decomposition of rock are nutrients, which are absorbed by the root system of plants and conveyed through the medium of water to the leaves for generation of food by the process of photosynthesis. It is then conveyed to flowers, fruits, branches, and trunks of the tree for their growth. Except the water consumed in the process of photosynthesis which takes place in the leaves during daytime, remaining water gets continuously released from the leaves of trees and plants which is known as evapotranspiration, and it then forms part of the world water cycle.

One more notable property of water is that, except only mercury, its surface tension is highest amongst all liquids. If a tube of glass is put in water, the water rises in the tube due to its high surface tension. As the diameter of the tube reduces water rises higher and higher, which is known as capillary action. Nutrients and salts dissolved in water in the soil are absorbed by roots of trees and are carried upwards to the leaves through very small veins called 'Xylems' because of the capillary action of water. Xylem transports water and nutrients from the roots up to other parts of the plant, while 'Phloem' transports sucrose and amino acids produced by the leaves to other parts of the plant. However, for conveyance of nutrients to the treetop over considerable heights against gravity, capillary action and osmotic pressure work together. The significance of these two properties of water would be understood when we come to study the complex process evolution of plant life on the earth.

You would now have realized how the multifaceted properties of water had contributed significantly to moderate the climate and make it suitable for the commencement of life on our earth. Being too familiar with the water, we all perpetrate the mistake of taking it for granted and are oblivious to its unparalleled properties. Scientific reasons for all the above unique properties and characteristics of water have been researched by scientists, although it is not considered necessary to go into those technical details here. But it would certainly be interesting to understand the circumstances which prevailed on the earth many millions of years before and realize the role played by the water which laid the pathway for kindling the 'Spark of Life' in the lukewarm sea water!

As per 'Big Bang' theory, which is acceptable to most of the scientists today, our Universe was born out of the explosion which took place sometime around 14,000 to 15,000 mya (million years ago) and the Universe has been continuously expanding since then. It is further estimated that, from out of the very hot mass scattered in the Universe, the Sun was born around 5,000 mya. Subsequently, parts of the very hot mass got separated from the Sun to give rise to planets which revolved around their own axis and also revolved around the Sun because of the force of attraction towards the Sun. The process of formation of such planets, including Earth as one of them, continued over millions of years to give rise to a greater number of planets revolving around the Sun. This system of the Sun and the planets revolving around it is called 'Solar system', which again is one of the many such systems in our Galaxy. Our Universe is very vast and beyond our imagination because millions of such Galaxies exist in the Universe and it is expanding still at a very fast pace. Many of these developments which came to light were because of the progress made by the scientists during the last 3-4 centuries in the field of various disciplines of science.

Earth formed around 4540 mya, approximately one-third the age of the universe, by the process of accretion from the solar nebula. Volcanic outgassing probably created a primordial atmosphere and then the oceans. The early atmosphere contained almost no oxygen. Earth existed then onwards as one of the planets in the solar system. At the time of formation, earth was a sphere of molten material which revolved around its own axis and around the Sun continuously since then. With the passage of time, it gradually cooled down from the surface because of the transfer of heat into the atmosphere. However, the heat generated in the process of intense radio activity of the molten material inside the earth continued to get transferred towards the surface of the earth. High density minerals such as Iron, Nickel etc. gravitated towards the center of the earth and lighter minerals remained in the outer layers. The speed of revolution of the Earth around its axis was very high at that time and the day (time of revolution around its axis) was only 4-5 hours duration. In due course of time the speed of revolution gradually reduced, and the present day it is 24 hours duration.

You would be surprised to know that water did not exist at that time on the extremely hot surface of the earth. As the pressure of various hot gases and water vapour in the semisolid magma inside the earth increased, it caused earth's crust to rupture where it was relatively thin. Due to sudden release of pressure, the semi-solid magma got liquified and erupted through openings in the earth's crust and started flowing out on the earth on all sides in a liquid form known as 'Lava'. Some lava around the hole was solidified, but it continued to flow out till the pressure of magma reduced. It thus formed a mountain-like structure around the hole, which is called 'Volcano'. Lava also used to flow out very slowly along either side of very long contraction cracks which were formed at some places in the earth's crust. This semisolid lava was solidified in due course of time, to form a layer of igneous rock. At some locations magma continued to outpour after some interval, duly forming several layers of varying thicknesses of basalt rock. At some places, crust of the earth was only pushed up due to pressure of magma inside, but it did not rupture. Such movements of the earth-crust and eruption & solidification of the lava resulted in the formation of mountains, valleys and depressions on the surface of the earth. A substantial quantity of water vapour was also released into the atmosphere through these volcanic explosions, which was the main source of water on the earth. In addition to the vapour released from volcanoes, our planet held plenty of water, largely seeded by asteroids during our solar system's early formation. Gases such as carbon Dioxide, Ammonia, Methane & Hydrogen Sulfide etc. along with vapour released from the volcanoes remained in the atmosphere. The concentration of these gases gradually increased due to frequent release of gases and vapour from the volcanoes. Water vapour released from volcanoes also formed part of the atmosphere around the earth. However, since water vapour was lighter than the gases which composed the atmosphere, it travelled upwards in the sky. As it moved further upwards, vapour condensed and caused rainfall or snowfall as explained above. Since the surface of the earth was very hot then, raindrops were immediately evaporated by absorbing heat from the atmosphere and the earth surface and the vapour so formed travelled upwards again. This water cycle of 'evaporation-condensation-rainfall-evaporation' continued incessantly over millions of years, thereby transferring heat from surface of the earth into the atmosphere continuously through the medium of water. It resulted in gradual cooling of the surface of the earth.

In due course of time internal heat due to radio activity from within the earth also gradually reduced and surface temperature of the earth reduced sufficiently. Intensity of the cycle of 'evaporation-cloud formation-rainfall-evaporation' gradually reduced after the sustained activity over millions of years. Hence only part of the rainwater evaporated, but the rest of it started flowing over the surface of the earth along slopes to meet water bodies which were formed in the depressions. Some of the water was stored in the depressions formed due to movements of crust of the earth to form lakes. In due course of time, very large water bodies were formed and were called 'Sea'. However, the activity of release of magma from cracks in the earth's crust as steady flow to form thick or thin layers, which later solidified as rock, continued at some places. At some other places, the magma would suddenly erupt through extinct volcanoes to flow as Lava along slopes and get solidified when the activity stopped.

Raindrops which fall on the earth have sufficiently high velocity to cause impact on the earth surface and to cause displacement of some rock material resulting in to very slow disintegration of rocks. As the surface of the earth cooled down, a web of some shallow and some deep cracks formed due to contraction of rock by its cooling. In the temperate zone, the water which entered in such cracks turned into ice during winter season. Because volume of ice is about 9% more than water, it exerted pressure on the rock resulting in widening and deepening of the cracks to accelerate disintegration of rock. Some of the gases in the atmosphere were dissolved in water to form mild chemicals which entered through these cracks to enhance the process of decomposition of rock layers near the top. These chemicals also entered in the joints between two layers of rock to cause decomposition of rock at that location. Such chemical actions taking place with the assistance of water and extended over millions of years resulted in slow physical disintegration and chemical decomposition of rock and formation of a layer of soil at the surface of the earth. This top layer of soil, rich in certain minerals, nutrients and salts, was to support trees, plants & grass and the terrestrial ecosystems, when they evolved on the earth after several million years.

When the rainwater started flowing along the surface of the earth, it revealed another notable property of flowing water. It was in the form of erosion of the soil and other material from the surface of the earth by the action of flowing water. Flowing water caused its transportation downstream and its deposition at different places along the river course where its velocity got reduced. When particles of the soil get displaced by rain drops falling on the surface layer and are carried with the flowing rainwater it is known as sheet erosion. When the surface water joins to form streams, brooks, rivulets and then the rivers, velocity of flowing water depends on bed gradient (slope) of the stream/river. Water flowing in rivulets carry the material formed by the disintegration of rock to the rivers. Rivers carry that coarse material downstream and erode rock from the riverbed due to abrasion, to form rock fragments of various sizes. One would not believe about the carrying capacity of a stream of flowing water. When the velocity of flow increases, carrying capacity increases by the fifth power of the diameter of the particle. When the velocity of a stream is doubled, capacity to carry size of rolling bed material increases by 64 times. Flowing water causes the bed material to roll over continuously which wears out sharp corners of rock fragments and gradually turns them into fairly rounded particles of various sizes, called gravel and sand. In the upper reaches of rivers bed material is coarse, varying from small size boulders and gravel. In the lower reaches of rivers, we get naturally formed finer material such as coarse and fine sand. This sand is the best construction material for the construction of houses, multistoried apartments, factory buildings, concrete roads, masonry and concrete dams, etc.

The coarse material rolls along the riverbed as explained above, but the finer particles of silt and soil displaced and carried with the rainwater due to sheet erosion are conveyed by the river in a suspended form. Coarse silt and soil get deposited along the inner curve of river where water is shallow, and the velocity of flow is less close along the riverbank. Very fine soil particles held in suspension are carried further to get deposited near the estuary where the river meets the sea, and the velocity of flow is very slow. This region is known as 'Delta Region' which is of a triangular shape, in which the river splits into several streams before meeting the sea. The land here is very fertile and has a very flat slope. Simply by diverting the flow of the river from upstream of the delta region to provide irrigation facilities, two or three seasonal crops can be taken every year in the deltaic region. This practice of irrigation was practiced in Peninsular India during last 10-15 centuries and also in deltaic regions of many rivers in the world. In this manner the rivers have been causing erosion of bed rock and conveyance of that material towards downstream, transportation of soil particles displaced by sheet erosion by carrying it in a suspended form and its deposition along riverbanks and deltaic regions, to create vast patches of fertile land. The role of water in the form of flowing rivers to create a platform for establishing fertile land on its banks and in the delta region on the earth would now be well understood.

When the intensity of activity of the water cycle reduced because of cooling of the earth, the cloud cover was no longer continuous in the sky. It then used to rain intermittently on the earth and during some specific months depending on the location and topography. The energy of solar rays in the form of light and heat used to fall on the earth incessantly during daytime where there was no cloud cover. In addition to that, harmful ultraviolet rays (UV Rays) from solar energy were also falling on the earth. Solar energy was intense along equator and its intensity gradually reduced towards North and South poles where it was least. Such large natural variation in solar energy would have resulted in confinement of life on the earth in a limited area, when it evolved on the earth in due course of time. But the hot air and the vapour formed in the equatorial zone, being lighter used to move upwards in the sky during daytime. The dry and cold air around the polar zone, being heavier used to move along the land slowly towards the equatorial zone, thereby moderating the climate on the earth to a certain extent.

One more activity has taken place on our earth, after cooling down its crust, and formation of land mass, mountains & large water bodies in the form of lakes and oceans. Land on the earth, which existed as one contiguous land mass got slowly separated into many continents due to tectonic movement of plates in a period of millions of years and reassembled afterwards in some more millions of years. This activity had taken place on the earth several times in the distant past. The last such activity was in the formation of a supercontinent consisting of a contiguous land mass, which was called as 'Pangaea'. It was assembled from the earlier continental units of Gondwana, Euramerica and Siberia, approximately 335 mya and existed for about 155 million years. The concept that the continents once formed a contiguous land mass which was then divided into continents was hypothesised, with corroborating evidence in 1912, by Alfred Wegener (1880-1930), the originator of the scientific theory of Continental Drift. It was vindicated from the evidence of observations made later during the twentieth century.

The Pangaea began to break apart about 180 mya, initially by dividing into two supercontinents, the Northern supercontinent was known as 'Eurasia' and the Southern supercontinent was known as 'Gondwana'. Gradually, both the supercontinents were further subdivided into many continents and subcontinents. The break-up of Gondwana began in 150–140 mya, when some of its landmass viz. South America & Africa separated from Antarctica into continents. Later South America started to move westward away from Africa. At the same time, India began to separate from Antarctica and moved northward toward Eurasia at a speed of 15 cm (6 in) per year and eventually collided with Eurasia some 50-55 Mya, forming the Himalayan mountains. After separating from Antarctica, the Indian subcontinent travelled more than 8,000 km towards North, which was the longest journey by any continent on the earth at that time. Indian subcontinent is still moving northwards at a speed of about 5-6 cm per year resulting in increasing the height of Himalaya Mountain. Australia also moved in the North-East direction at the speed of about 5-6 cm per year and has travelled about 3000 km so far. Formation of these continents and subcontinents resulted in formation of ocean currents as explained below, which also helped in moderation of climate in substantial parts of the earth.

The heat received from solar rays and absorbed by the sea water gets redistributed to temperate zones on the earth on a very large scale and over very long distances, through the medium of several streams (currents) formed in the oceans. Because of the difference in temperature of ocean due to variations in the intensity of solar energy at different places, due to rotational movement of the earth and due to some other reasons, warm ocean currents flow from near the surface towards polar region. On the other hand, cold ocean currents flow from much below the sea surface from the polar region towards equatorial region to replace the warm water moving as warm ocean currents close to surface of the oceans. Velocity of earth surface due to its rotational movement is highest at the equator and reduces gradually being negligible at the poles. *'Coriolis effect'* describes the pattern of deflection that takes place by the objects such as air and water which are not firmly connected to the ground, as they travel long distances around the earth. In effect the air in the atmosphere and water in the sea travel to the right side i.e., counterclockwise in the Northern hemisphere and to the left side i.e., clockwise in the Southern hemisphere. Hence all these natural actions are responsible for many large-scale favourable changes in the weather patterns on the earth.

Warm ocean currents originate near the equator and move towards the poles or higher latitudes, while cold currents originate near the poles or higher latitudes and move towards the tropics or lower latitudes. Besides moderating the atmospheric temperature in the temperate regions, warm oceanic currents carry and nurture high levels of phytoplankton with associated copepods and krill, and resultant food chains which support the aquatic life over there. The volume of water carried by these sea currents is enormous, and beyond one's imagination. Discharge of the *'Gulf stream'* of warm water for example, ranges from 30 mcumecs (million cubic meters per second) to 150 mcumecs and is very large in comparison with the total flow of 0.6 mcumecs from all rivers discharging in the Atlantic Ocean. It rises in the bay of Mexico from near South-East coast of Florida state of America and its one branch travels close to West coast of England and further to the West coast of Norway, which moderates the cold temperature in these countries. It plays an important role in the poleward transfer of heat and salt and serves to warm the European subcontinent. It is about 50-100 km wide, having depth of 1.5 km, has an average speed of 6.4 km/hr and is the fastest current in the oceanic world.

The Antarctic Circumpolar Current (ACC) is the planet's most powerful and arguably most important current, which has an estimated flow of 100-150 mcumecs or possibly even higher, making it the largest ocean current. It is the only current to flow clear around Antarctica in a closed circulation unimpeded by continents, without being diverted by any landmass. It connects the Atlantic, Pacific, and Indian Oceans, and serves as a principal pathway of exchange among them. There are in all about 19 warm and 15 cold ocean currents, which have been moderating the temperature of most of the oceans and the atmosphere on the earth, to make it habitable for life on the earth. By now you must have realized the vital role played by water in the oceans as a large-scale activity in moderating climate on the earth, by absorbing excess heat from solar energy received in the tropical regions and transporting it over very long distances in the oceans to convey it to the temperate regions of the earth.

In short, high specific heat, high latent heat of evaporation and melting, lesser density of ice than water, melting of ice under pressure, being a universal solvent, water vapour being lighter than air, etc., are the unique properties of water. We have also realised the vital role played by water, because of these inimitable properties, in moderating the climate in major parts of the earth to make it habitable for the living world.

# Chapter 2

# History of Evolution of Life on the Earth and role of Water in the Evolution

*History of the very gradual developments which took place on the earth after its entry into the solar system about 4540 million years ago (mya), up to the commencement of life around 3650 mya, is miraculous and incredible. We have seen in the earlier chapter about the vital role played by water during this period, in moderating climate on the earth to make it suitable for entry of living organism on the earth. Water, because of its many Inherent properties, was one of the important factors which contributed to the preparation of the stage for kindling the 'Spark of Life' in lukewarm sea water on the earth. In this chapter we would see the evolution of life in the sea from 3650 mya and then on the land up to about 12,000 years before, when the man started the practice of tending animals to supplement his food needs. It means that it would take first two chapters to review history of the earth from 4,540 mya to 12,000 years before the present. However, please keep in mind that it is going to take all the remaining chapters, to cover the ingenuity(!) shown by the 'Homo Sapiens – the wise man' in this very short period. It was primarily in the form of development of water resource and other natural resources endowed free of cost by the Nature, for their use by the humans, though at the cost of destruction and degradation of terrestrial and aquatic ecosystems on the earth.*

The origin of 'Life' on the earth stands as one of the great mysteries of science. Various theories have been proposed, all of which remain unverified so far fully and conclusively. History of genesis of 'Life on the Earth' and its evolution to the present stage, spans over about 3500 to 3800 million years. Because of the dedicated efforts taken by several scientists in various disciplines such as physics, chemistry, geology, biology etc. during the last 2-3 centuries, and advancements in the technology available to verify and supplement the presumptions, it has been possible to come to reasonable conclusions about it now. We have seen in the last chapter how the earth cooled down and how the glaciers, rivers and large water bodies were formed on the earth. But you would not believe that atmosphere on the earth then was totally lacking in the presence of oxygen in its pure form, which we find as vital for all living beings today. The atmosphere then contained only water vapour, and gases such as ammonia, methane, carbon dioxide, hydrogen sulphide, sulphur dioxide etc. which is called as an 'anaerobic condition'. Total lack of free oxygen gas in the atmosphere was because, it is a highly active element to react chemically and combine with many elements to cause their oxidation. Solar energy in the form of heat and light together with intense Ultraviolet (UV) rays, was incessantly falling on the earth. In addition to that, intense energy was also plummeting on the earth very frequently then in the form of lightening from clouds. But very surprisingly, all these severe conditions were setting up the stage for entry of 'Life on the Earth'.

According to Hindu mythology, the Universe, and the Earth, along with humans and other creatures, undergo repeated cycles of creation and destruction. Time is infinite with a cyclic universe, where the current universe was preceded and will be followed by an infinite number of universes. In Hindu cosmology, age of earth was stated as about 4,320 million years, incidentally which is very close to the presently estimated age of about 4,540 million years. In some religions, different ideas prevailed about the origin of life on the earth and its evolution. Usually they are in the form of stories which concern about the origin and nature of the world and the lives & activities of deities.

The origin of life on the earth is a natural process by which life has arisen from non-living matter, such as simple organic compounds. The prevailing scientific hypothesis is that the transition from non-living to living entities was not a single event, but an evolutionary process of increasing complexity that involved prebiotic synthesis of organic molecules, molecular self-replication and the emergence of cell membranes. Russian scientist Alexander Oparin in 1924 and British geneticist J.B.S. Haldane in 1929 had independently proposed that, the first molecules constituting the earliest cells slowly self-organized from a primordial warm soup in the shallow sea. They imagined the young earth as a huge chemical factory, with multitudes of carbon-based chemicals dissolved in the waters of the early oceans. Earth's prebiotic oceans near its shallow coast were having warm water saturated with many dissolved salts and minerals, to form a 'lukewarm soup'. When it was subjected to intense sustained external energy from sources in the form of lightening, ultraviolet rays, cosmic rays, and earth's internal radiation; amino acids (Building blocks of protein) might have been formed. From the chemical action between amino acids and proteins, nucleic acids might have been formed. Oparin reasoned that in due course of time, increasingly complicated particles were formed, culminating in carbohydrates and proteins to develop into formation of micro spheres having thin cover, which he called as 'Cocervates'. These could move in the sea water and divide into two, but still there was no life in them. How and when the spark of life was kindled in them was not known then and is still not very clear. Some scientists argued that the life began in vents on the seabed, where warm alkaline water seeped up from geological formations below. Interactions between warm water and rocks would provide chemical energy that would first drive simple metabolic cycles. Recent research suggests that the key molecules of life, and its core processes, could form only in places such as relatively shallow body of water in the estuaries, which are subject to alternate dry and wet conditions, since they were fed by the streams.

In the year 1952, Stanley Miller and Harold Urey carried out a chemical experiment at the University of Chicago, to demonstrate how organic molecules could have formed spontaneously from inorganic precursors under prebiotic conditions like those posited by the Oparin-Haldane hypothesis. They used a highly reducing (lacking oxygen) mixture of gases viz. methane, ammonia, and hydrogen, as well as water vapor. To simulate the effect of lightening, the mixture was subjected to frequent electric sparks/discharges to impart external energy. After three days of such sustained activity, it was seen that the mixture contained simple organic monomers such as aldehydes, carboxylic acids and amino acids – the building blocks of proteins. Miller and Urey realised that this process could have paved the way for the molecules needed to produce life. The experiment demonstrated that most amino acids, the chemical constituents of proteins, could be synthesized from inorganic compounds under conditions intended to replicate those of the early earth. External sources of energy may have triggered these reactions, including lightning, radiation etc.

The earliest life forms we know of were microscopic organisms (microbes) that left signals of their presence in the form of biogenic carbon signatures and stromatolite fossils discovered in the 3700-million-year-old metasedimentary rocks from western Greenland. As per another theory based on some fossil evidence indicated that, life on earth might have commenced between 3500 to 3800 mya, possibly through atmospheric entries of micro-meteorites from space.

**Theory of Evolution** - Anaximander, Greek philosopher from Miletus (about 500 BC) proposed that all life began in the sea because fishes hatch from eggs and immediately begin living with no help from their parents, as against human babies which are born helpless. He speculated that humans must have descended from some other type of creature who's young could survive without any help. English doctor Erasmus Darwin (1731-1802) – grandfather of Charles Darwin - talked about how competition and sexual selection could cause changes in species. He thought that *'The final course of this contest among males seems to be, that the strongest and most active animal should propagate'*. Whereas 'Theory of inheritance of acquired characters' was proposed by French naturalist, Jean Baptiste de Lamarck in 1794 in his book 'Philosphic Zoologique'.

Charles Robert Darwin (12-2-1809 to 19-4-1882), was a English naturalist whose scientific theory of evolution by natural selection became the foundation of modern evolutionary studies. He had just graduated in theology but was selected to serve HMS Beagle ship's sea voyage as a geologist and naturalist at the age of only 22. During this long voyage from December 1831 to October 1836, he explored many places on the East and West coast of South America, the Galapagos Islands and some other islands. He visited several places, studied many species of birds and animals, collected several sample specimens, recorded his observations and then at the end of the trip, the concept about evolution of life was crystalised in his mind. However, it was contrary to the view of the 'Creation' held at that time by most scientists as well as the Church, maintaining that all species were fixed and unchanging. His innate qualities of enquiring critically with an open mind into the whys and wherefores of every one of his observations had given rise to doubts in his mind about the correctness of the views as above. Hence, for the next more than 20 years, he made correspondence with many scientists on the subject and collected more evidence on related issues in support of his theory. He had written broad outline and the first draft of his theory of evolution, but still it was not finalised by him. In the meantime, Alfred Russel Wallace who had come up with a virtually identical theory, though with less supporting evidence, sent his paper on the 'Evolution' to Charles Darwin. The joint Darwin-Wallace papers were then presented in outline, to the Linnean Society of London in 1858.

Then Darwin decided and started writing his book on the theory of evolution and completed it within a year. Finally, the book titled as *'On the Origin of Species by Means of Natural Selection, or the Preservation of Favoured Races in the Struggle for Life'*, was published on 24 November 1859. According to Darwin, all organisms had one common ancestor at some point in time and it kept on diverging ever since. Evolution was a very slow and gradual process which took place over a very long period of time, extending over billions of years. The generation of a new species from another species, is a very slow and steady process as the changes and adaptations take a long time to stabilize and give rise to a new species. Darwin's concept of evolutionary adaptation through natural selection became central to the modern evolutionary theory, and it has now become the unifying concept of the life sciences.

Many of you may not know that Alfred Russel Wallace (8-1-1823 to 7-11-1913) was a British naturalist, explorer, geographer, anthropologist, and biologist, who had studied Nature and life in the Amazon River basin for 4 years (1848-52). Then from 1854 to 1862, he also travelled around the islands of the Malay Archipelago or East Indies (now Singapore, Malaysia, and Indonesia) to study the evolution of life. Based on this study he forwarded his paper to Darwin in the year 1858 as stated above.

**Evolution of life in the oceans -** First unicellular living organism is likely to have evolved from inorganic matter in the lukewarm sea water, as indicated above. Water has played one more role in protecting the early unicellular life forms from harmful effects of the ultraviolet rays, which become ineffective at a depth of about 10-15 meters below the water surface. Hence the living unicellular organism which originated near surface of the water could survive and thrive only in the water below that depth. Since there was no oxygen in the water that time, energy required by the cells could be obtained from the anaerobic exothermal chemical reactions. Without oxygen, microbes most likely had obtained energy through exothermal reactions of sulphur compounds. However, there was limitation on the reproduction of cells because, the energy released in this chemical reaction was much less. About 2300-2400 mya, a bacterium emerged in the sea that could convert sunlight into usable energy. This blue-green microbe called a cyanobacterium was likely to be the first photosynthetic organism, and it was a game changer in the story of life on earth. They were photo-synthesizers, making food from water, carbon dioxide & chlorophyl, with the help of solar energy, by releasing oxygen as a biproduct. Besides that, the level of energy released during this process was much higher than that under anaerobic conditions, resulting in increased pace of the evolution. They set the stage for a remarkable transformation, which can be called a 'Milestone' in the history of evolution of life on the earth. Over millions of years, oxygen generated by the photosynthetic plants continued to accumulate in the atmosphere. It was this oxygen that would allow complex life forms to evolve and thrive in the millennia to come. This action very gradually catalysed a dramatic rise in the oxygen level, making the environment less hospitable for other microbes that could not tolerate oxygen. Even though the actual process of photosynthesis is the most complicated one, it can be explained in simple chemical reaction as below: $6CO_2$ (Carbon dioxide) + $12H_2O$ (Water) + (Chlorophyl + Solar energy) = $C_6H_{12}O_6$ (Glucose) + $6H_2O$ (Water) + $6O_2$ (Oxygen). In simple terms it means that, leaves of trees absorb carbon dioxide from the atmosphere to generate glucose from water with nutrients dissolved in it, with the help of solar energy, to release oxygen and half the quantity of absorbed water back into atmosphere as evapotranspiration.

Due to action of ultraviolet rays on oxygen in the atmosphere, some of its molecules were gradually getting converted into ozone ($O_3$). It being lighter than the air, ozone molecules moved upwards in the atmosphere and eventually formed a continuous layer containing ozone around the earth in the stratosphere. Over the globe, thickness of this layer varied from region to region and with the season. At present about 90% of the ozone in the atmosphere lies in stratosphere, between 15 to 35 km above the earth surface. This ozone layer or ozone shield is a region of earth's stratosphere which contains less than 10 parts per million of ozone. But still, it absorbs 97 to 99 percent of the Sun's medium-frequency ultraviolet light, which otherwise would potentially damage exposed life forms near the earth surface. The principal marine primary producers such as cyanobacteria, phytoplankton, red, brown and green algae and marine plants which then existed below surface of the oceans could then come to surface safely, absorb more solar energy and evolve more rapidly. Living plant matter also released more oxygen in the atmosphere and produced more food that provided all other organisms with the chemical energy they needed to survive and thrive.

**Evolution of plant and animal life in the oceans** – As stated above, life on the earth as first cellular organism evolved in warm water of the shallow sea by about 3650 mya. Those single living cells further divided into two live cells and then multiplied in a geometric proportion. Next step of evolution meant finding a way for small single-celled organisms to work closely together to form the first multicellular life on the earth. How this happened is also not entirely well understood but evidence suggests that once it did evolve, there was no going back. Multicellular life evolved under the influence of both the non-biological and the biological environment, but how the balance between these factors changed remained largely unknown. With the emergence of cyanobacterium in the oceans about 2350 mya, which could convert sunlight into usable energy in the form of glucose as stated above, revolution in the living world commenced. It was the start of 'Plant Kingdom' in the oceans. Plants floated on water and produced glucose by the process of photosynthesis for their growth. Since minerals and salts necessary to produce glucose were available in the sea water, these bacteria absorbed them while floating on sea water. They later evolved plant like structure which consisted of leaves connected by thread-like shreds to produce food in all its parts. Many of the earliest groups continue to thrive, as exemplified by red and green algae in marine environments.

By the time such earliest plants evolved, animals were already the dominant organisms in the ocean. Plants were only constrained to the upper layer of water that received enough sunlight for photosynthesis. Therefore, plants never became dominant marine organisms. These bacteria were to be consumed as food for their growth by the organisms then evolved in the oceans. They further evolved into different forms as a part of the 'Animal Kingdom' and survived by consuming other organisms but could not produce food on their own. Animals are multicellular eukaryotes and are distinguished from plants by lacking cell walls. The earliest animals to evolve in oceans were marine invertebrates, which are cold-blooded animals having no backbone or spine. They are generally soft-bodied animals that lack a rigid internal skeleton for the attachment of muscles, but often possess a hard outer skeleton that serves for body protection. They lay eggs from which young invertebrates are produced. More than 90 percent of all living animal species in the world are invertebrates. Marine invertebrates include jellyfish, crabs, lobsters, squids, clams, corals etc. The earliest 665-million-year-old animal fossils in the South Australia are of invertebrates. Next to evolve were vertebrates. The evolution of fishes began in the sea water about 530 mya during the Cambrian-explosion. Early fish had no jaws, but most went extinct when they were outcompeted by jawed fish, but two groups survived. Jawed fish fall into two main groups: fish with bony internal skeletons and fish with cartilaginous internal skeletons (Sharks and Rays). Fishes are cold blooded vertebrates and breathe oxygen dissolved in sea water with the help of gills. They lay eggs from which young ones are hatched.

**Evolution of plant and animal life on the Land -** Plants also lived in freshwater communities on land as early as 1000 mya and that communities of complex, multicellular photosynthesizing organisms existed on land around 850 mya. The principal marine primary producers were cyanobacteria, algae and marine plants, which evolved into red, brown and green algae and then invaded the land to start evolving into the land plants we know today. About 500-450 mya, plants and fungi started colonising the land. The evolution of plants has resulted in a wide range of complexity, from the earliest algal mats, through multicellular marine and freshwater green algae, terrestrial bryophytes, lycopods and ferns, to the complex gymnosperms and angiosperms (Flowering plants) of today. When plants moved onto land, everything was wide open. Without plants growing on land, there was nothing for other organisms to feed on. Land could not be colonized by other organisms until land plants became established. Many of the earliest groups continue to thrive even today, as exemplified by red and green algae in marine environments. The plant kingdom is broadly divided into two major groups, the algae, fungi, bryophytes & ferns; and the gymnosperms & angiosperms. Grasses were the last to evolve around 66-55 mya i.e., after the last mass extinction.

About 365 mya amphibians evolved from fishes in the swampy habitats like shallow wetlands, coastal lagoons and large brackish river deltas which existed at that time. Amphibians evolved adaptations that allowed them to stay out of the water for longer periods, but they still required water bodies for their reproduction. Hence Amphibians lived in sea water and fresh lake water as well as on land only in coastal and moist areas around rivers and lakes. Evolution of animal life on land started with the evolution of cold-blooded amphibians. They were the forerunners for their further evolution into cold blooded reptiles from 315 mya, warm blooded mammals from 250 mya and birds from 160 mya, and they all were to occupy terrestrial ecosystems on the earth then onwards.

**Evolution from Mammals to Man** – Let us now see in more detail the evolution of mammals from about 252 mya to 0.3 mya to *'Homo sapiens'* and then to 'Modern Man' about 12,000 years ago. Mammals is a group of vertebrate animals, in which females give birth to live babies, not eggs, and the young are nourished with milk from special mammary glands of the mother. These characteristics distinguish them from reptiles (including birds). Mammals evolved about 252 to 201 mya i.e., after the fourth mass extinction about 252 mya, from members of the reptilian order. Mammals are warm blooded and have either four legs or two fore limbs and two hind legs. The earliest placental mammals may have evolved about 110 mya. The placental mammals evolved into primates around 85 mya, which include lemurs, tarsiers, monkeys, apes, and **humans**. Primates led arboreal life (in trees) till extinction of dinosaurs about 66 mya and the first true primates evolved by 55 mya or a bit earlier. Scientists have long assumed that the extinction of dinosaurs about 66 mya had opened many niches for mammals to exploit. The characteristics and evolution of primates is of particular interest to us as it allows us to understand the evolution of our own species. Primates are divided into two groups: prosimians and anthropoids. Prosimians include bush babies, lemurs, lorises and tarsiers. These primate species possess adaptations for climbing trees, as they all probably descended from tree-dwellers. Anthropoids include monkeys, apes, and humans. One characteristics of primates is the stereoscopic vision, two overlapping fields of vision from the eyes, which allows for the perception of depth and for gauging distance. Other characteristics of primates are, brains that are larger than those of most other mammals, claws that have been modified into flattened nails, typically only one offspring per pregnancy, and a trend toward holding the body upright.

Primates are among the most social of animals. Monkeys evolved by 40 mya and Apes evolved from them approximately 25 mya. Apes are generally larger than monkeys and they do not possess a tail. Within the superfamily apes, the family diverged from the gibbons some 15–20 mya; African great apes diverged from orangutans about 14 mya. About 8-9 mya, gorillas separated from humans, chimpanzees, and bonobos. Around 7 mya, a further divergence occurred which separated chimpanzees and bonobos from the early hominins (human-like primates) that were our direct ancestors. Finally, humans and chimpanzees diverged approximately 6 mya. Hominins were predominantly bipedal and include those groups that likely to have given rise to our species—including Australopithecus, Homo habilis, and Homo erectus—and those non-ancestral groups of modern humans, such as Neanderthals. The earliest humans developed out of Australopithecine ancestors about 3 million years ago, most likely in Eastern Africa in the Kenyan Rift Valley, where the oldest known stone tools were found. Australopithecus is a genus of hominin which went extinct about 2 mya. The human genus, Homo, first appeared between 2.5 and 3 mya and Homo erectus appeared approximately 1.8 mya. Number of species, apparently evolved from Homo erectus starting about 500,000 years ago. *'Homo sapiens'* – Modern man who designated himself as 'Wise man' - is believed to have emerged in East Africa about 300,000 years ago.

The Great Rift Valley is a series of contiguous geographic trenches, approximately 7,000 kilometres in total length, that runs from Lebanon in Asia to Mozambique in Southeast Africa. The valley is 48 to 64 km wide on an average but reaches nearly 480 km at its widest section. The valley is situated in a region where three tectonic plates meet. The rift has been forming for some 30 million years because the plates began to move apart because of violent subterranean forces that tore apart the earth's crust. As the valley developed, the precipitation pattern changed after its formation. Much forest area in the East African part of the valley gradually turned into 'Savannah' i.e., grass land interspersed with some trees, which promoted evolution and development of primates into bipedal man.

Early Homo sapiens might have migrated out of Africa about 200,000 years before as seen from the fossils found in Palestine and Greece. The recent African origin paradigm suggests that the anatomically modern humans outside of Africa descend from a population of Homo sapiens migrating from East Africa roughly 70–50,000 years ago and spreading along the southern coast of Asia and to Oceania by about 50,000 years ago. Modern humans spread across Europe about 40,000 years ago. During successive migrations Homo sapiens travelled out of Africa and reached Asia, Europe, Indonesia, China and Australia. Finally, around 15,000 years ago, humans crossed from Asia to North America and from there to South America.

Milestones in the 'History of Evolution of Life on the Earth' could be summarised as below:

4,540 mya – Entry of Earth in the Solar System. (mya – million years ago)

3,650 mya – Kindling the spark of Life on the Earth.

2,350 mya – Evolution of photosynthesising Cyanobacteria in the Ocean.

1,000 mya – Entry of plants in freshwater lakes on Land.

530 mya – Evolution from invertebrates to vertebrates in the Ocean.

365 to 300 mya – Evolution of plants on Land from Ferns to Gymnosperms to Angiosperms.

365 mya – Evolution of amphibians living close to coastal area.

315 mya – Evolution of reptiles on Land.

300 to 150 mya – Evolution of four main groups of Insects.

250 mya – Evolution of Mammals.

201 to 66 mya - Age of Dinosaurs.

160 mya – Evolution of Birds.

110 mya – Evolution of Placental Mammals.

85 to 55 mya – Evolution of Primates from Tree living to Land living.

65 mya – Evolution of Grass on Land.

40 to 25 mya – Evolution from Monkeys to Apes.

6 mya – Humans separated from Chimpanzees.

0.3 mya – Evolution of *'Homo Sapiens'* – Wise Man.

12,000 years before – Entry of *'Modern Man'* on the earth.

**Interruptions in the Evolutionary process -** The history of evolution of life on the earth which has been explained briefly as above was not so smooth and gradual as is narrated. There were some natural events such as 'Ice ages' which extended over millions of years and constricted the pace and scope of evolution. There were some 'Mass extinctions' which also extended over millions of years or occurred as a catastrophic event, to cause large scale destruction of many species evolved till then. Evolution, however, started afresh from the plant & animal species which survived after all such events and finally culminated into evolution of 'modern man' after the last ice age. Details of these events which changed the course of evolution are as below:

**Ice Ages** – An ice age (Glaciation age) is a long period – millions to tens of millions of years – of reduction in the temperature of earth's surface and the atmosphere, resulting in the presence and expansion of continental and polar ice sheets and alpine glaciers, covering large areas of its surface. Such periods of large-scale glaciation would last several million years and drastically reshape surface features of entire continents. Earth's climate alternated between ice ages and greenhouse (warm) periods, during which there were no glaciers on the planet. Scientists have recorded five significant ice ages throughout the earth's history:

The Huronian (2400-2100 mya), Cryogenian (850-635 mya), Andean-Saharan (460-430 mya), Karoo (360-260 mya) and Quaternary (2.6 mya to present).

Peak of the second ice age, and probably the most severe one, occurred from 720 to 630 mya and may have produced a 'Snowball Earth' in which glacial ice sheets reached the equator. The Quaternary Ice Age, the most recent activity of widespread glaciation (formation of the Arctic Ice Cap) occurred during the period 2.6 mya to about 11,700 years ago.

Individual pulses of cold climate within an ice age are termed as glacial periods, and intermittent warm periods within ice age are called as interglacial periods. When most people talk about the 'ice age', they are usually referring to the last glacial period (sudden climate warming event), which began about 1,15,000 years ago and ended about 11,700 years ago. Right now, we are in the most recent ice age's warm interglacial period of the Quaternary called the Holocene, which began about 11,700 years ago. A lesser, recent glacial stage called the 'Little Ice Age' began in the 16$^{th}$ century and advanced & receded intermittently over three centuries in Europe and many other regions. Its maximum development was reached about 1750 AD, at which time glaciers were more widespread on earth than at any time since the last major ice age ended about 11,700 years ago. The amount of anthropogenic greenhouse gases emitted into Earth's oceans and atmosphere is predicted to prevent the next glacial period for the next 500,000 years, which otherwise would have begun in around 50,000 years.

**Mass extinctions** – Extinction is a way of life, but there have been mass extinction events when a whole array of species of plant and animal life got wiped out on the earth. There were 5 such 'Mass extinctions' in the history of the earth. About 445 mya, Ordovician-Silurian extinction event occurred that eliminated an estimated 85 percent of all species then existing. Next mass extinction was Devonian extinction about 370 mya (419 to 359 mya) which was responsible for the elimination of 70 to 80 percent of all animal species then existing. About 252 mya, Permian extinction the largest extinction ever in the history of earth resulted in elimination of about 90 percent of marine species over the course of about 60,000 years. About 201 mya, Triassic-Jurassic global extinction event occurred (252 to 201 mya) that resulted in the demise of some 76 percent of all marine and terrestrial species. It is thought that it was the key moment that allowed dinosaurs (Giant Reptiles) to become the dominant land animals on the earth. Last mass extinction (Cretaceous-Paleogene), consequence of a catastrophic event, occurred about 66 mya. Now, the bulk of the evidence suggests that a bolide (asteroid) 5 to 15 km wide impacted/smashed to earth's surface in the Yucatán Peninsula 66 mya, forming a crater and creating a 'kill mechanism' that triggered the extinction event. The impact caused tsunamis, acid rain, wildfire, and global cooling and with such a catastrophic change, many species went extinct worldwide, including complete disappearance of the dinosaurs.

Next mass extinction named as 'The Holocene Extinction' hasn't been defined by a dramatic event like a meteor impact. Instead, it is made up of the nearly constant string of extinctions that have shaped the last 12,000 years or so, by a single species—*Modern Humans*—which came to dominate the earth since then. Some have even suggested that the Holocene Extinction would be more aptly named the 'Anthropocene Extinction', after the role humans have played in this ongoing loss of biodiversity around the world.

If we consider existence of about 3650 million years of the life on our earth as equivalent to *'One year'*, one day of that year would be of about 10 million years, one hour would be of about 4,20,000 years and one minute would be of about 7,000 years duration. Then we can say that the dinosaurs became extinct on the 359$^{th}$ day (last mass extinction 66 mya) of that year and evolution of the primates started concurrently. Our ancestors – monkeys, entered on the scene on the 362$^{nd}$ day (40 mya) and 'Homo Sapiens' i.e., the 'Wise man' entered on the last day (6-7 mya) of that year. Whereas 'Modern humans' came on the stage of the earth just about two minutes before today (12,000 years). For 364 days, 23 hours and 58 minutes evolution of life on our earth was taking place on the principles of 'Natural selection' or 'Survival of the fittest'. The progress of evolution, however, hindered for millions of years during the five 'Ice ages' as above. Whereas most of the species then existing perished during the five 'Mass extinctions' which also extended over millions of years. But after every such event, life on the earth restored gradually back to the new normal automatically after several millions of years by following the above principle.

*'The Holocene Extinction'* appears to have just started about 2 minutes (12,000 years) before, not because of any natural causes or events as before, but only due to man-made causes. When man started destruction of the terrestrial ecosystems (land under forests) around 12,000 years before to grow pastures and then to cultivate land to grow crops, it was the first small step in that direction. Destruction of forests by 'slash and burn' method also released the carbon sequestered in the trunks and branches of the trees, back into the atmosphere as carbon dioxide ($CO_2$). Concurrently methene gas ($CH_4$) was also released in the atmosphere due to ponded paddy (Rice) cultivation and from the digestion process of domestic flatulent animals. Over a 20-year period, methane gas is 80 times more potent at Global Warming than the carbon dioxide. Methane has hence accounted for roughly 30 per cent of global warming since pre-industrial times. Next major activity by man was the start of industrial revolution around 250 years before. Together with other developments of human society such as urbanisation, industrialisation, men & material transport and related activities, it has resulted in a continuous increase in the consumption of fossil fuels in the last 150 years. Such emission and accumulation of carbon dioxide and other 'Green House Gases' such as Methane in the atmosphere has given rise to 'Global Warming and Climate Change' (GW & CC), a potential hazard looming large on the horizon. Industrialisation and urbanisation have also resulted in pollution of the air and pollution of most of the riverine ecosystems.

We would review all the activities of man in making use of all the natural resources such as air, water, solar energy; and land, to meet his needs for survival and greed for his wellbeing. We will also see in all the foregoing chapters some undesirable ill effects arising out of it and possible remedial measures to mitigate the situation.

# Chapter 3

# Characteristics of Surface Water Resource and its Assessment to meet needs of Nature and Man.

*Precipitation is the primary source of 'Water Resource' which has been endowed free of cost on the Earth by the Nature, either in the form of rainfall or as snow fall. Since water resource, either in the form of surface water or ground water, is the most important life support system, let us firstly try to understand its characteristics. When modern man started making use of the water resource to meet his needs of drinking water, domestic use, irrigation, and industrial use, in that order, in some developed countries/river basins, the water demand increased appreciably. Hence making river basin wise assessment of natural availability of surface water resource was felt and procedure for the same has been covered in this chapter. However, due to several natural and other constraints, it is usually not possible to make available all the water resource in the river basins for human use. Secondly, water requirements for terrestrial and aquatic ecosystems have to be considered in the planning of water for human use. Figures of basin wise natural availability of surface water resource and the part of it which is available for our use have been given basin wise in India. Characteristics of Ground Water Resource have been covered separately in chapter No.9.*

Air, Water, Solar energy, and Land are the four life support systems on our earth. Out of these, nature has provided the *'Air'* abundantly, which mainly composes of Oxygen, Carbon dioxide and Nitrogen gas. *'Water'* is given free by nature as rainfall or snowfall, but its availability varies with location and time of the year. Solar energy is also given free by nature, but its availability varies with the location on the earth, reducing from the equator to the polar region. Plants make use of carbon dioxide from *'Air'*, and *'Water'* containing minerals & nutrients sucked from the soil by their roots, to produce food with the help of *'Solar energy'*, by the process of photosynthesis and generate oxygen and water as a biproduct. Animals including man consume food generated by the plants, inhale oxygen for their survival and exhale carbon dioxide. This is a symbiotic relationship between the plants and the animals. Fixation of Nitrogen from atmosphere in the soil by means of some compounds is helpful for plant growth. Plants are the primary producers of food on the earth, and hence they are essential and vital for all animal species on the earth. Lastly, even though the *'Land'* resource is given free by nature on the earth, because the nature cannot protest, man has destroyed fertile forest land extensively during last 12,000 years and acquired ownership of the land for his personal use. Its ownership had traditionally been with the person who encroached on the forest land to grow pastures or to grow crops on it. Now the ownership of land rests broadly with the Nation/State and the individuals, as per the Constitution of every country.

Large scale destruction of natural terrestrial ecosystems during the last 12,000 years, has also destroyed many species of insects, reptiles, animals, and birds supported by them. Besides that, burning of trees from forest land has caused releasing of sequestered carbon dioxide gas in the atmosphere. Practicing ponded paddy crop and tending of flatulent animals had caused to release methane gas in the atmosphere. After the industrialisation, carbon dioxide gas is being released in the atmosphere on a large scale due to burning of fossil fuels. However, till second half of the last century, we were not aware about the hazardous effects of release of all these 'Green House Gases' (GHG) in this manner on the 'Climate' of the earth. Hence in retrospect it can be said that, inadvertently, it has perhaps been the contribution of modern man, which has not only caused pollution of the atmosphere, but also has culminated into the potential hazardous effects of 'Global Warming and Climate Change' (GW & CC). We will see about the important issue of 'Climate Change', in a separate chapter.

Nature had provided a protective shield in the form of 'Ozone layer' in the stratosphere, which had protected life on the Earth from the harmful effects of Ultraviolet rays (UV) from the 'Solar energy', as explained in the earlier chapter. But during use of chemicals as coolant in refrigeration process & in the aerosol sprays, 'Chlorflor Carbon gas' (CFC) was released in the atmosphere, which gradually decomposed ozone gas to cause puncturing of that protective ozone shield at some locations around the earth. Falling of UV rays from those openings, because of the above action by man, though inadvertently, without knowing its harmful effects on the ozone shield, had caused incidence of potential harm to life on the Earth. Awareness about hazardous effects of emission of CFC on the ozone layer and necessity to reduce their emission was discussed in the World Conference in Kyoto, Japan in December 1997 and 'Kyoto Protocol' was signed. Necessity to act by all the developed countries of the world to contain such emissions within reasonable limits, had come to the forefront at the Global level since then. Subsequently, due to coordinated efforts taken by all the developed and developing countries in the world by reducing the use of CFC and other potent gases, now the ozone shield has been partly restored within safe limits.

Out of the above four life supporting systems, we do not have any control on the natural availability of air and solar energy, but we have only degraded their quality as explained above. Land is owned by the individuals, and one can supplement the soil with organic manures/chemical fertilisers and adopt improved agriculture technology to increase land productivity. So let us see in more detail about the important element *'Water'* from amongst the four life support systems because, it is amenable for its use to meet most of the basic human needs. Solar energy is the prime mover for the sustained 'Water Cycle' that provides water resource in the form of rainfall or snowfall on the earth every year, as explained in the Chapter No.1. This natural cycle of 'evaporation-cloud formation-condensation-precipitation' takes place every year on the earth. Hence first characteristic of precipitation and so the water resource is that it is a recurring or renewable resource. This is unlike other natural resources such as minerals, coal, oil and gas etc.

Water resource is endowed free of cost by the nature, but Its availability varies according to its location on the earth. By and large, it is high in the equatorial region, decreases towards the polar region and is least at the driest places in some deserts on the earth. Hence there is large variation in the quantum or magnitude of available annual precipitation from place to place. Orographic precipitation is recorded as highest in the World in the village Mawsynram in the northeast India in Assam state, as about 11,800 mm annually (Average of 48 years). Earlier it was in Cherrapunjee village near it, where it is 11,360 mm as average of 48 years. On the 16th of June 1995, Cherrapunjee recorded the highest rainfall received in one day (24-hour period) aggregating to 1563 mm. Rainfall is least in the Atacama Desert in the South America where it even does not rain every year. As against that, it rains practically every day in the evening in the equatorial region. In the countries along East coast of Africa, there are two rainy spells in a year, whereas it rains practically every month in England. In the Mauritius island and near the southern tips of many islands of the Philippines, rainfall is well distributed over the year and is adequate to sustain even the rain-fed sugar cane crop.

Precipitation pattern in India is as shown in the map below:

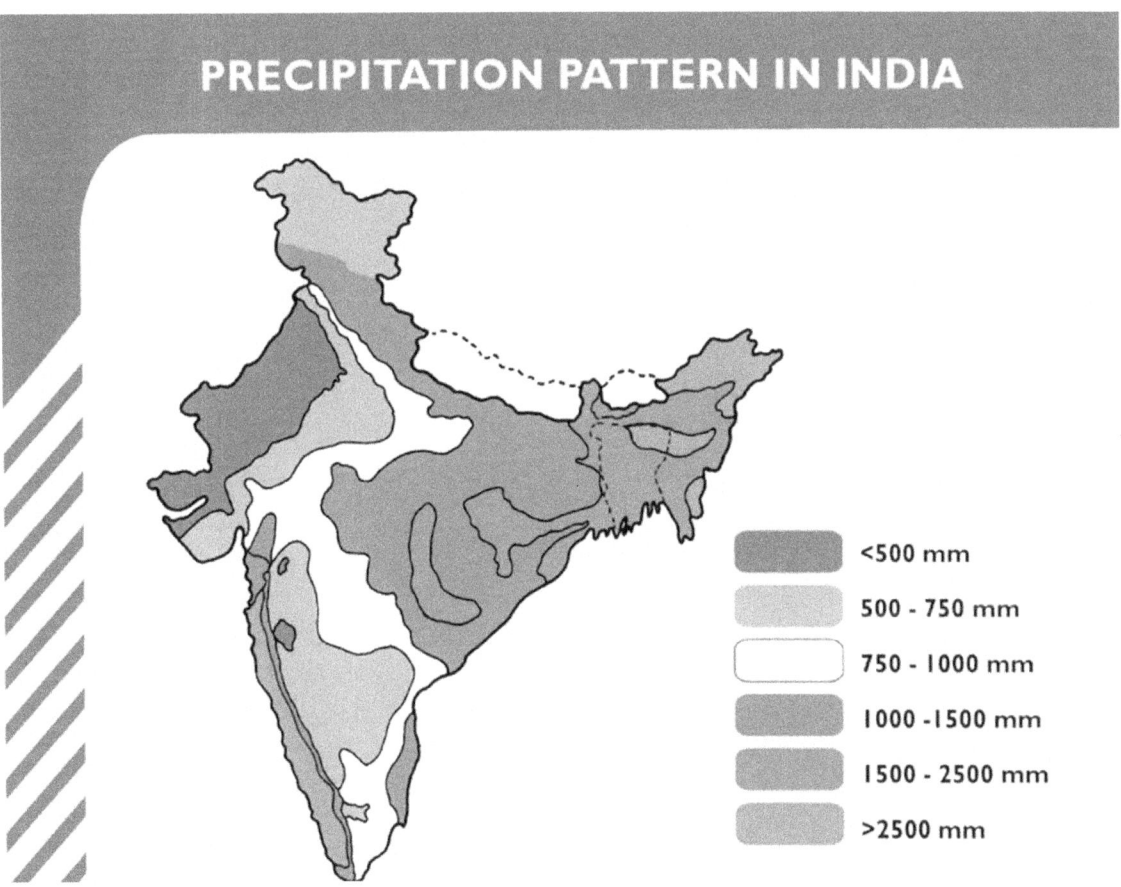

In India, precipitation is more than 2500 mm in the North-East region (Brahmaputra River basin) but is hardly 150 to 450 mm in the North-West region. To the West of North-South running Sahyadri mountain range close to the West coast of Peninsular India, annual orographic precipitation ranges from about 2500 mm to 5000 mm but reduces to only about 400 to 500 mm within 70-80 km towards East, in the rain-shadow zone. In short, the precipitation depends on the topography, latitude, monsoon pattern each year and hence is location specific. Month wise distribution of annual rainfall also varies from place to place. In India, South-West monsoon commences from S-E corner around 1st of June and covers the entire country by mid-July in the N-W corner. It starts receding in the 1st fortnight of September from N-W corner and gradually leaves the country from the S-E corner in the second fortnight of October. States along eastern coast of India also receive some rain from the returning monsoon in the months of November-December. There are only about 80 to 100 rainy days in a year in India.

Third peculiarity of precipitation is that it is variable from year to year in its magnitude and its month wise distribution. It may rain 1000 mm at a place in one year but may rain much more, or much less in the next year. In some years it may fall in lesser number of rainy spells with each of high intensity, causing damage to crop and causing floods to rivers. In some years it may fall evenly distributed during the entire rainy season in short spells, which would be ideal for the crop growth and there would not be any floods. In some years, it may be inadequate even to sustain rain-fed crops. Even though there is such variation in the pattern of rainfall and its magnitude from year to year, it is observed that average rainfall value measured at any place for any 30-40-year-cycle, remains nearly constant in India. It is also observed from long duration rainfall record of past years that, when total magnitude of total average annual rainfall is high, percent variation of lowest & highest value as recorded in the 30-40-year cycle is less when compared with the average value. On the contrary, where magnitude of total average annual rainfall is low, percent variation of lowest & highest value compared with the average value is quite high. For planning of water resource development infrastructure, estimate of availability of water resource in a river basin is usually worked out based on average rainfall in the basin, as computed from the latest 30-40-year cycle.

Now let us see the inter relationship between precipitation and the water resource. When it rains, all natural terrestrial ecosystems on the earth viz., rain forests, deciduous forests, savannas etc., and man-made ecosystems viz. pastures, cultivated fields, and all the open land, have first claim/charge on the rainwater. But you would not believe that in reality, 'Evaporation' has the first claim/charge on the rainwater even before it falls on the earth because, evaporation continuously takes place from the air in the tropical region before rain drops fall on the ground. Evaporation also takes place continuously from the land. We have no control on such evaporation and substantial part of water resource (about 42% as seen from Table No. 2 below) is thus lost due to evaporation. But then that water vapour moves upwards in the atmosphere and joins the water-cycle again. Part of the rainwater that falls on the land gets continuously absorbed in the soil, recharges the ground water and only the rest of it flows as 'surface water' through streams, rivulets, and rivers finally into the sea. Part of the flowing water also evaporates continuously into the atmosphere. When upper layer of soil gets saturated, water seeps further below in the ground into decomposed rock strata and flows below through cracks, crevices in rock and joints between two rock layers as Ground Water (GW). On saturation of the substrata, GW travels laterally very slowly through the sub strata towards the river and finally flows into it. Water in the ground below the riverbed level remains stationery but can be exploited by man for his use by means of a dug well. All water thus absorbed in the soil & the substrata below is known as 'Ground water'. So, we have dynamic water resource in the form of water flowing through rivers as surface water resource and ground water as relatively stationary resource which is temporarily conserved in the ground. Water that flows from rivers and that seeps into ground but flows towards the river is known as 'Blue water'. Water that is consumed by the trees and plants on the terrestrial ecosystems and by the crops and plants on the cultivated land from the ground water is known as 'Green water'. Some part of the water stored in the topsoil and from the GW is absorbed by roots of the plants and trees to produce food by photosynthesis; and balance water that is transpired from leaves as vapour, which is known as evapotranspiration, joins the water-cycle again.

Let us now see characteristics of the water resource. We have seen that the average rainfall at any place in a river basin is nearly constant. First characteristics would then be that total quantity of 'blue water' i.e., available water resource for its use by the nature and the humans in any river basin is limited and finite. Second characteristics of surface water resource is that it is a dynamic resource. If we don't make use of the flowing water in the river at any place, it would flow further downstream and finally into the sea. However, the Nature is not so unkind and has given us two 'savings accounts' to conserve this dynamic resource. First savings account in 'The Bank of Nature' is in the form of ground water. Plants withdraw from that savings account continuously for their survival, growth and to produce plant food for all the animal kingdom. We also can withdraw from that savings account to meet our drinking water needs and to irrigate fields. But if we don't make use of the ground water, it would flow into rivers slowly to feed them in the fair-weather season every year. Second savings account is in the form of snow that gets accumulated on mountain peaks above snow line in the tropical region, and on the land and mountains in the temperate region of the world. Snow accumulates during entire winter season and remains there till the atmospheric temperature starts to rise above $0^0$ C. Hence one cannot withdraw from that savings account during winter season to meet ones' needs. During hot weather season, the snow automatically melts and slowly flows into the rivers to sustain aquatic ecosystems and to enable us to make its use when it is needed the most for domestic/industrial/irrigation use and for power generation through hydroelectric projects.

Third characteristics of water resource is that it is a recurring/renewable resource. Even if river runs nearly dry during some summer months, with the onset of rainy season next year, it will start flowing again and would continue to do so year after year. It means that once we construct an infrastructure such as a Reservoir-Canal system or a River diversion Weir/Barrage-Canal system, water resource would be available every year for our use from the same infrastructure. We would only have to spend very nominal annual cost towards operation, maintenance and repairs of the infrastructure. Water resource would then be available up to the useful life (till it gets silted up) of that infrastructure, which is usually planned to be more than hundred years. Other natural resources such as minerals, coal, oil, natural gas etc remain in the earth till we exploit them. But once we exploit and use these physical resources, they would not be replaced in future in the mines or in the deep substrata by the nature. Secondly, unlike water resource, every year we would have to spend more and more money due to inflation in the cost of exploiting/harnessing these physical resources.

Fourth characteristics of the water resource is that it is a reusable resource. Some part of the water used for irrigation is lost permanently as evaporation from the irrigation system infrastructure. Some part is lost from the water conveyance system of canals, distribution network and from the cultivated land by way of deep percolation into the ground below. It can, however, be reused for irrigation by pumping it as ground water. If not so used it meets the river and then also it can be pumped and used for irrigation and other purposes. After urban use of water for domestic purposes, if the sewage generated is treated adequately it can be reused for irrigation. In the case of industrial use of water, except the quantum of water consumed in making the final produce (soft drinks, wine, beer etc.), rest of the water used in the manufacturing process must be treated prior to its release in the river, which can then also be used for irrigation. Alternatively, such effluent can be treated and recycled for industrial use any number of times. However, in both the cases, one must spend money for the treatment of effluent every time to get that much quantity of water for its reuse. That cost of treatment to get same quantity for reuse increases every year due to inflation and depreciation of the effluent/sewage treatment plants.

Fifth characteristics of water resource is that it is vulnerable to pollution. You can also call it a virtue because, all organic and inorganic pollutants which are dissolved, remain suspended, float, or settle at the bottom of the river, are carried free of cost by the river finally to the sea. Some of the solid material such as gravel, sand, and silt etc., carried along the riverbed gets settled on riverbanks to form fertile land and the balance finer material is carried up to the sea to get deposited there to form most fertile land in the Delta region. Coarse material such as gravel and sand carried by the rivers is used as engineering material during construction of buildings, roads and masonry/concrete dams. Since river water remains in contact with air while flowing on its way downstream, oxidation of some organic matter and inorganic chemical compounds take place to convert them into harmless stable compounds, to cause some natural purification of the pollutants. But because toxic chemicals & heavy metals from industrial effluent and some pathogens & phosphates from urban untreated sewage are carried by the river water, it gets polluted and cannot be reused for irrigation directly. When such polluted river water enters in a man-made reservoir on downstream, it starts polluting the lake water as well. All types of these pollutants are harmful if the river water is used for drinking purposes without providing adequate treatment. Hence this property of water can be considered as a vice because it gets polluted in the process, which prevents its direct reuse as a water resource to meet human needs.

**Estimation of availability of Surface Water Resource** – Any country is normally divided into States, Districts, Tehsils (sub districts), towns, and villages for the sake of administrative purposes. But rivers and its tributaries flow as per topography of the country or the region to form their river basins. At any point on the river course, total area from which the rainwater flows into it, is known as catchment area of the river at that point. When the river meets the sea, entire catchment area at that point is known as that particular 'River basin'. Estimation of availability of water resource is always done river basin wise, usually based on the average rainfall in the basin. In a large river basin where rainfall magnitude variation is notable, catchment is divided into sub basins, and estimation of available water resource is then done sub basin wise. These figures are then consolidated to get total availability of water resource in that river basin. When sub basin wise availability is known, on equity considerations, it is possible to plan transfer of water from relatively water-surplus sub basins into relatively water-short sub basins, which is then known as Intra-basin (within the basin) water transfer. On similar lines, it is possible to plan transfer of water from relatively water-surplus river basins into relatively water-short river basins and is then known as Inter-basin (from one basin to other basin) water transfer.

When a river basin extends over two or more than two countries, it is known as International River Basin. For such River basins, principles of sharing the surface water resource amongst the co-basin countries is decided either as per mutual agreements between the co-basin countries, or as per decision of the 'International River Water Disputes Tribunal' set up by the co-basin countries by mutual consent. On similar lines, principles of sharing the surface water resource amongst co-basin states is decided either as per mutual agreements between the co-basin states or as per decision of the 'Inter State River Water Disputes Tribunal' set up by the co-basin states by mutual consent. It is not possible to share the GW between co-basin countries or co-basin states, and hence right to exploit GW usually rests with every co-basin country and co-basin state within their boundaries.

Since rainfall is the primary source of water resource, availability of correct record of daily rainfall, extended over several years in the past is the basic information needed for its realistic estimation in any river basin. Usually, the rainfall cycle has some periodicity in a country or a region according to its rainfall source and storm pattern. It means that if we have actual rainfall data of the past 40 years and take average of every 10 years starting from the first year, then from the second year onwards and finally from the $31^{st}$ year, we will get 31 values of average rainfall for each 10-year cycle. If there is not much variation in these values, rainfall cycle can be said as 10 years. If there is substantial variation, similar calculations are done for 15-, 20-, 25-, and 30- year cycle. The rainfall cycle period of that region is the minimum number of year's cycle for which average value of all cycles is nearly the same. In India the monsoon rainfall cycle is taken as 30 years. Availability of rainfall record for 30 years is considered as adequate for correct estimation purposes for planning of WR development projects.

To measure actual daily precipitation, it is essential to install manually operated rain gauge stations at several places in the river basins. Locations and number of stations to be installed in a river basin depend on the pattern of variation in the magnitude of rainfall in the catchment area. If the variation is large, greater number of stations must be installed and the otherwise. The principle behind selection of locations of such rain gauge stations is that each station would be a realistic representation of the surrounding area covered by it. Actual rainfall during a 24-hour period is measured every day manually at 0800 hours, for all the year round. If connectivity of mobile phone is there, daily rainfall record is transmitted to the control room. But it does not record hourly intensity of rainfall, which is essential for correct estimation of floods to the river. Hence at some selected representative locations, automatic rain gauge recording stations are installed to record hourly intensity and total rainfall every day. At such stations, arrangements can also be made for automatic transmission of hourly intensity of rainfall data and daily rainfall data to the control room. Based on such real time data from all automatic rain gauge stations in the catchment, and the daily rain gauge record data, it is possible to estimate probable magnitude of flood to the river on a real time basis at different locations on the downstream. If such estimated magnitude of flood is above pre decided danger level, it is possible to forewarn people from towns and villages likely to be affected by the flood. It becomes a continuous process till the flood spell recedes.

In addition to measurement of rainfall by rain gauges, it is also essential to measure actual daily flow of main river and also its major tributaries if any, by installing river gauging stations at some selected locations along the river course. These stations are located where river course is stable, straight, and well confined within riverbanks. Some vertical standpost gauges are installed on one bank, starting from the riverbed up to and above the probable high flood level. Actual flow of river is then measured at different magnitudes of relatively steady flood water levels by measuring velocity of river water at different depths by a current meter all along cross section of the river at the gauging station. Such flow measurements can be taken in a better manner at a bridge location on its upstream or downstream, not very far from the river gauging station. For any nearly steady flood level, velocity of flow is measured by a current meter at different depths for each vent of the bridge and depth of flood water is also measured in each vent. Taking such measurements for representative vents (about 15-20 % of the total operative vents), we can get average velocity of flow of that flood. Knowing the area of flow under the bridge and average velocity as above, we can compute flood discharge for that flood level. By taking similar measurements of discharge for different flood levels, a stage-discharge curve can be prepared for that river gauging station. It is then possible to know magnitude of discharge of the river by recording gauge of river once in a day during fair weather season and more than once i.e., 3-4 times a day or more during rainy season. Knowing these values of average river discharge for every day, we can compute total quantum of water that has flown every week, month, monsoon season and in the year, at that river gauging station.

As we have seen above, part of the rainwater evaporates, part of it percolates into ground and balance only flows through the river, which is called as runoff at that place. On dividing the volume of water in the month/year as computed from river gauging record; by the total volume of water in the month/year as computed from the rainfall record of all stations above the river gauging station in the respective month/year, we get some factors. These factors represent monthly, monsoon seasonal and annual 'runoff-rainfall corelation'. They are generally on the lower side where total magnitude of rainfall in the catchment is low and are on the higher side where total magnitude of rainfall is on the higher side. For 30 year-cycle, if we compute the average factor of runoff and rainfall volume, it represents characteristics of that catchment in the river basin. For any other similar river basin of similar size, topography, forest cover and similar rainfall characteristics, if river gauging data is not available, this factor can be applied to the available average rainfall to get probable annual runoff from that catchment.

Central Water Commission, Govt. of India had carried out an exercise to estimate natural water resource availability in each river basin and in India as a whole. Those figures of River basin wise availability of water are as shown in Table No.1 below:

| Table No. 1 Water Resource availability in Major River Basins in India | | | |
|---|---|---|---|
| River basin | Average Annual Availability in Cubic Kilo meters | Per person Per year Average availability In Cubic meters | Per Hectare Per Year Average availability for Cultivable Land In Cubic meters |
| **A) East flowing rivers** | | | |
| 1. Ganges | 525 | 1,470 | 8,730 |
| 2. Brahmaputra-Barak | 586 | **16,620** | **44,180** |
| 3. Suvarnarekha | 12 | 1,320 | 6,530 |
| 4. Brahmani-Vaitarni | 28 | 2,920 | 8,900 |
| 5. Mahanadi | 67 | 2,510 | 8,370 |
| 6. Godavari | 111 | 2,050 | 5,840 |
| 7. Krishna | 78 | 1,290 | 3,850 |
| 8. Pennar | 6 | <u>650</u> | <u>1,770</u> |
| 9. Kaveri | 21 | 730 | 3,690 |
| 10. Remaining rivers | 70 | ------ | ------ |
| Total | 1,504 | 2,270 (Average) | ------ |
| **B) West flowing rivers** | | | |
| 11. Indus | 73 | 1,760 | 7.600 |
| 12. Luni | 15 | 680 | <u>640</u> |
| 13. Sabarmati | 4 | <u>360</u> | 2,460 |
| 14. Mahi | 11 | 1,150 | 4,980 |
| 15 Narmada | 46 | **3,110** | **7,730** |
| 16 Tapi | 15 | 1,010 | 3,290 |
| 17. Remaining rivers along West coast strip | **201** | -------- | -------- |
| Total | 365 | 2,030 (Average) | -------- |
| Grand Total | 1,869 | 2,220 (Average) | 5,680 (Average) |
| | | | |

With a view to assessing naturally available water resource potential in each river basin, it is expressed as 'Per person availability' and also as 'per hectare availability for cultivable land' as shown in the Table above. Per person availability mainly indicates average water availability for population for irrigation, domestic and industrial use. Per hectare average availability for cultivable land indicates maximum availability of water for irrigating the cultivable land. It would be seen that there is large variation in these figures from basin to basin. For the East flowing rivers, per person availability varies from 16,620 to 650 cubic meters and per hectare availability varies from 44,180 to 1,770 cubic meters. For the West flowing rivers, per person availability varies from 3,110 to 360 cubic meters and per hectare availability varies from 7,730 to 640 cubic meters. However, all these figures are only to be considered as indicative because they are based on the maximum availability of water resource in the river basins. Hence it becomes necessary to work out how much water resource is likely to be actually available for human use in each river basin

**Estimation of utilisable Surface and GW Resource** - Once River basin wise natural availability of surface water resource is estimated as above, next step would be to estimate how much water would be actually available for human use in every river basin. It depends on many factors such as topography, forest cover, actual status of irrigation development and urbanisation in the basin at the time of planning of projects etc. Usually there are limited sites available on the main river and its tributaries to locate storage reservoirs or diversion weirs. Where topography is suitable to locate the storage dams in the upper reaches, sometimes presence of substantial forest land under the lake submergence area makes it an unviable proposal. In the lower reaches even if topography at some place is suitable to locate a dam, lot of irrigated land or small town & some villages may get submerged, which then becomes a difficult social problem to resolve. Hence initially locations of all possible dam sites in every river basin are identified on topographical maps. Then preliminary field survey is carried out at such sites to construct a dam to store estimated water resource available at that site. Rough command area survey is also carried out to cover the area irrigated from that storage. Based on rough cost estimates and possible benefits from the project, its economic viability is decided. Such surveys are carried out in the entire river basin and based on the tentative feasible sites out of them, basin wise estimation of possible utilisable surface water resource by constructing suitable water resource development infrastructure is worked out.

Estimation of average annual natural ground water (GW) recharge in India is 432 cukm and utilisable recharge is 396 cukm in India. It has been worked out by the Govt. of India, with the help of Central Ground Water Board as stated in Ch. No. 9. Based on this information, figures of total surface water and GW available in India and utilisable water from all the river basins are as shown in Table No.2 below:

**Table No. 2 – Available and Utilisable Water Resource in India**

1. Total Water Resource available in India: 4000 Cubic Kilo meters
2. Total average evaporation loss from it: 1699 Cubic Kilo meters (42%)
3. Water percolating as GW on average each year: 432 Cubic Kilo meters (11%)
4. Average utilisable GW recharge -: 396 Cubic Kilo meters (10%)
5. Water flowing through rivers on average each year: 1869 Cubic Kilo meters (47%)
6. Utilisable surface water on average each year: 692 Cubic Kilo meters (17%)
7. Utilisable surface water & GW on average each year: 1088 Cubic Kilo meters (27%)

1 Cubic Kilo meter = 1000,000,000 (1000x1000x1000) Cubic meters = 1 Billion Cubic meters

1 Cubic meter = 1000 litres

**Identification of Water Surplus and Water Scarce River Basins in India** – In some basins, it is not possible to make use of the water resource available there fully. As against that there may be some basins which have very low availability of utilisable water resource. On the consideration of equitable development, it is desirable to transfer water from water surplus basins to water scarce basins. However, it is difficult to classify the river basins in any country clearly as 'Water surplus or Water scarce'. If more water is available in a river basin, it would be possible to develop it in the long run to make full use of it for different purposes. For some river basins, if the natural availability of water resource is inadequate, it puts restrictions on the water related development of the population residing in that basin. Such situation is likely to create inequitable development of the society. Based on the principle of social justice and equity it would hence be desirable to transfer water from relatively water surplus basins to relatively water scarce basins, to prevent lopsided development of the country. In the democratic set up classifying any basin as 'water surplus', becomes a contentious issue. Implications of this issue are covered in full details in Ch. No.10, in the paragraph on 'Interlinking of Rivers'. We can broadly classify the river basins in 3 categories as below:

1. Water surplus but not much water can be transferred to other basins.
2. Water surplus and some water can be transferred to other basins.
3. Water scarce basins – Based on per capita & per hectare poor availability.

Based on such analysis, a map of India showing major river basins and their classification as Water surplus, Transferable water surplus and Water scarce river basins is as below:

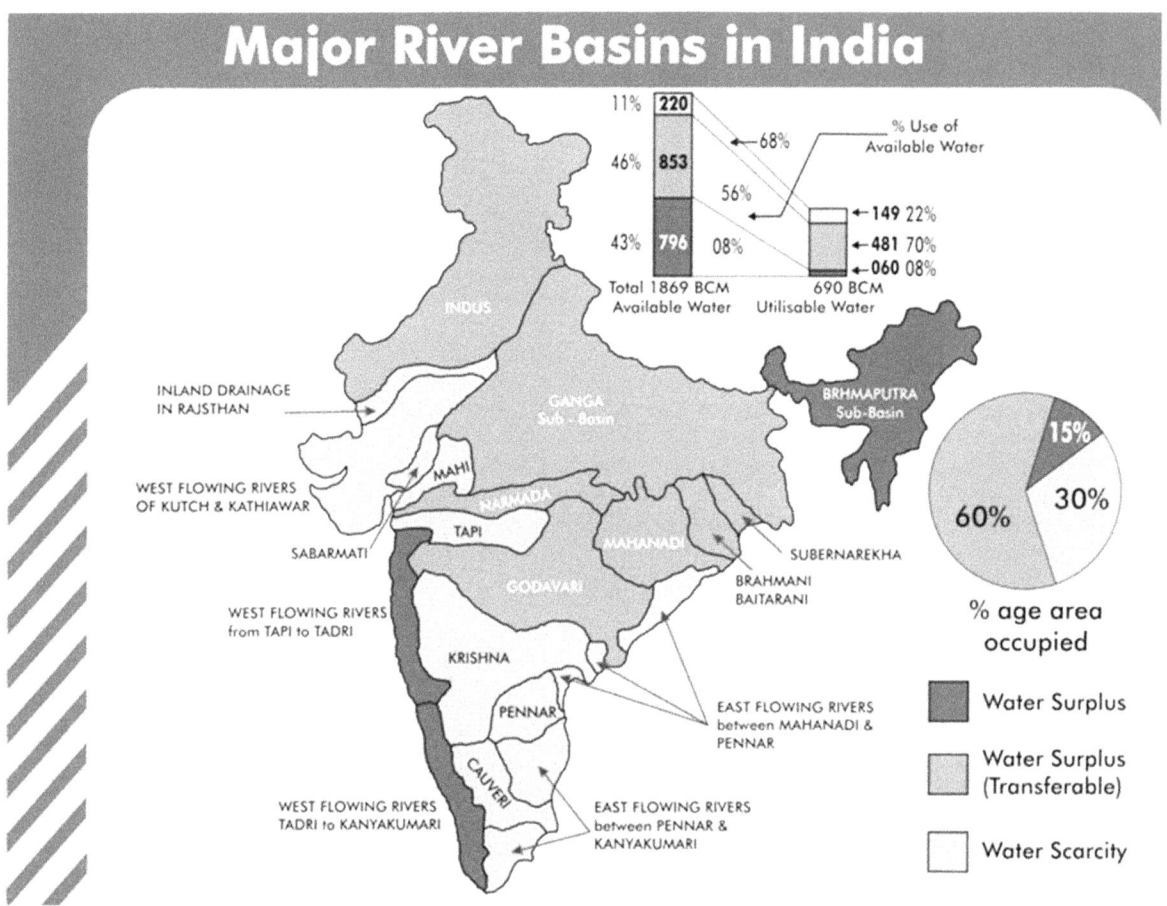

Detailed break up of WR availability and utilisable water in these three categories is shown in the map. There are water surplus river basins along the West coast in the Peninsular India and in the North-East region in the Brahmaputra sub basin as shown in the map. Along the West coast, land slopes are steep and good sites to locate dams are not available. Some small size dam-canal irrigation projects are constructed there, but there is weak response to irrigation due to sufficient rain in the area. If a dam is constructed there at lower altitude, the stored water can be best used by lifting it by 300 to 350 meters over the Sahyadri mountain to provide irrigation in the water scarce region in the East. Even if that area in the rain shadow zone is drought prone, such lift irrigation projects become economically unviable. In the Brahmaputra sub basin in the N-E corner of the country, land is mostly covered by rich forest and hence dam construction projects become unviable. Some storage dams are possible only on the northern tributaries of the river.

A map showing water available in water surplus and water short river basins and corresponding utilisable water in them is as below:

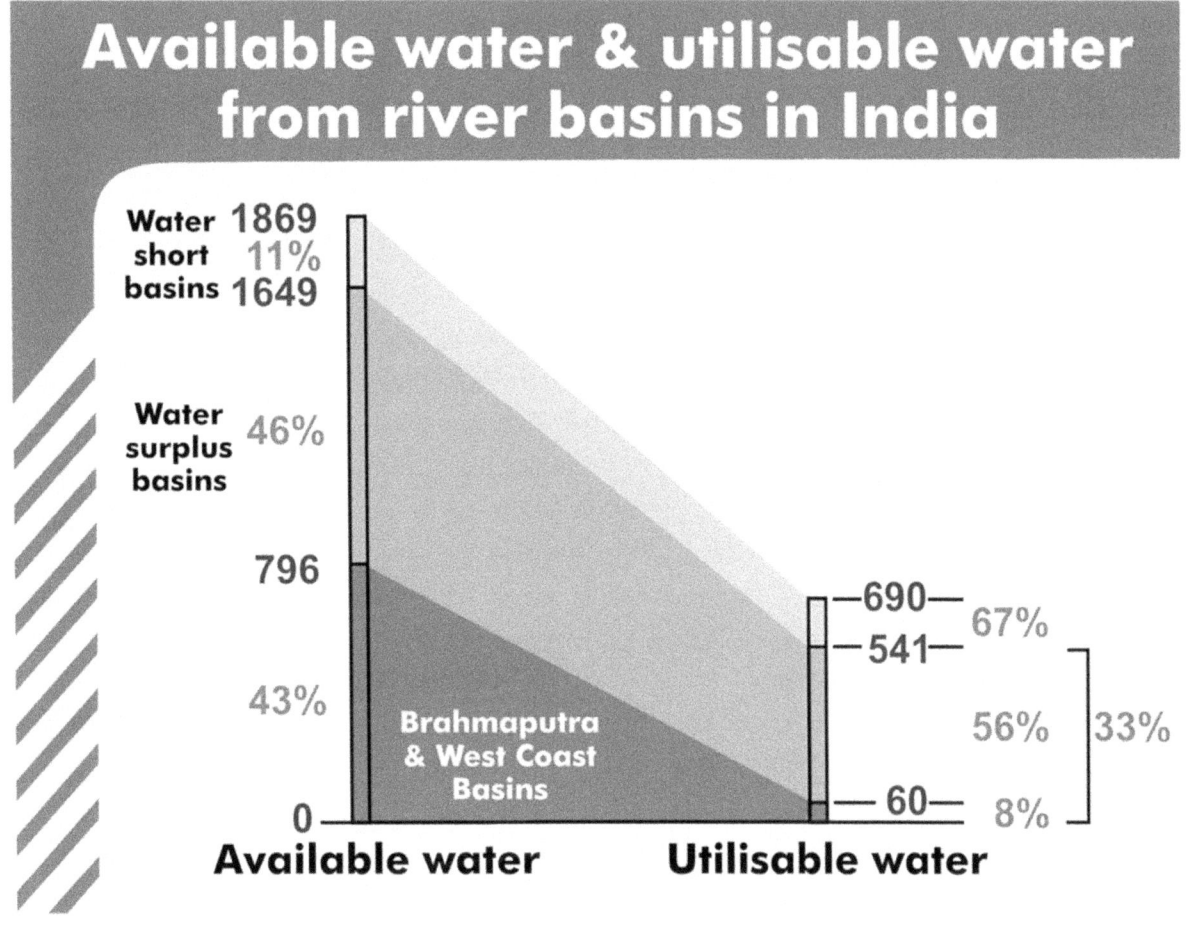

It would be seen from the map that, only 60 bcm i.e. 8% of 796 bcm can be used from these water surplus basins. In the 2nd category of water surplus basins, 481 bcm i.e. 56% of 853 bcm can be used. In the 3rd category of water scarce basins, 149 bcm i.e. 67% of 220 bcm can be used. Hence it is planned to transfer water from rivers in the 2nd category to rivers in the 3rd category under the 'Interlinking of Rivers'. Maharashtra state has also planned to transfer water from water surplus sub basins in the Godavari basin to water scarce sub basins in the Krishna and Tapi basins, within the state boundary.

**Conclusion** – While planning optimum use of available water resource in the river basins, water transfers from relatively water surplus basins to water scarce basins is essential on considerations of equity and social justice. Even if it involves extra cost in transferring water from one basin to other basin by gravity or by lifting the water, if necessary, it becomes unavoidable to ensure balanced water resource related development of the country.

# Chapter 4
# Water Resource Development Infrastructure Constructed in India Prior To Independence In 1947.

*Ingenuity of man motivated him to start practicing agriculture to grow food crops on land about 10,000 years before. Gradually some ancient human civilisations originated on the banks of some major rivers during the last 6 to 7 thousand years. They prospered because man innovated various types of infrastructure either to divert rivers or to store water and practice irrigated agriculture. Let us see the gradual historical development in India, in the types of infrastructure designed by the resourceful man to meet his basic needs of food and water. Even then, from the record of the last millennium it would be seen that there were many severe famines in India when millions of people had died due to starvation. Infrastructure to provide irrigation facilities for increasing food grain production was seen to be inadequate even during British rule. Chapter broadly covers historical evolution of such water resource development activities in India and in the Maharashtra state, up to the time the country became independent from the British rule in the year 1947.*

**Ancient Civilisations in the World -** All the ancient civilisations had originated on the banks of major rivers, because of the assured availability of water and that of the fertile land on its banks for agriculture, which fulfilled man's basic needs of food and water. The four oldest civilizations in the world were on rivers Tigris-Euphrates in Mesopotamia (Modern Iraq), on river Indus (Sindhu) in the Indian Continent, on river Nile in Egypt, and on rivers Huang He (Yellow River) & Yangtze (Blue River) in China. These rivers provided the basis for continuous cultural development in the same geographic locations extended over some millennia. Some of the important civilisations were as below:

Sumerian Civilization (4500 BC to 1900 BC) - Mesopotamia is the site of the earliest human developments and has been identified as having inspired some of the most important developments in human history, including invention of the wheel, planting of the first cereal crops, and the irrigated agriculture. Other Mesopotamian innovations include the control of water by weirs and the use of aqueducts, to resort to the irrigated agriculture. It originated about 6700 years ago and is recognised as the cradle of some of the World's earliest civilizations.

Indus Valley Civilization (3500 BC to 1500 BC) - It flourished in the alluvial plains of the Indus River, in the north-western regions of South Asia, lasted from about 5500 to 3500 years ago, and in its mature form from about 5000 to 4000 years ago. It is also commonly referred to as the Indus-Sarasvati Civilization and the Harappan Civilization. By the time of its mature phase, the civilisation had spread over an area larger than the other civilisations, which included a core of 1,500 kilometres up the alluvial plain of the Indus and its tributaries. The Indus cities are noted for their urban planning, a technical and political process concerned with the use of land and design of the urban environment. They are also noted for their baked brick houses, elaborate water supply systems, drainage systems, and clusters of large, non-residential buildings. The climate change which caused flooding, critical mega droughts, and famine, possibly caused collapse of the Indus Valley Civilisation, which finally collapsed around 3500 years ago.

Ancient Egypt civilization (3100 BC to 30 BC) - It prospered along banks of the Nile River and is recognized as one of the oldest cultures in the human history. Nile river's seasonal flooding was extremely important to ancient Egyptian civilization because, it deposited layers of silt rich in nutrients and natural fertilizers which created excellent agricultural land along the banks, an area that otherwise would have been desert. Humankind harnessing the bounty of this fertile area encouraged the earliest areas of sustained settlement and civilization, from about 5000 years ago. The civilisation is known for the detailed record of floods to the Nile River and that of the various dynasties which ruled there. It is also known for the world-famous pyramids and the temples of the deity.

Ancient Chinese civilisation (2070 BC to AD 220) - The well-evidenced Yellow River Valley Civilization (with an ordered society and written records), or 'Huang He' civilization is located in the present-day China. It first coalesced and developed in the middle and lower reaches of the river about 4,300 years ago. The name "Yellow" comes from the yellow-coloured silt carried across the land by the wind and the rivers in the basin. The Yellow River meets the Chiang Jiang River creating a fertile area suitable for cultivating crops. Agriculture was started in the flood plain of the Yellow River, and before long, through flood control and irrigation along the Yellow River. About 4,000 to 5,000 years before, banks of lower Yangtze River in the South China were also major population centres occupied by the earliest cultivators of rice. Their civilisation was influenced later by the people migrated from the Yellow River due to droughts there. Yangtze River Valley civilization, Yellow River civilization and other ancient Chinese civilizations have influenced each other and merged together in long time, eventually forming the Chinese civilization.

In addition to these, there were some civilisations such as Ancient Maya Civilization, Ancient Greek Civilisation and Ancient Roman Civilisation etc. in the ancient World.

**Historical development in the types of water resource development infrastructures in India** – Civilisations consisted of many families staying together near riverbanks for safety, security, and social life. In the years of good rainfall, crop yield was sufficient, but during years of inadequate rainfall it was insufficient to meet family needs. As the population increased, one alternative was to encroach on the forest land away from the village for crop cultivation. Instead of that, a group of some resourceful people came together and thought of a novel idea. By digging a channel along riverbanks, they diverted fair weather flow of the river to their fields, for taking a second or even a third crop in a year on the same land. Once it was successful, adjoining villagers also started practicing the same system of irrigation. Such works used to get damaged during high floods to the river. They then adopted the 'Trial and Error' technique, to refine and improve the infrastructure during the coming decades and centuries. Some innovative people also thought of constructing some permanent river diversion structure to serve the same purpose. Some rulers provided money to meet expenses for such works. Such developments in some of the civilisations can be traced from the remains of some of these structures. Brief details of the type of such structures and the systems which evolved in India and the Maharashtra State are explained below.

For that purpose, it would be necessary to study topography of the country because it decided courses of main rivers, their tributaries, and formed the main river basins. Northern India comprises mainly of basins of Rivers Ganga, Yamuna, & Brahmaputra, which rise in the snow laden Himalayan ranges and flow south-eastwards to meet sea in the Bay of Bengal. River Indus (Sindhu) and its main tributaries rise in the Himalayan ranges, flow south-westwards through India and Pakistan and meet the Arabian sea. Major part of these basins which is located below the mountainous region is very flat and the substrata consists of very deep alluvial deposits of sand, gravel and silt. At some places, depth of such strata exceeds even a kilo meter. In the central India, some tropical rivers rise in Vindhya Mountain ranges running East-West in the central India and flow northwards to meet rivers Yamuna and Ganga. River Narmada rises in Vindhya mountains and flows westwards to meet the Arabian sea. Further South, River Tapi rises in the East-West running Satpuda Mountain ranges and flows westwards to meet the Arabian sea.

In the Peninsular India, Sahyadri mountain range runs North-South, close to the West coast. All rivers (Except Narmada and Tapi) in the Peninsular India rise in the Sahyadri mountain ranges and either flow westwards to meet the Arabian sea or eastwards to meet the Bay of Bengal. Substrata in the river basins of all rivers in the central and Peninsular India (except Tapi river basin) consist of *in situ* formed soil, decomposed parent rock and different types of rock below such as, Basalt, Granite, Sedimentary and Metamorphic. Substrata in major part of the middle and lower Tapi basin consists of deep alluvial deposits of sand, gravel and silt. Along the West coast, soils are formed mostly by the decomposition of Lateritic rock.

Rivers rising in the Himalayan ranges are perennial because of runoff in the monsoon season and flow from the snow melt in the summer season. Hence in the Indo-Gangetic plains, use of river water for irrigation, by means of diversion canals, has been the common practice since ancient times. It consisted of a river water intake structure in masonry on one bank and flood embankment on its upstream & downstream to protect the off taking canal from river floods. The off taking diversion canal conveyed river water to the fields as per needs of the crops grown. Such irrigation is described in scriptures and mythological books written more than 2,000 years ago. Megasthenes, a Greek historian and ambassador who was in India, recorded the use of irrigation in the 4th century BCE. Irrigation was then highly developed during the period of Muslim rule from the 12th century onwards, and by the Mughal kings later who constructed several canals for irrigation purposes in the Gangetic basin. Firoz Shah Tughlaq had built many canals, the longest of which was about 240 km and was built in 1356 on the Yamuna River. Now known as the Western Yamuna Canal, it has fallen into disrepair several times during high floods to the river but had been restored subsequently many times. The Mughal emperor Shah Jahan built an irrigation canal on the Yamuna River in the early 17th century.

In the Central India, since lands were fertile, and rainfall was adequate to support monsoon and winter crops, hence historically, not many irrigation canals were constructed there. In the west flowing Tapi river basin in the Peninsular India, a very ingenuous system of irrigation known as

'Phad system' evolved and developed between about 17th to 19th century. It consisted of constructing a series of masonry bandharas (diversion weirs) and canals, on the left-bank perennial tributaries of the Tapi river, to divert river flow for irrigation. Command was divided in four phads (parts) and monsoon crop, two seasonal crop, winter crop and sugar cane crop were cultivated in them each year turn by turn by rotation. On equity considerations, crops would be rotated in a four-year cycle. Cost of bandhara and the canal was borne by the then rulers, but beneficiaries had contributed as labourers in the construction of all these bandhara and canal works. Management of irrigation and maintenance of bandhara and canal systems on all these works was being done by the beneficiaries. Use of water for irrigation by the beneficiaries was charged by increasing the land tax rates suitably.

Rainfall near coastal region located along East coast of India was adequate to support rainfed ponded paddy crop which was cultivated there on a large scale. But in some years, there used to be dry spells at the time of paddy transplantation or at the time of grain formation. In some years, there used to be early cessation of the monsoon season before the crop maturity. Crop yield used to get appreciably reduced during such years. Many centuries before, some innovative cultivators constructed small earthen dams on streams to store water in them in the monsoon season. Irrigation could then be done from the water stored against these dams by constructing canal to provide field to field irrigation to paddy crop during such occasional dry spells, which improved the crop yield substantially. Such earthen dams were constructed by the time-tested technology of 'Trial and Error' and with the experience, their technique was refined during years to come. Several groups of skilled labourers were formed in these regions, which would plan and carry out work of construction of such earthen dams and canals. They were replicated during 16th to 20th century along all the East coast states and even in some other states in India where rainfall pattern for ponded paddy cultivation was similar. It is said that at one time about 1 million such tanks and canals were existing in the country, though some of them used to get frequently damaged due to floods and some got silted up with the passage of time. Capital cost of earthen dams was usually borne by the then rulers and/or big landlords, but all the beneficiaries used to contribute to all the labour component of the dam and canal work. Management of irrigation and maintenance of the system used to be done entirely by the beneficiaries. Land revenue and water tax was being paid by the beneficiaries to the rulers or the big landlords.

Due to silting up, damage due to floods and mismanagement/negligence by the beneficiaries, number of tanks in use has been appreciably reduced during the last century. In the absence of accurate data across all the states, the number of such tanks in India at present is reported to vary from 0.25 million to 0.35 million. In terms of irrigated area, the tank irrigated area in India has declined from about 3.3 million hectares (mha) in the mid nineteenth century to about 1.67 mha in 2018.

In the Southern India, there were East flowing major rivers such as Godavari, Krishna, Kaveri and Pennar. In the distant past, substantial upper part of these river basins was under forest cover. Hence even if monsoon season in the river basins was limited to only about 3–4 months of the year, middle and lower reaches of these rivers were having perennial flow. Vast delta regions of all these rivers had very fertile and flat lands, which were ideal to grow ponded paddy (rice) crop. One such notable ancient river diversion structure located just on upstream of delta region of Kaveri River is described below:

**Kallanai Barrage** – It is the fourth oldest water diversion or water-regulating structures in the world and the oldest in India that is still in use. It was originally built by the King Karikalan of the Chola Dynasty in about 150 AD. The purpose of the Kallanai barrage was to divert water of the Kaveri River across the fertile delta region for irrigation via canals to its northern delta branch Kollidam. Downstream of the barrage, the river Kaveri splits into four streams and the flood waters used to be diverted, by opening the barrage gates, to pass through the remaining three delta branches to join the sea. The barrage was 329 m long, 20 m wide & 5.4 m high and was constructed from unhewn stone masonry spanning the Kaveri River. The area irrigated by the ancient irrigation network was about 28,000 ha. The barrage is thought to be the oldest river diversion structure in the world that's still in use. The fact that the original design lasted for more than 16 centuries is a testament to the incredible minds of the ancient Indian engineers who designed, constructed and successfully operated the structure to provide irrigation facilities. The barrage is still in excellent condition and has provided a model to later engineers.

**History of famines in India in the distant past and during British Regime up to 1947 –**

India receives rainfall from South-West monsoon during about 3 to 4 months from June to October every year. For want of adequate irrigation facilities existing in the country in the $17^{th}$ and $18^{th}$ century, except the ones described above, most of the agricultural land used to have rain-fed monsoon crops. On fertile lands having good soil moisture, winter crops could also be taken as rainfed crop. During years having inadequate rainfall to support such rain-fed crops, food grain production would appreciably reduce. If such conditions prevailed over extensive area covering some provinces, it used to result in drought or severe famine conditions. Due to lack of adequate grain storage facilities to have a buffer stock of grains, and/or due to lack of facilities for transport of grain by road from the adjoining provinces where it was surplus, sometimes there were large-scale deaths of people during such famines.

There were many severe famines in India in the distant past, but no authentic record of deaths during such famines is available. Most severe famines were those which occurred due to failure of monsoon rains extended over successive years. One of the most severe famines which occurred due to successive failure of monsoon rains for twelve years during the years 1396-1407, is known as 'Durga devi Famine'. Lady *Durga* from 'Lakha Vanjara' community then owned tens of thousands of bullocks. She used to sell bullocks and also was engaged in the profession of transport of food grains and other material between Northern India and the area around the present Maharashtra state in the Peninsular India. Over the years she acquired huge wealth in the profession and became a multimillionaire. At the time of this famine, she had seen plight of the poor people dying due to starvation. She purchased food grain from grain surplus areas from the Ganga basin, transported it to the famine hit areas and distributed it free of cost to the famine affected poor people. She had used her acquired wealth for purchasing, transporting, and distributing food grains to the poor people during twelve years of that most severe famine in the history. For such noble task on her part for the good of the humanity, she was called as 'Durga devi i.e., *Goddess Durga'*.

Many famines also occurred during British Regime in India and fairly reliable record of probable causes of such famines and casualties occurred during these famines is presently available. In India, traditionally, agricultural labourers and rural artisans have been the primary victims of the famines. In the worst famines, land holding cultivators have also been susceptible as victims. Deaths due to starvation were in millions during these famines, as would be seen from the details of 12 major famines which occurred in almost all provinces in the country as shown below. British administration can be said as responsible in not providing immediate relief to the affected people in the form of starting famine works. It also failed in not purchasing food grains from surplus states, transporting it, and distributing it free or at subsidised rates to the famine affected people. It also failed in not taking actions in the form of long-term permanent measures in the drought prone areas of the country. Works such as planning, designing, and constructing necessary infrastructure works such as dams and diversion weirs on rivers to provide additional irrigation facilities to the rainfed land from the chronic famine affected area were the capital-intensive. But they would have provided sustained relief from the droughts. Some such works which were taken during British rule are detailed below. However, looking to the deaths which occurred during these famines, such measures were too inadequate to meet needs of the famine affected areas in the country.

Details of locations and approximate mortalities (including the Princely States) in these famines are as below:

(Approximate population of India at the time of each event of famine and the percentage of deaths with the population at that time is given in bracket)

1769–1770 -   Bihar, Western Bengal – Deaths 2 to 10 million - (about 3% of 190 million)

1782–1784 -   North-Western India – Deaths 11 million - (about 6% of 195 million)

1788–1794 -   Southern India, Gujarat – Deaths 11 million - (about 6% of 198 million)

1837–1838 -   North-Western India – Deaths 0.8 million - (about 0.03% of 220 million)

1860–1861 -   North India – Deaths 2 million - (about 0.9% of 233 million)

1865–1867 -   East & South India – Deaths 4 to 5 million - (about 2% of 236 million)

1868–1870 -   North-West & North – Deaths 1.5 million - (about 0.6% of 238 million)

1873–1874 -   Bihar famine - No significant mortalities due to relief measures.

1876–1878 -   South India, Bombay Province – Deaths 6 to 10 million - (about 3% of 248 million)

1896–1897 -   All over India – Deaths 5 to 15 million - (about 3% of 290 million)

1899–1900 -   All over India – Deaths 5 to 10 million - (about 3% of 293 million)

1943–1944 -   Bengal famine – Deaths 3.6 to 4.5 million - (about 1% of 362 million)

Bengal Famine, the last one during British Regime was worst of all because of the inhuman approach taken by the British Govt. in England under leadership of Sir Winston Churchill in London. The Delhi Government sent a telegram to London, painting a picture of the horrible devastation and the number of people who had died in the Bengal famine. Even then British Govt. in London casually diverted all the supplies of food grains and medical aid that was being dispatched to the starving victims, to the already well supplied soldiers of Europe during the World War II. Here I refrain myself from quoting the derogatory remarks expressed by Sir Churchill about the fast-rising population of India then, in his reply to the Viceroy of India. Those who are interested may visit the relevant web sites. This action by the British Govt. aggravated the situation resulting in deaths of more than 20% population of the Bengal state due to starvation and due to the resulting epidemics during that famine.

During the British rule, some permanent measures by way of providing irrigation facilities on some major rivers were taken up in some provinces of India. Some such measures were also taken by the rulers of some Princely states. They were in the form of constructing necessary large size infrastructures on rivers (diversion weirs/dams and canals) to provide irrigation facilities to the agricultural land from the famine/drought prone area in some river basins as detailed below:

Upper Ganga Canal - Northern India experienced famines in 1837 and 1840 when, according to estimates, the population of the area fell by 20%. Hence to ward off drought and famine in the western part of the current Uttar Pradesh state, Upper Ganga Canal was the first British canal in India which was built between 1842 and 1854. It was first contemplated by Col. John Russell Colvin in 1836 but was eventually taken up and completed by its architect Sir Proby Thomas Cautley in 1854. The Upper Ganga Canal takes off from the River Ganga at the Bhimgoda weir near Haridwar. From there, a 560 km long canal, with another 480 km of branch line was constructed, to provide irrigation facilities to an area of 0.7 million ha. Width of the canal at the head was 61 m and the depth at full supply level was nearly 3.3 m. There are two super passages, one level crossing and one Solani aqueduct in the initial reach of the canal. These structures which were constructed in brick masonry in lime-surkhi (burnt brick powder) mortar, are still standing well after nearly 170 years. At the time of commissioning Ganga canal in 1854, Solani Aqueduct (Design based on Alcantara aqueduct in Portugal) was ranked as one of the most remarkable massive structures in brick masonry in the whole world. It was the largest canal ever attempted in the world at that time and still is recognised as one of the most exquisitely constructed civil engineering structure. At the time of commencement of that work, science of soil mechanics was not known, whereas hydraulic engineering was in its primitive stage. Mr. Cautley was then working in 'Saper Unit of Army' but was not an engineer by qualification. After its part completion, when there was a problem about non availability of funds for this work, he went back to England, convinced the British Parliament, and ensured that adequate funds are provided for the work till its completion. He came back to India and completed balance work of the project in 1854. Sir Cautley used his common sense and judgement in the planning and designing cross section, bed gradient of the canal & cross drainage structures as above. Finally, on completing and commissioning this commendable work single-handedly, he proved that he was truly a genius.

Anicut on Kaveri River - In the 1800s the British decided that the then 1650-year-old Kallanai barrage needed modernization. It is said that famed British irrigation expert Sir Arthur Cotton modelled his own dam designs after the Kallanai barrage. In 1804, Captain Caldwell, a military engineer, was appointed by the British to study the Kaveri River at the existing barrage and to promote scheme to provide additional irrigation to the delta region. The main change was implemented in the form of raising the weir crest level by 0.69 meters, to increase its storage capacity and to increase the amount of water being diverted to the fertile delta region for irrigation. Under sluices were provided in the barrage across the river, with outlets leading to the Kollidam part of the river to drain out bed silt. Due to such modernisation, by the early 20th century, the irrigated area had been increased to about 400,000 ha. The Lower Anicut built by Sir Arthur Cotton in the 19th century across Kollidam, the major tributary of Cauvery is said to be a replicated structure of Kallanai barrage.

Anicut on Krishna River – First Anicut on Krishna River was designed by Sir Arthur Thomas Cotton and its construction was implemented by Capt. Orr during the years 1852-1855, at a cost of Rs 17.5 million in those days. It had a length of 1223 meters and was located below the confluence with Musi River. It is one of the first major irrigation projects undertaken in South India. The Anicut at the head of Krishna delta controlled the flow within the deltaic plains and provided irrigation facilities to about 0.28 million ha of agricultural land. The anicut was breached during 1952 and was remodelled later as Prakasham barrage during the years 1954-1957. It now helps to irrigate over 0.48 million hectares of land.

Anicut on Godavari River - Anicut on Godavari River at Dowleswaram was designed and built by British irrigation engineer, Sir Cotton during the years 1857-62. The anicut of height 4.5 meters and 3.5 kilo meter long was constructed in four sections and has 175 crest gates to pass river floods. It provides water for irrigated agriculture to the East and West Godavari districts. Godavari Delta System is an established old irrigation system in operation since 1862. It has served for more than a century to provide irrigation to the Godavari delta region. But subsequently since the anicut was showing signs of distress, it was replaced during the years 1970-82 with a new larger barrage at a cost of Rs. 9530 million with the financial assistance from the World Bank and was named as Sir Arthur Cotton Barrage. Height of the new barrage was increased to 10.6 m and the reservoir created had gross storage of 3.12 Tmc (88.3 Mcum) and dead storage as 2.02 Tmc (57.2 Mcum). At present water stored in Polavaram dam, medigadda dam, sammakka sagar and Donkarayi reservoir is released to divert it from the barrage for irrigation. Total irrigation potential of about 0.4 million hectares has been created in the scheme and actual irrigation was about 0.36 million hectares.

Before these anicuts were constructed by Sir Arthur Thomas Cotton on the Krishna and Godavari rivers, several hectares of land used to get flooded with water and remained unused. The water would be worthlessly going into sea. But when these anicuts were built and the existing anicut on the Kaveri River was remodelled by a new anicut, those unused lands were brought into cultivation with the water that was stored, diverted, and used for irrigation. They averted famines to a certain extent and stimulated the economy of southern India.

Kurnool-Cuddapah Canal - It is located in Kurnool and Kadapa districts in Andhra Pradesh, India and was constructed between 1863 and 1870, originally as an irrigation and navigation canal. However, navigation was abandoned during 1933. The Sunkesula Anicut supplying the canal was built across Tungabhadra River near Kurnool. It is 1370 meters in length, founded on rock, has a clear overfall, and is furnished with a set of under-sluices. The canal runs for a total length of 306 km and transfers water to the Pennar river. In actual practice, on an average, about 12,000 ha area was irrigated. It was the first man-made conveyance scheme to transfer water from the Krishna River basin, where it was then abundant, to the Pennar River basin, where it was scarce and could be better utilised for human development. It has made it possible to utilize the water resources more equitably and economically to yield significant food grain production output in drought areas of Kurnool and Kadapa districts thereby achieving socio-economic development in the region.

Mulla-Periyar dam – By constructing a storage dam on Periyar river which flows westward of Kerala to the Arabian sea was diverted eastwards to flow towards the Bay of Bengal to provide water to the Vaigai River basin. The Mulla-periyar dam is on the Periyar River in the Western Ghats in the then Indian state of Kerala. It is a gravity dam made with concrete prepared from limestone and 'surkhi' (burnt brick powder) and faced with rubble. The dam is 54 meter high and of length 366 meters. Its crest is 3.6 meter wide while the base has a width of 42 meters. Its reservoir has a gross storage of 443 million cubic meter (Mcum) and live storage of 299 Mcum. After making an agreement to divert water eastwards to the then Madras Presidency area (present-day Tamil Nadu state), the dam was constructed between 1887 and 1895 by Major John Pennycuick. The diversion scheme could provide irrigation facilities to the rain shadow region of Madurai in Madras Presidency, which was in dire need of a greater supply of water than the Vaigai River could naturally provide. Diverted water was stored in the Vaigai Dam to provide a source for irrigating about 69,000 ha drought prone area from 5 districts.

Krishna Raja Sagar dam - Mandya region of the Kingdom of Mysore had historically been dry and had witnessed mass migration to adjoining areas in the hot summers. A severe drought in 1875–76 had wiped out one-fifth of the population of the Kingdom. Crop failures were common due to lack of water for irrigation. Kaveri River was seen as a potential source of irrigation water for the farmers in and around Mysore. Hence Krishna Raja Wadiyar IV Maharaj of Mysore decided to construct a dam on Kaveri River below the confluence with its tributaries Hemavati and Lakshmana Tirtha. It was planned, designed and constructed by Bharat Ratna Sir M. Visvesvaraya as a masonry dam in lime-Surkhi mortar. It was constructed between 1911 to 1924. The dam is 2,621 metres in length, 39 metres in height, and the spillway has 48 automatic gates. Its reservoir has live storage of 1,244 Mcum and the lake is spread over 130 sqkm, which was the largest in Asia at the time when it was built. It provided irrigation facilities to over 40,000 ha land and provided drinking water to Mandya, Mysore and Bengaluru.

Dams near Hyderabad - Hussain Sagar dam was built by Ibrahim Quli Qutb Shah in 1563. It is built on a tributary of Musi River to cater to the irrigation needs and water needs of the Hyderabad city.

Osman Sagar dam was created by damming the Musi River, to provide an additional source of drinking water for Hyderabad city and to protect the city after the Great Musi Flood of 1908. In that flood, about 15,000 lives were lost, 19,000 houses collapsed, and around 0.1 million people, which was roughly one quarter of the city's population, were left homeless. The dam had the storage capacity of 3.9 Tmc (110.4 Mcum) and was constructed between 1912 to 1920.

With the intention of protecting the city from floods and providing a drinking water source for Hyderabad city, Himayat Sagar dam was also built on the Esi River, a tributary of the Musi River. It was constructed in 1927 and had the storage capacity of 3 Tmc (85 Mcum). Both the dams were planned, designed and constructed under the chief architect Bharat Ratna Sir M. Visvesvaraya, during the reign of the last Nizam of the Hyderabad State.

Dam-canal projects in the Maharashtra State –

During some severe famines during the British rule, part labour intensive works of some small size earthen dams viz. Visapur, Mhasvad, Ner, Mayani, Shirsuphal etc., were taken up as productive famine works to provide work as a relief to the famine affected labourers. In the subsequent years, balance work of the dams, canals and distributaries for these dams was completed to provide permanent irrigation facilities from the water stored in these storages.

Khodashi diversion weir - Severe droughts during the 19th century prompted engineers to take up major irrigation works to provide relief to the drought prone area towards East in the rain-shadow zone of Sahyadri mountain range. Hence a masonry bandhara (Weir) was constructed on Krishna River which had perennial flow then. It was completed in the year 1864 to provide irrigation facilities to about 9400 ha land. It was the first irrigation development work taken up in the then Bombay Province during the British Regime.

Khadakwasla dam - Subsequently, Captain Fife of the British Army carried out detailed surveys and investigations for constructing a masonry dam in lime mortar on the Mutha River, below the confluence of Ambi and Mose rivers. It was constructed between 1869 to 1879, at a cost of Rs. 6.5 million and is one of the oldest masonry dams in India. It has length of 1940 meters, height 32 meters and has total capacity of 341 Mcum. The reservoir is the source of water for the 112 km long right bank canal which then supplied drinking water to Pune cantonment and irrigates about 45,000 ha of land. The left bank canal provided irrigation to some area along left bank and to the Agriculture College, Pune.

Bhatghar dam – A masonry dam on Yelvandi river in the Nira River basin was constructed around 1885. It was also designed to store water for providing irrigation facilities to the drought prone area towards East by constructing Nira canals. Subsequently, a large size masonry dam was constructed just on its downstream to make full use of the yield available at that site. The new Bhatghar dam was constructed in 1930. It is a masonry dam constructed in lime-Surkhi mortar. It is 1625 meter long and is having height of 57.91 meters to store 650 Mcum (22.93TMC). A 16 MW powerhouse was constructed in the dam in the year 1977. Stored water is released in the river which is picked up in a pick-up weir on Nira River on the downstream to irrigate land in the drought prone area by Nira Left Bank and Nira Right Bank canals.

At the location of the pick-up weir, Veer dam – a rubble concrete dam – was constructed on the Nira River in the year 1965 to store 266 Mcum (9.38 TMC) of water, to supplement Bhatghar dam. Nira Left Bank and Nira Right Bank canals take off from Veer dam now. There is also a 9 MW powerhouse constructed on the Veer dam.

Radhanagari dam – It is a gravity dam on Bhogawati river near Radhanagari in the Princely state of Kolhapur, presently in the State of Maharashtra. Its construction was initiated by the Visionary Chhatrapati Shahu Maharaj in February 1907. Height of the dam above lowest foundation is 43 m, while the length is 1,143 m. Gross storage capacity is 237 Mcum (8.36 TMC). The dam is famous for its automatically operated 7 gates as spillway, a technology which was novel when it was constructed. Construction of the dam was done during the period 1909 to 1918. Another novel feature of the project was that the stored water was released back into the river and was picked up from a series of several Kolhapur type weirs constructed on downstream one below the other on the river. Water for irrigation was lifted from these weirs by means of diesel pumps to provide irrigation to sugar cane and other crops. In the second stage, a powerhouse was constructed at the foot of the dam to generate hydro power from the water released into the river.

Vidarbha region of Maharashtra was a part of the C.P. and Berar State prior to independence. It had fairly good and dependable rainfall which traditionally enabled to grow rainfed paddy crop. On many small earthen dams, cultivators used to take follow-on summer paddy crop in good years. With a view to promoting crop diversification, in the first half of the 20th century, seven medium size earthen dams viz. Ramtek, Asola Mendha, Chandpur, Chor Khamara, Ghorazari, Bodalkasa, and Naleshwar were constructed by that State. But even then, cultivators preferred to grow paddy on paddy crop instead of diversifying the cropping pattern.

Between 1915 to 1930, the Tata Hydroelectric Power Co. had built 6 gravity masonry dams near Lonavala in the high rainfall zone along eastern slope in the Sahyadri ranges. Water stored in these dams was diverted westwards through tunnels to get advantage of the substantial natural drop, to generate hydro power by constructing power houses at the foot of the Sahyadri mountain. In all six masonry gravity dams viz. Mulshi, Walvan, Andra, Shiravata, Thokarwadi and Lonavala, were constructed. Stored water was released to generate hydro power through three powerhouse stations constructed at Khopoli (72 MW), Bhira (150 MW), and Bhivapuri (75 MW). These power houses were the India's first clean energy generating plants set up with the intension of providing clean and abundant power to the city of Mumbai and industries around it. In due course of time, water released from the power houses was being used by several industries set up in these valleys and was also used to irrigate ponded paddy and other crops in the Konkan region of the Maharashtra State.

Famine Commission - Between the years 1896 to 1900 about 10 to 25 million people (Including some from the Princely States) died due to severe famines in many provinces of India. Deaths of about 17 million people in all in these two famines, which was more than 5% of about 290 million population of India then, were quite substantial. British administration can be said as partly responsible for not taking immediate measures for providing work to famine affected people. They also did not make arrangements to transport food grains from grain surplus provinces and making arrangements for its free distribution or at subsidised rates. Long before the famine, they also failed by not taking long term measures of creating infrastructure to provide additional irrigation facilities. As an afterthought, British Govt. appointed a 'Famine Commission' under the Chairmanship of Sir Colin Scott-Moncrieff in the year 1901, to suggest structural measures to mitigate the undesirable effects of droughts in the country and to handle situation in such natural calamities in the future. The Commission visited the provinces affected by the famine, studied about possible long-term measures to provide relief to the famine affected Provinces and submitted its Report in the year 1903. In this Report, one of the recommendations for the then Bombay Province (now Maharashtra state), was as below: *'Protection in the Deccan must be sought for in a system of canals depending for their supplies on large storage works which will be filled from rivers whose sources are in the Western Ghats, where the monsoon rainfall is unfailing even in a year of drought'*.

Sahyadri mountain range runs North-South close to the West coast of Maharashtra state. Precipitation from SW monsoon ranges from 3000 to 5000 mm at the top of the mountain range but reduces to about 450 to 500 mm within a distance of about 70-80 km towards eastern side in the rain-shadow zone. Hence about 30 to 40 percent area of the State is considered as drought prone. In view of the above recommendation of the 'Famine Commission', during the British regime, some large masonry dams were constructed in the high rainfall zone along eastern slope of Sahyadri ranges, during the next 2-3 decades. Water stored in the reservoirs created by these dams was released back into the rivers and was picked up in the masonry diversion weirs (pick-up-weirs) located just above the drought prone area. The water was then conveyed to the fields in the drought prone area by means of canals constructed along both banks of the rivers. All dams and pick up weirs were designed according to the technology of gravity dams which was available then. These dams were founded on solid basalt rock and were constructed in lime-Surkhi mortar masonry. Canals were designed as unlined contour canals having ridge distributaries and minors. Following major irrigation projects were taken up during the years 1910 to 1930.

Chankapur dam and Girna canals (1911) - It includes masonry dam at Chankapur of height 41 meters and length of 3705 meters to store 68.81 Mcum (2.43 TMC), a pick-up weir at Thengoda, and Girna Left Bank and Right Bank canals.

Darna dam and Godavari canals (1916) - It includes a masonry dam of height 28 meters and of length 1634 meters to store 215.38 Mcum (7.60 TMC), pick up weir at Nandur Madhmeshwar and Godavari Left Bank and Right Bank canals.

Bhandardara dam and Pravara canals (1926) - It consists of a masonry dam (highest at that time in India) to store 313 Mcum (11.04 TMC), pick-up weir at Ozar about 85 km on downstream and off taking Pravara Left Bank and Right Bank canals. Bhandardara dam suffered due to earthquake near Koyna dam in Maharashtra in the year 1967. Hence it was strengthened by providing masonry buttresses to support the existing masonry dam. Hydro electricity is generated since June 2001, from Bhandaradara Hydroelectric Project Phase I (12 MW) & Bhandaradara Hydro-electric Project Phase II (34 MW), from the water released from dam.

Bhatghar dam (New) (1930), Veer dam cum pick up weir (1965) and Nira Left Bank and Right Banak canals. - Details are given above.

All these four large dam-pick up weir-canal works, together with other diversion weirs and small dam-canal works, had provided irrigation facilities to about 0.27 mha in the Maharashtra state as at the time of independence.

# Chapter 5

# Achieving Food Security to The Country After Independence by Green Revolution and Meeting the Challenge of Droughts in India.

*Issue of acute shortage of food grains perceived by the country in the second decade after independence, had to be resolved by importing food grains from America under some undesirable conditions. However, revolutionary changes in the approach taken by the Indian Govt. to bring 'Green Revolution' in the country had paid good dividends in the next two decades. It was brought about by the first activity of development of water resource infrastructure to create additional irrigation facilities on a large-scale. Irrigated agriculture was then supplemented by adopting modern technology in agriculture in the form of use of High Yielding Varieties of seeds, chemical fertilisers & pesticides, as a part of the green revolution. As a result of such measures, per hectare productivity of food grains increased phenomenally and the country became self-sufficient in food grains during the next decade. During some famines faced by the country in the last 75 years after independence, the critical situation was handled very effectively by immediately providing deployment to the famine affected labourers on productive works and by supplying them adequate food grains at subsidised rates. With the result, there were practically no casualties during all those famines. The chapter covers details of the 'Green Revolution' which resulted in achieving food security to the country on a sustainable basis and about the various famine relief measures taken to ameliorate its ill effects.*

During latter half of the last century, some fallow land and land under forest in the country was brought under cultivation. However, some cultivable land was required for the developmental works such as roads, railways, dam-canal works, expansion of urban growth centres, and for setting up several new Industrial Estates. Hence by and large, the area under plough in the country had remained nearly constant since independence till today. Due to increase in the area under irrigation after independence because of many large dam-canal projects being constructed in the country, there was increase in the food grain production. But the food grain demand was rising every year due to increase in population of the country. In the fifth and sixth decade of the last century, due to inadequate monsoon rains in some states, total food grain production in the country reduced appreciably in the sixties of the last century. To meet immediate needs of the 450 million population then, food grains to the tune of 7 million tonnes had to be imported immediately (ultimately about 10 MT) from America under PL 480 scheme, with some inescapable conditions. It could tide over the critical situation then prevailing and could prevent the possibility of deaths of the people due to starvation.

Learning from this lesson, the necessity of taking long term measures to ensure food security to the growing population of the country and resolve the issue permanently became very clearly evident. Between 1947 and 1964 the initial agricultural infrastructure was laid by the founding of organizations such as the Central Rice Institute in Cuttack, the Central Potato Research Institute in Shimla, and Universities such as the Pant Nagar University. Finally, well planned action was taken in the form of introducing 'Green Revolution' which commenced in the 1960s during which agriculture in India was converted into a modern industrial system. In essence, it was achieved by the adoption of technology, such as use of High Yielding Variety (HYV) seeds, mechanised farm tools, use of pesticides & chemical fertilizers and by providing additional irrigation facilities. It was led by agricultural scientist Bharat Ratna Dr. M. S. Swaminathan in India, as a part of the larger Green Revolution endeavour initiated by Norman E. Borlaug, which leveraged agricultural research and technology to increase agricultural productivity in the developing world. Swaminathan's collaborative scientific efforts with Norman Borlaug, spearheading a mass movement with farmers and other scientists and backed by public policies were the main activities initiated by him. Green Revolution within India commenced in mid-sixties with the use of hybrid varieties of maize, Jowar (Sorghum), Bajra (Pearl millet) and rust-resistant strains of dwarf varieties of wheat (by Norman E. Borlaug) & dwarf nonlodging varieties of rice (by M. S. Swaminathan). These varieties were responsive to the use of chemical fertilisers and assured irrigation. Along with high-yielding seeds, chemical fertilisers and irrigation facilities, the enthusiasm of farmers mobilized the idea of agricultural revolution. Other measures such as consolidation of land holdings, land reforms, improved rural infrastructure, contour bunding of dry land to conserve soil & water, supply of agricultural credit, and use of advanced machinery in agriculture operations etc. helped the rural community in improving land productivity per hectare.

The Green Revolution in India was first introduced in Punjab as a part of the development program issued by International Donor Agencies and the lead taken by the Government of India. Within a decade or two, the State of Punjab earned the distinction of being the "breadbasket of India". Such measures ultimately led to appreciable increase in food grain production, especially in Punjab, Haryana, and Uttar Pradesh States, and the country became self-sufficient in food grains within a short span of 6 years (1965-66 to 1970-71). In the twenty-year period between 1965 and 1985 gaps in the infrastructure were bridged by establishment of The National Bank for Agriculture and Rural Development (NABARD). During times of famines, droughts, and other natural calamities, NABARD provided loan rescheduling and loan conversion facilitates to eligible Institutions such as State Cooperative Banks and Regional Rural Banks for periods up to seven years. All these actions ensured establishing the food security on a sustainable basis. Because of such coordinated efforts taken in all the states in India, food grain production increased appreciably during the coming decades as would be seen from the figures below:

**Table 1 - Achievement of increase in the food grain production in India**

| Item / years | 1951 -52 | 1970 -71 | 1990 -91 | 2011 -12 | 2020 -21 |
|---|---|---|---|---|---|
| Food Grain production (mt) | 52 | 108 | 176 | 259 | 309 |
| Area under Food Grains (mha) | 97 | 124 | 128 | 125 | 129 |

| | | | | | |
|---|---|---|---|---|---|
| Irrigated area (mha) | 18 | 30 | 45 | 60 | 70 |
| Area under HYV variety (mha) | nil | 15 | 60 | 125 | 140 |
| Fertiliser consumption (mt) | nil | 2 | 13 | 28 | 33 |

(mt - million tonnes, mha - million hectares)

Note – Between 1951-52 and 2011-12, total area under wheat in the country increased by 41% and rice by 15% and so the total production increased appreciably. Even if area under Sorghum and Pearl millet decreased by about 30%, still the production increased by about 37% due to adoption of HYV & HYB varieties.

**Table 2 - Decadal Growth of Population and Food Grain production in India**

| Year | Population in millions | % Increase in previous decade | Food Grain Production in million Tonnes | % Increase in previous decade |
|---|---|---|---|---|
| 1950-51 | 361 | - | 51 | - |
| 1960-61 | 439 | 22% | 82 | 61% |
| 1970-71 | 548 | 25% | 108 | 32% |
| 1980-81 | 683 | 25% | 129 | 19% |
| 1990-91 | 846 | 24% | 176 | 36% |
| 1999-2000 | 1002 | 18% | 209 | 19% |
| 2011-2012 | 1220 | 22% | 259 | 24% |
| 2020-2021 | 1309 | 07% | 309 | 19% |
| **1950-51 to 2001-21** | | **3.63 times** | | **6.06 times** |

(Food Grain production during the year 2021-22 was 324 million Tonnes)

Table 3 - State wise Irrigation Coverage and Productivity

| State | Agri. Productivity in mt | %age of actual prod. | Productivity in mt/ha | %age of cultivated area under irrigation |
|---|---|---|---|---|
| Punjab | 27.8 | 11.6 | 4.8 | 98.1 |
| Andhra Pradesh | 20.4 | 8.7 | 2.7 | 63.0 |
| Rajasthan | 16.6 | 7.1 | 1.2 | 26.4 |
| West Bengal | 16.3 | 6.9 | 2.4 | 48.2 |
| Haryana | 15.6 | 6.6 | 5.3 | 87.6 |
| **Subtotal** | **96.2** | **40.9** | | |
| Remaining States | 138.2 | 59.1 | | |
| **Grand total** | **234.4** | **100%** | **1.9 MT** | **48.3%** |

mt – million tonnes, mt/ha – million tonnes per hectare

Note – Agricultural Productivity is arranged in descending order, giving state wise details for the first five top ranking states in the agriculture productivity.

Table 4 - State wise Irrigation Type, Capacity and Actual area

| State | Total crop Area mha | Crop area irrigated by GW mha | Canal mha | Total mha | Total actually irrigated mha |
|---|---|---|---|---|---|
| Rajasthan | 21.1 | 3.98 | 1.52 | 5.50 | 5.12 |
| Maharashtra | 19.8 | 3.12 | 1.03 | 4.15 | 3.36 |
| Uttar Pradesh | 17.6 | 10.64 | 4.21 | 14.85 | 14.49 |
| Andhra Pradesh | 16.6 | 2.50 | 2.70 | 5.20 | 4.19 |
| Madhya Pradesh | 15.8 | 2.74 | 1.70 | 4.44 | 4.19 |
| **Subtotal** | **90.9** | **22.98** | **11.16** | **34.14** | **32.06** |
| Remaining States | 68.7 | 16.45 | 11.32 | 27.77 | 26.07 |
| **Grand total** | **159.6** | **39.43** | **22.48** | **61.91** | **58.13** |

mha – million hectares

Note - Total cropped area is arranged in descending order, giving state wise details for the first five states top ranking in the cropped area.

---

As a result of all such planned and coordinated efforts taken by the Central & the State Govts. and the cultivators, the Green Revolution had become a reality. As at present, India is now largest producer of milk, banana, mango, coconut, tea, ginger, turmeric and cashew nuts. India is second largest producer of rice, wheat, fruits and vegetables. Food grain reserve is about 20% of the total production of food grains. India's annual export of agro products is now in the range of Rs.18,00,000 million per year. This comprises mainly of cotton (raw, yarn, fabrics, garments), Basmati & non-Basmati rice, wheat, sugar, spices, grapes, tea, & coffee.

**Policy for the future to ensure sustainable food security** – Let us now take review of India's present population and its future projections till the population is likely to stabilise.

**Table 5 - Projected population of India and food requirement**

| Year | Projected population in million | Food requirement per day per person in grams | Annual food requirement in million Tonnes |
|---|---|---|---|
| 2000 | 1000 | 550 | 200 |
| 2025 | 1400-1500 | 650-800 | 330-390 |
| 2050 | 1700-1800 | 800-1000 | 500-590 |

**Note** – Food consumption in the year 2005 in the USA was 2850 gm/day/person and 980 gm/day/person in China.

Population of India in the year 2023 is about 1400 millions. It is expected that it would stabilise before the year 2050 to about 1800 million and may start declining then onwards. As the average living standard of people increases, per day per person food consumption also increases as shown in the Table. Hence annual food requirement in 2025 and 2050 has been computed accordingly. India must plan for increasing the food production in future in such a manner that the country remains self- sufficient in food grains for the population which is likely to stabilise before 2050. Future targets in food grain production would have to be achieved from nearly constant or possibly from slightly reduced cultivable area and by the judicious use of finite availability of water resources for irrigation. It would be seen from the Table above that, after the year 1999-2000 the rate of increase in population and the productivity of food grains has nearly matched. It appears that, after reaching the peak productivity under the Green Revolution, a plateau has been reached in the food grain productivity. It is essential to take suitable measures in the water sector and the agriculture sector to increase land productivity per hectare and create a buffer stock of food grains to tide over the situation during any droughts in the future. It appears to be a stupendous task which needs all out planned efforts by putting in all the resources in a very coordinated manner in the coming 2-3 decades. It also calls for involvement of all sections of the society and mainly the irrigation water users. It has been predicted that, frequency of droughts and floods hereafter would increase due to the effect of 'Global Warming and Climate Change'. Hence in addition to that, we must plan to keep a buffer stock of at least 10% of the total food consumption, to take care of possible reduction in the production of food grains during occasional drought years.

**Global scenario of expected rise in the World population** - In the year 2022 the United Nations has updated the future projections about population of all continents and the World. Details are shown in the Table below:

**Table 6 - Population of the world, SDG regions and selected groups of countries, 2022, 2030 and 2050 according to the medium scenario**

| | Population (in millions) Region | 2022 | 2030 | 2050 |
|---|---|---|---|---|
| 1. | World | 7,942 | 8,512 | 9,687 |
| 2. | **Sub-Saharan Africa** | **1,152 (15%)** | **1,401(16%)** | **2,094(22%)** |
| 3. | Northern Africa and Western Asia | 549 | 617 | 771 |
| 4. | Central and Southern Asia | 2,075 (22%) | 2,248(26%) | 2,575(27%) |
| 5. | Eastern and South-Eastern Asia | 2,342 (29%) | 2,372(28%) | 2,317(24%) |
| 6. | Latin America and the Caribbean | 658 | 695 | 749 |
| 7. | Australia/New Zealand | 31 | 34 | 38 |
| 8. | Oceania* | 14 | 15 | 20 |
| 9. | Europe and Northern America | 1,120 | 1,129 | 1,125 |
| 10. | **Least developed countries** | **1,112 (14%)** | **1,328(16%)** | **1,914(20%)** |
| 11. | Landlocked developing countries | 557 | 664 | 947 |
| 12. | Small island developing States | 74 | 79 | 87 |
| 13. | **Total of Sr. Nos. 2 & 10** | **2,264 (29%)** | **2,729 (32%)** | **4,008 (41%)** |
| 14. | **Rest of the World** | **5,678 (71%)** | **5,783 (68%)** | **5,679 (59%)** |

Note – 1) Figures in bracket show the percentage of population with the World population of that year.

2) Population of Sub-Saharan Africa & Least Developed Countries together of 2,264 million in 2022 would increase to 4,008 million (77% rise) in 2050. Rest of the World population would remain nearly constant from 2022 to 2050.

Source – World Population Prospects 2022 – United Nations Department of Economic and Social affairs.

It would be seen from the figures given in the above Table that, population of 1,152 million of *Sub-Saharan Africa* in 2022 would increase to 2,094 million (82% rise) in 2050. Population of 1,112 million of *Least developed countries* in 2022 would increase to 1,914 million (72% rise) in 2050. **Both taken together, population would increase from 2022 to 2050 by 77%.**

Earlier projections of the World population by the United Nations were as shown in the graph below:

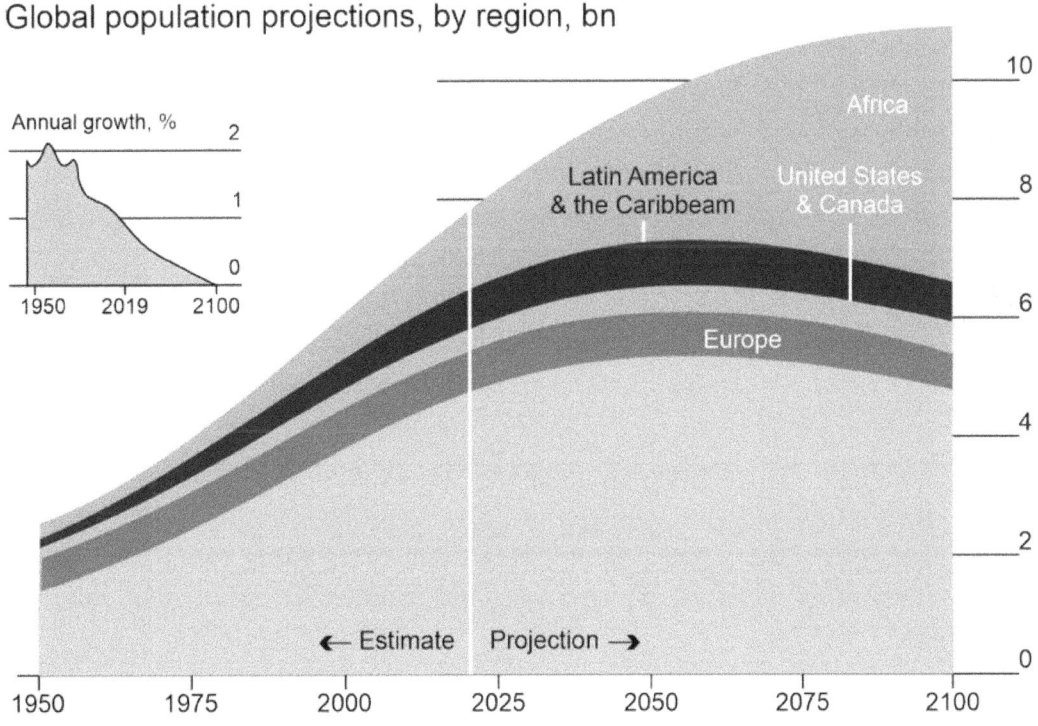

**Source** – Article titled as Graphic detail Demography 'Missing Millions' – The UN revises down its population forecasts; in the *Economist* dated June 22nd 2019.

As per the above graph, it is predicted that population of Asia & Oceania, Europe, United States & Canada, and Latin America & the Caribbean would marginally increase up to 2050 and is likely to reach their peak value between the years 2050 to 2065. Their population would decline then onwards from a peak value of about 7.2 billion to about 6.6 billion in the year 2100. However, population of the African Continent which is increasing at a very fast rate at present would continue to rise at a slightly slower rate beyond 2050. Population of Africa is likely to increase from its present population of about 1.3 billion (out of present World population of about 7.8 billion) and may stabilise to about 4.3 billion (231% increase in 80 years) by the year 2100 (out of World population of 10.9 billion then). These figures appear to be much on the higher side than the latest figures as shown in the Table 6 above. Hence figures in Table 6 may be considered as valid.

**This is a very alarming situation for the World at large.** With increase in the population of Sub-Saharan African countries and the least developed countries as shown in the Table 6 above, their annual demand for food grains would increase proportionately in the future. Besides that, with the gradual increase in the standard of living of the people there, per capita daily food grain requirement would also increase slowly from its present average value. Their demand of water for drinking purposes, domestic and industrial use would also increase appreciably due to industrialisation and urbanisation. As shown in the Table 6, World population of 7.94 billion in 2022 is expected to rise to 9.69 billion (22% increase) by the year 2050, mainly from the contribution of countries from Sub-Saharan Africa and least developed countries. Population of all other countries taken together would remain constant during these 80 years. Present food grain demand of 9.5 billion MT is, expected to rise to 19 billion MT (100% increase) by 2050 and furthermore by 2100. Uncertainty of seasonal monsoon rains, presence of sizeable drought prone area and inadequacy of water resource development infrastructure is the cause of poor land productivity in most of the countries in Sub-Saharan Africa & least developed countries. To increase food grain production to meet the ever-rising demand of food grains, one alternative would be to bring additional land under cultivation by destroying forest on a very large scale from these countries. Such mass destruction of rich terrestrial ecosystems should be totally unacceptable. Secondly, it would cause large scale carbon emissions due to 'Slash and Burn' activity on the fertile forest land and would also stop the carbon sequestration which is at present continuously taking place by the trees in those forests. Both the above causes would aggravate the intensity of Global Warming and Climate Change. Intergovernmental Panel on Climate Change (IPCC) has made following broad regional projections; *'Africa is one of the Continents, most vulnerable to increased water stress and low food productivity along the margin of arid and semi-arid areas.'*

In view of this situation, a viable and desirable alternative to increase land productivity would be to create additional irrigation facilities by constructing capital-intensive water resource development infrastructure consisting of a mosaic of large size to small size dam-canal and river diversion projects, to make optimum use of the finite water resource available in these countries. It would be worth highlighting here that out of the 48,000 large dams constructed in all countries of the World as in the year 2000, only 1,300 (3% of the total) large dams have been constructed in the African continent. Number of small size dams existing in Africa is also insignificant. Taking up the WR infrastructure development works of all sizes would hence have to be planned right now in all the Sub-Saharan countries as well as in the least developed countries as above. Immediate action in that direction is essential because of the long gestation period from estimation to construction, completion, and commissioning of the dam-canal and river diversion projects before getting their benefits of irrigation. Necessary technical guidance should also be provided to these countries for preparing long term River Basin-wise Water Resource Development plans and their time-bound implementation in the next 2-3 decades. Once such an infrastructure is created, it would continue to provide irrigation facilities for the next more than 10 decades to the country, by incurring very little expenditure every year for their annual maintenance and operation.

However, countries in the Sub-Saharan Africa and the least developed countries, would certainly not have the necessary financial resources to take up such capital-intensive works on the required large scale. Secondly, they would also not have the necessary technical expertise to investigate, plan, design and implement projects on such an extensive scale. Hence International Financial Institutions like World Bank (WB), Asian Development Bank (ADB), United States Agency for International Development (USAID), Japan International Cooperation Agency (JICA) etc., would have to take a proactive role in providing financial assistance and technical guidance for taking up above activities in these countries. Even India should think of establishing Financial Institutions (International Bank) which can extend low interest loans to Sub-Saharan countries and the least developed countries, for undertaking water resource development projects. Having vast experience in the investigation, planning, designing, implementation, and operation of WR development projects of all sizes, India has the expertise to provide necessary technical guidance along with the financial assistance. This important issue should be taken up by the United Nations to coordinate all the activities enlisted above. Once the irrigation benefits start getting realised from the completed irrigation projects, assistance and guidance would also have to be given in the Agriculture Sector to bring 'Green Revolution' to increase the land productivity on the lines of India. It would be in the form of using high yielding/Hybrid varieties of food grains and adopting latest techniques in agriculture duly supported by the increased irrigation facilities, to ensure food and water security on a sustainable basis. Irrigating the rain-fed land would then result in 'More crop, cash and jobs per drop of water'. Resulting rise in the agriculture produce because of the green revolution would provide additional employment to the people from the rural areas. They can then handle the food grain shortage situation themselves on a sustainable basis, even during drought years till their population stabilises.

**Besides that, taking adequate steps to bring down the rate of population growth in all these countries within the acceptable limits, should be made a precondition for providing such financial aid and technical guidance to take up construction of irrigation projects.** Then only there is possibility that the rising food grain demand and the increased food grain production because of above measures is likely to match sustainably in the future. In the case of any severe droughts or famines in the African continent or in other least developed countries occurring in the near future, food grain surplus countries of the world would have to export food grains to them to prevent deaths due to mass starvation. Countries like India and China having some surplus food grain production can provide it to them to reduce heavy casualties during such calamity. If these countries also do not have sufficient surplus food grains to transfer during such drought years, deaths of people from those countries due to starvation would be unavoidable. Substantial food grain production was possible in India, China and some other countries in the Asian Continent because of the construction of 31,500 large dams (out of 48,000 large dams in the World) up to the year 2000, together with thousands of small size dam-canal projects. Increase in the area under irrigation and supporting measures in the agriculture sector has achieved sustained food and water security to the nearly 60% population of the world. However, importing food grains during drought years from grain surplus countries of the world should be considered as a temporary solution to meet the food grain shortage arising from droughts or famines only in the next one decade. Frequency of droughts and floods is likely to increase in the future due to the adverse effects of the Climate Change. If above actions are taken right earnestly, these countries could become self-sufficient in foodgrains within less than the next 2 decades by creating permanent assets in the form of adequate water resource development infrastructure. These measures would provide food and water security on a sustainable basis to these underdeveloped countries, and they themselves can face the drought situation effectively thereafter.

Ultimate aim before them should be to become self-sufficient in producing sufficient food grains not only to the present population, but also to the strictly controlled population which is likely to stabilise in the distant future. It is sincerely felt that gravity of the problem of likely shortage of food grains due to severe droughts and famines in the Sub-Saharan countries and least developed countries in the future, is not recognised by the developed countries of the World. Unfortunately, if there is not enough buffer stock of food grains to export with other developed countries like India and China on such occasions, it may result in deaths of millions of people from these famine-affected underdeveloped countries. In the 18$^{th}$ to 20$^{th}$ century, twelve such famines in India had resulted in deaths of millions of people as stated in Chapter 4 of the Book. Similarly, during the 19th and 20th century millions of people had also died in China in each of the five major famines as stated in the paragraph below. We should not forget the catastrophic consequences of famines faced by India and China in the past.

**How China achieved sustainable food security to the country** - People's Republic of China had largest population in the World till 2022, but in 2023 population of India has exceeded that of China. In the distant past, China also faced many catastrophic events of famines in the last century when millions of people had died. Famine in 1876-79 (10-13 million deaths), 1906-07 (20-25 million deaths), 1928-30 (6 million deaths) and 1936-37 (5 million deaths) were the notable major famines in China. Besides these instances, there were many other smaller famines in the past which were faced by China. After independence to China, 'The Great Famine', which began in 1959 and lasted three years up to 1961, was probably the deadliest famine in the human history, killing between 30 and 45 million people in the Republic China. Chinese farmers under the Chairman Mao were organized into collectives that worked on common land. All these collectives worked very inefficiently, and the farms weren't very productive. Then everything changed in 1978 when farming families across China took quasi-ownership of plots of land and were granted more freedom to sell their yields in the open market. That single change created incentives to work hard and make investments for increasing land productivity. Heavy investment by the Republic in water resource development infrastructure began more than a decade before de-collectivization and after the famine of 1959 to 1961. **When there was not even one Large Dam (Dam having height more than 15 m and/or storage more than 3 million cubic meters) in China in 1950, by the year 2000 China had made very heavy investments in the water sector and constructed 22,000 large dams out of total 48,000 large dams existing in the world then.** This notable planned activity carried out entirely with the technical and financial resources of the country might be ranked as first notable and commendable activity in all countries of the world so far. It has dramatically changed the living conditions of the people of China because of the food & water security and the employment generation resulting from it. Today, more than half of Chinese farmers cultivate irrigated fields, making the country one of the most intensively watered farming economies on the planet. Besides that, China accelerated use of chemical fertilisers, insecticides, and initiated research on new varieties of grains, fruits, and vegetables that could, when paired with improved irrigation, produce more food on less land. Such improved agriculture practices had increased the land productivity of many crops when compared with those in India, which would be evident from the Table below:

**Table 7 - Crop productivity in Tonnes per hectare in India and China**

| Type of Crop | Per Hectare Productivity in Tonnes | |
| --- | --- | --- |
| | In India | In China |
| Wheat | 3.52 | 5.81 |
| Rice | 4.14 | 7.11 |
| Maize | 3.33 | 6.29 |
| Sorghum (Jowar) | 0.98 | 4.76 |
| Soyabean | 0.95 | 1.95 |
| Ground nut | 1.21 | 3.85 |
| Cotton | 0.44 | 1.90 |

Source – Foreign Agricultural Service; USDA Global Market Analysis August 2022

From these figures it would be seen that there is considerable scope in India to improve land productivity per hectare of most of the main crops. If such comparison is made only for irrigated crops in both the countries, the difference may not be so large. But it still emphasises the need to review the situation in India and take all possible measures to improve land productivity by making judicious use of all inputs and of the relevant technology.

There are some constraints and challenges in India's Agricultural sector and some measures are possible to overcome these constraints and to meet the challenge of achieving food grain productivity targets as above on a sustainable basis till 2050. These could be summarised as below:

1. Between 1971 and 2006, number of land holdings in the country increased from 70 million to 129 million, but the net cropped area remained constant at 162 million hectares (mha). Average size of operational holdings reduced from 2.28 ha to 1.3 ha. It was due to the prevailing Land Partition Act which gives equal rights on the family land, to all the male and female children. There is inverse relationship between productivity and farm size group and hence land ceiling and wasteland development need a fresh look if our agriculture is to remain globally competitive. Possibility of cooperative farming or commercial farming would have to be

explored. It would then be possible to mechanise the farms and increase per hectare productivity.

2. Literacy has a positive and significant relation with the crop productivity and a strong link between literacy and farm modernization. Literacy has emerged as an important source of growth in adoption of the latest technology, use of modern inputs like machinery, fertilisers, plant protection measures, alternative cropping systems and the like. Literacy will play a far more important role in the globalized world than it did in the past. As future agriculture will be increasingly technology-led and will require modern economic management, high return for investment on education is expected. Agriculture Department of Govt. machinery should provide more efficient service in the transfer of latest technology in agriculture, from Agriculture Universities to the farmer.

3. The total area of degraded soils in India out of 329 mha of total geographic area, is estimated to be 146 mha, comprising 94 mha affected by water erosion, 9 mha by wind erosion, 16 mha by acidic degradation, 6 mha by salination and 14 mha by physical degradation like water logging and 7 mha as a complex degradation. Suitable measures would have to be taken to restore such land and bring as much of it under cultivation as is possible. It is a slow process but coordinated efforts would yield good results by creating such permanent assets.

4. Use of chemical fertilisers and insecticides/pesticides in some states in the North India has resulted in pollution of the ground water. Toxic chemicals and carcinogens finding way into rivers and ground water after use of water for agriculture and industries has increased incidence of cancer. There is good potential to upgrade soil quality through green manuring, judicious recycling of residues into soil, compost/vermicompost application, biological 'N' fixation, use of bio-fertilisers including phosphate, sulphur and potash solubilizing microbes.

5. It is observed that for most of the rain-fed cereal crops grown, there is not much increase in the land productivity per hectare during the last 75 years. This was due to cultivator's inability to apply costly inputs because of uncertainty of timely and adequate rainfall availability. It is expected that little less than 50% area under crops may still remain as rain-fed, despite harnessing most of the surface and ground water resources. Hence it is necessary to make research to develop new strains of rice, wheat, maize, and millets which are more drought or water shortage resistant. In addition to that, measures to provide protective well irrigation to rain-fed crops during occasions of dry spells in monsoon rainfall should also be taken. These would be in the form of carrying out watershed development works in mini watersheds (250 to 400 ha each), by conserving rainwater where it falls and conserving the soil, by undertaking structural and non-structural measures. It would augment natural ground water recharge, enable providing protective well irrigation and increase land productivity per hectare.

6. It may be borne in mind that besides increasing land productivity to ensure food security to the country, the Green Revolution has achieved poverty alleviation in the rural areas. Generally, there is higher concentration of poor people in rainfed areas in comparison to the irrigated tracts. Even with 20% irrigation intensity there is sharp fall in the level of rural poverty. This indicates that extension of irrigation to unirrigated areas and popularizing locally

adaptable better crop husbandry will prove to be much effective in poverty eradication and social development.

7. Climate Change is bound to cause adverse impacts on the agriculture sector and the water sector during the coming decades. It would increase the frequency of droughts and floods. Rise in average temperature would reduce the duration and the average yield of cereal crops especially wheat and rice, though in some presently colder areas yield may increase. It would be necessary to develop new strains of crops which would not have much effect on the yield despite higher atmospheric temperatures. These weather-related issues call for greater understanding of crop weather relationship to develop crop weather models to devise efficient agricultural production strategies.

8. Comparison of figures of average productivity per hectare of crops like wheat, rice etc. in India and China are given in the Table above. Comparison of crop productivity figures in other developed countries like USA & Japan with those in India also indicate that there is need and scope for improvement in productivity India. Agriculture Universities should study the field conditions in some representative farms and suggest measures to improve crop productivity per hectare for all crops. These measures should then be replicated by implementing on large scale at the field level through the Agriculture Departments of all the states. Analysis of these results would help in deciding the policy for adoption by farmers in all the states in India.

9. It is felt that a 'Second Green Revolution' is now necessary because gains of the first are already plateauing. It is necessary to evolve seeds for crops which would survive flooding, tolerate droughts, extreme heat and salty soils, to make even poor-quality lands more productive. A revolution has been made possible by sequencing the rice genome which enabled the farmer to keep seeds from one harvest to plant in the next year with no reduction in yield (unlike maize and wheat).

Since the Author is not an expert in the agriculture sector, efforts have been taken to cover various aspects of Green Revolution by highlighting the important and vital issues, which have led to achieving food security to the country. Important issues which need to be attended to hereafter about the agriculture sector in the future to achieve sustainable food security till the year 2050 are also highlighted as above.

It should, however, be borne in mind that after independence, assured availability of water to the crops because of the increased irrigation facilities from surface irrigation schemes and ground water harnessing schemes (dug wells & bore wells), was the real prime mover of the Green Revolution. All other inputs such as High yielding variety & Hybrid seeds, chemical fertilisers, insecticides etc. are effective only if there is assured and timely availability of water to the crops. These inputs are not so effective for rain-fed/dry land crops and hence there has not been much improvement in the per hectare productivity of rain-fed crops during the last 75 years. Per hectare productivity of irrigated crops after applying all other inputs in the agriculture sector as above, could be 2.5 to 3 times that of the rain-fed crops. Report of 'World Commission on Large Dams' titled as *'Dams And Development - A new Framework for Decision-Making'* published in the year

2000 mentions that average productivity of irrigated land is about 2.67 times that of unirrigated crops.

Progress in science, climatology, hydrology, and engineering, prompted us to adopt modern technology in constructing all types and sizes of water resource development infrastructures to conserve water. In addition to the large dam-canal projects, construction of many medium size and small size dam-canal projects were taken up in India to ensure optimum development of water resource in the river basins, and to achieve social equity in the allocation of water within the basin. Pace of development of water resource was aimed to meet challenges of the dynamics of changing water demand patterns over time. How India met with the challenge of meeting competing and conflicting demands on water for irrigation, urban and industrial use, to ensure sustained food and water security to the country since independence, is very thought provoking for study. It would be a lesson to all the developing countries of the world to follow. Hence all aspects of water resource development and management for its use for irrigation in the country and for other competing uses of water have been covered in much more details in some chapters of the book.

**Measures taken to face droughts in India during last 75 years** – Green revolution has increased food grain productivity in the country on a sustainable basis as explained above. But still occurrence of droughts which was a natural climatic event, could not be avoided. Many coordinated actions had to be taken at the country/state level to face that calamity of droughts effectively to avoid casualties, the way they had occurred during the pre-independence period.

Failure of monsoon rains over sizeable area of the country resulting in failure of monsoon crop was the main cause of many severe famines in India in the pre independence period. As seen in the last chapter, large-scale famines in the second half of the 18th century, in the 19th century and first half of the 20th century had devastating effects on the population of India. There were about 2 to 10 million deaths in each of the eight out of twelve severe famines which occurred between 1750 to 1947. Total inadequacy of immediate relief measures such as providing work to the famine labour and not transporting food grains to supply them at subsidised rates to the famine affected people, were the main reasons for heavy casualties during these several famines during the British regime up to 1947. Due to lack of long-term planning to reduce intensity of such famines by implementation of water resource development infrastructure and other developmental works, such famines continued to have their disastrous effects in the past periods. With this background, let us now review how the Indian Govt. handled the situation during several severe famines which occurred during last 75 years after independence to the country in the year 1947.

There were some famines in some parts of the country during last 75 years, but the State Govts and the Central Govt. took proactive steps in a planned manner to handle the situation. To start with, some long-term measures were taken by starting works of several dam-canal works in many states to provide additional irrigation facilities on a large scale for the rainfed cultivation. It was supplemented by introducing 'Green Revolution' as explained above to increase land productivity per hectare by taking suitable measures in the agriculture sector. In the case of actual occurrence of drought, immediate action to provide works to the affected people near their villages was taken. Food grains were transported from the grain surplus states and were supplied to the labourers at subsidised rates. Such actions provided immediate relief to the famine affected people and hence there were no casualties of drought affected people. The economist Amartya Sen had won the 1998 Nobel Memorial Prize in Economic Sciences in part for his work on the economic mechanisms underlying famines. He has stated in his 2009 book, 'The Idea of Justice' that, *"Though Indian democracy has many imperfections, nevertheless the political incentives generated by it have been adequate to eliminate major famines right from the time of independence. The last substantial famine in India —the Bengal famine —occurred only four years before the Empire ended. The prevalence of famines, which had been a persistent feature of the long history of the British Indian Empire, ended abruptly with the establishment of a democracy after independence"*. No major famines have occurred since Indian independence and there has been a declining number in famines which had been of short durations and had limited adverse effects. 'Jean Drèze' finds that the post-independence Indian government largely remedied the causes of the famines which occurred during British regime, an event which must count as marking the second great turning point in the history of famine relief in India over the past two centuries.

**Famines occurred during post-independence period** - India still faced threats of some severe famines in some States such as in Bihar in 1966-67, Maharashtra in 1971-72, West Bengal in 1979-80, Gujarat in 1987-88 and Maharashtra again in 2013.

**Bihar famine 1966–67** - It was a famine in Bihar and eastern Uttar Pradesh state. Annual production of food grains in Bihar had dropped from 7.2 million tonnes in 1965–1966 to 4.3 million tonnes in 1966–1967. The national food grain production also dropped by about 19% between 1964-65 to 1965-66. Import of food grains from the United States of America had provided a relief to all the affected population that time. Rise in prices of food grains in Bihar caused migration and starvation, but the public distribution system, relief measures taken by the state governments and voluntary organizations have been instrumental to limit the adverse impacts of famine. Official death toll from starvation in the Bihar drought was 2353.

**Maharashtra drought 1971-72** – Before this drought, the state had faced scarcity conditions in some Districts in the North and Central Maharashtra in the year 1951-52. At that time works such as earth work for rural roads and breaking of road metal required for construction of water-bound macadam road were provided to the drought affected labourers. Earthwork of one major dam was also got done partly from the affected labourers. Subsequently, Maharashtra State passed an Act in 1963 to delete the term "famine" in the Bombay State Famine Relief Fund Act, 1958. In the preamble it was asserted that *'The Agricultural situation in the State is constantly watched by the State Government, and relief measures as warranted by the situation are provided as soon as signs of scarcity conditions are apparent, so that there is now no scope for famine conditions to develop'*. Despite such awareness of keeping watch on the situation during each monsoon season, they were unable to foresee the severe drought in the Maharashtra in 1971-72 when at its peak period, about 25 million people (more than 70% of rural population in the State) needed immediate relief and help.

In the annals of Indian agriculture, 1972 will be remembered as another 'Year of the Drought'. It was not the worst recorded, yet it was bad enough and extended over large areas of the country to create sufferings for tens of millions of people. Varying in degree of intensity, it occurred in Maharashtra, Andhra Pradesh, Gujarat, Rajasthan, and large pockets of Mysore, Orissa, Madhya Pradesh, and parts of UP. Something can be said about its scope and aftermath before this drought became just another one in the long chain of similar episodes. In the Maharashtra state, the administration promptly took coordinated actions at all levels to face and handle the drought situation. Immediate relief measures which were undertaken by the Government of Maharashtra (GoM) included providing employment to the drought affected people on works such as earthwork for rural roads, breaking of stone from quarries to form road metal required for construction of metal roads etc. Construction of many water-bound macadam roads in the rural area was also started as famine works. One advantage of such road works was that all the landowners had given their consent to acquire land required for all such roads, due to pressure from the needy famine labourers. Most of all these roads were completed during the next 5-6 years through State funds, to create a very good network of roads in the rural area. Such network of roads later on provided very good facilities to transport agriculture produce to the urban area and to transport other goods from urban area to meet needs of rural population.

When there was no scope to take up any more road works, it was decided to carry out productive works such as construction of lentic water bodies like village ponds, small earth dams, percolation tanks etc., by deploying labourers from the drought affected population. Looking to this situation, working estimates were prepared in advance for many such works in the rural area (within 5 km radius from their villages) which aimed at creating permanent productive water resource development infrastructure. Irrigation Department took a leading role in the activity of survey and preparation of estimates for such works and to approve them. Implementation was done by them as well as by Zila Parishads (District Councils), Public Works Department etc. Such works provided employment to labourers during peak period of the drought. Out of the 14 drought affected Districts having 137 Talukas, 87 Talukas were drought affected. About 9,412 percolation tanks were completed through labourers and 3671 were partly completed when the drought ended in 1972. In the remaining 15 Districts of the State, 609 percolation tanks were completed and 375 were partly completed through drought affected labourers. All the partly completed percolation tanks were completed during later years through State finds. On all the scarcity works, labourers were paid every week on the basis of the total work/turnover done by them in the week. Food grains were transported by the State Govt. from other states and were distributed by the public distribution system through fair-price shops to the labourers. Nutritional supplement viz. 'Sukhadi' was also provided free of cost to all the labourers. Arrangements of drinking water to the labours were made from nearby wells which had enough water and from nearby reservoirs. In spite of the drought conditions in the area, water was available in many wells because GW exploitation was on a low key in the drought affected area at that time. Due to all these planned activities, no deaths from starvation were reported in this famine. However, some cattle were either sold to the butchers or there were some deaths of cattle for want of adequate fodder.

Earth work for many dams & canals of the State sector major, medium, and minor irrigation projects was also got done from famine affected labourers. Such relief works initiated by the Government helped employ over about 5 million famine affected labourers at the height of the drought in the Maharashtra leading to an effective famine relief for them. The Maharashtra drought in which there were zero deaths, is the one which is known for the successful deployment of famine mitigation policies. While the famine relief program in Bihar was somewhat poor, Jean Drèze calls the one in Maharashtra was a model programme. The author of the Book has first-hand information of all the famine relief measures taken during this drought because, about 8,000 to 10,000 drought affected labourers were deployed under him as Executive Engineer in the Irrigation Deptt. of GoM. Unskilled components of earth dams & canals of some medium/minor size projects and those of some village tanks, percolation tanks were got done by the author through such drought affected labourers.

**Droughts after the 1971-72 Maharashtra drought -**

Subsequently there were some droughts in the Maharashtra state in the eighties and nineties. Following were the significant changes in the situation in the rural area and in the relief measures during these subsequent droughts, when compared with the 1971-72 drought.

1. Due to reduction in the size of family land holding from about 4 to 4.5 ha at the time of independence to about 2 to 2.5 ha during the next 30-40 years, it was becoming difficult to sustain the family from the rain-fed crop cultivation from the reduced family land holdings. Hence pace of harnessing ground water in the drought prone area increased appreciably in the eighties and nineties. This was also due to the subsidies given by the GoM towards the cost of digging/drilling wells and for installing pumps on wells. Electrically operated pumps were deployed due to spread of electricity distribution network and availability of electricity at subsidised rates in the rural area. Availability of drilling rigs and multi-stage submersible pumps enabled exploitation of shallow and deep-seated GW aquifers by means of bore wells.

2. Completion of many major, medium, and minor surface irrigation schemes had increased the area under irrigation in the drought prone area of the state. Financial assistance provided by the World Bank (soft loans) and other Financial Institutions helped in early completion of irrigation projects.

3. Above activities of increased GW exploitation on large scale and increased area under irrigation by the surface irrigation schemes, had provided all the year-round employment to the landless farm labours. With the result, there were much less labourers who needed employment on drought relief works in these subsequent droughts.

4. Some cattle camps were set up near major and medium projects where sufficient water was available to provide it in the cattle camps where cattle from nearby villages were provided with shelter. Fodder was procured by the Govt. and was also provided in these cattle camps free of cost. Hence there were no deaths of cattle during these droughts.

5. However, due to increased exploitation of GW for well irrigation as mentioned above, supplying drinking water to the drought affected labours by transporting it from long distances from reservoirs by water tankers was seen to be essential during these droughts.

6. Only productive works such as village ponds, percolation tanks and earthwork for dams and canals of state sector and local sector irrigation projects were taken up during all these droughts.

**West Bengal drought of 1979–80** - The drought was the next major drought and caused a 17% decline in food production with a shortfall of 13.5 million tonnes of food grain. Stored food stocks in other states were leveraged by the government, and there was no need to import food grains from other countries. The lessons learned from the Maharashtra and West Bengal droughts led to the Desert Development Programme and the Drought Prone Area Programme, as a long-term measure. The intent of these programmes was to reduce the negative effects of droughts by applying eco-friendly land-use practices and conserving water. Major schemes in improving rural infrastructure, extending irrigation to additional areas, and diversifying agriculture were also launched. The lessons from the drought relief measures brought to light the need for employment generation, watershed planning, and ecologically integrated development.

**Gujarat drought 1987-88** - Failure of monsoons in year 1987-88 had catastrophic consequences for the State of Gujarat, when 16 out of the State's 19 districts were affected by the severe drought. There was a severe economic crisis in the Saurashtra region, with groundnut mills closing and agriculture being deeply impacted. However, due to immediate famine relief measures taken by the State on the lines as above, there were no casualties in this drought.

**Maharashtra drought of 2013** - According to Union Agriculture Ministry, over 11,800 villages in Maharashtra were declared drought affected. This drought was considered the second worst to date, exceeded only by the drought in Maharashtra in 1971-72. It was also well managed by providing productive works to drought affected people and by providing other facilities as above. Hence there were no deaths of people and the cattle in this drought.

People from various walks of life, such as social activist Smt. Vandana Shiva and researcher Mr. Dan Banik, agree that famines and the resulting large-scale loss of life from starvation have been eliminated after Indian independence in 1947.

# Chapter 6
# Water Resource Development Infrastructure Evolved in India After Independence.

*'Development of Water Resource' in the river basins to create irrigation facilities was one important factor behind the success of the Green Revolution, which ensured sustainable food security to the country. In addition to that, it has also ensured sustainable 'water security' mainly to the urban and partly to the rural population of India. It also provided adequate dependable water needed for industrial development which had taken place in many states in the country after independence. All water resource development infrastructures are compatible to the topography of the river basin, climatic conditions, rainfall pattern, and its magnitude. They are planned and constructed to meet present and future water demands for all its competing uses. Holistic planning needs to be done to ensure optimum and equitable development of available water resource in the river basin, without sacrificing the water needs of terrestrial & aquatic ecosystems and the environment. On considerations of equitable allocation of water resource in the basin for irrigation purposes, water resource development structures of varying sizes, storage capacities and types were planned and constructed in the basins as per the topography. Hence it is known as integrated development of water resource. The chapter covers full details of all such structural measures taken after the independence, to create surface irrigation facilities in India in general and in the Maharashtra State in particular. Review of status of water resource development infrastructures constructed at the world level is also taken.*

Water is a very powerful/potent agent in providing food and water security and in achieving/ensuring socio-economic development of the society. Optimum development of Water Resource (WR) in every river basin, duly considering needs of the terrestrial and aquatic ecosystems, should be the basic approach in the planning of water resource development projects. Integrated development means achieving optimum development and equitable allocation of WR in every river basin by Intra-basin transfer of water and holistically, for all the river basins in the country by planning Inter-basin transfer of water wherever necessary. On an average, availability of WR in any river basin is finite, though it is variable from year to year in its magnitude and its timewise distribution each year. Type of infrastructure suitable for development of WR needs to be compatible to the rainfall magnitude & pattern, and to the topography of the basin. If rainfall is well distributed and occurring in almost all months in a year, rivers would usually have perennial flow, and a river water diversion structure could cater to the needs of irrigation to the crop and other water needs. If the river rises in the cold temperate region, there is snowfall in the upper reaches which gets accumulated there in the entire winter season. Such rivers have flow from seasonal rainfall in the lower parts in the monsoon season and have flow in the summer season due to snow melt from the upper reaches. Hence such rivers also have perennial flow and river diversion structures are adequate to meet needs of irrigation to the crop and for other non-irrigation uses of water.

When the monsoon rains are confined only to some months of the year, and there is not much land under forest cover in the catchment, such rivers may only have seasonal flow for 5 to 8 months in a year. In that case, a Masonry/Concrete/Earth dam of designed storage capacity needs to be constructed at a place on the river, according to suitability of topography and substrata foundation conditions. Height of the dam is decided according to the planned design storage capacity of the reservoir created at that place on the river. In India, planning of man-made reservoirs is done on the basis of estimated dependable rainfall in a river basin. If we have a series of 40-year rainfall data of past period and arrange it in descending order, rainfall value of the 20th year is considered as 50% dependable rainfall. It means that on an average, in 2 out of 4 years we can expect rainfall likely to be more than that value. If we take rainfall value of the 30th year, it is considered as 75% dependable rainfall and on an average in 3 out of 4 years, we can expect the rainfall likely to be more than that value. Average value of rainfall of all the 40 years would give average rainfall value for planning, which is generally close to 50% dependable rainfall worked out as above. In India and the Maharashtra state, major projects (more than 10,000 ha irrigable area each) are designed for 75% dependable rainfall and medium projects (between 10,000 to 2000 ha irrigable area each) are designed for 60% dependable rainfall. Whereas small size projects (below 2000 ha irrigable area each) are designed for 50% dependable rainfall. All projects irrigating drought prone area are, however, designed for 50% dependable rainfall. Since observed rainfall cycle is of about 30 years duration in India, past rainfall data of at least 30 years is required for planning optimum design capacity of the storages. Different practices for planning storage capacity of the reservoirs are followed in different countries.

Once the dependable rainfall is decided as above, next step is to work out the coefficient of rainfall-runoff relationship. It is then possible to estimate how much quantity of water having designed dependability would be available for use at that dam site. The coefficient depends on the climate, magnitude & pattern of rainfall and characteristics of the catchment area. If the catchment is flat and has sizeable land under agriculture, much of the rainfall gets arrested on the surface, gets absorbed in the soil and there is less runoff. In the tropical climate region, lot of water is lost by way of evaporation when compared with temperate climate region. If the catchment has steep slopes and light soils, less water would be absorbed in the soil and there would be more runoff. If sizeable land is covered by forests, there is less runoff in the monsoon but there would be some steady runoff in the fair-weather season due to gradual release of ground water into the river. Generally, runoff to rainfall ratio in percent is higher for high magnitude of average rainfall, than for the lower magnitudes of average rainfall. Rainfall-runoff relationship can be best established for a catchment where daily river discharge data at a river gauging station and corresponding rainfall data from many rain gauge stations in the catchment for the past period is available for the same years. For completed dam works, record of daily rainfall data from rain gauge stations in the catchment and very reliable actual daily inflow in the reservoir and daily outflow data from the spillway after its filling, is available after completion of the dam. From this more reliable record of actual runoff, coefficient of rainfall and runoff relationship can be computed very accurately.

If we plan to construct new storage dam on a river where record of rainfall is available for many years, but there is no river gauging station on it, such coefficients established for other similar catchments as above, can be adopted to get dependable runoff computed from the available rainfall data. Care should, however, needs to be taken to see that such factor shall be taken for the catchment which has nearly same rainfall magnitude and similar other characteristics such as climate, size of the catchment, extent of forest cover, cultivated land, land slopes etc.

**Principles behind selection of storage for a reservoir** – A major dam planned to store large quantity of water has some inherent advantages as below: Average depth of water stored in the reservoir is much more than small size dams and hence, area under submergence per unit of stored water is less and so has less cost of land acquisition. Total value of evaporation loss in meters in a year from the reservoir water depends on the climatic conditions at that place and it is nearly constant irrespective of the capacity of the reservoir. Hence for reservoirs of major dams which have high average water depth, evaporation loss in percent is less when compared with small size dams which are having lesser average lake water depth. By and large, design flood discharge for spillways is proportional to square root of the catchment area. Hence design discharge per unit of catchment area is less for large size dams than the small size dams and so the spillway costs. Due to all these reasons and also because of the scale effect, cost of storing per unit of water for large size dams is least and it increases as the storage capacity of the dam reduces. Hence from the economic point of view preference is given for construction of large size major dam projects where the topography permits.

But usually, there are limited number of sites available on any river, which are suitable to locate a major dam. They are planned on main river or on major tributaries of the river at a location where river valley is narrow (to reduce cost of the dam) & there is rocky strata at shallow depth below the riverbed. So also, rock should be of good quality to locate spillway in the main gorge or to locate it on either bank as per availability of stable rock, where site is suitable to locate spillway tail channel. It is also necessary to ensure that there is adequate construction material such as soil, murum i.e. semipervious decomposed rock, for earthen dams and stone/rubble/sand for masonry/concrete dams, available at short leads. Other requirements are that the lake should not submerge much irrigated fertile land, forest land and towns/villages as far as possible. Due to such constraints, available sites to locate major dams in any river basin are usually limited. Major dams in India are generally planned to provide irrigation to certain percentage of perennial crops like sugar cane, banana, horticulture - fruit trees etc., in their design cropping pattern. Because the water availability in major dams is more dependable (75% dependability), they are also planned to provide water for non-irrigation purposes such as urban water use and industrial water use. Such non-irrigation demand needs to be fulfilled from quantity of water available when computed at 90 to 95% dependability. Not only that, to take care of the contingency of late outbreak of monsoon season, non-irrigation requirement of water for about one and half to two months i.e., up to end of July or up to mid-August is required to be kept in the reservoir at the end of summer season i.e., up to mid-June. Major dams are located on large rivers and usually the land commanded on either bank of the river by canals is relatively deep, fertile, and flat.

Major dams hence do not cater to the water needs of less fertile shallow lands located in the upper reaches of the river basins and sub basins. Hence next best choice would be to explore sites to locate medium size dams and then to locate minor size dams, on the same principles for locating major dams as above. On the consideration of achieving optimum development of water resource in the river basin and also for ensuring equity in water allocation in the river basin, construction of many medium and minor dams becomes essential. Even if they are costlier per unit of stored water than the major dam projects and provide only seasonal irrigation to crops, their implementation is necessary to achieve dispersal of irrigation benefits in the basin to ensure social equity. With a view to reducing loss due to evaporation from these small size reservoirs, all medium and minor projects in India/Maharashtra are usually planned to cater to provide irrigation only to seasonal crops in Kharif (monsoon) and Rabi (winter) season. Reservoirs are hence planned to be empty by end of winter season i.e., by end of February each year, which avoids heavy evaporation loss that would have taken place from the reservoirs during the summer season. Next step to achieve social equity would be to take up irrigation projects which irrigate area below 250 ha each. In the Maharashtra State, all projects above 250 ha irrigable area each are planned, designed, implemented, and operated by the Water Resource Department in the state sector. Whereas projects below 250 ha are planned, designed, implemented, and operated by the District Councils (Zilla Parishads).

**Review of the Activity of construction of Dams, at the World level** – To meet various needs of water such as irrigation, household & industrial use and hydropower generation, activity of construction of water storage dams was started in the twentieth century, in some countries of the world such as America, Spain, India etc. Awareness about non submergence of forest land in their reservoirs was not a serious issue that time. Since most of those dams which were constructed in the first half of the twentieth century were located in mountainous/hilly region, not much cultivated land was getting submerged in them. But during second half of the twentieth century, the situation started to change. In some countries of the world, substantial land under cultivation was getting submerged in some of these reservoirs constructed in lower reaches of the major rivers. Awareness about protection of forest ecosystem also came to the forefront in many countries of the world. Main issue was about the social problems arising out of the involuntary resettlement of Project Affected People (PAP) whose land and their villages were getting submerged in these reservoirs. Emphasising on the unsatisfactory resettlement of the PAPs due to inadequate facilities provided to them in the resettled villages and degradation of the environment caused by the submergence of forest land etc., social activists and environmentalists from some developing countries raised voice against construction of such large size dam-canal projects. In some extreme cases, the social activists demanded to stop the activity of construction of such large dams on that account.

It was hence decided to examine all the related issues at the world level, to study adequacy and suitability of the 'Large Dams' as a development model to meet water needs for the people. With a view to exploring all such aspects, 'The World Commission on Dams' (WCD), a global multi-stakeholder body was initiated in 1997 by the World Bank and the World Conservation Union (IUCN). It was set up in the year 1998 and after taking review of status of construction of large dams in all countries of the world and deliberating on all the related issues, the WCD submitted its Report *'Dams and development - A new framework for decision-making'* in the year 2000. It established the most comprehensive guidelines for dam building which described an innovative framework for planning water and energy projects that were intended to protect dam-affected people, the environment and ensure that the benefits from dams are more equitably distributed.

The Report covers status of completed 'Large Dams' constructed in the countries of the World up to the year 2000, as shown in the Table below. Definition of Large Dam has been made in this Report as – 'a dam having height more than 15 meters and/or storage capacity of more than 3 million cubic meter (mcum)'.

Table 1 - Number of Large Dams constructed in all countries up to the year 2000.

| Country | Number of Large Dams by 1950 | Number of Large Dams between 1950 - 2000 | Total |
|---|---|---|---|
| China | 22 | 21,978 | 22,000 (46%) |
| America | | | 6,600 (14%) |
| India | | | 4,300 (9%) |
| Japan | | | 2,700 (6%) |
| Spain | | | 1,200 (2%) |
| Rest countries | | | 11,200 (22%) |
| Total | 5,000 | 43,000 | 48,000 (100%) |

Table 2 - Continent wise number of Large Dams constructed up to the year 2000.

| Continent | Number of large dams | Percentage |
|---|---|---|
| Asia | 31,500 | 65% |
| North America | 8,000 | 17% |
| Europe | 5,600 | 12% |
| Africa | 1,300 | 3% |
| South America | 1,000 | 2% |
| Australia | 600 | 1% |
| Total | 48,000 | 100% |

One notable feature in the activity of construction of large dams in the developing and underdeveloped countries of the world was by way of the financial assistance and technical guidance provided by the several International Financing Agencies during the period 1950 to 2000. World Bank and Asian Development Bank took a lead role in this activity. During the period of 50 years from 1950 to 2000, total financial assistance of about 126 billion US dollars - @ 1998 price, was provided by all the international funding agencies. The assistance was 3 billion US dollars during 1950-55, which gradually increased to reach a peak value of 22 billion US dollars during 1980-85 and then gradually reduced to 11.5 billion US dollars during 1995-2000. As in the year 2000, about 695 to 960 (as per different sources) large dams were in progress in India, which was the highest number in all countries of the world then. China had 209, South Korea 132, Japan 90 and Iran had 98 large dams in progress.

Increase in the pace of construction of large dams in India after independence in 1947 and completion of 4,300 large dams by the year 2000, had ensured sustained food and water security to the country. Relatively cheap and the environment friendly hydropower was also generated from many of these large dams. By systematic and coordinated operation of spillway gates of all large dams in the river basins, some moderation of floods could also be done.

After the world-wide 'Great Depression' of the nineteen thirties, America took the initiative to take up capital intensive works such as construction of many large dam projects and that of the National Highway projects across America. Immediate objective was to provide employment to the depression affected people, and long-term objective was to create permanent assets for future development of America. Because of the activity of construction of many dams across major rivers and their completion later, per capita availability of stored water in America was probably highest in the World by 1950. Vast stretches of the earlier rain-fed cultivated areas were provided with sprinkler irrigation facilities to grow wheat by mechanised farming. Production of wheat and milo increased appreciably, and hence the country could export about 10 million Tonnes of food grains to India in the sixties of the last century, to tide over the critical food grain shortage situation there. Substantial hydroelectric power was also generated from most of these large dams. It provided cheap electricity for the sprinkler irrigation, for food processing & other industries and for electrification in several towns and villages.

After the Great Famine of 1959-61 in China which resulted in casualties of about 30 and 45 million people, the country radically changed its policy about construction of water resource development infrastructures. From the figures above it would be seen that China, which had only 22 large dams up to the year 1950, had constructed 21,978 large dams in just a period of less than 50 years, out of the 43,000 large dams constructed by all countries in the World during the period from 1950 to 2000. Such large-scale activity had increased irrigation facilities appreciably and increased land productivity to achieve food & water security to the people of China from seventh decade of the last century. Because of the buffer stock of food grains created on that account, there were no deaths due to droughts in China after the catastrophic 1959-61 drought. Assured supply of water from these dams also provided adequate water for urban & industrial use and hence China could achieve phenomenal development of the industrial sector during that period. Because there was no possibility of exercising any control or regulation on the floods during the period before 1950, there were very heavy casualties due to flooding of many rivers and due to breaching of dykes constructed in the lower reaches of the rivers to confine river flow and floods. Construction of several large dams on rivers enabled regulation and moderation of floods to most of the major rivers in China. With the result, there were very few severe floods and there were negligible casualties and limited loss of houses and property in China since then due to river floods.

**Water Resource Development activities taken by the Govt. of India -** After independence, India contemplated to take up many large irrigation projects and hydroelectric projects, which would benefit one or more than one State. For implementation of such major projects involving substantial technical input in the planning, design, and implementation stage, Govt. of India (GoI) set up Central Water and Power Commission (CWPC) under the Ministry of Irrigation and Power to look after all activities related to the water resource development infrastructure. CWPC had set up Damodar Valley Corporation, Bhakra Project Control Board etc. for centralised implementation of these large multipurpose projects. Besides that, planning and designing of dams i.e., head works for many major projects which were taken up by some states was also done by the CWPC by following the practices standardised by them or had provided the states necessary guidance for design of dams. Maharashtra state had large number of major projects planned for construction. Hence a separate Central Designs Organisation was set up in the state for carrying out planning and designing of all major projects in the state. All the states would prepare project reports themselves as per standard guidelines of CWPC and get clearance from them prior to start of the projects. Work of giving Administrative Approval, Technical Sanction and starting their construction after making budget provision would be the responsibility of the states. Implementation of all projects excepting those implemented by the River Valley Corporations or the Control Boards, was done by the respective states. Implementation of Interstate projects was done by each co-basin state for all the projects within their boundary. Even if 'Water' is a 'State' subject, under the Constitution of India, such monitoring and governance at the country level, by following uniform standardised practice and procedure in the work of WR development infrastructure was essential under the circumstances.

Another important activity was taken up by the GoI was by way of promoting implementation of the irrigation projects in the country. Firstly, it was in the form of providing additional funds by the GoI to the State Govts., for certain projects by assigning them as National Projects. Such action expedited completion of these projects so that benefits due to creation of additional irrigation facilities were accrued early by the country. Besides that, Irrigation and Power Deptt. of GoI. negotiated with the World Bank (WB) for granting low interest long term loans for expediting construction of some irrigation projects in some states. Maharashtra state which had maximum number of ongoing Dam-Canal irrigation projects amongst all states in India, had received funding from the WB for many such ongoing major projects, which expedited their completion. With the funding from the WB in many states in India, projects of 'Dam Safety Review' consisting of review of completed major, medium, and minor dams for improving their performance and their safety were also taken up. Due to this activity, the state engineers learnt about the latest practices and trends in the planning, design, and implementation of irrigation projects in the developed countries. Under one project funded by the WB, special units were set up in some states to compile and publish hydrological data of all river basins in the state. WB also provided funding to set up Water and Land Management Institutes (WALMI) in some states where appreciable land was brought under irrigation. With the funding from the United States Agency for International Development (USAID) which was established in 1961, many engineers from some states in India were deputed to participate in different short-term courses on specialised technical subjects in America, Israel, and some other countries. Financial assistance received from these funding agencies had expedited completion of irrigation projects in these states and ensured that there was improvement in the quality of works during construction of all components of the projects.

**Construction of Large Dams in India and in the Maharashtra State** – Major part of North India is covered by the Ganga-Brahmaputra and Indus River basins. These rivers rise in snow laden Himalaya Mountain ranges. Beyond the foot of these ranges, lands are fertile and have very flat slopes. Middle and lower reaches of rivers get monsoon rainfall but in the uppermost mountainous region, the snow gets accumulated in the entire winter season. In the summer season it melts so that all rivers then have good flow even in the summer season. With the result, Himalayan rivers have perennial flow. A diversion weir located in upper reaches of the plains and having canals on either bank to convey water to the fields for irrigation is the most economical and viable infrastructure to cater to the irrigation needs of the plains. After independence, the strategy was slightly changed, and it was planned to construct large dams in the mountain ranges to store water and to generate hydropower while releasing stored water for irrigation. Stored water of Bhakra dam was conveyed (Inter-basin water transfer) to irrigate parched lands in the Rajasthan state in the North-East India. Before start of the snow melt in the summer season, monsoon water stored in the reservoir is released for winter irrigation & for power generation. Adequate space is thus created in the reservoir to accommodate the snow-melt runoff in the summer season. That water is then released from the reservoir in summer season to generate hydropower and to irrigate perennial and summer season crops. Other major project was construction of Farakka Barrage in the plains to divert river flow for irrigation.

In the Central India and the Peninsular India, most of the rivers are seasonal, being compatible to the four-month seasonal monsoon pattern. Some large rivers in the South India had perennial flow in the lower reaches and in their Delta region. In the pre independence period, as detailed in the earlier chapter, river diversion structures were constructed to irrigate delta regions of East-flowing rivers in the South India. After independence, many large Masonry/Concrete/Earth dams and canals were constructed in upper reaches in the central and southern India to provide perennial irrigation to crops. Krishna and Godavari Rivers rise in the Maharashtra state in the N-S running Sahyadri mountain ranges and flow eastwards to meet Bay of Bengal. Because of the 3-4-month monsoon rains, they do not have perennial flow in the upper reaches. Hence many large dams have been constructed in the Sahyadri mountain ranges along eastern slope in the high rainfall zone, to provide irrigation to drought prone area in the rain shadow zone towards East. Because about 30 to 40 percent area of the State is drought prone, highest number of completed large dams (up to 2020) in the country (2,069 i.e., about 40% of 5,264) are in the Maharashtra state and about 285 large dam-canal projects were then under construction.

Within two to three decades after independence, appreciable cultivated land was provided with irrigation facilities created by construction of several large dams in many states. It helped to increase land productivity and the total food grain production through the 'Green Revolution', to make the country self-sufficient in food grains since then. Many medium size and minor size dams were also constructed in the states as per local topography, to meet irrigation needs of the small cultivators who were bypassed from the benefits of large irrigation projects. It also ensured optimum development of WR in the river basins. Some large lift irrigation schemes were also constructed in some states to provide irrigation facilities to the lands located at high level plateau, which were bypassed by the surface irrigation schemes. Existing 'Anicuts' i.e., diversion weirs constructed during British regime and earlier to irrigate lands of delta region of the East-flowing Peninsular rivers were remodelled to increase their area under irrigation.

Activity of construction of major projects in the country had slowed down in between because of the problems associated with the resettlement and rehabilitation of PAPs. A movement was initiated by some social activists on behalf of PAPs of Narmada Project in the Gujarat state. Central and/State Govts. then reviewed their policies and made many improvements in the facilities provided to the PAPs of all developmental projects. But the social activists continued 'Narmada Bachao Andolan (NBA) – Save Narmada Movement' and filed a Public Interested Litigation (PIL) in the Supreme Court to stop construction of the Sardar Sarovar Dam on the Narmada River in the Gujarat state. However, through a decision given by the Supreme Court in October 2000, the case was dismissed by a majority decision. The Supreme Court noted: *"If one compares the living conditions of the PAFs in their submerging villages with the rehabilitation packages first provided by the Tribunal's Award and then liberalised by the States, it is obvious that the PAFs had gained substantially after their re-settlement."* (Para 170). At one place it said: *"Public Interest Litigation should not be allowed to degenerate to becoming Publicity Interest Litigation or Private Inquisitiveness Litigation."* (Para 226). Due to the litigation by the NBA, construction of the Narmada dam was kept suspended for six years, entailing heavy financial loss to the Gujrat state. The benefits that accrued from the project were also postponed, which had an adverse impact on a large number of beneficiary cultivators and urban population. The activity of construction of large dams in the country then gained momentum which continued since then.

Table 3 - Large dams completed and under construction in India.

| Name of State | Completed large dams up to the year - | | | | | | | | |
|---|---|---|---|---|---|---|---|---|---|
| | 1900 | 1901 -1950 50 yrs | 1951 -1980 30 yrs | 1981 -2000 20 yrs | 2001 -2020 20 yrs | Year NA | Total | Under construction | Total |
| (NA – Not available) | | | | | | | | | |
| Maharashtra | 21 | 38 | 795 | 833 | 382 | 0 | 2069 | 285 | 2354 |
| Madhya Pradesh | 3 | 86 | 321 | 394 | 67 | 28 | 899 | 7 | 906 |

| | | | | | | | | |
|---|---|---|---|---|---|---|---|---|
| Gujarat | 6 | 57 | 295 | 212 | 45 | 5 | 620 | 12 | 632 |
| Chhattisgarh | - | 11 | 70 | 136 | 30 | 1 | 248 | 10 | 258 |
| Karnataka | 6 | 24 | 99 | 71 | 14 | 16 | 230 | 1 | 231 |
| **Total of 5 States** | **36** | **216** | **1580** | **1646** | **538** | **50** | **4066** | **315** | **4381** |
| Rest 24 States | 32 | 86 | 447 | 363 | 126 | 144 | 1198 | 122 | 1320 |
| **Total for India** | **68** | **302** | **2027** | **2009** | **664** | **194** | **5264** | **437** | **5701** |

**Source** - NATIONAL REGISTER OF LARGE DAMS (NRLD) is a compilation of the dams in the country prepared as per information received from the State Government/Authority concerned. In NRLD the definition of "large dams" has been adopted as per the norms of International Commission on Large Dams (ICOLD).

ICOLD Specification for Large Dams -

• A large dam is classified as one with a maximum height of more than 15 metres from its deepest foundation to the crest.

• A dam between 10 and 15 metres in height from its deepest foundation is also included in the classification of a large dam provided it complies with one of the following conditions:

  a) length of crest of the dam is not less than 500 metres, or

  b) capacity of the reservoir formed by the dam is not less than one million cubic metres, or

  c) the maximum flood discharge dealt with by the dam is not less than 2000 cubic metres per second, or

  d) the dam has especially difficult foundation problems, or

  e) the dam is of unusual design.

It would be seen from the above figures that, within 30 years after independence, 2027 large dams were completed and within the next 20 years additional 2009 large dams were completed in India. That activity had resulted in increase in the area under irrigation appreciably and so the land productivity per hectare of the irrigated area. Since that activity has continued after 2000 onwards, though at a slightly slow pace, the increased food grain production on that account has ensured sustainable food security to the population of India up till now. It has also provided adequate water for industrial development and for the increased urban population.

**Water Resource Development in the Maharashtra State -** Maharashtra state has geographical area of about 3,08,800 sqkm which is about 9.4 percent of the geographical area of India (32,87,300 sqkm). State has about 18% area under forests of which about 14% is under savannas & grass lands and only 4% under mixed forests. Crop land is about 78% (2,40,000 sqkm). The Gross Cropped Area in Maharashtra is about 2,26,000 sqkm (225 lakh ha) and the Net Cropped Area is about 1,75,000 sqkm. In majority of the area, residual soils are formed due to in-situ disintegration and decomposition of parent base rock, which is primarily basalt, and metamorphic/schist only towards the eastern side. Deep alluvial soils are met with in the Tapi basin and Poorna basin in the northern part of the state. Laterite and lateritic soils are occurring in the narrow strip along the West coast, called as Konkan region. To the West of N-S running Sahyadri mountain range, orographic precipitation ranges from 5000 mm to 3000 mm (S to N) in the Konkan region. It, however, reduces to only about 450 to 550 mm within a distance of about 70 to 80 km towards East in the rain shadow area, resulting in about 30 to 40% area of the State as drought prone. Rainfall then increases gradually to about 1300-1400 mm up to the State border in the East. Construction of dam-canal projects of varying sizes is the main stay of WR development activity. Total number of WR development structures i.e., dam-canal projects, Kolhapur Type weirs, Lift Irrigation Schemes, weir /bandhara, percolation tanks etc., of various sizes in the Maharashtra State is very large, details of which are given in the Table below:

Table 4 - Details of Major and Medium projects in the Maharashtra State

| River Basin | Area Square km | No. of Projects | Live/Gross storage Mcum | Irrigation Potential ha | Remarks |
|---|---|---|---|---|---|
| Godavari | 1,54,000 | 215 | 24,900/20,600 | 29,65,000 | East flowing |
| Krishna | 70,000 | 111 | 19,500/16,200 | 14,53,000 | East flowing |
| Tapi | 51,000 | 73 | 6,000/4,800 | 7,23,000 | West flowing |
| Narmada | 2,000 | 1 |  | 3,000 | West flowing |
| West coast | 32,000 | 30 | 4,600/3,900 | 1,85,000 | High rainfall |
| Total 3,09,000 (100%) |  | 430 | 55,000/45,500 Mcum | 53,29,000 hectares |  |

Table 5 - Details of State Sector & Local Sector Minor irrigation projects in the Maharashtra State

| Type of project | Irrigation Potential created by projects | | Total Potential in hectares |
|---|---|---|---|
|  | State Sector Minor projects (2000 to 250 ha) | Local Sector Minor projects (below 250 ha each) |  |
| Dam-canal | 11,83,000 | 4,51,000 | 16,34,000 |
| K.T. Weirs | 3,57,000 | 3,31,000 | 6,88,000 |
| Lift Irrigation | 19,000 | 54,000 | 73,000 |
| Weirs/Bandharas | - | 53,000 | 53,000 |
| Percolation Tanks | - | 4,84,000 | 4,84,000 |
| Total | 15,59,000 ha | 13,73,000 ha | 29,32,000 ha |

**Source** – 'Integrated Water Resource Management' Volume I, (Year 2022) book by Lead Author Dr. S.V. Dahasahastra, and four engineer co-authors.

Year-wise record of actual crop-wise area irrigated is available for State sector projects (above 250 ha each). However, no such record is available for actual irrigation under local sector projects (below 250 ha each), which have irrigation potential of 13,73,000 ha.

**Basic data and organisational set up necessary for WR development works** – Following basic data is essential for planning of WR development works.

Survey maps - The Survey of India is India's central engineering agency in charge of mapping and surveying, set up in 1767 to help consolidate the territories of the British East India Company at that time. It is one of the oldest Engineering Departments of the Government of India. The Great Trigonometrical Survey (GTS) was a project that aimed to survey the entire Indian subcontinent with scientific precision. It had begun in 1802 by the British infantry officer William Lambton under the auspices of the East India Company and was completed by James Walker in 1871. With that survey, altitudes i.e., levels above mean sea level, at many points in the entire country (including Princely States) and distances between them were established very accurately. Based on above information by the GTS, Survey of India very painstakingly and very accurately then carried out detailed ground survey of the entire country. Contour maps were then prepared showing locations of cities, towns, villages, roads, rivers, tributaries, water bodies and all major landmarks on them. These maps drawn to a scale of 1 inch equal to 1 mile were called as 'Toposheets' and maps drawn to a scale of 1 inch equal to 4 miles were called as 'Degree sheets.' These maps were very useful to understand topography of the river basins and to select tentative sites suitable to locate storage dams on the rivers. In the then Bombay Province, British Engineer Mr. Henry Fitzerald Beal had selected sites of almost all possible major dams in the Maharashtra State with the help of these toposheets. He also visited all these sites personally by travelling either on horseback or by walking in the mountainous region of the state, to confirm suitability of their locations. Before and after independence, most of the major dams in the Western and Northern Maharashtra State (Erstwhile Bombay Province) were constructed at these locations.

Rainfall data and river gauging data – During British regime, manually operated rain gauge stations were established at most of the District and Tehsil (sub district) places in the country. Very valuable record of daily rainfall data was hence made available for planning and design of WR development infrastructure after independence. Many more manually operated rain gauge stations were established after independence in almost all the river basins. In addition to that, during last 4-5 decades many automatic-recording rain gauges were also established in several major river basins. Besides the daily rainfall data, they provided very valuable information about intensity of precipitation (centimetres per hour) during storms, cloud bursts and intense rain spells. Estimation of probable flood during storms could hence be done more accurately from that information. Such estimation of probable maximum flood in the river basin was of much use in finalising the design flood discharging capacity of spillways on some large major dams. For small size dams, spillway capacity is usually designed as per empirical formulae. In some river basins in which there were many flood-prone cities, towns and villages, arrangements of tele-transmission of the data enabled estimation of probable flood magnitude at these vulnerable places on real time basis. It was then possible to forewarn the affected people about the magnitude of floods and to reduce possible damage. Many River gauging stations were also established on most of the major rivers in the country. By comparing estimated floods and actual floods at different places, refinements in the procedure of estimation of floods for large size dams could be done. Record of rainfall measuring stations and river gauging stations is compiled and published every year by the hydrology units established in some states under the financial aid from the World Bank.

For correct estimation of crop water requirement of various irrigated crops, it is essential to establish climatological stations at regional headquarters or at the district places. They have instruments to record information such as temperature, sunshine hours, wind velocity, humidity, evaporation etc. This data is required for estimation of crop water requirement for different crops taken in their field of influence. Evaporation pans established on reservoirs also provide accurate information to compute evaporation loss from the reservoirs. Because the climatic observations as above do not change much from place to place, there are much smaller number of climatological stations in any state than the rain gauge stations.

Organisational set up required to implement WR development projects – Setting up of following organisations/offices is essential for planning, designing, implementation, management, and performance monitoring of WR development projects.

- Project investigation Unit – For carrying out preliminary and detailed survey of their command areas & canals, distributaries etc., for the dam sites selected from toposheets, and for preparing tentative designs, drawings & estimates of projects for getting administrative approval to the projects to be undertaken.

- Testing laboratory for construction materials – Testing the properties of all construction materials such as soil, murum (decomposed rock), stone, sand, cement, mortar, concrete, steel etc., to evaluate their strengths and other properties as required for their detailed design. Hydraulic model testing laboratory may also be necessary for assessing effectiveness of the proposed spillways and energy dissipation arrangements. Field testing laboratories should also be established at selected Major dam sites for day-to-day testing.

- Design wing – Preparation of detailed designs of all components of the dam such as dam cross section, spillway, head regulator etc., based on availability and suitability of construction material at site and as per sub strata/foundation conditions at the site. Design of important and major structures on canals.

- Mechanical and Electrical wing – For manufacturing head regulator gates and radial/vertical lift gates for spillway and installing them at dam sites, mechanical wing is essential. A mechanical unit for drilling holes and getting cores of the foundation rock is necessary for assessing foundation conditions at the prospective dam sites. For planning, designing, and constructing hydroelectric projects, electrical wing is necessary.

- Project construction – Preparation of detailed working estimates of various components of dam, get them approved, get required funds for implementation and then take up construction of dams. Carrying out detailed survey for selecting alignment of canals and distribution system, preparation of their estimates and carrying out their implementation as above.

- Irrigation management – Firstly allocating stored water for the first-priority non-irrigation requirements such as urban & industrial use, and then carrying out management of balance water for irrigation on canals every year as per actual water available in the dam. Preparation of bills for the actual water use for irrigation and non-irrigation purposes and effecting their recovery. Maintenance and repairs of dams and water distribution network consisting of canals and distributaries.

- Performance evaluation of projects – On completion of the projects, collection & compilation of various data each year such as, rainfall in the catchment, actual runoff & flood magnitude, evaporation from the reservoir, water actually released at the canal head, crop wise actual irrigation, balance water at the time of first replenishment next year, etc. is to be collected every year. After every 10 years of functioning of the project, it is necessary to carry out comparison of actual performance and review correctness of various assumptions made at the time of planning and designing of the project. Preparation of revised guidelines, if necessary, for planning & designing of future projects.

- Dam safety monitoring – Review of record of instruments such as piezometers, seismometers, plumb bobs installed in the body of dam, relief wells, etc. Record measurement of seepage from drains below earth dams and through drainage galleries of masonry & concrete dams and their review. Review the performance of side channel spillway and energy dissipation arrangements below gated/ungated central spillway. Routine inspection of dam and major structures on canals is to be carried out by the irrigation management staff every year. For important and major projects, inspection of dams for their safety and review of their performance is to be carried out by a separate 'Dam Safety Organisation' set up at the state level for that purpose. It explores the necessity of improvements in the structural measures which are seen to be necessary, for ensuring long term safety of the structure.

- Regulatory mechanism – An independent organisation is essential to review and ensure rectifications where necessary, to ensure optimum and equitable WR development in the river basin and in the state/country. It should also ensure establishing regional/river basin wise balanced development and allocation of water resources, without sacrificing needs of environmental and other ecosystems. It should enforce Govt. and semi-Govt. agencies to treat the entire sewage/effluent generated after urban/industrial use of water and ensure its reuse for irrigation or industries. It should ensure use-treat-reuse policy for industrial use for achieving ultimate aim of 'zero effluent' target for the industrial use of water. At present release of partial or untreated effluent has caused pollution of most of the rivers in the states in India and hence the necessity.

**Conclusion** – In India and in all the states, construction of WR development works to meet all the water needs for the society is carried out in the public sector. Build-Own-Operate-Transfer (BOOT) mechanism is used (without the construction cost of the dam) only in case of some hydroelectric projects. But because Water Resource is a renewable resource, by spending very small amount for operation and maintenance of dams each year, water gets stored in the dams for its use year after year for several decades. Loss of storage capacity due to siltation in the Maharashtra state ranges from 0.3% to 1% and hence useful life of dams is decidedly more than 100 years. The rate of siltation is least in the reservoirs having their catchment in the high rainfall zone. There is no depreciation for dams like that for STPs and ETPs, but on the contrary there is appreciation in the value of dams every year. Hence in the long run, heavy investment done to construct the dam infrastructure is most economical in the long run to meet basic needs of ensuring sustainable food and water security to the people.

After completion of the projects which are under construction in the Maharashtra state and in most of the states in India, there would be limited scope to take up new dam-canal projects thereafter. To meet additional food and water needs of the rising population of India, which is expected to stabilise before 2050, following actions would be necessary. Implementation of Inter-basin water transfers from water-surplus river basins to water-short river basins within the state, which are economical as on today. Schemes of diversion of water (by gravity and by lifting) from high rainfall zone along West coast to eastern part of the state should also be taken as per economic viability. Besides that, implementation of National River Linking Project is essential during the next 2-3 decades because it is expected to increase the usable surface water availability in the country by about 25% of the presently usable surface WR. Details of this ambitious project are given in Chapter 10.

# Chapter 7

# Use and Management of the Water Resource for Irrigated Agriculture

*Water Resource is a natural resource, endowed free of cost by the Nature and is amenable for its development and use by the humans. It has been the primary life support for all plants and animals - including man - in the terrestrial and aquatic ecosystems on the earth. But when 'Modern Man' entered on the scene around 12,000 years ago, the situation started to change. Man started utilising more and more water & land resources to meet his basic needs of food and water for his survival, and then for his wellbeing. He started with the use of water for irrigating the rainfed crops to increase food grain production. Little more than two centuries before the present, industrial development commenced in Europe and was gradually introduced in many other countries since then. Consequent increase in the urban population increased the demand for urban and industrial water use. Management of water for use in irrigation became a very complex issue due to continuous rise in such non-irrigation demands. All these uses of water for the man were at the cost of corresponding reduction in the water availability for the natural ecosystems. The chapter covers details of development of various systems adopted by man for achieving optimum development and improved management of water for irrigated agriculture and their gradual evolution to the sophisticated water-use efficient modern irrigation techniques.*

In any country, pace of development of infrastructure constructed to develop water resource always remained compatible to the nature and magnitude of demand for water by the humans. With gradual development of the society, dynamics of changes in the water demand pattern had to be responded to by making appropriate changes in the management of water available from the existing and the planned new infrastructure. At the time of independence to India, agriculture was the predominant developmental activity and majority of the population was residing in the rural area. To ensure food security to the rising population, one option was to disforest fertile forest land and bring it under cultivation to increase food grain production. But better alternative which would protect the terrestrial ecosystems was to create infrastructure to provide irrigation facilities to the rain-fed land, to increase per hectare land productivity and ensure food security. Hence in the fifties and sixties of the last century, in the Maharashtra and in many other states in India, many major dam-canal projects were taken up for construction to provide irrigation facilities to the dry land as explained in the earlier chapter.

Before coming to the present stage of its' development, let us start with the beginning of irrigated agriculture from the known historical activities. It was the first activity initiated by the 'Man' by diverting river water to the crops to increase their productivity. This was done more than 5,000 years before in the Tigris & Euphrates River basins in Mesopotamia, and later in the Nile River basin in Egypt. A temporary river diversion structure used to be constructed on one bank, to divert part of the river flow by digging a channel on that bank to convey water to fields to irrigate the crops. This work used to be taken up every year after the rainy season when the river was not likely to have floods anymore and when the crop needed water either for growth of the standing crop or for sowing new crop. With the experience, the technology improved by constructing a relatively permanent river diversion structure, duly protected on its upstream and downstream by constructing flood banks of sufficient height and length. They protected the canal from washing out during normal floods, but it used to get damaged during occasional high floods and had to be repaired or reconstructed. Improvements were done continuously by using the time-tested technology and by learning from the use of such technology at other places in the same river basin or in the other river basins.

Some small sub channels off taking from the main canal at suitable distance would be constructed, to deliver water to all fields in the canal command area. Water would be delivered from these sub channels to the fields one after the other turn by turn, to complete one round of watering in about 10 to 15 days, depending on climate and the types of crops grown. Then the second and further rounds/rotations of irrigation would be continued up to maturity of the crop. If the river had enough flow and more area could be provided with irrigation, discharging capacity of the canal would be increased by increasing its cross section and by extending it further as needed. By and large, the same practice of irrigation was continued in all the ancient civilisations which prospered along banks of rivers such as Indus, Ho hang ho, Yang tze etc. Subsequently, during the last few centuries even when water was being stored by constructing storage dams on rivers as explained in the earlier chapters, the practice of delivering stored water to the fields was by and large the same as above. Since this source of water was more dependable, perennial crops such as sugar cane, plantain, fruit trees etc. could be grown on their canals.

To facilitate dispensing of water to the crop, some arrangements had to be made on the field. For high density crops like wheat, maize, sorghum, millets etc., field would be subdivided in small compartments having soil banks/ridges on all its four sides to confine the delivered water. Water would be delivered at high-level-end of the compartment, and it would flow as sheet flow slowly along the field slope to cover the entire compartment in which crop is standing. When the water flows along slope, part of it percolates in the soil and the rest of it flows further to cover entire compartment. If soil is clayey and heavy, field slope is kept flatter to give sufficient time for water to get absorbed in the soil before it flows further. On the contrary if the soil is light or sandy, steeper slope is provided to the compartment. Objective is to deliver the water in a reasonably uniform manner within the compartment. On completion of watering of one compartment, water would be diverted manually to the next compartments one by one till all the field is covered by irrigation. Water would then be diverted to the next farmer.

'International Crops Research Institute for Semi-Arid Tropics' (ICRISAT) has recommended raised bed cultivation. In this system, high density crops are grown on narrow raised beds and water is delivered on all its four sides. Water then seeps below the raised bed to the standing crop, which reduces evaporation loss from the soil surface. For vegetables like Onion, Tomato, Brinjal etc. (i.e., low density crops) and even for sugar cane, water is delivered through furrows and plants are grown on ridges in between on its one side or either side. Since lesser area of the field gets wetted than the compartment method, there is less evaporation loss from the field. For fruit trees like mango, Guava, Oranges etc., circular compartment is prepared around the tree and water is delivered in them from the field channels turn by turn. For ponded paddy (rice) crop, canal water is delivered in the uppermost field from where it flows to the next field at lower level and then to the next field and finally up to the lowermost field. This is how entire command area having paddy crop is provided with irrigation.

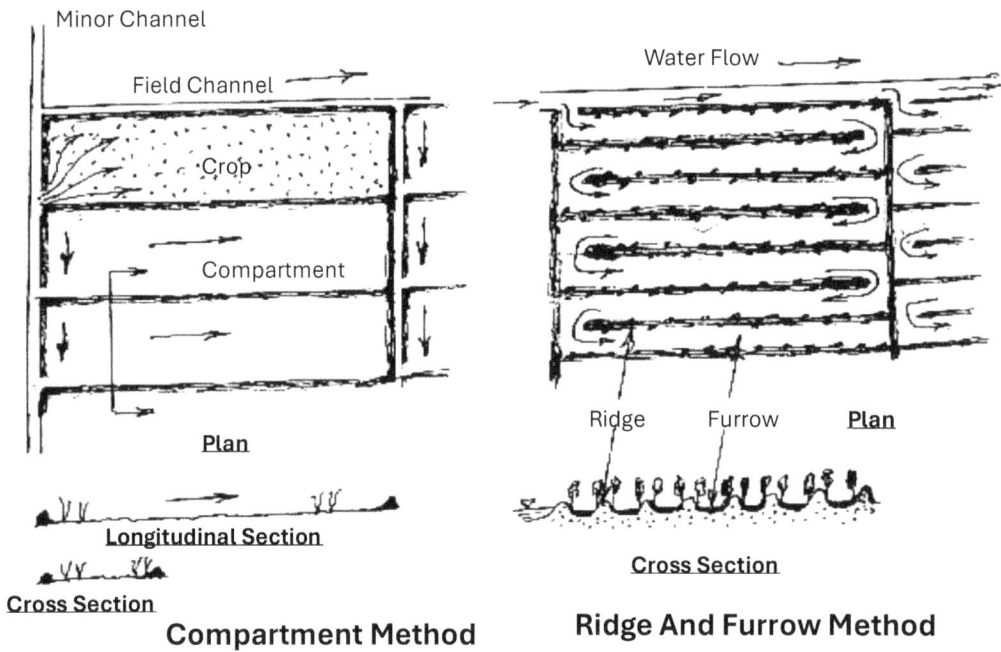

**Compartment Method**  **Ridge And Furrow Method**

Because of these limitations of the water delivery system, water is delivered to the field normally once in every 12 to 14 days. But because roots of the crop absorb water from the ground continuously during daytime, there is some water stress on the crop during last 4-5 days before start of the next rotation of water. Secondly, irrespective of what is the actual need of water for the crop from sowing to maturity, we cannot deliver less than about 8 to 10 cm average depth of water on the field during every rotation. Hence if any crop needs less water per day during its initial stages of crop growth or at the time of its maturity, large part of the applied water percolates in the ground below to recharge GW or gets evaporated from the field and is lost. Because different crops are usually taken by farmers in the canal command area and their sowing dates are also different, rotation period of 12 or 14 days or more as suitable to all the crops is observed in practice. Question then can be raised as to who is the customer of irrigation water? Is it the farmer who pays for the irrigation water, or is it his field on which crop is grown? Neither is true and the real customer of water should be the crop which is grown in the field. But because of the constraints in water delivery system as above, in practice we deliver water not to the crop but to the field on which crop is incidentally standing. These are the main limitations of delivering water to the crops by the traditional surface irrigation water delivery system, which is also known as flood irrigation system.

Shortcomings of flood irrigation system – Water released from the reservoir at the canal head is conveyed to the field through a network of channels consisting of main canal, distributaries, minors, sub minors and finally the field channels. During such conveyance, some water evaporates from surface of the channels and some percolates below into the ground through channel banks and from the channel bed. When water is applied to crop on the field, water evaporates from the soil surface continuously day and night. Some water also comes to surface continuously from below due to capillary action and gets evaporated, more so when the vegetative growth of crop is less in the initial stages. Some water from the soil below is absorbed by the roots. Part of it is used by the plant for its growth and the rest is lost as evapotranspiration from the crop, but it is unavoidable. Water lost by evaporation and evapotranspiration from all these places is lost permanently from the irrigation system. But water percolated in the ground recharges the GW and can be reused from wells in the command area or from rivers into which it ultimately flows from below the ground. Because of all such losses in the process of conveyance of water from the canal head to the crop, water-use efficiency of this system is generally poor. Cultivator is also required to prepare the land beforehand each year to suit the type of crop he is growing. There is less seepage and evaporation loss with furrow irrigation and the raised bed cultivation. Labour input is essential during every rotation for channelising of water from one compartment/furrow to the other and for managing delivery of water to the entire field till its completion.

Where the soil is retentive, clayey, and deep, it is advisable to take only seasonal crops in it. Sometime perennial crops are taken in such rich soil to get more income than the seasonal crop. The applied water does not percolate much below and gets retained in the soil which gradually results in raising the Ground Water Table (GWT). During the next rotations, GWT rises further. Aeration of root system of the crop is essential for good crop growth. As the GWT rises to encroach on the root zone (which is about 1.5 to 2.5 meters deep according to type of crop), growth of the crop starts getting affected. When the GWT comes very close to ground level, the standing crop wilts & withers. This process is known as 'Water logging' of the land which ultimately makes it uncultivable. If the water contains more minerals and salts dissolved in it from the soil below, only water evaporates from the surface of such soil, but solidified salts and minerals remain in the top layer of the soil. In due course of time when concentration of these salts increases in the upper layers of the soil, it becomes uncultivable. It is then known as land affected by 'Salt efflorescence'. To restore such waterlogged or salt affected land, it is essential to lower down GWT below root zone of the crop. This is achieved by digging open trenches at some interval in the affected land, to drain out the ground water into these open drains and then to nearest streams. Slowly in some months, it lowers GWT and makes the land cultivable again. However, lot of land is required for these open surface drains, which also make the cultivation operations on the land difficult. Hence alternatively, open-jointed pipes with inverted sand filter around the joints are provided at the bottom of open drains and in the trenches. A layer of soil is then laid on the top of these trenches, which then provides continuous field for cultivation. But the cost of such closed drains is high, and its maintenance becomes difficult. Hence better way in such soils is to take only seasonal crops under flood irrigation or to adopt drip or sprinkler irrigation if perennial crops are to be taken.

Crop Water Requirement – Crop water requirement (CWR) is defined as the depth of water (in millimetres) needed to meet the water consumed through evapotranspiration (ETc) by a crop during the period of crop growth from its sowing to maturity. Water escaping from the soil surface and on the leaves and stem of a plant is called 'evaporation'. Some part of water absorbed by roots of the plants is utilised for growth of the plant and to produce grains/fruits etc., with the help of water, carbon dioxide & minerals, by the process of photosynthesis. But in this chemical process, some water escapes to the atmosphere as vapour through the plant's leaves. This process is called 'transpiration', which happens mainly during daytime. Water need of a crop thus consists of transpiration plus evaporation, which is called as 'evapotranspiration' (ET). Scientific experiments were carried out in America in the last century, to estimate daily crop water requirement for different crops right from its sowing to their maturity. It was the first step to estimate how much water the real customer of irrigation – *the crop* - needs for its growth. An instrument known as 'lysimeter' which is used to estimate crop water requirement was built initially by Edward Lewis Sturtevant, a botanist from Massachusetts, in the United States in 1875. But actual experiments to estimate water requirement for various crops were carried out in America in the twentieth century, with the help of a lysimeter working on the same principle but on a large-scale size improved model.

Detailed guidelines for computing water requirement for various crops by several methods then in vogue, were established and mentioned in the United Nations Food and Agriculture Organization's FAO-24 publication, which were in use for many years. These guidelines were later updated, and a standardized method of estimating ET was outlined in the FAO-56 publication. Several Agro-scientists have done experiments with the help of different types of lysimeters, to compute crop water requirement (ETc) for different crops and evolved empirical formulae to compute ETc as below: Thornthwaite (1948), Penman (1948), Blane-Credal (1950), Ansin-Christie (1968), Penman and Modified Penman formulae. In India and Maharashtra state, 'Modified Penman Formulae' is used to estimate ETc. Most of these formulae work out ETc from the data of Atmospheric temperature, Humidity, Sunshine hours, Wind velocity etc., as obtained from the nearest Climate Observation Centre. Effective rainfall (Pe) during crop growth period is computed by deducting runoff, evaporation, and deep percolation from the total rainfall. Net CWR i.e., Irrigation Need (IN) is computed by deducting Pe from Etc (IN = Etc - Pe). Potential evapotranspiration (ETo) is defined as *'The evaporation in mm from an extended surface of a short green grass of uniform height which fully shades the ground and is always well supplied with water'*. In Maharashtra State, ETo is measured to be minimum of 4 mm/day in December (winter), increasing to about 8.5 mm in May (summer), then reducing to 4.5 mm in July and again increasing to 5 mm in October. For any crop – say wheat – actual daily ETc has been worked out for the period from sowing to maturity. Total of such fortnightly ETc (Evapotranspiration or water requirement) divided by total of fortnightly ETo at that place gives a factor which is called as Crop Coefficient (Kc). These values as computed for Pune city in Maharashtra for wheat crop are as below:

**Table 1 – Fortnight wise crop water requirement**

| Sr No | Details | Nov | | Dec | | Jan | | Feb | | Total |
|---|---|---|---|---|---|---|---|---|---|---|
| 1 | ETo in mm | 62 | 57 | 57 | 57 | 62 | 65 | 68 | 75 | 503 |
| 2 | Crop Coeff Kc | 0.29 | 0.57 | 1.02 | 1.15 | 1.15 | 1.15 | 0.96 | 0.42 | |
| 3 | Water Req. in mm | 18 | 32 | 58 | 66 | 71 | 75 | 65 | 32 | 417 |

<u>Water-use efficiency</u> – Once the exact water requirement of different crops from their sowing to maturity was known, it was possible to compute water-use efficiency of any irrigation system. In the case of a canal off taking from a reservoir and having different types of crops, each type covering certain command area, it was possible to compute total water requirement for all the crops in a season from their sowing to maturity. Reduction in the total volume of the reservoir could be known by taking lake level before and after completion of the season. Deducting observed depth of evaporation from the reservoir (by pan evaporation method) during that time, net depth of water and the net volume of water released into canal from the reservoir could be known. Dividing total water requirement for all the crops computed as above for the season, by the quantity of water released at the canal head during that season, we would get water-use efficiency for that season. For an unlined canal and unlined distribution system, water-use efficiency lies between 0.25 to 0.35 depending on size of the area irrigated, type of crops grown and intensity of the cropped area out of the total command area.

It means that about 65 to 75% of water released into the canal at its head is lost from the system. Water that percolates below from the water delivery system and from the fields is not lost because it recharges the GW and can be reused from wells in the command area. Rest of the GW gradually flows into the river, which can be pumped and used to grow crops along the riverbank. However, water that is lost by evaporation & evapotranspiration is lost forever from the system. Transit losses due to percolation from the water conveyance system could be reduced by providing concrete lining, preferably selective concrete lining (only in reaches of high seepage), to the canal and distributaries. Alternatively, water could also be conveyed through closed pipes for canals and distributaries. It is preferable to carry out cost economics study for all such viable alternatives and if economical to adopt them at the time of construction stage itself. Once the canal system starts functioning, it becomes very difficult to stop irrigation and implement such structural improvements later. Even if transit losses can be reduced by such measures, losses in the flood irrigation system are unavoidable.

<u>Evolution of Micro Irrigation Systems</u> – With the flood irrigation, after every watering, water availability in the soil slowly reduces every day and there is stress on the crop due to water shortage for some days before the next rotation. It is said that 'Necessity is the mother of invention'. Micro Irrigation Systems (MIS) aim at delivering water to the plants/crops directly through closed pipes, on every day or on alternate days to just meet their actual crop water needs. Accordingly, some experiments were carried out in the past to deliver water to the crop at shorter intervals. First experiment was done in Germany in 1860 in which water was delivered to the crop

at certain interval of one or two days, through Galvanised Iron (GI) pipes having holes. Water was delivered through holes in the pipe close to the plants to reduce evaporation loss. But it was seen that the holes in the pipe used to get choked frequently and installing of several GI pipes to irrigate the entire field was found to be a costly and cumbersome affair to operate. Hence that experiment proved to be impractical.

Then around 1930, sprinkler system of irrigation evolved in America and Australia, primarily not for reducing water losses thereby improving water-use efficiency, but primarily to solve the problem of shortage of labour which was critical with the conventional flood irrigation water delivery method. Wheat crop was grown extensively in America and pastures were grown extensively in Australia for tending of Merino sheep. Farm/pasture sizes in both the countries were very large and all other operations for cultivation could then be done with the help of machinery such as tractors, dozers, harvesters etc, to counter the problem of labour shortage. However, providing water to the crop by flood irrigation system needed large number of labourers.

<u>Central Pivot System</u> - After trying several systems, finally two systems were established and adopted on a large scale in America and Australia. One was the 'Central pivot system', which consisted of pumping water from the source such as river, reservoir or well and delivering it under pressure through the central pivot pipe to which a freely rotating long lateral pipe was attached. The lateral pipe was supported by means of 3-4 wire ropes having one end attached to the extended central pivot and the other ends were attached to the lateral pipe. Outer end of the lateral pipe was supported on a steel column having rubber wheel trolley at the bottom, and an electric motor was installed on it to move the wheel trolley radially. Nozzles were fitted on the lateral pipe at suitable interval (their spacing and water delivering capacity increasing towards the outer end) through which water would come out like a fountain each covering a circular area, having some overlap with the adjoining fountains. The wheel trolley would slowly move radially with the help of an electric motor. In one round of rotation, with the circular spray of water from each nozzle, entire circular field of wheat, maize, soyabean or grass would be provided with irrigation in a reasonably uniform manner and to just meet the daily need of the crop at that time. Speed of wheel trolley could be adjusted - fast in the initial stages of crop growth and gradually slowing down as the crop water demand increases. Next rotation could be given on the next day or after one or two-days interval as per the crop water needs, and it would be continued till maturity of the crop. However, with this system, slightly triangular shaped parts of the field at all the four corners remained fallow i.e., without crop. Only one person could operate this system to irrigate many such circular fields simultaneously. It thus solved the problem of shortage of labour in America and Australia and incidentally also saved quantity of water used for irrigation.

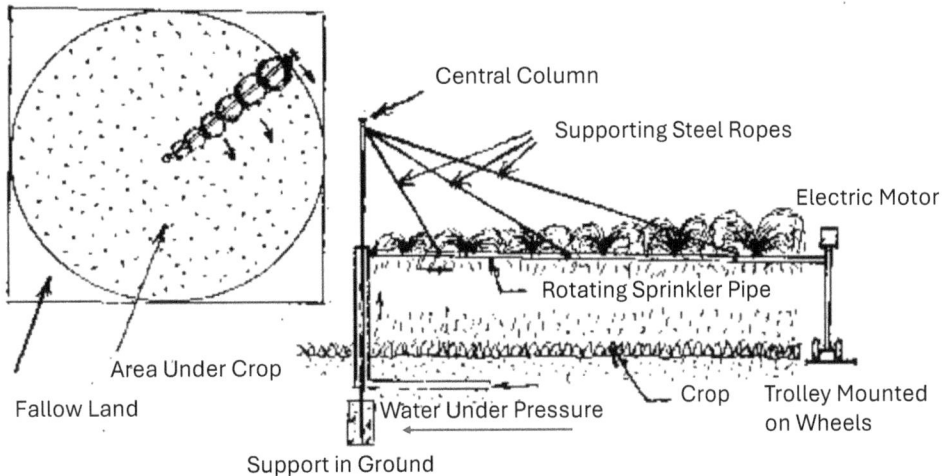

**Central Pivot Sprinkler Irrigation System**

Linear Moving System – In this system, a pipe having nozzles fitted on it at a fixed same spacing is structurally supported by a steel truss, which is supported at both the ends by trollies moving on wheels which are operated by electric motors. Water pumped from the source such as river, reservoir or well and delivered under pressure enters at one end of the pipe (other end is closed) and comes out as fountains (adjacent fountains having some overlap) through the nozzles fitted at fixed spacing. As per stage of the crop growth, forward speed of the trollies can be adjusted to meet actual crop water needs during that turn. Next rotations could be given on the next day or after one or two-days' interval as per the crop water needs, and the system would be continued till maturity of the crop. This system irrigates a rectangular field and the strip on which wheels move would only remain fallow i.e., without crop.

Main advantage of sprinkler irrigation is that water is applied uniformly to the crop and at short intervals as per actual need of the crop from its sowing to maturity. It relieves water stress on the crop (like flood irrigation), which reduces crops maturity period and increases the crop yield. It is not necessary to level or prepare the field and there is minimum loss of water in sandy soils and there is no possibility of water logging or salt efflorescence in heavy soils. However, because the water is applied like a fountain and the entire ground gets wet in the process, there is more evaporation loss in this system from the sprayed water and from the soil, when compared with the drip irrigation system. Secondly, it promotes growth of grass and weeds between the crop and its removal becomes a job. Sprinkler irrigation is, however, an ideal method for high density crops like wheat, maize, millet, barley, soyabean, ground nut etc. By using one set of equipment, only one person can apply irrigation to several hectares of land in a day.

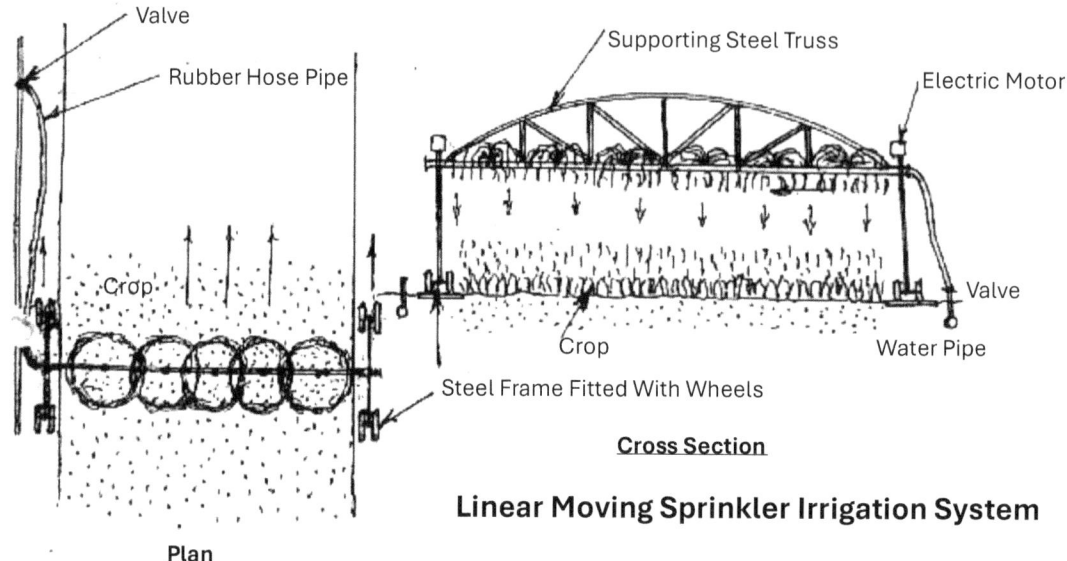

**Cross Section**
**Linear Moving Sprinkler Irrigation System**
**Plan**

For gardens or small farms, movable Sprinklers or Rain guns (to cover large area) can also be used. They spray water in one direction and slowly rotate to cover circular area by uniform spray of water during adjustable pre-decided rotational movement time. They can be shifted manually on completion of one round of irrigation to the next adjoining area. There can be a chain of such movable sprinklers to cover a strip of the farm. The entire chain of movable sprinklers can be shifted to cover adjoining strip until entire field is irrigated, but it requires more labour.

Drip Irrigation System – This system of irrigation delivers water drop by drop near the plants, so that it percolates into ground and can be sucked by the plants through their root system. Water from the source is to be pumped and conveyed through pipe near the field, and then into the field right up to the plant. Up to fourth decade of the last century, use of steel/galvanised iron pipes and flexible rubber pipes for drip irrigation was in practice, but it was seen to be costly to install and was inconvenient to operate it. But invention of plastics and polymers around the time of the second world war, brought forth a material which was very convenient for manufacturing of pipes on a mass scale and being very light weight was easy to lay on the field. It was also convenient to manufacture other equipment (filter tank, fertiliser tank, venturi, drippers etc.) required for drip irrigation system in plastic or polymers. Water is pumped from wells or farm ponds and is conveyed to the field or group of fields (for a common drip scheme) through rigid polyethylene pipes of suitable diameter (75 to 100 mm diameter). Pumped water passes through a sand filter provided to arrest any floating/suspended matter which is likely to choke the drippers. A venturi is then provided which sucks liquid fertiliser from a tank in desired quantity and desired rotations, as required for the crops grown. Liquid insecticides could also be mixed in this tank during some waterings as per requirement of the crop. Water is then conveyed near the field through small diameter rigid pipes branching from main pipe. Main pipes and branching pipes could be installed about 0.5 to 0.6 m below the ground so that they do not disturb farming operations on the field.

Small diameter (16 mm diameter) flexible lateral pipes off take from the rigid pipes with their spacing according to type of crop grown. Spacing of drippers which are fixed on the laterals also depends on the type of crop grown. Drippers have different capacities to deliver such as 8, 10, 12 or more drops of water per minute. Drippers of suitable capacity are installed to suit water requirement of the crop grown, and periodicity of irrigation is changed as per stage of the crop growth. At a time 8 to 10 laterals deliver water simultaneously near the plants, and on completion of their irrigation, next set of laterals is operated. Next watering can be applied next day or after one-or two-days interval as per crop needs.

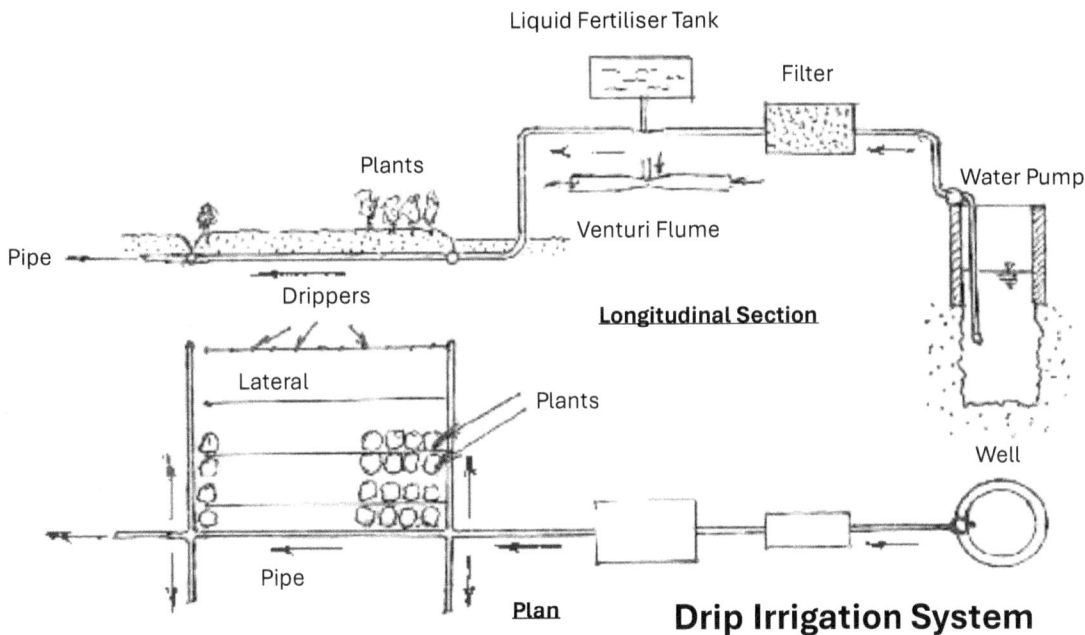

**Drip Irrigation System**

Since water is applied close to the root system of the plants directly, there is negligible loss of the applied water due to evaporation from surface of the soil. Because there is no growth of grass and weeds in between the plants, there is no problem of their removal. Liquid fertilisers and insecticides could be applied conveniently with the irrigation water. Because the water is applied every day or on alternate days, there is not much stress on the crop, which reduces its maturity period and increases the crop yield. Drip irrigation is suitable for low density crops like tomatoes, brinjal, radish, sugar cane, flowers etc. Sometimes laterals are removed and shifted to irrigate the next plots turn by turn. Fruit trees like oranges, pomegranate, guava, mangoes etc. could be provided with water by means of 4 to 6 drippers installed around the tree to cater to the underground root system spread around the trees. One labour can look after drip irrigation to cover a large size farm. It is not necessary to level or prepare the field and there is minimum loss of water in sandy soils and there is no possibility of water logging or salt efflorescence even in heavy deep soils. MIS can be installed very conveniently for well irrigation. It can also be used on canal irrigation system by constructing a farm pond of suitable capacity near the group of fields of size about 15 to 20 ha. Canal water would be stored in such farm ponds and a pump set should be installed on it. Irrigation water would be pumped from there and conveyed through polyethylene pipes near every field and then delivered to the crop in the field by means of laterals turn by turn by drip or from one pipe for the sprinkler system as above.

**Adoption of Micro Irrigation Systems in India and other countries of the World –**

**Table 2 - Area covered by Micro Irrigation in different States of India as on 31-3 2022**

| Sr. No. State | Sprinkler. Irri. area mha | Drip Irri. area mha | Total Micro Irri. area mha |
|---|---|---|---|
| 1 Karnataka | 1.60 | 0.83 | **2.43** |
| 2 Rajasthan | **1.78** | 0.32 | 2.10 |
| 3 Maharashtra | 0.63 | **1.41** | 2.04 |
| 4 Andhra Pradesh | 0.52 | 1.40 | 1.92 |
| 5 Gujarat | 0.79 | 0.92 | 1.71 |
| 6 Tamil Nadu | 0.39 | 0.87 | 1.26 |
| 7 Haryana | 0.64 | 0.04 | 0.68 |
| 8 Madhya Pradesh | 0.30 | 0.36 | 0.66 |
| 9 Chhattisgarh | 0.34 | 0.04 | 0.38 |
| 10 Telangana | 0.09 | 0.22 | 0.31 |
| 11 Uttar Pradesh | 0.24 | 0.06 | 0.30 |
| **Subtotal** | **6.47** | **7.32** | **13.79** |
| 11 Remaining 18 States | 0.21 | 0.49 | 0.70 |
| **Grand Total** | **6.68** | **7.81** | **14.49** |

Note – States are arranged as per descending order of total area under Micro Irrigation.

These are the latest figures up to 31-3-2022, as per Department of Agriculture and Farmers Welfare of Govt. of India

**Table 3 - Area covered by Micro Irrigation in the Developed countries of the World.**

| Sr No | Country | Total Irri. area mha | Sprink. Irri. area mha/ % | Drip Irri. area mha/ % | Total Micro Irri. area mha/ % | Year |
|---|---|---|---|---|---|---|
| 1 | USA | 23.48 | 14.12/60 | 1.98/8 | 16.10/68 | 2017 & 13 |
| 2 | Spain | 3.64 | 0.89/24 | 1.79/49 | 2.68/73 | 2015 |
| 3 | France | 2.60 | 1.38/53 | 0.10/4 | 1.48/57 | 2017 |
| 4 | Italy | 2.42 | 0.96/40 | 0.42/17 | 1.38/57 | 2017 |
| 5 | Australia | 2.15 | 0.82/38 | 0.22/10 | 1.04/48 | 2017 |
| 6 | Saudi Arabia | 1.62 | 0.72/44 | 0.20/12 | 0.92/56 | 2004 |
| 7 | Canada | 1.05 | 0.68/65 | 0.01/1 | 0.69/66 | 2017 |
| 8 | Germany | 0.54 | **0.52/96** | 0.01/2 | **0.53/98** | 2005 |
| 9 | Japan | 2.90 | 0.40/14 | 0.10/3 | 0.50/17 | 2014 |
| 10 | Slovak Rep. | 0.31 | 0/0 | **0.31/100** | **0.31/100** | 2000 |
| 11 | Israel | 0.23 | **0.06/26** | **0.17/74** | **0.23/100** | 2000 |
| 12 | (9 countries) | 3.37 | 0.44/13 | 0.16/5 | 0.60/18 | |
| | **Total** | **44.31** | **20.99/48** | **5.47/12** | **24.46/60** | |

**Table 4 - Area covered by Micro Irrigation in the Emerging economy countries & Developing countries of the World -**

| Sr No | Country | Total Irri. area mha | Sprink. Irri. area mha/ % | Drip Irri. area mha/ % | Total Micro Irri. area mha/ % | Year |
|---|---|---|---|---|---|---|
| 1 | India | 62.00 | 6.68/11 | 7.81/13 | 14.49/24 | 2022# |
| 2 | China | 65.87 | 3.73/6 | 5.27/8 | 9.00/14 | 2017 |
| 3 | Brazil | 5.80 | **3.86/67** | 0.62/10 | **4.48/77** | 2013 |
| 4 | Russia | 4.50 | 2.50/56 | 0.05/1 | 2.55/57 | 2012 |

| 5 | Turkey | 6.65 | 1.43/22 | 1.12/16 | 2.55/38 | 2019 |
| 6 | Iran | 8.46 | 1.00/12 | 1.02/12 | 2.02/24 | 2019 |
| 7 | South Africa | 1.67 | 0.92/55 | **0.37/22** | **1.29/77** | 2017 |
| 8 | (16 countries) | 28.97 | 2.91/10 | 0.51/2 | 3.42/12 | |
| | **Total** | **183.92** | **23.03/12.5** | **16.77/9.1** | **39.80/21.6** | |

Note – Countries are arranged as per descending order of total area under Micro Irrigation.

\# These are the latest figures up to 31-3-2022, as per Department of Agriculture and Farmers Welfare of Govt. of India

mha – million hectares, Sprink. Irri. – Sprinkler Irrigation, Irri. – Irrigated, MIS – Micro Irrigation System i.e., Drip plus Sprinkler, Year – Year of information.

**Table 5 - World scenario of Micro Irrigation**

| Status of Countries | Number | Total Irri. area mha | Sprink. Irri. area mha/ % | Drip Irri. area mha/ % | Total Micro Irri. area mha/ % |
|---|---|---|---|---|---|
| Developed | 21 | 44.31 | 20.99/48 | 5.47/12 | 26.46/60 |
| Emerging & Developing | 23 | 183.92 | 23.03/12.5 | 16.77/9.1 | 39.80/21.6 |
| Least Developed | 3 | 0.57 | 0.05/1 | 0.01/0 | 0.06/1 |
| **Total** | **47** | **228.80** | **44.07/19** | **22.25/10** | **66.32/29** |

**Source:** INTERNATIONAL COMMISSION ON IRRIGATION AND DRAINAGE (ICID), New Delhi, except for India as stated above.

From the above data of actual use of MIS, following observations could be drawn:

In USA, France, Australia, Canada, Germany, Brazil & Russia, sprinkler irrigation is much in use presumably due to labour shortage problem in those countries. Germany, Slovak Republic & Israel have 98 to 100% of the irrigated area under MIS.

China & India together have about **56 percent** (127.87/228.80 = 0.56) of the total irrigated area of the 47 countries. Area under MIS in India as in the year 2014-15 was only about 6.69 mha. Because of the systematic efforts taken under different schemes launched by the Central Govt (GoI) from that year, there was appreciable increase in the area under MIS (in million hectares) in India from the year 2015-16 to 2022-23 as shown in the Table below.

**Table 6 - Year wise area in mha brought under MIS in India between 2015-16 to 2022-23**

| 2015-16 | 16-17 | 17-18 | 18-19 | 19-20 | 20-21 | 21-22 | 22-23 | Total in last 8 years |
|---|---|---|---|---|---|---|---|---|
| 0.57 | 0.84 | 1.05 | 1.16 | 1.17 | 0.94 | 1.02 | 1.05 | 7.80 million hectares |

**Table 7 - State wise area brought under MIS in India**

| Sr No | State | Area under MIS up to 2014-15 in mha | Addnl. area under MIS during 2015-16 to 22-23 in mha | Total area under MIS on 31-3-2023 in mha |
|---|---|---|---|---|
| 1 | Karnataka | 0.68 | 1.75 | 2.43 |
| 2 | Rajasthan | 1.50 | 0.60 | 2.10 |
| 3 | Maharashtra | 1.10 | 0.94 | 2.04 |
| 4 | Andhra Oradesh | 1.07 | 0.85 | 1.92 |
| 5 | Gujarat | 0.72 | 0.99 | 1.71 |
| 6 | Tamil nadu | 0.25 | 1.01 | 1.26 |
| 7 | Haryana | 0.68 | - | 0.68 |
| 8 | Madhya Pradesh | 0.35 | 0.31 | 0.66 |
| 9 | Chhattisgarh | 0.34 | 0.04 | 0.38 |
| 10 | Telangana | - | 0.31 | 0.31 |
| 11 | Uttar Pradesh | - | 0.30 | 0.30 |
|  | **Sub Total** | **6.69** | **7.10** | **13.79** |
| 12 | Rest of the 18 States | - | 0.70 | 0.70 |
|  | **Grand Total** | **6.69** | **7.80** | **14.49 mha** |

mha – million hectares

<u>Non-structural measures to improve water-use efficiency</u> – As explained in the earlier chapter, there were number of small paddy (rice) tanks in the area close to the East coast of India and there were some bandharas (weirs) in the Tapi basin under 'Phad' system in the Maharashtra State. Management of irrigation and maintenance of structures under these traditional systems was being

done by the beneficiaries in an efficient manner because these systems were having command only in one or two villages. However, for large size dam-canal projects constructed during British regime where the command area was spread in some districts & sub districts, irrigation management and maintenance of dam & distribution system was being done by the Govt. agency. Cultivators were charged for the water used for irrigation by them as per actually measured irrigated area basis according to types of crops grown i.e., seasonal, two-seasonal or perennial. Rates were fixed and there was no incentive for the farmers to save water and irrigate more area with the same quantum of water. During discussions by the World Bank engineers with the engineers of WR Department of GoM, it was decided to explore possibility of entrusting the irrigation management of state sector schemes to small groups of about 200 to 250 ha area (preferably from one or two villages) through Water User's Association of the beneficiaries. After carrying out some pilot projects and holding discussions about all the related issues with the beneficiaries and Non-Govt. Organisations (NGO), an Act was drafted by the WR Department. It was passed by the Maharashtra Assembly and the Act titled as 'Maharashtra Management of Irrigation System by Farmers Act – MMISF Act 2005' came into force in the year 2005. Water User's Associations (WUA) were to be registered first and were to function as per specified rules and regulations. Canal water was to be delivered to the WUAs on volumetric basis at pre decided rates for each season. WUAs could make free use of GW in their area and use both sources conjunctively to grow any crop over as much area as decided by all the beneficiaries by consensus. Operation and maintenance of channels within their area was to be done by WUAs. Maintenance of dam, main canal and distributaries up to WUA was to be done by WR Deptt. For the first three years of operation, some financial incentive (reducing every year by one third and to nil in the fourth year) was also given to the WUAs. It was expected that they would make more equitable allocation of water among the members and make more efficient use of water, aimed at producing 'More crop and cash per drop of water'. In actual practice as seen during last more than fifteen years, response of the beneficiaries was not so encouraging and only small number of WUAs functioned in an efficient manner, where the promoters and motivators of the schemes were innovative and resourceful.

One project was implemented on some major and medium projects with the financial assistance from the World Bank. It included improvements in the canal and distribution systems to achieve volumetric distribution of water and construction of office building to facilitate formation of WUAs. But even then, there was not much response from WUAs on those projects. WR Department of GoM is hence exploring some measures to improve the situation to encourage formation of WUAs.

Maharashtra Water Resource Regulatory Authority (MWRRA) had issued Notification in the year 2015 to introduce MIS i.e., Drip Irrigation on experimental basis in the command area of 8 major projects in the Maharashtra State. Introduction of MIS needed construction of water storage ponds for every small group of farmers (20 to 25 ha) or a common pond of WUA for all the 200 to 250 ha in the canal command, installing electric pump on it and providing arrangements to deliver water through pipes up to each field and then by drip irrigation system to all fields in that group. Such system would make more efficient and equitable use of canal water to grow high value perennial crops. Water so saved by introducing MIS was planned to be used to provide irrigation to the farmers at the tail end of the canal system to grow seasonal crops. But response to the scheme had not been encouraging since then. WR Department of GoM is hence trying some measures to improve the situation. Both these measures would certainly improve water-use efficiency of projects, without making any capital investment by the WR Deptt.

**Modern Irrigation Systems –**

Green Houses – In the countries having tropical climate, though ample sunlight is available most of the time, dry weather and high temperatures affect the plant growth in summer season. So was the case in the countries having temperate climate during winter season when atmospheric temperature was very low and was unfavourable to grow crops in open fields. If large size permanent 'Green Houses' were constructed, ambient temperature and humidity in them could be controlled in any season as per requirement of the crop. Such investment becomes economically viable to grow high value crops like flowers, some fruits & vegetables etc., because the quality and yield of the produce improved appreciably. If any high value crop is grown in the greenhouses during out of their normal growing season, agriculture produce then fetches good price in the market. It is also possible to install sensors to automatically control humidity in the green house by operating fine spray nozzles and to control starting of drip or sprinkler irrigation automatically when the soil moisture reduces below certain limit. In Netherlands in the temperate region, modern green houses are lighted with LED lamps during night-time, which ensures crop growth during night-time also and reduces maturity period of the crops grown inside. Due to establishing of thousands of such greenhouses and by making use of such modern technology, such a small country like Netherlands is second largest exporter of high value agriculture produce, after America. Use of tissue culture for getting month old plants reduces growth period in the green houses. Use of organic fertilisers and bio measures to control pest problem improves quality of the produce. On a smaller scale, cheaper shed-nets can also be constructed to serve as green houses for growing high value crops.

On Demand Irrigation System – It is a very 'User friendly scheme', which is in operation for the last 3-4 decades on some surface irrigation and groundwater irrigation schemes in Italy and Spain. Water from the reservoir is conveyed through closed pipes/lined canal into the several lined farm ponds constructed near every group of farmers in the command area. Water is pumped from these ponds from a pump house having several electric pumps installed in it. These pumps are operated one by one in sequence in response to the consolidated irrigation water demand by all farmers in the group. Water pumped from these ponds is conveyed through pipes and delivered with nearly constant pressure to each farmer. On making advance payment, each farmer is given an 'Aqua card' for certain volume of water for each season. He gets water delivered under nearly constant pressure near his farm, which he can use directly for drip/sprinkler irrigation. He can take water on any day and at any time of the day as per his convenience, for any crop and over as much area he desires to irrigate, but by observing the total water volume limit permitted to him for that season.

When several farmers use water for irrigation, level of water in the common farm pond reduces, which automatically transmits message to release water from the main reservoir into that pond as per their actual consumption, to restore storage in their pond to full capacity. Water from the reservoir is released in response to the total water demand from all farm ponds on the canal system. This procedure continues in all the seasons round the year. Depending on the actual storage of water in the reservoir each year, allocation of water is done for each farm pond for each season and the same is informed in advance to the farmers. If the source of water is ground water available from extensive layers of alluvial sand-soil layers below, deep tube wells are drilled at several places, perforated steel pipes are fixed in them below normal GW level, and multistage pumps are installed on each tube well. All these tube wells operate one by one in sequence in response to the actual demand of water from the farmers served by the system. Based on GW level each year before start of the season, estimation of GW availability is done in advance and farmers are informed to plan their irrigation in every season accordingly.

Conclusion – From the simple traditional flood irrigation system of irrigation being practiced for the last more than 5000 years, many improvements have been made during last 80-90 years. Aim was firstly to improve water-use efficiency (ratio of crop water requirement to the actual water used in the system) of the system, secondly to respond to the daily crop water need during crop growth period and thirdly to make the system more user friendly. Sophisticated systems are generally used for high value crops. It would be seen that use of MIS, as a percentage of total irrigated area is very high in most of the developed countries but is increasing in many developing countries. In India, under almost all the surface irrigation schemes, water is delivered to the standing crop by the flood irrigation system. Most of the use of MIS at present is for GW irrigation on the wells.

# Chapter 8
# Integrated Management of Water Resource to Meet All Its Competing Uses.

*As the demand of water for industrial and urban use started increasing from the sixties and seventies of the last century in India, Urban-Rural conflicts emerged, emphasising the need to adopt an integrated approach in the use and management of the water resource. At the time of independence, only some major cities in India had captive reservoirs, and some cities could lift water from perennial rivers to meet their urban water demand. Most of the remaining small cities and towns were then managing their drinking water and domestic use demands from dug wells by lifting the water manually. Rivers were used for washing clothes and for bathing. Development of industries was on a low key then and their water demand was also not significant. Hence most of the major dams constructed in India after independence in the first two decades were primarily planned to increase irrigation facilities to improve crop productivity and to ensure food security to the country. From the sixties of the last century onwards, many new industries were set up in some progressive states, which started increase in the demand for industrial use of water. Because of the increased job opportunities so created in industries, people from semi urban and rural areas migrated to industrial and other cities, thereby increasing urban population and so also the urban water demand. Since both these non-irrigation demands had priority over irrigation, their demands were fulfilled by diverting water from many major reservoirs, though at the cost of corresponding curtailment of water for irrigation. In due course of time, because of the totally inadequate treatment to the sewage/effluent generated after such non irrigation use of water and releasing it in the rivers, had caused pollution of most of the rivers in the country. This situation called for an integrated approach in the use and management of water while responding to the dynamics of all its competing and conflicting demands. The chapter covers situation in India in general and that in the Maharashtra state in particular, by explaining historical development of all the related issues, their present status, and possible desirable actions necessary to improve the present situation.*

At the time of independence to India, Maharashtra state had only about 0.27 million hectares (mha) irrigation potential created by the surface irrigation schemes out of 22.5 mha of the cultivable land. Groundwater development was limited to irrigate some fields in rural area, primarily by lifting water from dug wells by means of the bullock power and by diesel pumps at some places. Drinking water demand of most of the small towns and all the villages was met with by means of small diameter wells (in cities/towns) and large diameter common dug wells (in villages), and also from the rivers. About 30 to 40 % area of the Maharashtra state has been drought prone, being in the rain shadow zone to the East of Sahyadri mountain range. Hence before independence, four major irrigation projects were taken up to increase irrigation facilities there. Few captive storages were also constructed then to meet urban and industrial demands of water for Mumbai city and some other cities in the state.

This situation started changing in the country in the fifth and sixth decade of the last century. Many major dam-canal irrigation projects were taken up in some states for providing irrigation facilities, primarily to achieve food security to the country. Some major dams, like Koyna in the Maharashtra state, were planned to provide cheap hydroelectric power for industries and cities. With the construction of several large dam-canal projects in the country such as Bhakra, Hirakud, Nagarjunsagar, Maithon, Panchet etc., area under irrigation increased appreciably. It also provided year-round employment to the landless labourers from rural area which was close to the canal command areas. With the introduction of 'Green Revolution' in the sixties, crop productivity appreciably increased and so the country achieved food security from the seventies onward as explained in the earlier chapters.

Simultaneously, many basic heavy industries (Steel, Thermal Power, Antibiotics, Vehicles, Rail engines & coaches, Aeronautics etc.) were established in the public sector by the Govt. of India in different states of the country. In some progressive states, several other industries were also started in the private sector, near some cities where electric power and dependable source of water was available. In some states where sufficient fallow land, electric power and adequate water was available, Industrial Estates were also set up to start several industries at one place in one industrial complex. With increase in the agriculture produce, some food processing industries and sugar factories were also set up near small towns in the semi-urban area. All these industries provided permanent employment opportunities to skilled, unskilled labour and to the technical & managerial personnel. People from rural and semi-urban areas migrated permanently to such cities to meet these needs of industries. Availability of good higher education facilities (Science, Arts, Commerce, Engineering, Medical, Management etc.) in some cities, was an attraction for migration of students from semi-urban areas to cities. Gradually, as the standard of living of urban population started increasing, the then prevailing system of ground water use for drinking and domestic use could not meet increased water needs of the urbanites Common water supply scheme from a more dependable source to deliver water by taps in every house had then to be planned and implemented.

All these actions resulted in increase in the population of many cities at a fast rate and so also the demand of water for industries and urban population in such industrialised states. Since demand of water for industrial and urban use is location specific and is nearly constant in all the twelve months of the year (unlike irrigation demand), it had to be met with from more dependable and reliable sources of water. Even major rivers in the state did not have much flow then in the summer season. As explained in earlier chapters, medium and minor size dams (each irrigating less than 10,000 ha) were planned to provide only seasonal irrigation and were emptied by end of February each year. Hence dependable year-round water for non-irrigation purposes could only be made available from major dams (each irrigating more than 10,000 ha) which provided all the year-round irrigation to certain percentage of perennial crops. In the Indo-Gangetic plains of the North India where rivers were perennial due to snowmelt in the summer season, water could be pumped all the year round directly from rivers, which were unpolluted then, to act as a dependable source of water for urban and industrial use.

Up to the seventies and even eighties of the last century, reservoirs, canals & distribution system of most of the major projects in the Maharashtra state were planned, designed, and implemented to utilise all the stored water to irrigate land in their command area. For very few projects, only some quantity of the stored water was reserved for urban use in big cities or for industrial use. However, rapidly increasing water demand for non-irrigation purposes during last 4-5 decades in the Maharashtra state, resulted in gradual curtailment in the availability of water which was originally planned for irrigation. Since there was no other dependable source of water in the state to meet urban and industrial water demand, water from many major reservoirs had to be diverted to meet these non-irrigation demands of water. Such curtailment was accommodated by diluting the existing crop pattern in the canal command. But the demand continued to rise at high pace and adequate water could not be made available to irrigate land located in the tail end of such canals. Expenditure incurred in the acquisition of land and construction of water distribution network in the tail reaches of the canals became infructuous. During drought years when quantity of water stored in the dams was much less than in a normal year, almost all water had to be utilised to meet the high priority non-irrigation demands, leaving negligible or even no water for irrigation. Such situation increased the intensity of Urban-Rural conflicts in the command areas of most of the Major projects in the state. With the unavoidable rapid growth of the Service sector and Information Technology sector, urban population and urban water demand had increased rapidly during the last 2-3 decades. It is bound to increase further in the near future, in the regional headquarters like Mumbai, Pune, Nashik, Aurangabad, Nagpur etc., in the state. More industries and thermal power plants would also be set up in the coming decades. Hence gravity of the problem of Urban-Rural conflict due to such increase in the non-irrigation demands of water is bound to increase hereafter.

As a solution to this problem, sewage generated after urban use of water was planned to be treated to make it suitable for reuse in irrigation (expected availability of about 80% of actual urban use of water), and it was to be pumped back into canals of such projects. Approval to the diversion of water for non-irrigation purposes was given only with that condition. Such action would have provided adequate relief by restoring the curtailed irrigation at least partly and would have solved the problem of river pollution. But that was not done in practice by the Municipal Corporations/Municipalities, and the partly treated and/or untreated sewage containing organic matter, faeces, nitrates, phosphates, and pathogen was continued to be released into rivers causing their total pollution. Effluent generated after use of water in industries was treated to some extent, but still it contained some toxic chemicals, heavy metal compounds, and carcinogens etc. Same was also released into rivers from the industries and industrial estates. In Punjab, Haryana, and some other northern states, when the Green Revolution commenced in the late sixties of the last century, irrigated wheat & rice was being grown on a very large scale. Heavy use of chemical fertilisers, insecticides and pesticides for these crops increased the crop productivity but had resulted in release of toxic chemicals and carcinogens in the water regenerated after irrigation. These were the main reasons for pollution of almost all rivers in India during last 4-5 decades.

Responding to the dynamics of these increasing non-irrigation demands and safeguarding interests of cultivators practicing irrigated agriculture in the command areas of major projects, has hence become a very complex issue for its management. Let us first see the characteristics of water demand for urban and industrial use and problems created by them in the management of water resource.

Urban use of water – Water demand for humans can be classified as 'Water for Food' and 'Water for the People'. Water that is consumed in the rain-fed agriculture and in the irrigated agriculture is called as water for food. Water that is required for drinking, bathing & household use and for industrial use, is called as water for the people. By the end of nineteenth century and even up to mid twentieth century, only big cities like Mumbai (having Tulshi, Vihar, Powai & Tansa dams) Pune (having Katraj & Khadakwasla dams), Nagpur (having Telang khedi dam, Kanhan river), Aurangabad (having Harsul dam) and few District places in the Maharashtra state had captive reservoirs to meet domestic needs of the urban population. In the Central and Peninsular India, upper strata of the land consisted of in-situ decomposed basalt, granite & metamorphic rocks underlain by layers of those rocks at most of the places. Hence ground water (GW) availability in such strata was at shallow depths, limited, confined and discontinuous. But still the shallow GW in such strata was adequate to meet water demand of people from most of the cities, towns, and villages. Source of drinking water was small diameter wells in towns and large diameter common dug wells in villages and water was being lifted by manual power at both the places. Because GW use for agriculture in the rural area was not much then, many rivers had some flow even in the summer season and the rivers were not polluted then. Hence river water was used for drinking at some places but for bathing and washing of clothes at many places.

Because of the extensive availability of deep alluvial soils (layers of sand, silt, and gravel) in the Sindhu, Ganga & Brahmaputra River basins (Indo-Gangetic basin) in the North India, GW availability was in plenty, and GW Table (GWT) was also not very deep below the surface. Hence for drinking water & domestic use, people from cities, towns & villages depended on small/large diameter dug wells by lifting the water manually. Since these rivers were rising from the snowed ranges of Himalaya Mountain, there was perennial flow in all the rivers because of the snow melt in summer season. Hence river water and water from dependable wells was pumped, treated, and provided by taps in some big cities near these rivers and was also provided for the industrial use. Most of the rivers were used for bathing and washing of clothes as well.

Let us now see the procedure and technology adopted at present in the use of water for drinking and domestic purposes. City water is supplied either from rivers, captive storages if available, or from reservoirs of major projects constructed by the WR Department (WRD) of state Govts. Even if the source of water was rivers in the North India and large reservoirs in the central and southern India, river/reservoir water remained muddy during 3-4 months of the rainy season. The water also contained some floating matter, algae, and bacteria. Hence some treatment was required to be given to such water prior to its use in cities and towns. Where the water to cities was conveyed through open canal, oxidation of some impurities takes place naturally, but it may also get polluted due to use by the people on the way. Where it is conveyed through closed pipes, both these possibilities were avoided. Water supplied by the state Govts. to the Municipal Corporations or Municipalities of cities and towns for urban use was charged on volumetric basis, normally at a subsidised rate. Treatment of water to make it suitable for drinking & domestic use was, however, their responsibility. Water treatment plants were constructed, operated, and maintained by them.

Water Treatment Plants - In the water treatment plant, to start with the raw water is cascaded so that it comes in contact with air and gets naturally purified to some extent. Then it is passed through a 'Clarifloculator' and 'Rapid sand filter' for removal of suspended silt particles, floating matter, and other impurities. Clarifloculator is a circular Reinforced Cement Concrete (RCC) tank whose bottom is sloping towards the centre. Water is mixed with alum solution which is released from the centre of the tank near its bottom. There is a circular vertical wall in the tank as shown in the sketch. Electric motor is fixed at the top of the central column. It continuously rotates the horizontal arm which is fitted with two vertical arms. Continuous rotation of the arm ensures mixing of alum solution with water, which causes coagulation and settlement of solid fine suspended particles in water at the bottom. Settled silt is then removed periodically from the bottom. Clear water then flows out from the circular channel provided near top of the tank near its circumference.

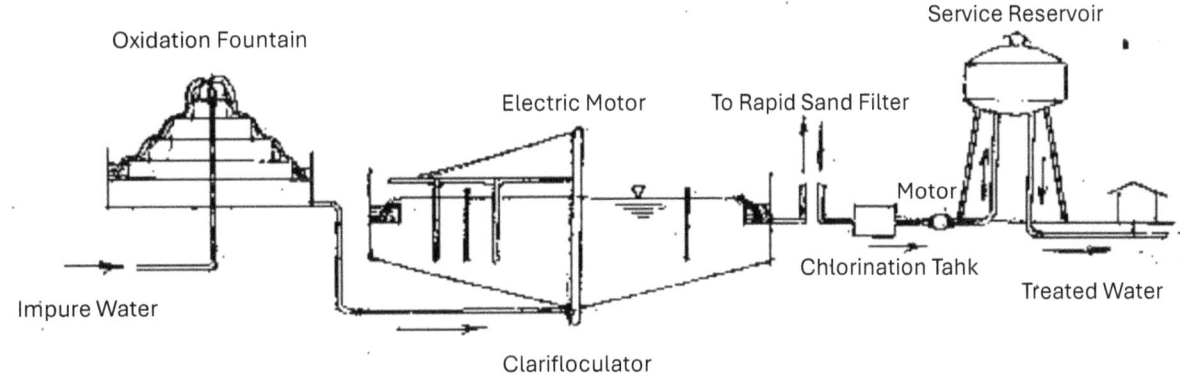

**Purification Process for Drinking Water**

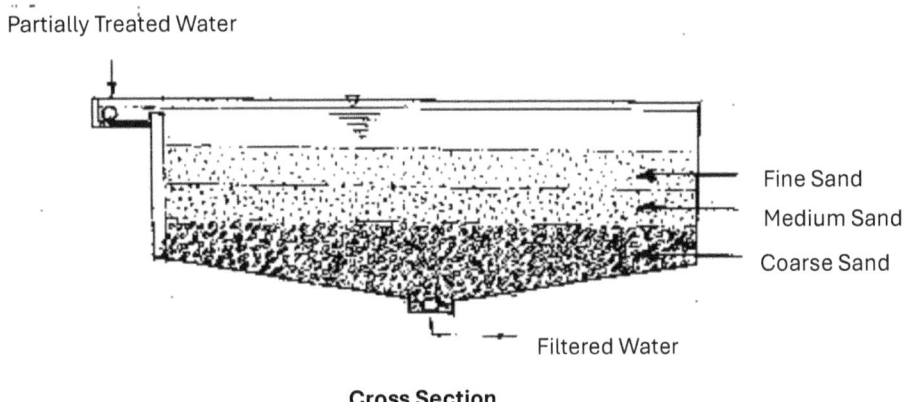

**Rapid Sand Filter**

But the treated water still contains some silt, floating matter, algae etc. Hence the water is passed through 'Rapid Sand Filter' as shown in the sketch. It is a rectangular RCC tank having RCC channel at the top from where water delivered from the clarifloculator is released in the tank. RCC tank is filled with a layer of coarse sand at the bottom, layer of medium size sand above it and a layer of fine sand at the top. Silt, floating matter, and algae present in the water is retained in the fine sand layer and the filtered water flows below which is taken out from the horizontal perforated pipe installed at the bottom. Because of the impurities arrested in the fine sand layer, it gets choked after some days. Water under pressure is then released from the perforated pipe at the bottom, which flows upwards, churns the water and removes impurities arrested in the sand layers, to flow out from channel near the top. Even then bacteria remain in the treated water, which are destroyed by the action of chlorine released from the weak solution of bleaching powder which is mixed in the water in adequate quantity from a small tank. Well treated water is then pumped and stored in a ground level or an elevated RCC tank near the water treatment plant. Treated water is then conveyed through underground pipes and stored in several elevated service reservoirs constructed in different parts of the city. It is then conveyed from there through underground pipes and supplied during specific hours of the day to the citizens in their houses by water taps. Recurring cost of treatment, maintenance & depreciation of the treatment plants and supplying water up to houses is recovered from water user citizens by levying 'Water Tax'.

Prescribed norm for cities having tap water supply is 140 litres/capita/day (including wastage in the underground pipeline system) in all states in India as at present. But in actual practice, most of the cities in the Maharashtra state provide water to the citizens much below these norms. During drought years and during summer months, number of days of supply in a week and daily hours of supply of water depend on actual availability of water in the reservoirs or rivers. Water in the reservoirs is normally reserved to last up to July end or mid-August, to meet the contingency of late outbreak of monsoon season (normal start of monsoon is from mid-June to end of June). Issue of drinking water supply to villages is covered in the next chapter on 'Ground water'.

Common problems associated with tap water supply and possible solutions -

1. There is no control on the actual use of water by taps by the citizens and there is no incentive for them to save water because water use charges are fixed as per diameter of the household supply from the main pipeline to the citizens. Hence water is commonly misused and wasted.

2. Usually there is lot of wastage of water due to leakages from underground network of pipes especially if the system is old. Municipal Corporations and Municipalities usually have no established mechanism to identify/locate such leakages and rectify them promptly. Annual audit of actual water use is also usually not done, and no efforts are taken to educate water users to economise on the use of water, which ultimately results in lot of wastage of treated water even up to 25 to 30% of the total water use against the expected wastage of about 10%.

3. Metered supply could be a possible solution to reduce total water consumption, but it is costly and difficult to implement and manage in practice. Even then, initially metered supply should be made compulsory to all residential hotels, hospitals, apartment complexes and all new colonies & redeveloped buildings to start with. Network of metered supply should then be

gradually expanded to all existing colonies, houses, and bungalows in the city. Meters should also be installed on water supply pipe at the start of each apartment complex and bungalow colonies. By monitoring such metered consumption in them, it would be possible to know the actual average per capita consumption of people in these human clusters.

4. To compel Municipal Corporations and Municipalities to take all the above measures to avoid wastage of water, telescopic rates based on actual consumption of water should be charged by the State Govts. who provide them the untreated water. It means that specific minimum rate should be charged up to pre-decided quantity of per day per capita water uses in every city. For any additional consumption, rates charged should be progressively increased for every 10% of additional use.

5. Many times, there are leakages of sewage from pipes of underground drainage system. Such sewage water is likely to seep into the leaking pipes of water supply system during their closure hours, to pollute the drinking water. Such locations should be investigated, identified, and rectified.

6. Providing of rainwater conservation/harvesting measures should be made compulsory/obligatory for all buildings, bungalows, apartment complexes, public places, gardens etc. It ensures additional GW recharge, which can be used by bungalow owners and apartment complexes by drilling bore wells, for use in gardening and even other household uses, thereby saving the costly treated water.

Sewage generation after use of water by humans, its treatment and reuse – Before independence, most of the houses in many cities and towns in India had individual or common toilets for sanitation purposes. Conservancy system i.e., removing human excreta through manual labour and depositing it at a common location away from city/town for natural treatment, was the most common system then in India. However, after independence the conservancy system was gradually discontinued, and human excreta was then treated by connecting toilets to the individual/common septic tanks. After defecation, anal cleaning by water had been the common practice all over India and it continues even today at most of the places. Most of the male and female population from villages then used to go for defecation in separate specified open fallow areas near villages. Excreta would dry up there and get washed away during rainy season. But during last 3-4 decades, subsidies are being given to villagers for construction of individual toilets in houses and specific funds are provided under different schemes for constructing common toilets - separate for ladies and gents. During this and the next decade, such facility is expected be available in all villages in India. Here also treatment of human excreta is by means of septic tanks or by making use of 'Two-pit Latrines'.

Underground drainage system was in use only in Mumbai much before 1947 and in Pune since 1942 in the Maharashtra State. Activity of providing underground drainage systems in some district places in the state was started in the sixties but it gained good momentum around eighties of the last century. It was started primarily in the cities and towns where source of water was more dependable, such as reservoirs or main rivers. At present many district places and few talukas (sub districts) in the state are having underground drainage system in operation.

As the urban water demand started increasing after rapid increase in population due to industrialisation, more and more water which was originally planned for irrigation use was diverted for urban use. Municipal Corporations and Municipalities were required to treat the sewage generated after the urban use adequately for its reuse in irrigation. Pune Municipal Corporation is a representative case as explained below. Additional water from khadakwasla, Panshet and Warasgaon major dams located on upstream side of Pune city was diverted by gravity pipe system for urban use, as per increasing requirement of the city. In the year 1992 additional quota of water was provided by the WR Deptt. of GoM, with the condition that 80% of the water shall be adequately treated, pumped, and delivered back into the Khadakwasla Right Bank Canal which was passing through the city. Had the action of constructing adequate Sewage Treatment Plants (STP) been taken promptly and the treated water was delivered in the canal, originally planned irrigation would not have suffered much. But in actual practice, action of constructing STPs was delayed by decades and even as on today only part quantity of the total sewage generated is treated and only some of that treated water is made available for irrigation. Hence, releasing of the partly treated or untreated urban sewage into Mutha River in the past 3-4 decades has polluted it completely. In this case, the polluted Mutha River water is further draining into Ujjani reservoir (largest capacity reservoir in the state) located about 105 km on downstream of Pune city and has also been polluting water stored in the reservoir. Even if Ujjani reservoir water is mainly used for irrigation, it is also used by Solapur city (District place) on its downstream and by some villages along banks of the river for drinking and domestic use. In all the cites where underground drainage system is introduced, condition of degree of treatment of sewage generated prior to its release in rivers is by and large the same as that of the Pune city. With the result almost all rivers in the state have been heavily polluted.

Let us now see the procedure and technology adopted in the treatment of urban sewage.

<u>Domestic wastewater treatment systems in cities having underground drainage system</u> -

Domestic wastewater treatment systems can be mainly categorized as follows:

i. Mechanised Wastewater Treatment Systems

   a) Aerobic Systems: Activated Sludge Process & its modifications, Trickling Filters, Rotating Biological Contactors are few of the technologies that are aerobic in nature.

   b) Anaerobic Systems: Septic tanks (for on-site treatment), Up-flow Anaerobic Sludge Blanket Reactors (UASB) are the anaerobic processes for wastewater treatment.

ii. Non mechanised Systems comprise following technologies:

   - Decentralised on site Waste Management Systems
   - Phytoremediation

**a) Aerobic systems –**

Activated Sludge Process (ASP) has been traditionally used as a wastewater treatment method for more than last 100 years. With stringent norms, the basic process has been upgraded and currently following advanced versions of this treatment are used:

1) Moving Bed Biofilm Reactor (MBBR) - Contaminants in the sewage from kitchen, bathrooms & toilets are treated to produce liquid and solids suitable for discharge to the environment or for reuse. Sewage treatment includes physical, chemical, and biological treatments to remove these contaminants. Primary treatment is to remove coarse free & floating suspended solids which are trapped by vertical bars and fine screens. The screened effluent is then collected in the collection tank which is provided with coarse bubble aeration to mix it properly, to avoid settling of solids and to prevent degradation of waste causing odour. Secondary treatment is then given in Aerobic Reactor Tank where aerobic microbes will grow and utilize the pollutants in the presence of oxygen thereby reducing Bio-chemical Oxygen Demand/Chemical Oxygen Demand (BOD/COD). The biomass generated is separated in the tube settler where flocculation & settling is done, and clear supernatant is pumped into filter feed tank for tertiary treatment. The sludge separated will be taken in the sludge holding tank. Tertiary treatment is given in the pressure sand filter and activated carbon filter. Effluent then becomes suitable for reuse in secondary requirements like gardening and/or flushing purpose after disinfection.

2) Sequential Batch Reactor (SBR) – Screened sewage is firstly conveyed into equalisation tank. Sewage gets temporarily stored in it during peak hours of inflow of sewage to ensure delivery at a nearly uniform rate into SBR. Arrangements are made for thorough mixing of the sewage and to keep it in a homogeneous condition and to avoid septic conditions. Bioreactor comprises of a tank fitted at its bottom with jet aerators. Bacteria in the sewage synthesize the organic matter under aerobic conditions into harmless products such as carbon dioxide and water. After specific time, aeration automatically stops and then the solid material settles at the bottom. After certain time, clear liquid from the tank above a specific level is removed and then the settled solids are removed.

**Non mechanised systems -**

1. Decentralised on site Integrated Waste Management System, which was developed by Padmashree Dr. Mapuskar can be adopted for apartments complex or a colony of apartments/bungalows in the city or town. Human night soil is collected in a tank without mixing it with sullage, where it gets anaerobically digested, and the effluent becomes hygienically safe. Biogas generated during digestion process can be used as a fuel. Sullage from bathrooms & kitchens (grey water) is connected to intercepting tank and then to stabilising tank, in which stabilised effluent from biogas tank gets mixed. Stabilised water from tank can be used for gardening and solid waste from biogas tank can be used as manure. Wet waste is vermi-composted and can also be used as manure.

2. Phytoremediation is a green technology that uses plant systems for remediation and restoration. It encompasses microbial degradation in rhizosphere as well as uptake, accumulation, and transformation in the plant. Plants in conjunction with bacteria and fungi in the rhizosphere transform, transport or store harmful chemicals. Pollutants are taken up by the plant and transformed into plant tissue.

Treatment of sewage generated from towns and villages not having underground drainage system – As stated above, in most of the towns in the Maharashtra state, actual supply of water for domestic use is much less than the norms of 140 litres/day/person. Norms of water supply for villages are 40 litres per day per person and the source is generally ground water from common dug wells. Hence not much quantity of effluent is generated from household use of water in many towns and villages which are not having underground drainage system. Effluent generated from household use of water in them is conveyed through open gutters - small size constructed open surface drains, along both sides of roads leading to the nearest stream or river. Since such effluent does not contain human excreta directly and contains much less pollutants, its partial natural purification takes place during its transit to the river. Hence, by and large, their contribution is not significant in the river pollution, provided timely actions as stated below are taken.

Human excreta from flush toilets in the houses from such towns is conveyed by underground pipes into individual septic tank or common septic tank for a group of houses/apartments. Septic tank systems are commonly designed as stabilising systems, not as treatment systems. Naturally, the effluent coming out from such systems is harmful from the health point of view because of the presence of pathogens due to limited hydraulic retention time. Therefore, it is expected that this effluent is absorbed underground in some kind of absorption or soak-away system. Unfortunately, it is experienced all over India that, the effluent from septic tanks flows either in open surface drains or accumulates in a cesspool adjacent to the septic tank. In septic tank, anaerobic or facultative anaerobic bio digestion takes place. During this process harmful greenhouse gases such as methane and carbon dioxide are produced, but unfortunately, this fact is overlooked in India and probably all over in the developing and underdeveloped countries of the world.

Partially stablised solid material settles below in the relatively less polluted liquid above in the septic tank. Before the septic tank fills, all contents of the septic tank shall have to be pumped out into special tankers, transported, and then pumped out into drying pits. When the solids settle below in these pits, upper water can be pumped out and used for irrigation. The solids below when dried, form very good manure for crops and can be sold to gardeners or farmers. Usually, the work of pumping out contents of all septic tanks in the towns, transporting, and then disposing it as above is entrusted to local contractors. Municipalities are required to monitor their work for ensuring timely emptying of all the septic tanks in the town, sequentially one by one and disposing the contents as indicated above all the year round. However, it is observed that such actions are usually not taken in time and polluted effluent containing partially treated excreta flows out from septic tanks into open gutters and then into rivers to pollute them.

To monitor this activity, a standing committee of representatives of Municipal elected members, State Govt. officials, citizens, and Social NGOs should be established in every such town and village. In the villages where individual toilets or common toilets are constructed and septic tanks are provided for effluent treatment, same precautions as above are required to be taken for ensuring timely treatment of sewage. In some villages, 'Two-pit latrines' are also provided where human excreta remain in dry state in the pits. After filling of first pit second pit is used. Excreta in the first pit naturally decays and gradually turns into manure, which is required to be removed before filling of the second pit. Village councils (Gram Panchayats) are responsible for ensuring that periodical cleaning of septic tanks and two-pit latrines is done in the villages.

<u>Industrial use of water</u> – Industrial use of water could be classified in three types. First would be the use of water as a coolant for condensing steam in the manufacturing process in Steel industry and in many other industries. Here water does not get polluted but is lost to some extent in the process due to evaporation and can be reused number of times. Second type is the use of water as a part of the end-product such as soft drinks, beer, wine, fruit juices etc., and hence the water used should be of drinking water quality. However, some effluent containing organic matter and chemicals is generated in their manufacturing process and it needs to be treated prior to its release in the river. Third type is the manufacturing of paper, pharmaceutical products, sugar, and similar many such industries. In these industries effluent generated contains toxic chemicals, heavy metal compounds, carcinogens, and organic matter. Such effluent is most harmful, and it must be treated fully prior to its release in rivers and needs to be monitored at all levels to reduce its harmful effects. In the Maharashtra state this responsibility is entrusted to the state 'Pollution Control Board'.

For industrial use of water, there are some captive reservoirs constructed by the Maharashtra Industrial Development Corporation (MIDC), but for most of the industries and industrial estates, water is obtained from reservoirs of the major projects constructed by the WR Deptt. of GoM. Water is then adequately treated by MIDC if necessary and is supplied to industries by charging it on volumetric basis. However, responsibility of providing adequate treatment to the effluent generated prior to its release in the rivers rests with the individual industry. It is monitored by the 'Pollution Control Board'. In some industrial estates, common effluent treatment plant is constructed, and industries are charged for treatment of the effluent based on the quantity and quality of the effluent generated by the individual industry. Maharashtra state is the second largest in the manufacture of sugar in India and there are more than 200 cooperative sugar factories in the state. Release of partly treated effluent in the river by some sugar factories have created problems of river pollution many times.

To economise on the industrial use of water and keep control on the release of partly treated/untreated effluent in rivers, following measures should be taken.

1. Industries should be encouraged to treat the generated effluent themselves and reuse it as much as possible by following use-treat-recycle-reuse practice. It would also reduce consumption of fresh water by them.

2. This objective can be achieved by treating the chargeable water rates per unit of volume as an economic instrument for regulation. High water rates would encourage/induce industries to treat and recycle the treated water instead of using fresh water.

3. For all existing industries located near cities (other than type two industries above), either the sewage treated adequately by the Municipal Corporations should be reused by such industries or the untreated sewage should be supplied directly to such industries, for them to treat and make use of it. It would partly solve the problem of pollution of rivers due to release of untreated urban sewage and reduce consumption of fresh water.

4. It is essential to review availability of treated/untreated sewage from cities and requirement of other than type two industries and prepare a time bound programme of gradual implementation of use-treat-recycle-reuse practice. All these actions should ultimately be planned to lead to 'Zero effluent' from industrial use. It would reduce quantum of industrial use of water and would also avoid pollution of rivers.

Status of Effluent Treatment provided in different states in India –

As per the seventh schedule of Constitution of India (Article 246) 'Water' is a 'State' subject and it is the responsibility of States/Union Territories to ensure cleanliness and development of rivers within their jurisdiction. However, based on the information provided by the states about the extent/percentage of treatment given to the sewage/effluent generated after urban/industrial use, prior to its release in the rivers, a map has been prepared by the Govt. of India. As indicated below, it shows the percentage of treatment provided by each state to the sewage/effluent generated.

In the states of Punjab, Haryana and Himachal Pradesh in the North India, less than 15 percent effluent is released untreated. In many states in the North-East part of the country such as Odisha, Bihar, Bengal, Assam, Jharkhand and Kerala in the South, about 90 to 100 percent effluent is released untreated in the rivers. In rest of the states in the country, about 30 to 80 percent effluent is released untreated in the rivers. National Average of untreated sewage released in the rivers is about 63 percent.

Mechanism for ensuring effective implementation of effluent treatment - Prevailing Acts and Rules do not compel Municipal Corporations and Municipalities to take timely actions to treat urban sewage prior to its release in rivers to reduce gravity of the problem. Enabling Acts should hence be drafted, passed by the State Assemblies, and necessary Rules should be framed to ensure their rigorous effective implementation. As per these Acts, statutory responsibilities should be fixed on Municipal Corporations, Municipalities for advance planning and timely construction of STPs for ensuring 100% treatment of the effluent generated. State Govt. should bear part capital cost of construction and subsequent replacement/modernising of STPs, but entire recurring cost of operation, maintenance, repairs, depreciation and restoration of STPs should be borne by the above non-Govt. agencies. On the principle of 'Polluter Pays', this recurring cost should be recovered from beneficiary citizens by levying 'Sanitation Tax' from them. Village Councils should also be made responsible for managing proper functioning of septic tanks and two pit latrines. State Pollution Control Boards should be held statutorily responsible for ensuring full treatment of effluent generated after use of water by the industries and in the irrigated agriculture.

All the above agencies should first estimate projections of urban population and trends of development of industries in the next 3 decades right up to 2050 and work out corresponding probable quantum of sewage/effluent generation. They should then prepare plans of setting up STPs/ETPs, work out requirement of funds each year and make provision of funds. Plan of restoration /replacement/modernising of old STPs/ETPs should also be prepared in advance. They should also take advance action for acquisition of land required for the new treatment plants. GoM should share part cost of the capital investment for all these activities. Aim should be to match programme of setting up of STPs/ETPs having adequate treatment capacity with the total generation of sewage/effluent by the year 2030-2035. Right from the next year, major part of the fully treated urban sewage & industrial effluent should be pumped into canals for irrigation use. Balance quantity of the treated sewage & effluent should be released in the rivers as 'Environmental flow'. End objective of treatment of industrial effluent should be 'Zero effluent' by 2040.

Conclusions – Providing treatment only to part quantity of sewage generated after domestic use of water from cities, towns and villages, and its release in the rivers is the main cause of pollution of almost all rivers in India. According to The Central Pollution Control Board, only about 20% urban sewage in India is treated. The remaining about 80% raw sewage is flowing untreated into rivers and various water bodies. Untreated sewage component results in pollution & disease transmission. The urban sewage contains nitrates, phosphates, organic matter, and pathogens. Inadequately treated effluent after industrial use of water contains toxic chemicals, heavy metal compounds, & carcinogens. Water regenerated after irrigated agriculture contains harmful residues of chemical fertilisers, insecticides, and pesticides. Hence after all such use of water, partial or non-treatment of the effluent generated primarily contributes to pollution of most of the rivers. Such issues have emphasised the need not only for taking an integrated approach in the use of water for various purposes, but also for ensuring proper governance and instituting some mechanism for regulation on the development, use and integrated management of water for all its competing demands.

# Chapter 9
# Development, Augmentation, Use and Management of Ground Water Resource

*Besides the surface water, ground water is an important component of the Water Resource. Out of the rainwater, part is lost by evaporation, part of it percolates in the substrata as ground water and the rest of it flows through streams to rivers and finally to the sea. Quantity of water that gets absorbed in the ground firstly depends on the magnitude and intensity of the rain spells, and secondly on the land slope & type of substrata below the topsoil. Main advantage of ground water resource is that unlike surface water resource, it is free from loss due to evaporation. In India, harnessing of ground water is done by means of dug wells or bore wells, entirely in the private sector unlike the surface water resource development which is done entirely in the public sector. Use of ground water contributes significantly to the total area irrigated and ensures equitable use of water resource in a river basin, to achieve social justice. Micro Irrigation Systems (Drip and Sprinkler) can be effectively introduced on well Irrigation to increase its water-use efficiency and area under irrigation. Groundwater is available in shallow aquifers as well as in deep seated aquifers. Natural shallow ground water recharge can also be augmented by taking structural measures to conserve soil and rainwater where it falls on small size watersheds which are having in situ naturally decomposed non-alluvial sub strata. However, management of ground water becomes a very complex issue especially when the demand starts increasing in comparison with the limited & finite availability of the ground water. The chapter covers all these issues in detail.*

As mentioned earlier, Ground Water is the first savings account in the 'Bank of Nature', other savings account being that of the 'Snow in the temperate & tropical climatic region'. Substantial part of rainfall is lost by way of evaporation during and after it rains on the earth, and the part which percolates in the ground is known as Ground Water (GW). Rest of the rainwater flows along land slope initially as sheet flow over the ground and then into the streams, rivulets, rivers and finally into the sea. Obviously, the quantum of GW mainly depends on the magnitude of rainfall at any place. However, in the spells of rain having low intensity (less rain per unit of time), more water percolates in the sub strata and less water flows along the surface. On the contrary if intensity of the rain spells is high, more water flows along the surface before it gets chance to percolate below. Other important factor is slope of the land. If the land slope is steep, velocity of sheet flow is more, and hence less water percolates in the strata below. If the land slope is flatter, because velocity of flow is less, more water percolates in the strata below and less water flows over the surface. If the topsoil and the sub strata are pervious, more water percolates to recharge GW, but if it is impervious less water percolates below.

When land plants evolved to encroach on the land, they absorbed nutrients & rainwater from the topsoil to survive and thrive. In due course of time, gradually the decaying plant material increased organic contents in the topsoil, and soil became more and more fertile for the plant growth. Growth of seasonal plants checked sheet erosion of the topsoil caused due to rainwater. When grasses evolved later, they provided excellent cover on the soil to arrest sheet erosion of the topsoil nearly completely. These actions increased thickness of the layer of fertile soil at the top, which promoted evolution of bushes, shrubs, and then finally the big trees. Roots of big trees penetrated deep in the soil, sub strata, cracks, joints and crevices in the rock layers thereby gradually increasing thickness of the decomposed/fractured strata. This is how the terrestrial ecosystems evolved on the earth by surviving and thriving by absorbing nutrients, rainwater, and GW in the fair-weather season. Let us now see characteristics of the Ground Water Resource.

Ground Water Resource – GW resource has many different characteristics when compared with the surface water resource. Firstly, it exists below the ground and hence unlike the surface water resource, it is totally free from the evaporation loss. It primarily meets water needs and nutrient needs i.e., minerals, chemical and organic fertilisers, nitrogen compounds etc. dissolved in water in the upper layers of soil, for the growth of all shallow rooted plant life on the land. Rainwater firstly seeps in the topsoil to fill pores in it. GW remains stationery in the upper layer of the root zone due to capillary action. On its saturation water moves further downwards to fill voids in the soil and pores in the decomposed layer and then further below to fill cracks, crevices, and joints in the rock layers. When the sub stratum gets saturated and GW attains some steady level, it is known as Ground Water Table (GWT). GWT level increases when there is inflow of percolating rainwater from the surface. Stored GW then also starts flowing very slowly laterally/horizontally, towards the river which is at a level lower than the GWT. Hence GWT has very gradual slope towards rivulet or river and has its lower end at the steady water level in the river. When rain stops, moisture in the top layer of soil does not flow below to join GW but is held in the soil pores by the capillary action and is available for plant growth. Depth of such layer of moisture which is retained in the topsoil depends on fineness of soil particles & presence of organic matter (humus) in the soil. Its depth is generally more in clayey soils and is less in sandy soils. When moisture in this top layer is absorbed by the plants, water from GW below comes up by capillary action to take its place. Roots of big trees penetrate further deep into the substrata and into cracks and crevices in the rock below to absorb GW from there.

Sub strata is broadly of two types i.e., in situ decomposed rocky strata and the river transported alluvial strata. In the South and Central India at most of the places, parent base rock below the decomposed strata is of igneous rocks such as basalt, granite, schist etc., or rarely of sedimentary rocks. In due course of time (millions of years) such rocks got disintegrated because of daily variations in the atmospheric temperatures and due to seepage of water through cracks and crevices in the rock. These rocks were decomposed due to the action of chemicals dissolved in the rainwater seeping through the cracks & crevices. Such actions resulted in the formation of a layer at the top of the parent rock consisting of in situ decomposed material having its thickness depending on the type of rock, rainfall, and the ambient climate. Decomposition of rock is usually more in the tropical zone and less in the temperate zone. Soil at the top usually contains organic matter called as humus. GW occurrence in these fissured rock formations occupying nearly two-thirds of the geographical area of the country, is mostly limited to topsoil, weathered zone below it (called as soft murum and hard murum) and in the jointed & fractured portions of soft rock and hard rock below it.

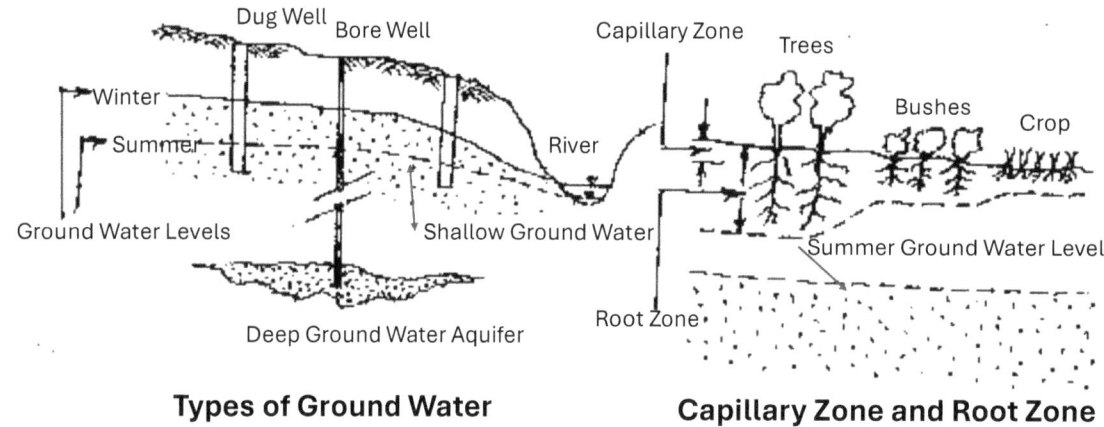

**Types of Ground Water**  **Capillary Zone and Root Zone**

Because of the above stated nature of rocky sub strata, GW availability in these shallow aquifers is limited, finite, discontinuous and is confined to a depth of about 20 to 30 meters, depending on the type of the sub strata. To exploit it for irrigation purposes, large diameter wells (10 to 15 meters) are dug, their depth depending on the location of GW availability. Since GW from all sides seeps into the well slowly, it gets stored in the large diameter well and can then be pumped out continuously or intermittently as per actual rate of inflow of GW into the well. Earlier, water used to be lifted from dug wells by means of bullock power and later by diesel operated centrifugal pumps. Now water from dug wells is lifted by installing electrically operated centrifugal pump installed in the well. Water in the shallow GW aquifers gets recharged every year during rainy season and it continues to flow through ground towards rivers all the year round till it depletes up to the riverbed level in summer season. If GW is exploited by digging a well, GWT gets temporarily lowered in its influence zone area. When the pumping stops, GWT in the influence zone of the well starts rising slowly and restores due to inflow from around or due to rainwater. When GWT goes below riverbed level due to overextraction from wells, river water recharges GW and raises GWT near it. Generally, it can be said that, besides the characteristics of precipitation in the area, magnitude of GW availability depends on permeability, retentivity, storability and transmissivity of the sub strata.

In this type of strata, GW occurs in shallow aquifers and also in deep aquifers. Shallow water aquifer is that, where GW flows downwards first and on saturation of the substrata, which flows very slowly towards the river. Shallow GW gets recharged/replenished in the same rainy season in every rain spell and in the next rainy season. In the Maharashtra state, depths of shallow GW aquifers are usually less than about 20 to 30 meters. It is, however, observed that, in this type of rocky sub strata, GW is also available at some places in rocky strata much below the shallow GW, which are called as deep GW aquifers. GW from shallow aquifers seeps further below very slowly through cracks and joints in the rock layers and gets stored in voids, joints, and crevices in the rock layers even up to a depth of 300 meters or more below the ground level. This process of accumulation of water in the form of deep GW may have taken thousands of years and the deep rocky strata having all its voids saturated with GW is called as 'Deep GW aquifer'. In the

Maharashtra state, such deep GW aquifers are usually met with below 50 meters and even up to 300 meters below the surface. It was not possible to harness it for human use till the technology and machinery for drilling deep bore wells up to 300 meters or more had evolved and was available for use. It was then possible to install casing pipe in the drilled bore only in the decomposed strata, fix multistage submersible pump at the bottom of the drill hole in rock and operate it with the availability of electricity network at the location. But GW availability in such aquifers is finite and it does not get recharged each year like the shallow GW aquifers. Hence exploitation of ground water from such deep GW aquifers is rightly called 'mining of water'. Identification of exact location of such deep GW storages is also not possible as per present technology and hence usually when several bores are drilled in the land holding of an individual cultivator, there is some possibility that one of the bores might tap the deep GW aquifer storage.

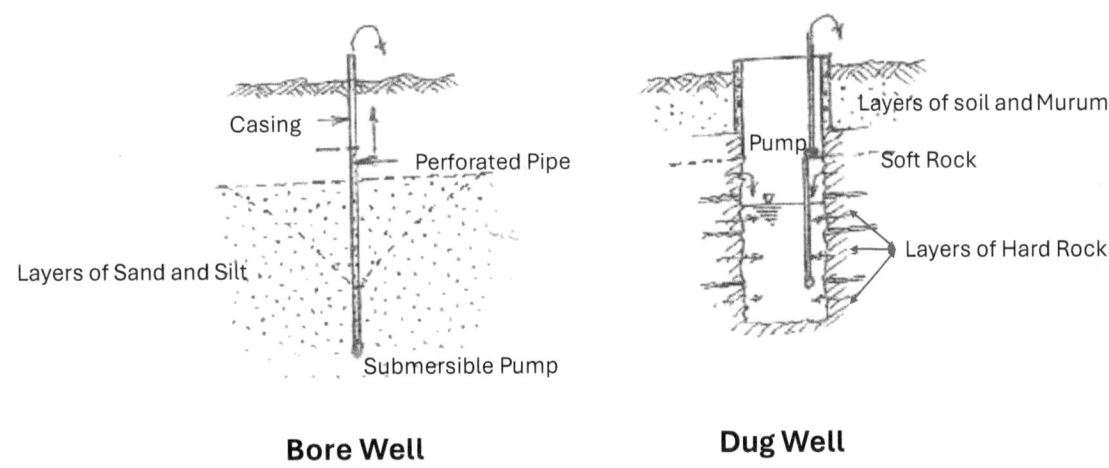

**Bore Well**    **Dug Well**

Other important source of GW is in the alluvial strata. In the Indo-Gangetic basin of the northern India, on downstream of the hill ranges of Himalayas, most of the strata in the vast plains consist of nearly horizontal layers of sand, gravel, and silt. These layers were formed by material transported by the Rivers Ganga, Sindhu, Brahamaputra and their tributaries into the ancient sea known as 'Tethys'. Depth of these layers of alluvial soil deposits is hundreds of meters at most of the places and is more than one kilo meter at many places. On downstream of the Himalayan ranges, the river basins have very flat land slopes. Enormous quantity of water has been stored in the Indo-Gangetic basin, and it is one of the largest GW storages in the World. Other nearly same size large GW storage in the World is Ogallala Basin spread over 0.45 million square km area, extended in eight states of the North America. Because the topsoil in the Indo-Gangetic basin is mostly silty, and land slopes are very flat, substantial part of the rainwater percolates into the ground to recharge GW. Recharge of GW also takes place continuously from the rivers and its tributaries from their beds and banks from the nearly horizontal layers of gravel, sand and silt. Hence GW in these alluvial river basins is contiguous, dependable, extensive, quantum-wise substantial and can be accessed from any place in the basin. Exploitation of GW used to be done in the past by constructing small diameter wells of masonry or precast concrete shells and lifting it by means of bullock power. In the twentieth century water could be pumped out by diesel engine operated centrifugal pumps. Subsequently where electricity was available, well water was lifted by electric motor driven centrifugal pumps. But due to over exploitation of GW in many such river basins in the recent past, GWT has now gone down appreciably at many places. It is hence essential now, to drill large diameter bores (20 to 30 cm) and install steel casing pipe having holes/perforations below the GWT level, for allowing continuous ingress of the GW from all sides into the bore well. Pumping of water is done with the help of an electrically operated multistage submersible pump installed at the bottom of the casing pipe. Since GW is naturally filtered, clean & potable, it was used for drinking and domestic use in all the villages, towns, and cities in the North India. It was also used for irrigating seasonal crops like wheat, rice, maize and perennial crops like sugar cane, banana, fruit gardens etc. Alluvial soils are also available in the North-West region in Rajasthan & Gujarat States (Extinct Saraswati River basin) but the availability of GW there is very poor due to very low rainfall in the area. Alluvial deposits are also there in the middle & lower reaches of Tapi & Purna river basins in the Peninsular India where availability of GW is fairly good. In the reaches on upstream of delta region of East flowing rivers in the Peninsular India, sub strata are of alluvial soils. For most of the rivers in the Central and South India, shallow alluvial soils are also met with locally along all the inner side banks of bends in the meandering rivers.

In comparison with the surface water resource, ground water resource has following advantages:

1. Because GW is stored below ground, there is no loss of water due to evaporation. This is a big advantage because more than 20% of the surface water is lost due to evaporation.

2. Command areas of all major and some medium projects are located in the narrow belts along the banks of major rivers where lands are flat, and soils are generally deep and fertile. Hence normally one crop in monsoon season can usually be grown there on the rains. Canal irrigation is generally provided for two seasonal or hot weather crops and for some percentage of perennial crops in the command areas. It means that we are providing irrigation to cultivators who are already assured of one crop and are not providing irrigation to cultivators in the upper reaches of river basins who are not assured of even one crop due to shallow & infertile soils. Some relief is, however, given by medium and minor projects to the land from the upper reaches. On the contrary, because GW is scattered all over the basin even in the upper reaches of watersheds, well irrigation benefits the cultivators in upper reaches to establish social justice by more equitable allocation of the water resource.

3. Very high investment for the development and management of surface water resource for construction of infrastructure of dams, canals, and distribution network has to be done under the public sector from the taxpayer's money. Secondly, revenue generated from the subsidised charges levied from the cultivators for the use of water for irrigation, barely meets the expenditure towards operation and maintenance of the projects. As against that, all investment for digging/drilling wells, installing electric motor-pump on it, paying for electricity charges etc., is done in the private sector by the cultivators. However, Govt. provides loans at low interest rates towards investment for digging/drilling wells and installing electric motor-pumps on it. Govt also bears capital investment cost for extending the electricity network in the rural area and for providing electricity at subsidised rates to the cultivators.

4. Water-use efficiency (ratio of water required by the crop and the water delivered at the canal head) of dam-canal systems is generally between 25 to 35%. As against that, water-use efficiency of well irrigation is high and lies between 60 to 70%. Hence more area can be irrigated from less consumption of GW.

5. Even if the crop consumes water every day for its growth, canal water is delivered once in every 15 to 20 days during the crop growth period. Hence there is water stress on the crop during the week before the next rotation of canal water. It affects crop growth and its yield. As against that, water from well can be delivered after every 3-4 days as per crop requirement and hence crop growth is better, crop maturity period reduces, and the crop yield improves.

6. Well irrigation is ideally amenable for introduction of Drip and Sprinkler irrigation i.e., Micro Irrigation Systems (MIS). Water pumped from wells can be conveyed through pipes on which laterals can be fixed for drip irrigation or sprinkler irrigation depending on the crops grown. It improves overall water-use efficiency even up to 80 to 90%. Area under irrigation increases by introducing MIS on well irrigation. Shed nets can also be used to grow high value crops.

Estimation of availability of Ground Water Resource – Estimation of GW assessment is rather a complex process. In the Maharashtra state, Groundwater Survey and Development Agency (GSDA) Pune, had started this work in the last decade of the twentieth century and published their first Assessment Report in the year 1998. The mechanism of assessment of availability of GW resource was continuously refined and finally area of the state was divided into 1529 small watersheds for the purpose of realistic GW assessment. In the state, about 80 percent area consists of watersheds formed by the in-situ decomposition of basalt and metamorphic rocks. Remaining watersheds, mainly in the Tapi river basin, are formed by alluvial material such as silt, sand and gravel carried and deposited by the river in nearly horizontal layers. Assessment of probable GW recharge in each small watershed is done every year based on its topography, type of substrata and rainfall record of nearest rain gauge station. If any such watershed is covered fully or partly by the command area of a surface irrigation scheme, estimation of likely recharge from deep percolation loss from actual irrigation is also done every year. Water levels in some dug wells in the representative watersheds are continuously monitored to assess actual GW recharge during every rainy season. Based on this information, annual quantum of GW recharge is first worked out for each small watershed. Then the GW recharge is compiled for each river basin/sub basin in the state. Probable GW recharge values were updated watershed wise in the Reports published by GSDA in the years 2004, 2007-08, 2008-09, 2011-12, 2013-14 etc. Since the year 1990, Govt. of Maharashtra has taken up watershed development works in the form of structural measures in many small watersheds below 250 to 350 ha each, to conserve water and soil to meet water and other needs of cultivators in the upper reaches of watersheds. It has increased artificial GW recharge in such watersheds. That is also accounted for in the calculations of annual recharge of GW by the GSDA.

Estimation of average annual natural GW recharge and usable recharge in India has been done by the Govt. of India, with the help of Central Ground Water Board, as below:

**Table No.1 - Average annual available and usable Ground Water recharge.**

| Rivers | Average Annual Natural GW recharge **Cubic Kilo meter** | Average usable Ground water recharge **Cubic Kilo meter** |
|---|---|---|
| East flowing | 357 | 396 (E & W flowing together) |
| West flowing | 75 | |
| **Total** | 432 | 396/432= (92%) |

Development and Management of Ground Water Resource – Source of GW is rainwater which falls on all the land to recharge GW. Hence logically every land holder should have proportionate right on the GW below his land. But then exploitation of GW by every individual cultivator becomes impractical and uneconomical especially due to heterogeneous aquifer within hard rocks and uncertain & discontinuous availability of GW. It may be possible when the aquifer is alluvial where GW is continuous and can be accessed from anywhere, but it may not be practical. At some places in the alluvial basins, big land holders drill deep bore wells, install high-capacity multistage pumps to irrigate their land, and then sell surplus available water to adjoining cultivators by charging as per the area irrigated or as per hours of pumping. It is a symbiotic operation benefitting both the parties. Because of such complex issues in the actual use of GW, instead of treating GW as a common pool resource, in almost all countries in the World, ownership of GW rests with the owner of the land who exploits the GW.

Up to the fifties of the last century, GW exploitation was not significant in India. Firstly, because water from wells was lifted by bullock power, and use of diesel pumps was limited and confined only in advanced states. Second reason for it was that average size of land holding per family was more than 5 hectares then and the produce could meet family needs, which incidentally were not much then of majority of the cultivators. Small & marginal land holders and landless families used to work for their livelihood as labourers in the farms of big land holders. However, in India 'Land Partition Act' had entitled every male child to have equal right on the land during transfer of landed property from one generation to the next generation. From the year 2005 due to modifications in the Act, even the female children also acquired equal right on the inherited landed property. Such land partition had resulted in gradual reduction in the size of family landholding, and the present average size of landholdings is less than 1.5 hectares. Naturally, now majority of the landowners are small and marginal land holders having land much less than 1.5 hectares. It then became very difficult to sustain the family with the agricultural produce generated from rain-fed cultivation with the reduced family landholding. With the development of the society, needs of the family also increased. Hence state Govts. on consideration of social justice, provided relief to the needy rural population by providing electricity at subsidised rates, granting loans for digging/drilling wells and for purchasing electric motor-pumps at low interest rates. After the 1971-73 severe drought in the Maharashtra state, rate of GW exploitation started increasing notably. Due to availability of machinery for drilling deep bores and that of the single stage/multistage submersible pumps, GW use increased appreciably from eighth decade of the last century and the trend continues thereafter even now.

About 30 to 40% area of the Maharashtra state, to the East of North-South Sahyadri ranges and lying in the rain shadow zone is drought prone. Harnessing of GW had provided much relief to the cultivators in the drought prone zone whose lands were located outside the command areas of irrigation projects. However, in due course of time, in some watersheds it resulted in over exploitation of GW exceeding the annual GW recharge. GW management is seen to be difficult in the drought prone area because of the inability to enforce restrictions on digging/drilling new wells. As a relief to such situation, 'Watershed Development' activities were taken up in such overexploited watersheds to augment GW recharge artificially as explained in paragraphs below. Some big landowners also drilled deep bore wells up to 300 meters or more to extract GW from deep aquifers. Because it was not possible to identify location of deep aquifers, they ventured to drill many such bores till they succeeded in tapping the deep GW aquifer even in one bore. It was then possible to recover cost of drilling of many bores, by taking cash crops like sugar cane, plantain, grapes etc., on the successful borewell and only if GW storage in the deep aquifer was enough to last for some years.

Except in villages located on the banks of big rivers, GW is the most common source or perhaps the only source for drinking water and domestic use in the rural areas of India. Most of the villages have one or more dug wells which provide water for drinking & domestic use for the villagers all the year round. Earlier, water was being lifted very commonly by manual labour. Later in some villages where water was adequate in the well, it was lifted by diesel/electric pumps and stored in tanks from where villagers could take it. Only in few large villages where water availability in the wells was adequate, water was delivered in houses by taps or through common public taps. For a group of villages on the plateau where GW availability was poor (difficult villages), water was pumped from nearby reservoir/river and was supplied to such villages by pipelines. However, during drought years when GW availability was insufficient due to poor natural GW recharge during that year, water from nearest reservoirs was pumped and supplied by water tankers to villages where the wells had gone dry. In fact, where water from deep aquifers was available near villages, it becomes a dependable source for drinking water in such villages. But indiscriminate exploitation of GW from deep aquifers by the influential cultivators for growing cash crops has become a problem in the management of GW in the Maharashtra state.

Even if enabling Acts were passed and Rules for harnessing/regulating use of GW were framed, their implementation at the ground level became very difficult. Govt. of Maharashtra (GoM) had proposed a comprehensive Act in the year 2009, which was approved by the Govt. of India in 2014, and it came into force as 'Maharashtra Groundwater (Development and Management) Act 2009-14'. Rules for the same have also been finalised by GoM but are yet to be passed. To ensure integrated development and management of water resource, GoM had passed an Act in the year 2005 and established 'Maharashtra Water Resource Regularity Authority (MWRRA) in the year 2005. Initially it was looking only after surface water resource. Subsequently, with a view to monitoring and regulating the development and management of GW in view of the provisions of the above GW Act passed in 2014, a separate post of 'Member Groundwater' was created in MWRRA in October 2017. Unfortunately, the post is not filled so far due to some Court litigation.

**Institutions looking after the work of Groundwater Development and Management –**

**Central Ground Water Board, New Delhi** - For ensuring 'Sustainable Development and Management of Ground Water Resources of the Country' Central Ground Water Board (CGWB) was established in the year 1970 under the Ministry of Jal Shakti, Department of Water Resources, Govt. of India. It is the National Apex Agency entrusted with the responsibilities of providing scientific inputs for management, exploration, monitoring, assessment, augmentation, and regulation of ground water resources of the country. The Board has 18 Regional offices, supported by 17 Engineering Divisions and 11 State Unit Offices for undertaking various field activities. Subsequently, Central Ground Water Authority (CGWA) was constituted under the Environment (Protection) Act, 1986 for the purposes of regulation and control of GW development and management in the country. The Authority is engaged in various activities related to regulation of GW development to ensure its long-term sustainability.

GW Resources Assessment is carried out at periodical intervals jointly by state GW Departments and CGWB under the guidance of the respective State Level Committees on GW Assessment at state levels and under the overall supervision of the Central Level Expert Group. Such joint exercises have been taken up earlier in 1980, 1995, 2004, 2009, 2011, 2013, 2017 and 2020. Based on such study carried out after 2020, a Report has been published as *'National compilation on Dynamic Ground Water Resources of India'* in October 2022. The assessment involves computation of dynamic GW resources or Annual extractable GW resource, total current annual GW extraction (utilization) and the percentage of utilization with respect to annual extractable resources (stage of GW extraction). The assessment units (Tahsils/sub tahsils) are categorized based on stage of GW extraction, which are then validated with long-term water level trends.

Salient findings of this Report are as under:

Availability of GW in India and status of GW Extraction

1. Total Annual GW Recharge –              438 bcm
2. Annual Extractable GW Resources –       398 bcm (60% of GW recharge)
3. Annual GW Extraction –                  239 bcm
4. Stage of GW Extraction –                60%

bcm - billion cubic meters which is equal to cukm – cubic kilo meter.

For making realistic estimation of GW availability and present state of extraction of GW, the country was divided in 7089 Assessment Units. Details of the findings as stated in the above Report are as under:

**Table 2 - Categorisation of Assessment Units**

| Sr No. | Category | Number of Assessment Units | | Recharge worthy Area in | | Annual Extractable GW Resource | |
|---|---|---|---|---|---|---|---|
| | | lakh sqkm | % | (in bcm) | % | Number | % |
| 1 | Safe | 4780 | 67 | 16.18 | 66 | 292 | 73 |
| 2 | Semi Critical | 885 | 13 | 3.03 | 12 | 47 | 12 |
| 3 | Critical | 260 | 4 | 0.77 | 3 | 13 | 3 |
| 4 | Over-Exploited | 1006 | 14 | 4.30 | 17 | 46 | 12 |
| 5 | Saline | 158 | 2 | 0.4 | 2 | NA | NA |
| | **Total** | **7089** | **100** | **24.69** | **100** | **398** | **100** |

The main source of replenishable GW resources is recharge from rainfall, which contributes to nearly 61 % of the total annual GW recharge. India receives about 1190 mm of rain annually on average, with high spatial variation from about 400 mm to 2500 mm. With an extraction of about 239 bcm/cukm of GW per year, our country uses about 20-25 percent of all GW extracted globally, ahead of USA and China. Because more than 60 to 70 percent of irrigated land in agriculture today is from GW as source, it will remain the lifeline of India's water supplies for years to come.

**Groundwater Surveys and Development Agency - GSDA, Pune (Maharashtra)** – In view of project agreement between International Development Association and Government of Maharashtra Groundwater Surveys & Development Agency (GSDA) was established during the year 1972, for the development of minor irrigation schemes based on groundwater. GSDA is engaged, in the exploration, development and augmentation of groundwater resources in the state through various schemes. This mainly includes rendering technical guidance under minor irrigation programme by locating suitable dug well sites, strengthening of groundwater sources by water conservation measures, artificial recharge projects for induced and drilling of bore wells/tube wells under Rural Water Supply Programme.

Based on the Overestimation Committee Report, first scientific GW resource assessment of Maharashtra was done in the year 1979. After due considerations of limitations in the earlier methodologies, GW Estimation Committee proposed revised methodology known as GEC 97. It was subsequently revised, which was known as GEC 2015 Methodology. Exercise of estimation of GW Resource in Maharashtra was done in 2004, 2007-8, 2008-9, 2011-12 and 2013-14 as per earlier CGWB guidelines. Estimation of GW Resource was then done in 2017, 2020 and 2022, based on GEC 2015 norms.

*'REPORT on the Dynamic Groundwater Resources of Maharashtra 2022'* prepared jointly by GSDA and CGWB has been published in the year 2023. Salient findings of the Report are as below:

Maharashtra State has geographical area of 3,08,000 sqkm of which about 62,000 sqkm (20%) is under forest. About 81% area is having basalt (Deccan Trap) as base rock, 13% having other types of rocks and 6% has alluvial strata. East flowing Godavari River basin occupies 49.8% area & Krishna River basin occupies 22.6% area. West flowing Tapi River basin occupies 16.8% area & West flowing coastal rivers occupy 10.8% area. Net sown area is about 188 sqkm and gross cropped area is about 232 sqkm. Present population is 112.4 million of which 45% is urban and 55% is rural. For administrative purposes, State has been divided in 36 Districts and 357 Talukas (sub districts). There are 336 cities & towns of which 40 have population more than 1,00,000. There are 40,785 villages and 45,528 hamlets (group of huts).

For the sake of estimation of GW, the state has been divided in 1,635 watersheds. Hilly area having land slope more than 20% is not considered for the purpose of estimation of GW recharge from rainwater. To monitor actual GW recharge, there are about 3920 observation wells from which water level is recorded in January, March, May, and September/October each year. Besides natural recharge of GW by rainfall, estimation of recharge of GW by canals of surface irrigation schemes, GW irrigation & other Water Conservation measures is also done each year. In the year 2022, GW recharge from rainfall and other sources was estimated as 21.26 bcm & 11.03 bcm, totalling to 32.29 bcm. Maharashtra State has about 2100 completed large dams, i.e., about 40% of the 5300 large dams in India. Irrigation potential of about 84 lakh hectares has been created by major, medium, and minor irrigation projects in the state. GW recharge is also augmented by watershed development works. Hence total GW recharge from the completed surface irrigation projects, tanks & ponds, water conservation structures, and GW irrigation is substantial being 11.03 bcm, which is 34% of the total GW annual recharge. Out of the non-rainfall components of artificial GW recharge biggest contributor (46%) is surface irrigation projects. After deducting natural discharge of 1.84 bcm, annual extractable GW works out to 30.45 bcm. Actual abstraction in the year 2022 was about 16.65 bcm i.e., about 54.66% of the extractable GW resource.

1. Number of bore wells - for irrigation 3.56 lakhs, for domestic use 1.71 lakhs.
2. Number of dug wells - for irrigation 20.83 lakhs, for domestic use 2.16 lakhs.
3. Number of wells for industrial use – dug wells 180, bore wells 620.

In the year 2022, annual GW recharge and actual extraction of GW in the State is as below:

1. Annual GW recharge - 32.29 bcm
2. Extractable GW recharge - 30.45 bcm
3. Total extraction at present - 16.65 bcm
4. Total extraction for irrigation use - 15.29 bcm
5. Total extraction for domestic use - 1.36 bcm

(Extraction for industrial use is negligible)

During assessment of GW availability and actual extraction it was observed that, in some watersheds extraction of GW was more than the annual recharge. Present status of GW exploitation i.e., percentage of annual GW extraction with that of the annual GW recharge in the 353 talukas is as below:

1. Over exploited i.e., > 100% -    watersheds from    11 Talukas.
2. Critical – Between 90 to 100% -    watersheds from    7 Talukas.
3. Semi critical – Between 70 to 90% -    watersheds from    62 Talukas.
4. Safe – Below 70% -    watersheds from    272 Talukas.
5. Saline –        1 Taluka
6. **Total -**        **353 Talukas.**

Augmentation of Ground Water – From the fifth and sixth decades of the last century, many states in India had taken up measures to conserve soil by preventing its erosion due to rains. States of Maharashtra, Gujarat, Tamil Nadu, Karnataka and Andhra Pradesh had carried out this activity on a large scale. It was observed that, fine particles from soil were getting washed away from the surface due to sheet erosion that was taking place with the rainwater. In the long run, it reduced thickness of the topsoil layer and fertility of the soil. Proportion of soil loss increased with slope of the land and extent of such loss in the Maharashtra state would be seen from the Table below:

**Table 3 - Soil Erosion Potential Status in Maharashtra**

| Sr. No | Category | Range of soil loss in tonne/ha/yr | Area |
|---|---|---|---|
| 1 | Very slight to Slight | <10 | 112 lakh ha |
| 2 | Moderate to Severe | 10 to 20 | 110 lakh ha |
| 3 | Severe to Extremely severe | >20 | 70 lakh ha |
|  |  | **Total** | **292 lakh ha** |
| Total area of Maharashtra state - |  |  | 307 lakh ha |

(Source – *'Initiative to make Maharashtra Soil and Water Secure'*, by Soil and Water Conservation Department, Government of Maharashtra)

To arrest erosion of the soil, activity of providing 'Contour bunds' in the cultivable land was taken up by the Agriculture Deptt. of GoM. It is an important measure that conserves soil and water in the arid and semi-arid areas with high infiltration & permeability and is commonly adopted on agricultural land up to a slope of about 6%. Contour bunding consists of building earthen embankments having their crest at one level across the slope of the land by following the contour as closely as possible, to act as barriers to the free flow of water, thus reducing velocity of the runoff and the amount of soil loss with the rainwater. Contour bunds can save soils from erosion to the extent of 25 to 160 tonnes/hectare annually. It conserved & maintained soil fertility, and increased water infiltration into the soil considerably. Contour bunds are not provided in deep black soils because they crack during hot weather season. Poor drainage properties of black soils also give rise to long stagnation of water against contour bunds and make them unstable. At the end of these bunds on either side, passages are made which are lined with stones for the excess rainwater to flow below and finally into the natural streams. Work of constructing contour bunds had provided employment to the needy landless labourers during the fair-weather months when there was no work for them in the farms.

**Watershed Development Works** – In the seventies and eighties of the last century, some enlightened and creative minded social workers visualised the idea of constructing structures in small watersheds, to conserve water at the place where it rained, to augment natural GW recharge. With the cooperation of the stakeholders, they implemented some such small water conservation works on streams through involvement of the beneficiaries, to complement large size water storage schemes taken up by Govt. and to increase GW recharge. They convinced and induced stakeholders to make equitable use of GW for providing protective irrigation to seasonal crops to benefit many cultivators in the watersheds. One such similar scheme was also taken up at the same time by the Soil & Water Conservation Deptt. of GoM. Looking to the benefits of these schemes to the small and marginal land holders in the upper reaches of small watersheds, from the year 1990 GoM decided to take up even such small water conservation works on a large scale, through soil & water conservation Deptt. Brief details of various types of engineering structures which form part of the 'Watershed Development Programme' implemented by the GoM are as below:

1. Stone bunds – Close to the ridge line of watersheds where stream slopes are steep and soil depth is less, stone bunds are constructed across streams. They arrest coarse soil particles, but the rainwater passes through them below. Gradually, coarse material gets conserved, and the stream slope gets flattened due to siltation on their upstream.

2. Earthen bunds – Further downstream across all streams, earthen bunds are constructed, to store some water on their upstream. Excess rainwater flows on downstream from the waterway provided on its one bank. Stored water continuously recharges GW, and when water level depletes, it gets replenished during the next rain spells during entire rainy season. Silt also gets accumulated on upstream, which is required to be removed every 3-4 years to restore storing and GW recharging capacity of the water stored against the bunds. The silt is spread in the fields to improve land fertility.

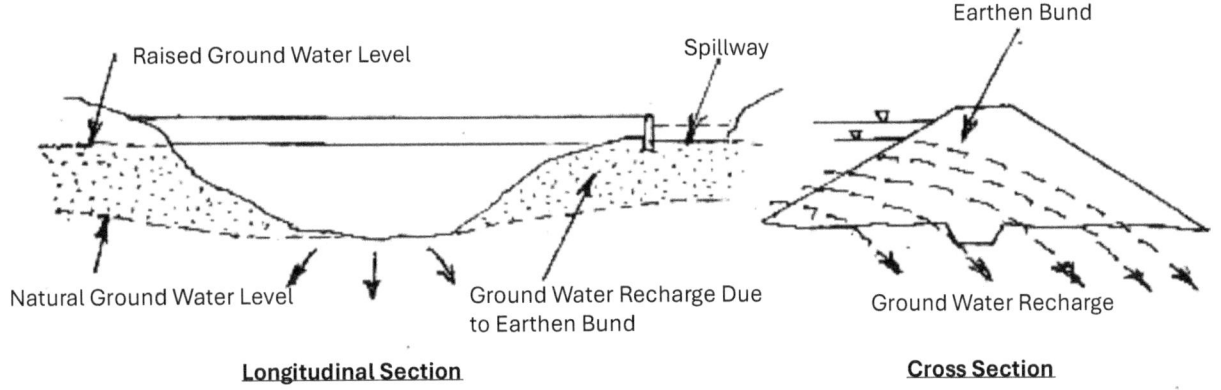

**Earthen Bund to Recharge Ground Water**

3. Masonry bandharas (weirs) –

In the lower reaches of streams where beds are shallow and land slopes are flatter, masonry bandharas are constructed if foundation rock is not very deep. Some openings are kept in them for the rolling silt to flow downstream with the flood water. These openings are closed by wooden needles/planks or with sand filled gunny bags at the end of monsoon season. Water then gets stored up to crest level of the bandhara and recharges GW on either bank of the stream during monsoon and the fair-weather season. Silt accumulated in the stream bed is required to be removed after every 3-4 years as above to restore GW recharging capacity of the bandhara. At some places where foundation rock is deep seated, Gabian bandharas (stone bandhara bounded by steel grill) or temporary bandharas consisting of layers of sand filled gunny bags are also constructed to serve the same purpose.

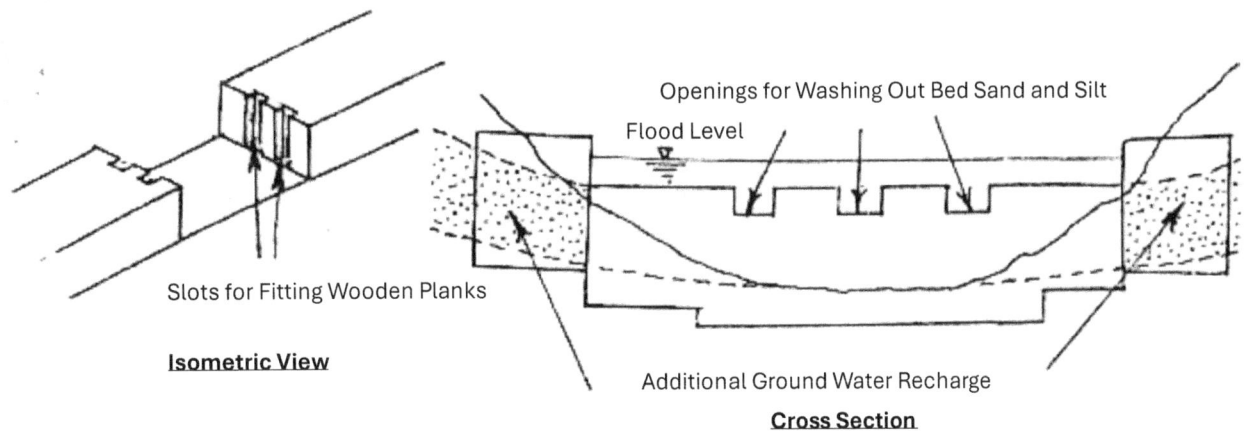

**Masonry Bandhara**

4. Underground bandharas – Where streams are shallow, foundation rock is very deep and bed material is sandy or pervious, a trench is dug in the riverbed and is backfilled with compacted soil to form an underground bandhara. It does not increase natural flood level and does not submerge additional land during floods, unlike earthen bunds and masonry bandharas. Water gets conserved below the stream bed on upstream side, which recharges GW on either bank

on the stream up to stream bed level. GW so stored can then be lifted and used for irrigation or other purposes.

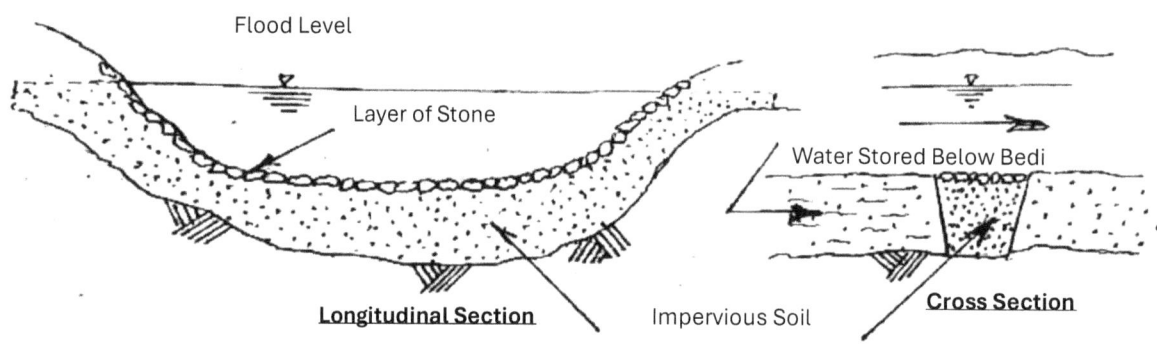

**Underground Bandhara**

5. Percolation tanks –

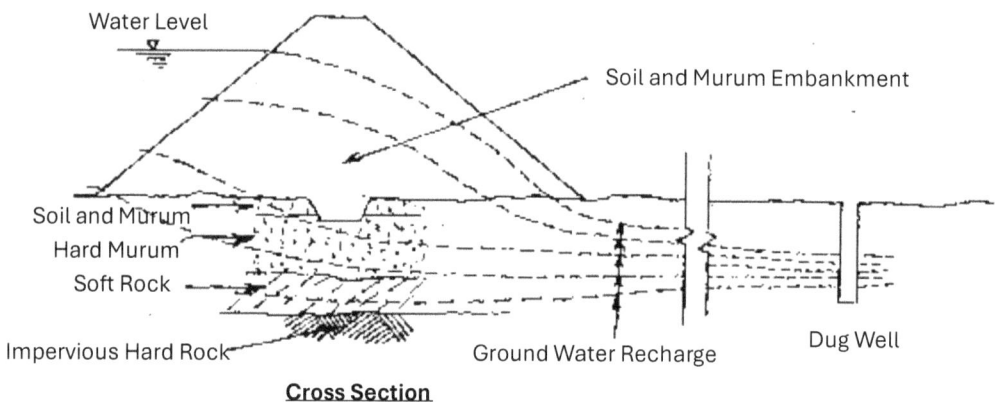

**Percolation Tank**

In further lower reaches of streams, small earthen dams of standard cross section, with a designed spillway are constructed to store substantial quantity of water. A shallow cutoff trench is provided below the earth dam in the stream bed, which allows safe seepage of stored water in the dam from below it towards downstream to recharge the stream bed and strata on downstream further. Stored water also recharges GW on either bank of the stored water on the upstream side. Water seeping from below both banks of the dam recharges GW for a considerable length on its downstream. As the lake level goes down due to such continuous seepage during monsoon season, it rises again during the next rain spells. Rate of seepage from tank bed gradually reduces due to accumulation of silt in the tank bed. Hence the silt conserved in the lake is required to be removed after every 3-4 years to restore GW recharging capacity of the percolation tank.

All the above water and soil conservation measures are taken on streams in the watersheds at specific locations as indicated above. To conserve rainwater and prevent sheet erosion of soil from the land, besides the contour bunding as explained above, following measures are taken on the land between the two streams.

7. Contour Trenches – They consist of digging continuous or discontinuous trenches on the land which is having somewhat steep slopes in the upper reaches of the watersheds where soil cover is also thin. Excavated material from the trenches is laid on downstream side of the trenches to form a continuous earth bank. Trees could be planted on their lower side, which can provide fodder for cattle and some firewood for cooking to the villagers in due course of some years. What is required is to nurture these trees at least for the first 3-4 years and protect them from the four legged and 'two legged animals' all the time. Spacing between rows of contour trenches depends on the land slope. Rainwater & soil flowing with it fills the trench and excess water flows from both ends of the trenches into the lower trenches. Water conserved in the trenches continuously recharges GW. Silt conserved in the trenches is to be removed and placed on the earth bank every 3-4 years to restore GW recharge capacity of the trenches.

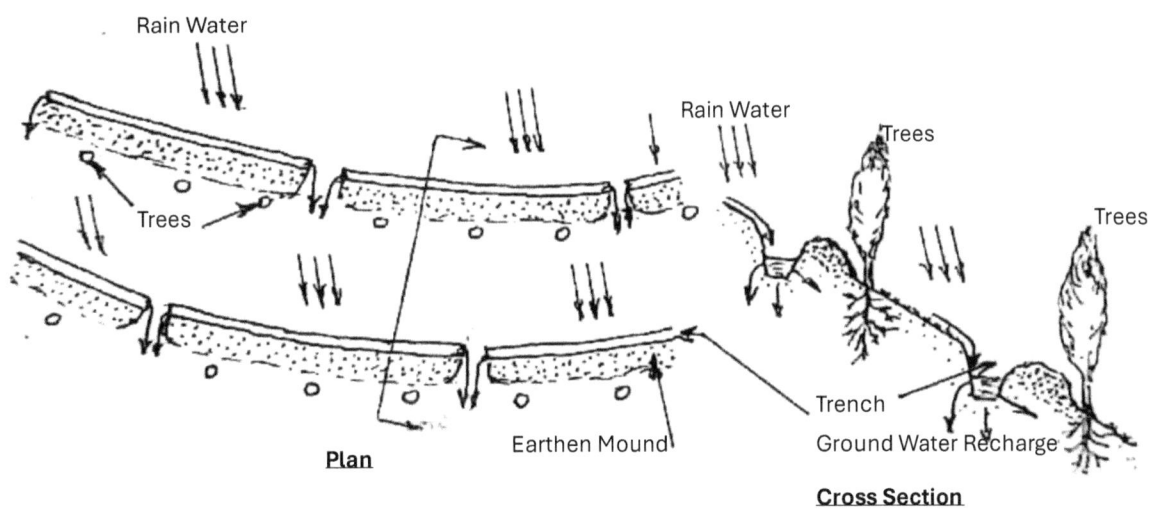

**Discontinuous Trench-Cum-Mound Construction**

6. Farm ponds –

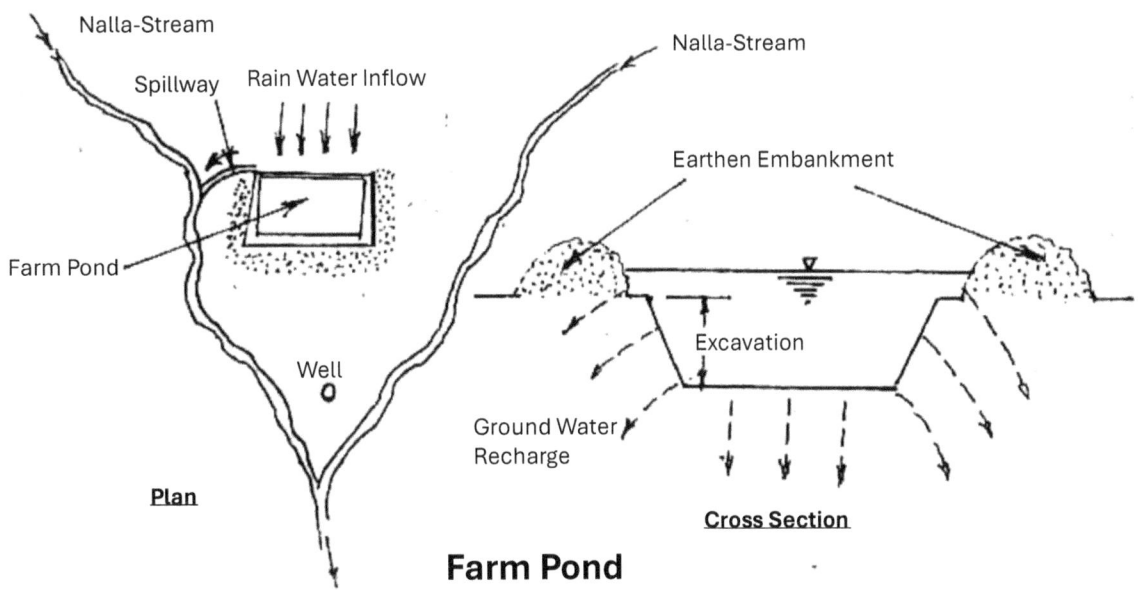

**Farm Pond**

Farm ponds are constructed on land preferably on upstream of confluence of two streams. A rectangular shaped pond is excavated, and the material is dumped on three sides as shown in the sketch. Rainwater from its catchment which enters from the fourth side gets stored in the pond to recharge GW on the lower side. Excess rainwater flows from one side of the pond into the stream. If a shallow well is dug on downstream side of the pond, its water can be used for providing protective irrigation to the crop at the end of rainy season. Sometimes storage capacity of the pond is increased, and it is provided with plastic sheet lining to store water pumped from a nearby river and use it to irrigate rabi crop. There are schemes to provide subsidy for providing such lined farm ponds. Silt due to sheet erosion gets stored in the pond and is required to be removed every 3-4 years to restore GW recharging capacity of the unlined pond.

Activity of 'Watershed Development Programme' has been taken up in the Maharashtra state on a large scale since 1990 as a Govt. scheme. Even then, it should be kept in mind that real benefits of increased GW recharge are possible only if they are shared equitably by maximum number of cultivators by providing them with one or two protective irrigations to seasonal crops. Some wells which are benefitted by the increased GW recharge should be reserved exclusively for drinking water use in the benefitted villages. However, it is observed that in many villages such cooperation in sharing the benefits is not there. Few influential cultivators only grow high value crops on their wells. With the result desired benefits of the scheme are not realised in practice. Hence it is necessary to select at random, some completed watershed development schemes in the state and make impartial/realistic third-party assessment of their actual performance in achieving the planned objective of equitable sharing of the benefits. This work of performance review should be entrusted to Agriculture Universities and some Non-Govt. Organisations (NGO) working in the water sector. It would indicate the need to do introspection, explore rectification measures to improve their performance and implement them. It would also provide good feedback to enable finalising revised guidelines for future watershed development works.

Conclusion – Groundwater is a very valuable resource which is free from evaporation loss and is naturally available at most of the places in a river basin to achieve equity in water resource allocation. All development of this resource is done entirely in the private sector. Govt. have only to spend on various subsidies given to the farmers to promote harnessing of the GW. Water-use efficiency of well irrigation is much higher than the surface irrigation schemes, which are developed entirely in the public sector. Well irrigation is easily amenable to adoption of use of Micro Irrigation Systems, which can improve the water-use efficiency up to 85-90%. It is also possible to artificially augment the GW by taking structural measures in mini watersheds where the sub strata are suitable. However, it is necessary to ensure that the GW does not get polluted because, once polluted it is very difficult to restore it to normal conditions. By and large it can be said that management and regulation of GW is the most difficult part in the use of this valuable water resource.

# Chapter 10
# Governance and Regulation on the Development, Use and Management of the Water Resource

*Water Resource is amenable for its Development and Management to meet human needs of water. Besides the basic need of drinking water, other main need is for domestic & drinking use of water. Next was the need of water to irrigate land for increasing crop productivity and ensuring food security. Last one was the need of water for industries, in that order. As the population of humans increased on the earth and various developmental activities as above were started by man, water demand continued to rise incessantly. It was met with by constructing necessary infrastructure for the development of water resource. But availability of water in any river basin was finite on an average, and there were natural limitations on the sites for construction of the development infrastructure. Hence issues such as ensuring optimum and equitable development & management of available water resource cropped up while responding to the dynamics of the competing and rising water demands. All river basins are formed as per natural topography, but because land of the major river basins is usually divided in some countries and states, it also attracted the issues related to equitable sharing of the finite water resource in the river basins amongst them. Inadequate treatment of the effluent after non irrigation use gave rise to the problem of pollution of rivers and even of some man-made reservoirs. On social considerations, issues related to sharing the benefits of water equitably amongst most of the people, had also to be settled amicably. To ensure that all such interrelated complex issues in the development and management of water were settled satisfactorily, some sort of governance and if necessary, some regulation, on the same was also seen to be essential. To resolve all such issues, some actions were taken by the Central Govt. and some by the Maharashtra Govt. The chapter covers all these aspects in detail.*

Aquatic ecosystems were the first to evolve on the earth in oceans and then in the rivers & natural lakes. Subsequently, terrestrial ecosystems evolved, developed, and stabilised in different parts of the earth, always being compatible to the prevailing climate, location, altitude, precipitation, & subsoil characteristics. During the last 3650 million years these ecosystems responded to the gradual or sudden changes in the climate and precipitation, caused by the ice ages or mass extinctions. Even after evolution of human genus about 3 mya, humans remained a part of the terrestrial ecosystems for quite some time, just like other animals. Nature was regulating and managing all the activities for sustaining life (*flora and fauna*) on the earth. These things started changing from about 12,000 years ago when 'modern man' started growing pastures to feed domesticated cattle and later when he started cultivating land to grow food grains. To make the forest land suitable for crop cultivation, the 'Slash and Burn' technique adopted by him caused quantitative destruction of forest land i.e., natural terrestrial ecosystems. However, hazardous effects of resulting carbon emissions causing 'Global Warming and Climate Change' and stoppage of carbon sequestration which was naturally taking place by the woody trunks and branches of the cut trees, was realised only in the latter half of the twentieth century. Development of the natural water resource for irrigation was the next milestone achieved by man. **It may be difficult to realise and accept, but it can be said in retrospect that, increase in the land productivity caused because of the increased irrigation facilities had appreciably reduced the rate of destruction of forest land for cultivation, thereby preventing further destruction of forest land for agriculture.** Ponded paddy cultivation and tending of flatulent domestic animals had increased emission of methane gas in the atmosphere, which is a more potent 'Green House Gas' than the carbon dioxide. However, awareness about it came only in the latter half of the twentieth century as above.

From the eighteenth century onwards, industrialisation and consequent urbanisation had increased location-specific demand of water, which had to be fulfilled from highly dependable sources of water such as perennial rivers and large reservoirs. Industrialisation, urbanisation and growth of transport sector also increased carbon and other Green House Gas emissions. Totally inadequate treatment of effluent generated after non-irrigation use of water and its release into rivers had caused severe pollution of most of the rivers in India and so also in most of the developing countries. Use of such polluted river water by lifting it for irrigation by the needy cultivators along the riverbanks had resulted not only in contamination of the agriculture produce but also that of the groundwater in such areas. Polluted river water also entered in some reservoirs on downstream and polluted them as well. Problems arising out of development & management of water resource and their adverse effects on global warming and climate change have been covered in a separate chapter. Problems related to inadequacies in the optimum & equitable development of water resource and that of the regional imbalance created during the water related development, had to be resolved amicably. Need for environmental considerations during construction of WR development infrastructure and severe pollution of aquatic ecosystems caused due to inadequate treatment of urban and industrial effluent were the other problems to be dealt with. All these issues have been covered in detail in this chapter. It is also elaborated as to how far the governance and regulation on WR development and management was effective in achieving these objectives.

Governance on Water Resource Development at the country level – India has been divided in 39 States as at present. As per Constitution of India, the subject 'Water' has been assigned as a 'State subject'. Hence every state is permitted to develop WR available in their state in the manner they desire to plan and harness to meet their water needs. However, for international river basins like Indo-Gangetic River basins in the North India, available WR needs to be shared by the co-basin countries in view of provisions of the International Agreements signed between them. For sharing water resource of Sindhu (Indus) river, 'Indus Waters Treaty', was signed on 19$^{th}$ September 1960, between India and Pakistan and brokered by the World Bank. The Treaty, however, was effective from 1$^{st}$ April 1960. The treaty had fixed and delimited the rights and obligations of both countries concerning the use of waters of the Indus River system. The treaty gave the waters of the western rivers - the Indus, Jhelum, and Chenab - to Pakistan and those of the eastern rivers - the Ravi, Beas, and Sutlej - to India. In the year 1977, the Ganges Waters Agreement was negotiated between India and Bangladesh, which regulated water distribution for five years. Subsequently, a

Treaty was signed between India and Bangladesh on the 12$^{th}$ of December 1996 on the sharing of Ganga (Ganges) River waters. The Treaty shall remain in force for a period of thirty years, to be renewable by mutual consent.

A Treaty known as "Mahakali Treaty" concerning the integrated development of the Mahakali River, was signed between India and Nepal on the 12$^{th}$ of February 1996. A Memorandum of Understanding (MoU) was signed between India and China to share hydrological information such as rainfall and water level of the Brahmaputra River. Even if China makes full use of Brahmaputra River water within their territory, India will have sufficient water from the catchment within its territory. Secondly, storage dams on the Brahmaputra River in India are difficult due to submergence of rich forest land. A Joint Expert Team was formed in 1979 to review the progress of scheme for the Forecasting Network on rivers common to India and Bhutan. A scheme titled "Comprehensive Scheme for Establishment of Hydro-meteorological and Flood Forecasting Network on rivers Common to India and Bhutan" is in operation since 1992. Many hydroelectric projects in Bhutan were designed, planned, financed, and constructed by India. Most of the environment friendly electricity generated from them is supplied to and used in India by paying the actual electricity use charges to Bhutan. Because of this symbiotic relationship, generated hydropower meets needs of electricity of India and the revenue from selling electric power to India is a major source of income in the economy of Bhutan. These are the actions taken by the GoI to ensure equitable allocation of WR available in the international rivers amongst the co-basin countries.

Many river basins in the Central and Peninsular India are Interstate River basins. For the interstate rivers, surface WR in the river basin can be shared by all co-basin states as per mutual agreements between them. If they cannot come to a mutual agreement, there is a provision in the Constitution of India that, GoI would set up a River Water Disputes Tribunal (RWDT) before which each co-basin state shall put forth their water demands duly giving supporting justification for the same. RWDT examines all such demands by all the co-basin states and declares their final Award which allocates specific quantum of water to each state, usually subject to some conditions. Provisions in the Award are binding on all the co-basin states. If the estimates of water availability in the basin at the time of RWDT deliberations were based on insufficient hydrological and other data, or for any other valid reasons, sometimes there is a provision in some such Awards to review the water availability and the state wise allocations made in the Award after a period of some 15-20 years, by setting up a new RWDT. This is how equitable allocation of WR available in the interstate rivers is done amongst the co-basin states.

Under these circumstances, it was essential to ensure that WR development projects in all states in the country were planned and designed by following a uniform standard practice. Hence Irrigation and Power Department of GoI had set up Central Water and Power Commission (CWPC) to issue standard guidelines for planning and designing all WR development projects and to monitor compliance of these guidelines by of all the states. CWPC had prepared detailed guidelines for estimation of water availability in the river basin, planning the storage capacity of reservoirs, and estimation of design flood for spillways etc., for Major projects (each irrigating more than 10,000 hectares). Project Report of each Major project prepared by the state Govts. as per these guidelines was to be submitted to CWPC, New Delhi. CWPC would review the Project Reports, get them modified if necessary and then would give clearance to the same. Then only the states could give 'Administrative Approval' to the projects and take up the work by making provision in the state budget. For Medium projects (each irrigating between 10,000 to 2000 ha.) in the states, CWPC would only review the planning of water allocation & its use and give clearance to the projects. States would then prepare Project Report with detailed estimates of various components and give administrative approval to them. For Minor projects (each irrigating below 2000 ha.) giving clearance and administrative approval to them was fully the responsibility of the states. For interstate rivers, provisions in the RWDT Award would guide and limit the total use of water by means of all projects in the state.

National Project of Interlinking of Rivers in India i.e., Inter Basin Water Transfer (ILR/IBWT) – With a view to sharing the water resources available in different river basins in the country in an equitable manner by all the river basins/states, following actions were taken by the GoI. There is large variation in the precipitation pattern in India. Indo-Gangetic basin in the Northern part of the country is relatively water-surplus (please see maps in chapter 3) and there is chronic scarcity in the North-West region of the country. There is heavy precipitation in the North-East region of the country and in the narrow strip along the coastline to the West of North-South running Sahyadri mountain range. Sizeable area in the Peninsular India, lying towards East in the rain shadow zone of Sahyadri range is drought prone. By and large, most of the river basins in the South India are relatively water-short basins whereas water availability in the central India is reasonably good. Due to such large variations in the precipitation pattern in the country, necessity of linking the water-surplus rivers in the North with the water-short rivers in the South was felt in the sixth decade of the last century. Such measures would bring equity in the allocation & availability of water for human use and bring better opportunities in respect of the water related development of the population living in water-short river basins.

Situation as explained above challenged ingenuity of many engineers and number of schemes to link northern rivers with southern rivers emerged on the national scene. First well drafted proposal was that of engineer Dr. K.L. Rao in the year 1972, who happened to be the Minister Irrigation in the GoI then. His proposal comprised linking Ganga River in the North with Cauvery River in the South by a 2640 km long canal having capacity of 1,430 cumecs (about 50,000 cusecs) of water, to irrigate about 4 million hectares of land in the Peninsular India. It involved lifting of water over 550 meters, but only to be operative during 5 months of the year. This was because of the necessity to have some minimum flow during summer season for functioning of the Hugli port on downstream in the Ganga River. Such lifting of water required about 5000 to 7000 MW electric power. High capital cost & heavy recurring expenses on electric power, made the proposal economically unviable.

Next one was by Capt. Dastur in the year 1974 titled as 'Garland canal scheme'. It consisted of collecting & storing water of most of the Himalayan rivers by means of a 4200 km long canal constructed along southern slopes of Himalaya Mountain ranges. Level of the canal was kept at such an altitude, which would make it possible to deliver the water beyond the Vindhya and Satpuda mountain ranges in the central India by gravity by means of an inverted siphons starting from New Delhi & Patna (5 rows of steel pipes of diameter 3.7 m at both the places). It thus envisaged dispensing with the pumping of water altogether and avoiding its heavy recurring expenses. The water would then provide irrigation during 12 months of the year to the land from the central & peninsular India by a 9300 km long canal. Two committees appointed by the GoI, however, concluded the scheme to be technically infeasible & economically unviable.

Since Inter-basin water transfer from water-surplus basins to the water-short basins had the potential to mitigate floods in the North & droughts in the South, a draft of necessary actions to be taken to achieve it was prepared by the Ministry of Irrigation, New Delhi in the year 1980. Same was discussed & deliberated upon in the National Development Council, having all Chief Ministers of the states as members & Hon. Prime Minister of India as the chairman. As per their recommendations, The National Water Development Agency (NWDA), an Autonomous Society was constituted in the year 1982 to carry out detailed survey & investigation of individual river link schemes & to prepare their feasibility reports. On practical considerations, NWDA was given directives to prepare separate proposals for interlinking of rivers in the Himalayan component and in the Peninsular component, priority being given to the later one.

First task before NWDA was to assess water availability in all major river basins in the country, to estimate present water demand for all competing uses of water in the river basins, make future projections of demands, and then decide upon the relative status of each basin viz. water-surplus or water-short. Next activity was to investigate possibilities of linking the water-surplus rivers with the water-short rivers by means of separate gravity canals wherever possible and to provide for lifting of water maximum up to 120 m, only where it was unavoidable. Construction of reservoirs on some rivers was essential to store seasonal monsoon flows of the rivers and to raise water level to facilitate water transfer by gravity. These reservoirs moderated flood intensities on the downstream and also generated hydropower while releasing the stored water into link canals. Between 1982 to 2002, NWDA investigated & prepared prefeasibility reports of the planned 30 link canal schemes and feasibility reports of 8 schemes out of them.

Scope of the project is displayed in the map and the Table below:

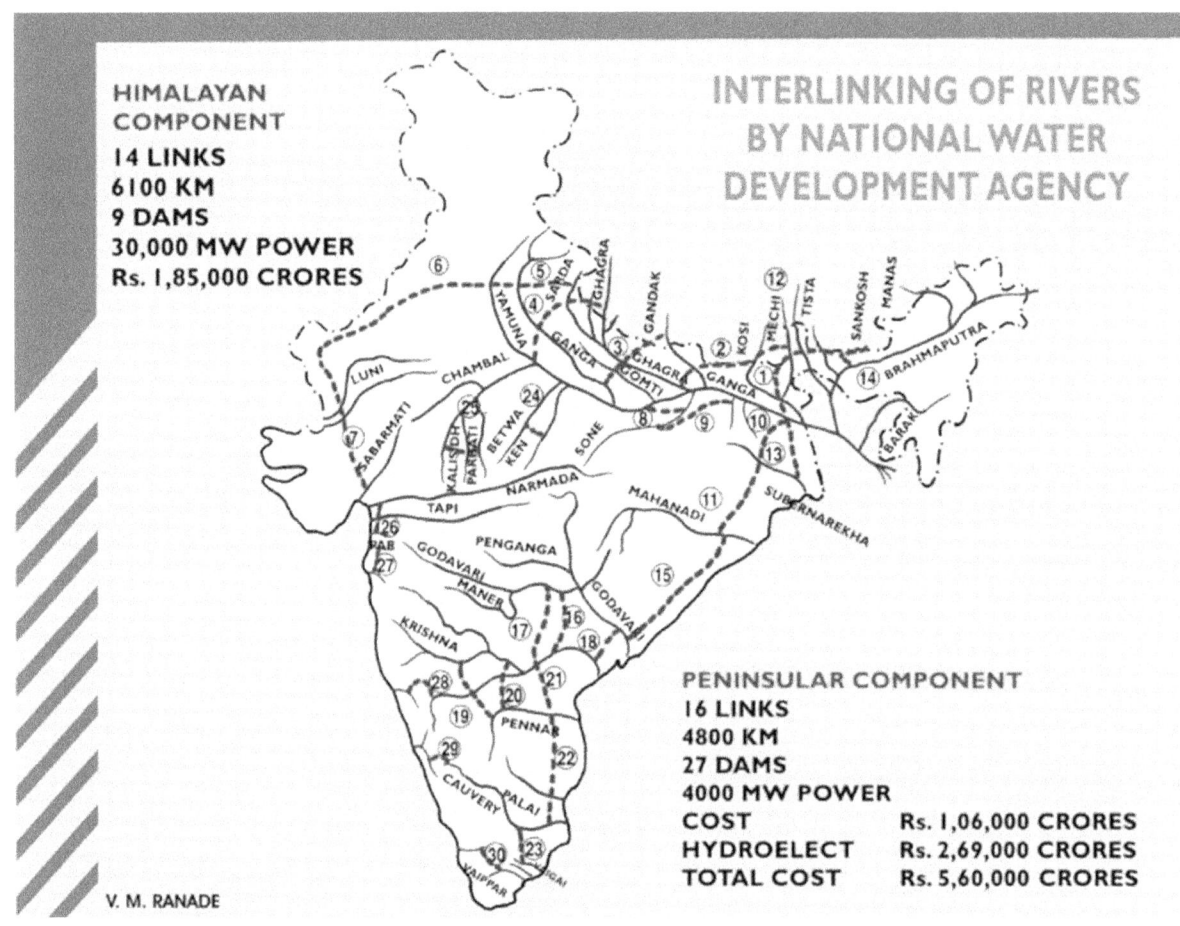

Table 1 - Scope of National Project of Interlinking of Rivers in India

| Sr No | Details | Peninsular Component | Himalayan Component | Total |
|---|---|---|---|---|
| 1 | Link canals | 16 | 14 | 30 |
| 2 | Major dams | 27 | 9 | 36 |
| 3 | Length of link canals km | 4,800 | 6,100 | 10,900 |
| 4 | Water diverted (cukm-bcm) | 141 | 33 | 174 |
| 5 | Power Generation (MW) | 4,000 | 30,000 | 34,000 |
| 6 | Cost in Rs. Crores | 1,06,000 | 1,85,000 | 2,91,000 |
| 7 | Hydroelectric Project cost in Rs. Crores | | | 2,69,000 |
| 8 | **Total cost of ILR Project in Rs. Crores (FY 2003-04 rates)** | | | **5,60,000** |
| 9 | Additional Irrigation Potential in million hectares (Considering additional groundwater recharge) | | | 34 mha |

(Note – cukm = cubic kilo meter = bcm = billion cubic meters, mha = million hectares, Crore = 10 millions)

**Table 2 - Available water resources in India and projected future demands.**

**In Billion Cubic Meters (BCM)**

| Year | Irrigation | Domestic | Industrial | Energy | Other | Total |
|------|------------|----------|------------|--------|-------|-------|
| 2000 | 541 | 42 | 8 | 2 | 41 | 634 |
| 2025 | 910 | 73 | 23 | 15 | 72 | 1093 |
| 2050 | 1072 | 102 | 63 | 130 | 80 | 1447 |

**Notes:**

1. Figures are as per CWC New Delhi study in August 2000.
2. Usable water availability by surface and groundwater   (690+396 =1086 bcm)
3. Additional possible water available by Inter Basin Water Transfer    174 bcm
4. Likely total usable water will be available by 2050 with IBWT    1260 bcm

**Table 3 - Future projections of population of India and expected food grain demand.**

| By the year | Population in millions | Food grains reqd./ day / person in grams | Food grains reqd. for country in Million Tonnes |
|-------------|------------------------|------------------------------------------|-------------------------------------------------|
| 2000 | 1000 | 550 | 200 |
| 2025 | 1300 – 1400 | 650 – 800 | 310 – 350 |
| 2050 | 1500 - 1600 | 800 – 1000 | 440 – 580 |

Note – Food consumption/day/person in the first decade of the twenty first century was about 2850 grams in USA and about 900 grams in China.

All climatologists agree that frequency of occurrence of the two extreme climatic events i.e., droughts & floods in all the river basins is likely to increase due to unavoidable impact of the Climate Change. Hence to take care of such contingency, about 10% additional food grains should be produced and kept as a buffer stock. Population of India is expected to stabilise before the year 2050 and may reduce then onwards. Hence, we must plan to achieve food and water security for the population of the country as projected by the year 2050. It would be seen from the figures of total water requirement and availability by the year 2050 as shown in the Table 3 above that, even after completion of Interlinking of Rivers Project, there is likelihood of shortage of water available for use to meet all water needs. This issue may have to be resolved by improving water-use efficiency of all irrigation schemes and making reuse of the adequately treated urban & industrial effluent for irrigation purposes.

Looking to this situation, Govt. of India took proactive step to draft 'National Water Policy 2002' and sought its approval from the Chief Ministers of all states in the country. Para 3.5 of the same states that," *Water should be made available to water short areas by transfer from other area including transfers from one river basin to another, based on National Perspective, after taking into account the requirements of the areas/basins*". Even if the subject of Inter Linking of Rivers was much discussed at the national level and at the state Level in the years 2004 and 2005, its actual implementation even for some links is still in a very initial stage. This is mainly because of the following complex issues involved in its implementation.

1. Problems of rehabilitation of project affected people, acquisition of private land and forest land etc. for the construction of dam-canal infrastructure would be handled by the water-surplus basin states, but benefits of the water transferred from there would be provided to the water-short basin states. This problem would be difficult to handle in the democratic set up, even if all states have agreed for such transfer of water as per National Water Policy 2002. In convincing the population and the ruling party from the water-surplus basin states for taking actions at the ground level for construction of the infrastructure and such transfer of water to other state, political acumen would be tested to its extreme in the implementation of this clause in practice.

2. Social activists have already exaggerated some adverse social and environmental impacts of the Inter Linking of Rivers project by totally conniving at the need of the project for ensuring sustained food and water security to the future generations till 2050 and beyond. As usual, they have also not suggested any viable alternatives to achieve this objective by any other more environment friendly project which would have minimum adverse social and environmental impacts and achieve sustainable food security to the country.

3. Many problems are anticipated in coming to terms in sharing of waters & hydropower, in respect of the International Rivers in the Himalayan component. These hydropower projects on the northern tributaries of Ganga River would have to be taken on priority because they would be generating about 30,000 MW of environment friendly power and round the year releases of water from them would provide year-round water for navigation through the rivers and for irrigation on the downstream.

4. Present actual cost of the project as in 2023-24 may be 6-7 times the estimated cost stated as above i.e., would now be totally about Rs.30,00,000 to 40,00,000 crores. Providing adequate funds by the GoI and the concerned beneficiary state govts. for construction of the links is going to be a most difficult problem. Financial assistance would hence have to be secured from international funding agencies such as the World Bank, the Asian Development Bank etc.

5. Because the gestation period of completing individual river links would be very high, following measures would have to be taken immediately by the Maharashtra state and other states to increase the present irrigation facilities.

- Completion of all the ongoing WR development projects in the states early, by giving priority to the projects in advanced stage of completion. Taking up other viable new projects wherever necessary.

- As a structural soft option, carry out performance evaluation of all completed irrigation projects and take possible structural measures to increase area under irrigation by them. This is more necessary even for all small irrigation projects each irrigating less than 250 ha each, which contribute about 17% of the total irrigation potential created by surface irrigation projects in the Maharashtra state. There is very scanty data about actual irrigation done by these small irrigation projects in the Maharashtra state.

- Developing use of GW by providing subsidies to the cultivators for digging/drilling wells, installing electric motor-pumps, and introducing Micro Irrigation Systems on them. Augmenting of GW shall be done by giving priority to the watershed development works in the semi critical, critical, and overexploited watersheds.

- As a non-structural soft option, measures such as entrusting irrigation water management to Water User's Associations, promoting adoption of MIS on surface irrigation major projects by the beneficiaries wherever possible, etc. should be taken up to improve water-use efficiency and to increase area under irrigation.

- As mentioned in the earlier chapters, average per hectare productivity of irrigated land in India is much less than that in China and other developed countries. Hence as a soft option, necessary measures should be taken in the agriculture sector (Second green revolution) to improve land productivity of rain-fed and irrigated land in the country.

Governance and Regulation on Water Resource Development and Management at the state level –

Optimum and equitable development of water resource – Water is a prime natural resource, fundamental to life, livelihood, food & water security, and for sustainable development of the society. Precipitation is the primary source of 'Water Resource' (WR), but in any river basin and its sub basins, it is subjected to spatial and temporal variability in a year and also has variability from year to year. Rainfall pattern in any river basin is decided by its location, latitude, and topography. This inbuilt inequity in the precipitation could be overcome by human efforts because 'Water Resource' is amenable for its development and use by the humans. Dictionary meaning of the term 'Equitable' is rightful, impartial, and non-discriminatory. But still, we must consider practical limitations and constraints in attaining these ideals in practice. Optimum development of WR within the river basin means constructing diversion weirs at suitable locations on perennial rivers and constructing large to small size dams on rivers and tributaries wherever feasible to suit the topography. Governance on WR development is necessary to ensure that the dams cause minimum social impacts on the Project Affected People by providing them with adequate facilities for their rehabilitation. It is essential to ensure that their status of living in the rehabilitated villages would be better than before and their lands are provided with irrigation facilities. It is also necessary to ensure that the WR development structures cause minimum degradation of the terrestrial ecosystems such as forests. In short, planning of all WR development structures in any river basin should aim at providing its equitable benefits to the society and causing minimum adverse impacts on the society and on the natural ecosystems.

If there is large variation in the magnitude of precipitation within the basin, WR development infrastructure should be planned to store water in the high rainfall zone and to utilise it to meet needs of the water-short zone in the basin. This was done in Maharashtra State even during pre-independence period by constructing 5 large dams along the high rainfall eastern slope of Sahyadri mountain range and diverting their water to irrigate land in the drought prone area towards East in the rain-shadow zone. After independence, 10 more large dams were constructed in the Sahyadri range from North to South to serve the same purpose. This is the equitable development of WR which is called as intra basin (within the basin) water transfer.

Large dams are generally most economical to store per unit of water than the small size dams because of the scale effect and other design considerations. But even then, on social considerations, a mosaic of large dams and several small size dams has been developed to benefit small and marginal farmers from parched lands in the upper reaches of river basins, who are bypassed by irrigation benefits provided by canals of large irrigation projects. Permitting project affected people to lift reservoir water by lift irrigation schemes or constructing some schemes to benefit them is essential on social considerations. Constructing lift irrigation schemes to provide irrigation facilities to the parched lands located in high level plateau in the river basin must also be done on social equity considerations, even if such schemes have very high recurring costs to operate and maintain them.

Providing low-interest-rate loans for digging/drilling wells & installing electric motor-pumps on them and supplying electricity at subsidised rates for promoting groundwater use is also done on social equity considerations. Taking up watershed development works to conserve rainwater where it falls, certainly benefits the farmers in the upper reaches of the watersheds. Even though it is very costly to create irrigation potential per hectare through watershed development works, it is taken up to meet water needs of small and marginal land holders. All such actions were taken in the Maharashtra state while planning and implementing WR development projects. **In short, governance in the water sector means to monitor and ensure implementation of all such actions to establish reasonably optimum development of WR and achieve equitable socio-economic development of the agrarian community.**

Regional imbalance in the Water Resource Development – Maharashtra state at the time of State re-organization on the 1st of May 1960 consisted of some districts from erstwhile Bombay State (Western, Northen and Konkan Regions), some districts from the erstwhile Nizam state (Marathwada Region) and some districts from the erstwhile C.P. & Berar state (Vidarbha Region). As in 1960, the Vidarbha Region had only 8 completed medium projects and the Marathwada Region had only one completed medium project. But Western & Northen Regions together had 5 major and some small size irrigation projects even at the time of independence. Many major and medium projects were already started and were completed or in progress between 1947 to 1960. Hence there was some imbalance in the development of water resources between Marathwada &

Vidarbha Regions and the rest of Maharashtra State in the 1960 itself. It took some time to set up organisation for investigation of new irrigation projects and start construction of irrigation projects in these two regions. In 1980 i.e. even after 20 years from the formation of the Maharashtra state, the situation of actual regional imbalance in the irrigation development did not improve much, primarily because more funds had to be provided for ongoing projects in the Western & Northen Regions. As per demands made in the Legislative Assembly by the elected representatives of the people from the Marathwada & Vidarbha region, GoM appointed in the year 1983 a 'Fact Finding Committee on Regional Imbalance' under the Chairmanship of Dr. V.M. Dandekar, a well-known economist. The Report of the Committee which was submitted in the year 1984 covered regional imbalance in 11 important development sectors of which, 'Surface Water Irrigation' sector was one of them. Regional imbalance in the 'Water sector' in physical and financial terms was estimated by the Committee, duly stating mechanism for redressal of the imbalance and given a time frame to implement it in practice. However, in practice implementation of the suggested time frame to remove regional backlog did not materialise as was expected in the Report. This was because works in progress in the other two regions had to be provided with more funds to complete ongoing projects and also due to some other reasons. Hence one more Committee was appointed to examine and suggest measures to expedite the process of removal of the regional imbalance. Despite that, the progress in removal of regional backlog in the water sector was not seen to be satisfactory. Finally, allocation of funds for the water sector for the Marathwada and Vidarbha regions had to be taken over by the Hon. Governor of Maharashtra state. With the result, the process of removal of regional imbalance in the water sector had finally achieved the objective in the year 2010, i.e. after more than 25 years from the recommendations of Dr. V.M. Dandekar Committee Report in the year 1984. Developing countries should hence take proactive measures of proper governance right from the beginning to avoid possibility of creating such regional imbalance.

<u>Initiative to provide relief to drought prone area and Project Affected People in the state</u> – About 30 to 40 percent area of the state lying in the rain shadow area of Sahyadri is drought prone. There are some major projects which provide irrigation to the drought prone area. Cropping pattern of most of the major projects includes about 3 to 5% area for providing irrigation to perennial crops like sugar cane and for some percent area under hot weather crops. One Committee of experts was appointed by the GoM to examine the possibility of providing more relief to the drought prone area located in the command area of Major irrigation projects. GoM considered recommendations of the Committee and took a conscious decision in the year 1987, to provide irrigation only for 8 months (instead of 12 months) on canals of major projects which benefit the drought prone area. Reservoirs of Major irrigation projects benefitting drought prone area would then be emptied by end of February, like medium and minor irrigation projects. It would then save appreciable quantity of evaporation loss taking place from reservoirs during summer months. Water so saved was planned for providing seasonal irrigation to additional drought prone area by extending the canal and the distribution system further if necessary. This pragmatic decision was taken by the GoM on social equity considerations.

However, in most of the major projects benefitting the drought prone area, objective of extending of the desired benefits of irrigation to such extended command area did not materialise in practice. Cultivators in the initial reach of the canals extensively planted sugar cane crop by providing canal irrigation for 8 months (monsoon and winter season) of the year as per the revised policy. Such flood irrigation for the 8 months caused to ensure good recharge of the GW in that area. Cultivators then dug wells in their fields and provided irrigation to the sugar cane crop during 4 months of the hot weather season from the wells. The cultivators whose land was located close to the river, had lifted water from the river to irrigate sugar cane crop during summer months because, river had some discharge due to regenerated water from 8 monthly irrigation. Water was also released in the river to meet drinking water needs of Solapur city on downstream and for many villages on the way. Sugar cane crop is a sturdy crop and does not have problem of insects and pests. Secondly, the produce had assured market from the sugar factories which were already established near all these major projects. Because of such intense irrigation of sugar cane in the initial reach of the canal, all the water stored in the reservoirs was consumed there and the tail enders in the command area were still left high and dry.

Govt. had given liberal permissions to set up new cooperative sugar factories in the drought prone area or located close to it. In some cases, permission was also given to the existing sugar factories in these areas to increase their daily cane crushing capacity. Despite this situation, no elected representative from these areas had raised their voice in the State Legislative Assembly against such injustice on the poor and the needy cultivators from the tail enders in the canal command. No NGO tried to educate, unite, and motivate the cultivators from drought prone area to raise their protest against such injustice on them. Pockets of prosperity were created due to such sugar cane cultivation, thereby causing social inequity. With the result, good initiative taken by the state Govt. proved to be futile in reality.

For many major projects, only part land from some villages was getting submerged in the reservoirs but the village itself was not getting submerged. In some cases, villages were getting submerged, but lot of land from the village was above the lake level. In such cases, these villages were resettled close to the reservoir but at a higher elevation. With a view to providing relief to the rehabilitated people, some lift irrigation schemes were constructed by the GoM to provide irrigation facilities to the land of the PAPs. Subsequently, Govt. also approved proposals of some cooperative lift irrigation schemes constructed by a group of villagers in which some PAPs were their beneficiary members. When the number of such proposals by the cooperative societies increased, approval was given subject to compulsory use of introduction of Micro Irrigation Systems for irrigating the crops.

However, same thing as above happened in practice here also. Most of the water lifted from reservoirs was used to irrigate sugar cane crop because of its benefits as above. It no doubt benefitted some PAPs, but majority of the beneficiaries were the other cultivators. Sugar cane crop sustained on canal gets water by rotation once in 15 to 21 days. But for lift irrigation schemes on the reservoirs, water could be delivered at short intervals of time by lifting it day and night from the reservoir whenever electricity is available. It consumed more water but improved productivity i.e., per hectare tonnage of sugar cane crop. Even if use of MIS was made compulsory on such cooperative lift irrigation schemes, in very few cases it was actually done in practice by the irrigators. WR Deptt. (WRD) had no control on the irrigation practiced on all these lift irrigation schemes. Because of the extensive plantation of sugar cane on canals of Major projects and on the lift irrigation schemes from the reservoirs, majority of the sugar factories in the state are in or close to the drought prone area. Out of more than about 200 cooperative and private sugar factories in the state, about 60% are in the drought prone area or close to it. Even if pragmatic decisions are taken by the Govt. to benefit cultivators from drought prone area, in actual practice vested interests of some elected representatives of the people and political expediencies of policy makers, come in the way of their actual implementation, as would be seen from the above two examples.

Regulation on the Development and Management of Water Resource – Issues related to governance and regulation as discussed above were discussed by the experts from the World Bank with the senior engineers of WRD, during implementation of one World Bank (WB) aided project in the Maharashtra state. It was suggested by the WB experts to consider the possibility of setting up a statutory regulatory authority to monitor all such activities of the WRD. It was then discussed and deliberated by the WRD, and an enabling Act to regulate functioning of the WRD was framed. The same was passed by the Maharashtra Legislative Assembly and the Act came into force as 'Maharashtra Water Resources Regulatory Authority Act 2005' – (MWRRA). WR Ministry and the elected representatives of the state should be complimented for passing the Act which brought some restrictions on their powers by the provisions of the Act. Let us now see how the provisions in the MWRRA Act which were supposed to regulate and streamline the functioning of WRD were implemented in practice. Salient points are as stated below:

1. As per Clause 15 of the Act, state was to constitute a State Water Board which was to prepare a draft Integrated State Water Plan (ISWP) consisting of WR development for the state and submit it to the State Water Council (SWC) headed by the Hon. Chief minister of the state within 6 months after the Act. Same was to be approved by the SWC within the next 6 months. No new project which was not included in the ISWP could be taken up for implementation. However, in practice it took about 13 years to prepare ISWP and get approval of the SWC to it. Before its approval, the action of taking up about 191 new projects by the WRD was stayed by the orders of the High Court on one Public Interest Litigation. Their implementation could resume only after approval of the ISWP by the SWC in the year 2018.

2. As per Clause 20 of the Act, MWRRA was to prepare Annual Report covering activities done and expenditure incurred during the year & giving status of Region/District wise irrigation backlog (Clause 21) and send it to WRD, but it was not done.

3. As per Clause 14 (4) of the Act, from the date notified by MWRRA, canal water for perennial crops could be used only after adoption of Micro Irrigation System (MIS). Water so saved was to be used for drinking purposes if necessary or was to be distributed equitably in the command area. Even then, Notification of introducing MIS for perennial crops on 8 Major projects was issued after 10 years in 2015, stating its implementation to be planned in 2018. But even in

2024 not much has been done in that direction so far. With the result, almost all irrigation to the sugar cane crop on canals and on the lift irrigation schemes lifting water from reservoirs, is being done at present by the conventional flood irrigation system, resulting in very high consumption of water. By introducing MIS on canal irrigation, lot of water could have been saved, which would have given relief to the tail enders of the canal in the drought prone area. Due to lack of follow up by the MWRRA with the WRD this proposal was ineffective in practice.

4. After passing of the 'Maharashtra Groundwater (Development and Management) Act 2014', it was seen that its actual implementation at the ground level was not satisfactory. Hence it was felt that the issue of development and management of GW should also be brought under the purview of MWRRA. With a view to monitoring and regulating the development and management of GW in view of the provisions of the above GW Act 2014, a separate post of 'Member Groundwater' was created in MWRRA in October 2017. But unfortunately, the post of Member GW is still vacant due to some litigations in the Court.

It would be seen from the instances as above that, during last 19 years after the constitution of MWRRA, it has not been effective in bringing regulation on the functioning of WRD. It would be seen that there is appreciable curtailment in the water available for irrigation due to increasing use of water for non-irrigation purposes during the last 3-4 decades. It could have been partly made good by providing adequate treatment to the sewage/effluent generated after urban & industrial use of water. The MWRRA should have enforced Municipal Corporations /Municipalities (by drafting and getting approval to the enabling New Acts if necessary) to treat generated effluent and provide such treated water into canals for reuse in irrigation. It would also have solved the severe problem of river pollution. The MWRRA should take more proactive role hereafter at least to ensure that development and management of water resource is done more effectively.

Conclusion – It would be seen from the forgoing paragraphs that, governance on the development and management of water resource is very much essential to ensure optimum development and equitable allocation of water resource. It was necessary to respond to the dynamics of changes in the competing and conflicting demands on water which were associated with the development of the society. Even in a progressive state like Maharashtra, lot of efforts were necessary to achieve proper governance in the water sector. To improve the shortcomings as observed in the efficacy of governance, a statutory regulatory body was also established by passing an enabling Act. It had improved the situation slightly in some respects but even then, many shortcomings were observed in its functioning as narrated above.

# Chapter 11
# Droughts and Floods – Two Extreme Events of the Climate

*Droughts and floods are the two extreme climatic events. Whenever the average precipitation pattern in a River basin change to much below the normal, it is likely to result in drought situation in that river basin. If it much above the normal pattern, it may cause flooding to the river during intense or long duration rain spells. In some river basins there may be chronic drought conditions due to very low average rainfall in the past many years. Whereas in some rivers occurrence of floods may be a more frequent event. It is primarily because there is natural variability in the total magnitude of rainfall from year to year, at any place. There is also variation in the number of rain spells in a rainy season and variation in the intensity of rainfall in each rain spell. Actual instances of droughts and floods in the past centuries in any river basin provide good information for taking advance actions to face such unavoidable contingencies in the future. First action would be to take structural measures to reduce the intensity of adverse impacts of droughts and floods as much as possible. Second action would be to be prepared to face the situation of droughts and floods in such a manner that there would be minimum adverse impacts of these natural calamities on the affected population. It is expected that, due to adverse effects of 'Global Warming and Climate Change', frequency of occurrence of these two extreme climatic events will certainly be increasing continuously in the next 2-3 decades and beyond. The chapter covers in detail all such aspects of these two natural calamities and about the structural and non-structural measures necessary to be taken to minimise their adverse impacts on the affected population.*

**Droughts -** Inadequate rainfall for a few weeks normally does not cause a drought. It is the persistent inadequate rainfall or lack of rainfall over a long period, that causes a drought. There are three kinds of droughts. Inadequate rainfall is the meteorological drought, intensity of which can be reduced if there is adequate storage in the reservoirs. If there is inadequate flow in rivers and also there is inadequate storage in the reservoirs, then it is a hydrological drought. If there is inadequate rainfall even to sustain the crops, it is called agricultural drought. If inadequate rainfall in the monsoon/rainy season persists, the meteorological drought leads to hydrological drought, and then to agricultural drought. If the drought conditions prevail for a very long time and cover extensive area of a country/state/river basin resulting in total loss of crop, it is then called as a 'Famine'. Even if less average annual rainfall in a year can be predicted in view of the present technology, absence of rainfall over a prolonged period leading to drought conditions cannot be forecasted at present. It emphasises the need to take advance action of constructing water resource development infrastructure to benefit the traditional drought prone area and to mitigate the effects of droughts in the future as much as possible.

Between the 18$^{th}$ to 20$^{th}$ century, there were 12 major famines (from 1769-70 to 1943-44) in India in which millions of people died, as would be seen from the details given in the Chapter No.4. During that time there were very few WR development structures available in India to provide irrigation facilities to ameliorate the hazardous effects of such famines. There were also shortcomings and inadequacies in the administrative structure in the British regime to handle the situation effectively during these famines. Number of deaths could have been appreciably reduced by providing deployment to the famine affected people on some road construction works and soil conservation works. Simultaneously, it was necessary to provide them with adequate food grains at subsidised rates by transporting them from grain surplus regions in the country. Due to lack of any such actions at that time, about 1 to 6% population of the country each time had succumbed to death due to starvation in each of the 8 major famines out of 12 major famines which occurred between 1769 to 1944.

Droughts or famines result from scanty rainfall for sustained period over extensive area. Man cannot exercise any control on the magnitude or the pattern of rainfall at any place in any year. Artificial rain has very limited scope and has very low efficacy in its performance as explained in chapter No. 12. Hence, we must consider the droughts as *fate accompli*, take suitable structural & non-structural measures to reduce its adverse effects and finally adjust to live with it. We can certainly take some long-term measures to initiate actions which would ameliorate the ill effects of droughts and famines on the affected population. They consist of creating water resource development infrastructure to store water that otherwise would flow through rivers to the sea during rainy season. Water stored in the man-made reservoirs would augment irrigation facilities to the rainfed agriculture from the drought prone areas. For perennial rivers in the Indo-Gangetic basin in the North India, in addition to storage dams, river diversion weirs and canals could serve the same purpose to augment irrigation facilities. Irrigated agriculture increases productivity of land per hectare by two and half to three times, and more so when supplemented by initiating reforms in the agriculture sector. Additional food grain production creates buffer stock of food grains for its use during droughts.

In any region/river basin if the soils are of poor quality and total seasonal rainfall is barely adequate (which also fails in some years) to support only seasonal monsoon crop (Kharif crop), it is called as chronic scarcity area. Such scarcity conditions exist in most of the Rajasthan state and in parts of Gujarat and Haryana states, all located in the North-West part of the country. As against that, about 30 to 40% area of the Maharashtra and Karnataka states in the Peninsular India, lying in the rain-shadow zone located towards East of the North-South running Sahyadri mountain range is called as 'drought prone' area. In this area, monsoon rain is adequate to support seasonal monsoon crop say in 7-8 years out of 10 years on an average. In the good rainfall years, it is also possible to grow follow on rainfed winter crop (Rabi crop) on the residual soil moisture in the heavy deep black cotton soils. But suddenly in some year at random, the monsoon rain gets totally inadequate even to support seasonal monsoon crop. There is also not much GW recharge in the existing wells in such years due to scanty rainfall in that year. If such conditions prevail over sizeable part of the drought prone area in any year, then it results in drought condition in that area. Similarly, droughts can also occur in other areas of the country, though less frequently, because entire country is covered by the South-West monsoon rains.

If a salaried person gets his monthly pay regularly as only about Rs.20 to 25 thousand, he can adjust his living style to suit it and will accept it. If some other salaried person gets his monthly pay regularly of about Rs.35 to 40 thousand continuously for 5 years, he will adjust his living style to suit it. But in the sixth year, if he suddenly gets pay of only Rs. 5 thousand per month or no pay at all for one year, his living conditions in the sixth year would be miserable. Difference between chronic scarcity and occasional drought conditions is just like that. However, it should be clearly understood that it is not their fault that people from such chronic scarcity or drought affected areas in the country/state were born & brought up there. They have lesser opportunities to get benefits of water resource-related development due to such natural inequity in water allocation vis-à-vis other regions of the country. On social considerations, it then becomes responsibility of the Govt. to take structural and systemic measures which would minimise ill effects such inherent inequities in the available natural water-related developmental facilities. It defines the scope of measures necessary to be taken to provide permanent relief measures to the people from chronic scarcity and drought prone areas. It is possible to achieve some equity in water allocation by transfer of water from water-surplus part of the same river basin (intra-basin water transfer) or by transfer of water from any other water-surplus river basin (inter-basin water transfer) in the state/country.

First time such measures were taken during British regime as per recommendations of the 'Famine Commission Report, 1903'. As elaborated in chapter No.5, in the then Bombay Province (now Maharashtra state), four large masonry dams were constructed along the eastern slope of Sahyadri mountain range in the high rainfall zone, to store water and use it to provide irrigation facilities to the low rainfall drought prone zone towards the East. Some small size earthen dams were also constructed in the state in the plains during famines, primarily to provide work to the affected labourers. These small dam-canal projects were completed later to provide irrigation facilities in the drought prone area. Even though they had provided some relief to some part of the drought prone area, they were much short because about 30-40% area of the state is drought prone.

After independence to the country in 1947, priority was given by the Maharashtra state to construct large size & medium size dams at these and other locations. In all about 25 major and medium dam-canal projects were constructed from North to South along high rainfall eastern slopes of the Sahyadri range, which provided irrigation facilities to most of the water scarce drought prone area. At the national level, priority was given for creation of large water resource development infrastructure in many river basins in some states. Within the next one-two decades, irrigation facilities started increasing in the command areas as the canals & distribution systems of these major irrigation projects was getting completed. Beginning from mid-sixties of the last century, several actions were also taken to commence 'Green Revolution' in the country to increase land productivity of irrigated land and achieve self-sufficiency in food grains as detailed in Chapter No.5. In the states of Punjab, Haryana and Uttar Pradesh in the North India, use of GW was extensively done to grow wheat and rice crop. Because of the availability of good road and rail facilities after the independence, it was possible to transport food grains from grain surplus states to such states during drought situations.

**Drought relief measures** – Long term permanent measures as stated above cannot prevent droughts but improve the availability of usable water in the river basins to reduce the intensity of droughts which occasionally occur. In addition to that, planning needs to be done to handle the situation during drought which may occur in any year without warning. Such drought relief measures consist of two parts, firstly it is by way of advance planning for providing work to drought affected labours. Secondly it is by making preparation of short-term action plans for effectively implementing relief measures for labours during actual droughts. Long-term measures consist of preparing in advance a shelf of sanctioned plans and estimates of many labour-intensive productive water-conservation works in the drought prone area for unskilled labours. It is also essential to prepare a 'Manual on drought relief measures' for the guidance of all planning, implementing and monitoring agencies. It is then possible to start such relief works at short notice by deploying drought affected labours during sustained failure of rains in any year. Out of the works for which estimates are ready, works close to the drought affected villages are chosen so that most of the labourers walk down daily from their villages to the site of the drought relief works. Arrangements to provide drinking water for the labourers have to be made as per availability of source of water near every drought relief work. Necessary tools such as pickaxes, shovels, crow bars, iron baskets etc., are provided to them free of cost by the supervisory staff. They allot specific work to each group of labourers, record measurements of the work done by them during every week and based on their actual turnover, make payment to them every week. Foodgrains were transported from foodgrain surplus states and arrangements were made to supply them at subsidised rates to the labours through fair price shops set up in nearby villages.

Making use of bullocks for ploughing fields and for other agricultural operations was then common with the farmers having big and small land holdings. During the 1971-72 drought in the Maharashtra state, arrangements of providing the farm animals with fodder and drinking water were, however, inadequate. Hence some farm animals were sold by their owners to butchers at throw away price and many of them died for want of fodder and water. During last 3-4 decades, in addition to the farm animals, some farmers started tending cows and buffaloes to supplement their income by selling milk through milk collection centres. Hence during subsequent droughts in the state, many cattle camps under temporary sheds were set up near major and medium projects where sufficient water was available to provide it in the cattle camps. Fodder was procured by the Govt. and was provided in these cattle camps free of cost. Hence there were no deaths of cattle during the subsequent droughts. Due to such coordinated efforts taken at the state level, there were negligible deaths in the 5 major droughts which occurred between 1966 to 2013. Details of each of these five droughts have been given in detail in the Chapter No.5.

**Manuals on Drought Management –**

After getting some experience of handling drought situation in the Maharashtra state, The Bombay Scarcity Manual (Drought relief - 255 pages) was prepared by the Revenue and Forests Department Maharashtra (India) in 1966. During the severe drought of 1971-72, drought situation was handled by all the concerned departments of the GoM in a coordinated manner. As intensity of the drought gradually increased, many circulars and Govt. Resolutions were issued by the concerned departments to guide and authorise field officers to take necessary actions to face the critical drought situation. Many radical decisions were taken by GoM which provided great relief to the rural population which was suffering due to drought. GoM subsequently published a compendium of all the important Circulars and Resolutions issued in the context of handling the 1971-72 drought situation. It served as good guideline for taking appropriate actions in the next droughts.

GoI New Delhi, Ministry of Agriculture, had published a comprehensive 'Manual for Drought Management' in November 2009. The Manual has been developed by the National Institute of Disaster Management (NIDM) through a consultative process involving the concerned Central Ministries, State Governments, scientific, technical and research organisations and the grass root level organisations working for mitigation and management of drought. NIDM is the apex training and resource centre of the GoI in the field of disaster management. It has provided various services and support to the GoI and the state Governments for disaster management in the country. It has published various manuals, guidelines, training literature, research papers and journals on various aspects of disaster risk management. Over a period of time, it has emerged as a premier institution specializing in disaster management in the South Asia. This Manual has been developed with support and guidance from the Department of Agriculture and Cooperation, Ministry of Agriculture, GoI.

**Various indicators of water scarcity condition** – Internationally accepted indicator defining status of availability of water in a river basin is known as 'Falconmark Indicator'. It defines that, if availability of water in a river basin is less than 1,700 cubic meters per person per year, water scarcity is felt there. When it reduces below 1,000 cubic meters per person per year, it decidedly induces a chronic scarcity condition. In India where about 80 to 85% of the total water use is on an average for the irrigated agriculture, it would be desirable to consider another indicator which is based on availability of water in a river basin in relation to the cultivable area as well as to the population in the river basin. For detailed analysis, such an exercise was carried out by subdividing the five major river basins in the Maharashtra state viz., Godavari, Krishna, Tapi, Narmada and the West flowing river basins in the coastal Kokan strip. These basins were sub divided into total 34 sub basins so that each of them had a fairly uniform rainfall pattern. Then these sub-basins were clubbed in 5 groups on the basis of total water availability per hectare of the cultivable area. These five groups are: severely water short, water short, average, water surplus and much water surplus, as shown in the Table below:

| Table 1 - Sub-basin wise water availability classification in the Maharashtra State | | | | | | |
|---|---|---|---|---|---|---|
| Sr. No. | Sub-basin classification | Water availability Per year per hectare In cubic meters | Number of Sub-basins | Geographic Area million hectares | Cultivable Area million hectares | Population (1991 census) millions |
| 1 | Severely Water short | Less than 1,500 | 5 | 32 (10) | 29 (13) | 72 (9) |
| 2 | Water short | 1,500 to 3,000 | 6 | 88 (29) | 74 (33) | 184 (23) |

| | | | | | | |
|---|---|---|---|---|---|---|
| 3 | Average | 3,000 to 8,000 | 9 | 102 (33) | 76 (33) | 221 (28) |
| 4 | Water Surplus | 8,000 to 12,000 | 2 | 22 (7) | 13 (6) | 55 (7) |
| 5 | Much water Surplus | More than 12,000 | 12 | 63 (21) | 34 (15) | 257 (33) |
| 6 | **Total** (Figures in bracket show percentage) | | 34 | **307 (100)** | **226 (100)** | **789 (100)** |

Source – Maharashtra Water and Irrigation Commission Report, September 1999.

It would be seen from above figures that, for severely water short, and water short sub-basins together, 46% cultivable area supports only 32% population of the state. People from these 11 sub-basins suffer the most during drought years. On the considerations of equitable allocation of water, it is necessary to take following actions to provide relief to the people from these sub-basins.

1. To make optimum use of available water resource, all possible surface irrigation projects should be taken up even by relaxing the normal financial yardsticks.

2. Schemes of transfer of water from adjoining water surplus basins should also be approved by relaxing the normal financial yardsticks.

3. In the major dams benefitting area from these 11 sub-basins, adequate carry over storage should be kept, which can be used if the next year happens to be a drought year or a year of late outbreak of monsoon season.

4. Since GW is totally free from evaporation loss, subsidies should be given for digging /drilling wells, installing electric motor-pumps and for setting up drip irrigation systems.

5. Watershed development works should be taken up in these sub-basins to augment natural GW recharge. Priority should be given for these works in the overexploited and critical small watersheds.

6. There should be complete ban on harnessing of deep GW aquifers (100 to 300 meters deep) for irrigation purposes. It should be reserved and used exclusively for drinking water purposes in the villages.

7. Industries which do not need much water should only be promoted in these sub-basins, which would provide employment opportunities to the farm labourers who get only seasonal employment in agriculture in these sub basins.

**Floods** – Variability from year to year in the total magnitude of rainfall is the inherent characteristics of the monsoon rainfall in India. We have seen as above the one extreme climatic event viz. drought, which is caused due to totally inadequate rainfall in the river basin to support crops. 'Floods' is the other extreme climatic event which is caused due to high intensity rain spells of long duration in the river basin. Sometimes very high intensity rainfall occurs for very short duration, and which is spread over localised area is known as 'Cloud burst'. It also causes very intense flood to the river locally to cause much damage even during the short duration of the flood. Such variations in the rainfall pattern in any river basin is a natural phenomenon and we cannot control or regulate it. Hence the only course available for us is to accept it and implement some structural measures which would moderate the intensity of floods to the river. If there are some reservoirs constructed on the river, some moderation of floods naturally takes place in the process of filling of the reservoir during initial months of the monsoon season. Initial floods to the river get stored in the reservoirs and there is no outflow on downstream till the reservoir fills to capacity. When there is flood to the river after filling of the reservoir, part of it is used to increase the lake level and only part of it flows out over the spillway thus moderating the incoming flood. Such flood moderation automatically takes place in the dams having ungated spillways, till the inflow rises to the design flood discharge and the lake level reaches Highest Flood Level (HFL). Then the outflow becomes same as the inflow flood and there is no moderation of the flood.

Controlled flood moderation can, however, be done by planned operation of spillway gates which are provided on large size storage dams constructed in the river basin. Out of the total design storage of the reservoir, appreciable storage is against the radial or vertical gates installed on the spillway. For planning effective flood regulation by their systematic operation, it is essential to install automatic rain gauge stations in the catchment area and get data of actual intensity and magnitude of rainfall by tele-transmission on real time basis. By analysing this data with the help of a computer programme, it is possible to get probable magnitude of incoming flood in the reservoir at any time. Water is initially stored in the reservoir against the gates up to pre decided level at the end of every month during the monsoon season, depending on the expected inflow every month based on past inflow record. If automatic rain gauge stations in the catchment indicate sizeable inflow, spillway gates can be opened to release some stored water thereby making space for the intense inflow and to moderate the outflow. For a large river basin having several dams having gated spillways, 'Real time' estimate of incoming flood should be made from the rainfall data in the entire basin and coordinated operation of spillway gates on all the dams shall have to be done to moderate flood to the river till it meets the sea.

For dams in the North India where flood is a recurring problem, separate 'Flood absorption capacity' is provided in the reservoir while planning design capacity of all the dams. Normally water is not stored against that capacity and whenever there is incoming flood especially in the late monsoon season, water starts getting stored against this reserved capacity temporarily. Spillway gates are then operated to moderate the outgoing flood by ensuring that lake level does not go below the full supply level. Flood absorption capacity can thus be used to moderate the outgoing flood. Such flood absorption capacity is not provided in the planning of most of the dams in the Central and the Peninsular India.

Depending on the topography and the nature of the river course, it is also possible to contain the floods locally within the river course by constructing embankments and/or masonry/concrete walls on either bank of the river to reduce damage due to floods. Earthen embankments are generally provided in the reach of the river on upstream side of the delta region of the river where land slopes are very flat, and land on the banks is very fertile. Construction of such earthen dykes is very common on many rivers in China but is not so common on the rivers in India. In some cities in India, masonry walls are constructed on one or both the banks of rivers to protect some low-lying flood prone area in the city from the river floods.

**Problem of floods to rivers in India -**

**Characteristics of Rivers in India –** Formation of the river course/channel from its start and then along its passage till it meets the sea, is a result of water flowing through it over millions of years. In the initial reach where the riverbed gradient is steep, flowing water having high velocity erodes the bed material which is carried by the river on downstream. When the river enters the plains, the bed gradient and the velocity of flow reduces, so the heavier material carried by the river gets deposited in the bed or along the banks. In the plains, lot of silt is carried by rainwater as sheet erosion from the fields on either banks of the river and its tributaries into the main river. Gravel, sand and the rolling silt flows further to settle in the bed and along inner curves of the meandering rivers. When the river meets the sea velocity becomes zero and all the rolling and suspended silt settles there to form vast triangular delta region on the upstream side close to the estuary. In the initial reach of most of the rivers, floods are not much a problem because river course is well defined to usually contains the high velocity flow within its banks. As the river reaches in the plains, river course is generally shallow and flood water spreads along banks to cause some damage to the crop if the land is under cultivation and causes damage to houses, and other property if there is human habitation close to the riverbanks. In the reach upstream of the delta region, river flood creates problems because of the back water effect of the sea. Flood water spreads on either bank for considerable distance. Problem becomes more serious when the flood coincides with the high tide to the sea. For some rivers, in the lower reaches earthen embankments are constructed on either bank to contain the flood within them and to avoid flooding of fertile flat land on either bank. Such dikes are constructed from the distant past in China in the lower reaches of Yellow River and its tributaries to contain the floods.

In the North India, northern rivers in the Indo-Gangetic basin rise in the snow-clad Himalayan ranges. Once the rivers reach below the hill ranges and enter in the flat plains, substrata consist of alluvial soils having very deep layers of sand and silt. Bed gradients of the rivers are very flat, and river courses are shallow. There are floods to rivers during monsoon season (July to October) and also in the summer season due to snow melt. Worst floods occur when the flood due to snow melt coincides with the occasional untimely rains during summer season. Very intense floods also occur due to breach of naturally formed snow-dams formed in the upper reaches of the rivers, which is called as 'Glacial Lake Out Bursts'. These floods are unpredictable about their timing & magnitude and may have the potential to cause very heavy damage on downstream & to the engineering structures such as dams, bridges etc. Land slopes in the plains are very flat and hence rise in the river flood level only by half a meter causes submergence of land, over more than a kilo meter on either side. Because of the slow velocity of flow, usually flood lasts for many days.

Floods to these rivers are more frequent and they cause damage to the standing crop on the land on either bank. However, during such floods there is deposition of fertile silt carried by the floods on the inundated fields, which improves fertility of the soil. Some of these rivers have tendency to migrate laterally during high floods. River channel migration is the geomorphological process that involves lateral migration of an alluvial river channel across its floodplain. This process is mainly driven by the combination of bank erosion and deposition over time, typically in reference to the meandering streams. Such meandering and migration of the river encroaches the land along one bank due to erosion and results in formation of new land on the opposite bank. It creates problems in the long run, because of changes in the ownership of land due to large scale erosion on one bank and formation of new land on the other bank.

In the Central and Peninsular India on the other hand, most of the rivers traverse through strata which consists of in-situ decomposed rock underlain by parent basalt, granite, metamorphic or sedimentary rocks. Riverbed gradients are moderate and sometimes river courses are serpentine, which are formed by erosion along outer bank and deposition of sand and silt carried by the river along the bank on the opposite side. Alluvial deposits hence exist along the inner bank of most of the rivers for some width. It is a very slow process involving erosion of the hard strata which might have taken many thousands of years to form. River courses are well defined and generally are not shallow. Land slopes on either bank are not flat but have moderate slope. Flood water in such reaches does not spread for long distance on either bank. Hence normal floods to the rivers are contained within the river course and they do not cause much damage to the crop or property. Occasional high floods to rivers cause some damage to the standing crop and submerge some structures in the low-lying villages. Floods cause more damage near cities and towns where there are obstructions to its flow due to bridges, causeways and due to encroachments along the riverbanks by the slums (temporary huts by the poor people) and high-rise buildings. In the reach of rivers close to their delta region, there are alluvial deposits on either bank over sizeable area extending kilo meters on the upstream side and forming a triangular shape delta region which is interspersed by several branches of the river. This region is often subject to floods to the rivers.

It would be seen from the map below that, flood prone area in India is primarily in the Indo-Gangetic basin in the North and in the delta regions of rivers along the East coast and in the Gujarat State.

# INDIA

## AREA LIABLE TO FLOODS

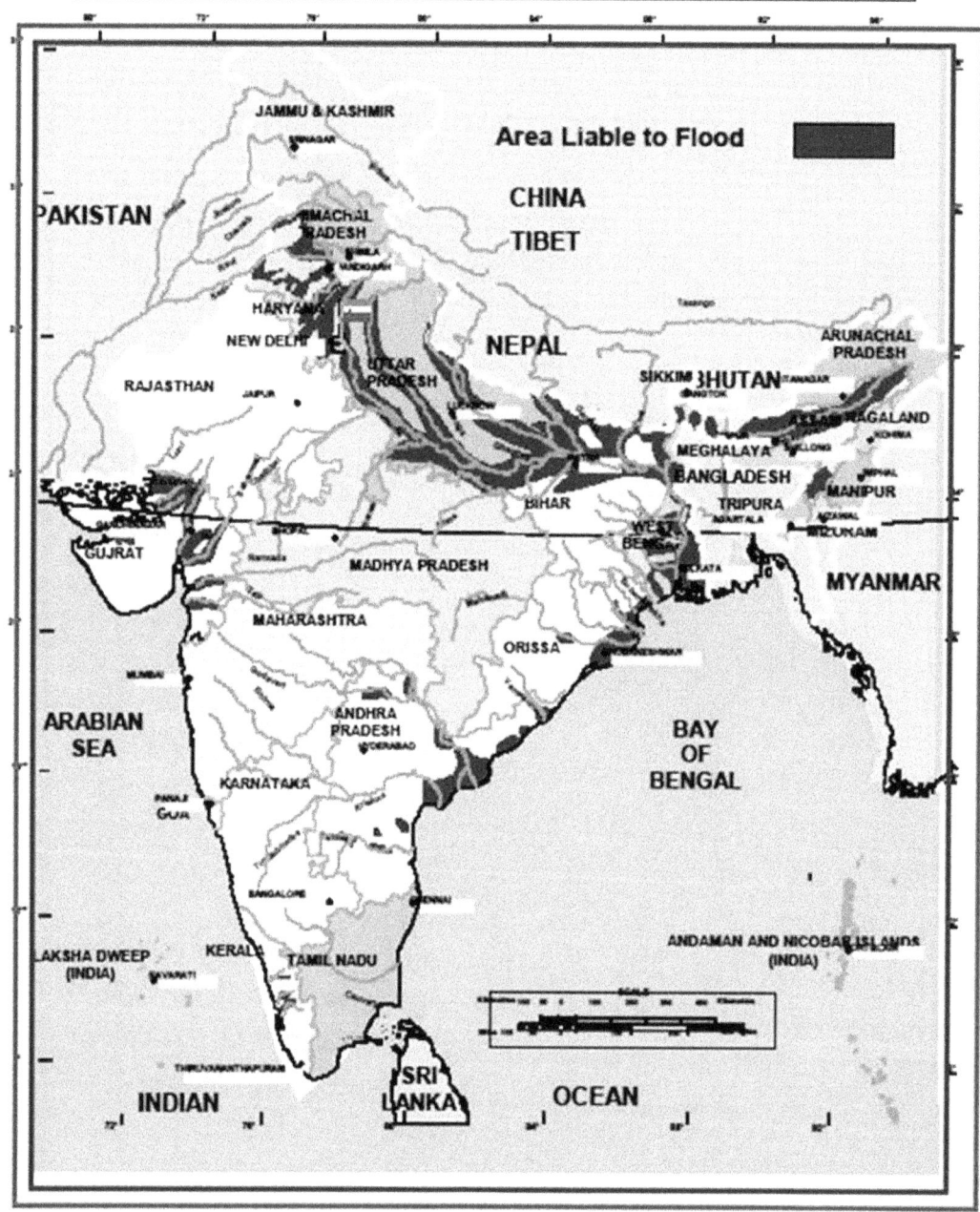

**Flood protection measures for the affected people** – With the help of structural measures suggested above we can take some actions to moderate intensity of floods to rivers. But still there remains possibility of occurrence of occasional heavy floods due to sustained rain spells which would cause risk to the lives of people and cause damage to houses & properties located close to the river. Hence the policy of 'Forewarned is forearmed' must be adopted to minimise risk to the lives of people and the property as much as is possible. For that purpose, it is imperative to set up several self-recording rain gauge stations in the catchment area of the rivers on which there are towns and villages close to the river or where the flood spreads for considerable distance on either bank and submerges lot of cultivated land and houses in the low-lying villages. It is necessary to set up control room where the automatic rainfall data would be analysed and probable magnitude of flood at all such vulnerable locations would be computed on real time basis immediately. Then only it is possible to forewarn people from the likely affected cities, towns, and villages about the likely flood level and its probable timing at all such vulnerable places. It is also necessary to prepare action plans which would be implemented in a coordinated manner by all the concerned departments of the Govt. at these cities and villages. As per expected flood levels, it is necessary to shift the likely affected people temporarily to pre decided schools/colleges located at higher levels in the city. Actions such as disconnecting electric supply in such areas, closure of affected roads etc are also to be taken in time. Normally collector of the district is in charge of implementing these flood protection action plans. In the Indo-Gangetic basins where floods may last for many days, arrangements of transportation of people by boats to safe places have to be made. Arrangements of distributing food packets and drinking water to the affected people by helicopters or boats may also have to be made.

In the Maharashtra State, in all the cities and towns which are likely to be affected by floods, 'Blue lines' and 'Red lines' are marked all along the river course on either bank of the rivers. Blue line is the likely flood level for a flood having frequency of 1 in 25 years, whereas red line is the likely flood level for a flood having frequency of 1 in 100 years. No encroachments of any type on the river course are permitted below the blue line. Low level bridges across the river have their level above blue line and they are to be so planned and designed that their piers and retaining walls at both ends would cause minimum obstruction to the flow of water in the river course. Between blue and red line, roads can be constructed on either bank, but construction of houses, buildings or any permanent structure is not permitted. High level bridges have their level above the red line. Floods of magnitude more than the 1 in 100 years frequency are also likely to occur in some years and rescue plan should also provide for measures to be taken in that contingency. All bridges, however, cause some obstruction to the flow of water thereby causing some afflux on its upstream side, but that is unavoidable as long as obstruction in river flow is only due to the bridge piers. Such obstruction can be reduced by having longer spans and lesser number of piers.

**Damage due to floods in the past -**

India is highly vulnerable to floods and the frequency of major floods is more than once in five years. Out of the total geographical area of 329 million hectares (mha), more than 40 mha is flood prone. Floods are a recurrent phenomenon, which cause huge loss of lives and damage to livelihood systems, property, infrastructure, and public utilities. It is a cause for concern that flood related damages show an increasing trend. According to the National Disaster Management Authority (NDMA), about 75 lakh hectares of land was affected every year, 1600 lives were lost and inflicted damage worth Rs 1,805 crore to crops, houses and public utilities every year in India. However, the average annual flood damage in the period from 1996 to 2005 was Rs. 4745 crores as compared to Rs. 1805 crores, the corresponding average for the previous 53 years. This can be attributed to many reasons including a steep increase in population, rising costs of buildings, rapid urbanization, growing developmental and economic activities in flood plains coupled with global warming. The maximum number of lives (11,316) were lost due to floods in the year 1977. According to data from Central Water Commission, the total flood-related losses in India were estimated to be over Rs 37 lakh crore from 1953 to 2017.

**Worst floods recorded in the history of the world** – Following are the three major floods in which millions of people have lost their lives.

1. Yellow River Flood (1887), Qing, China - Yellow River flood that started in September 1887 and lasted till October 1887, is thought to have killed 0.9 to 2 million people. It was China's deadliest flood ever and one of the worst natural disasters. Farmers who lived near the Yellow River for hundreds of years had built earthen dikes to confine/contain the floods. Around September 28, 1887, rising river flood broke through the dikes near Zhengzhou, Henan Province, in Huayuankou, because of days of sustained heavy rain. Because of the nearby low-lying plains, the flood quickly spread across Northern China, covering an area of about 1,30,000 sqkm. and hitting both cities and towns in the countryside. About two million people lost their homes. More people died because of the disease and lack of basic needs than from the flood itself.

2. Yangtze River Flood (1931), China - The Yangtze-Huai River flood happened from June to August 1931 in the areas of central and eastern China and flooded densely populated cities like Wuhan, Nanjing, and some other large cities. On August 25, 1931, a dike along Lake Gaoyou broke. Field investigations for the University of Nanking estimated that 50,000 people had died. The official story says that 1,40,000 people drowned and that 2 million people died during the flood, either from drowning or due to not having enough food. In the following year, from May 1932 to April 1933, there was cholera pandemic in which about 32,000 people died. The flood had affected the lives of an estimated 52 million people. Total death toll of the flood ranges between 0.85 to 4 million, depending on the source.

3. Banqiao Dam Failure (1975), Henan, China - The Banqiao Dam disaster happened in Henan, China, in August 1975, when Typhoon Nina broke the Banqiao Dam and 61 other dams. The Banqiao Dam was built for a one-in-thousand-year rainfall event of 300 mm/day. However, near the typhoon's centre, more than a year's worth of rain fell in just one day. The dam break caused an estimated death toll of between 26,000 and 2,40,000. It affected 10.15 million people and flooded 30 cities and counties over an area of 12,000 square kilometres. The flood also caused destruction of about 5 to 6.8 million homes.

There were some other major floods which occurred in China as below:

1938 Deliberate Man-Caused Yellow River Flood - In a tactic intended to halt the southward movement of Japanese soldiers from Manchuria before World War II, Chiang Kai-shek ordered his soldiers to breach the levees/dikes of the Yellow River and purposely divert its flow. At least 200,000, maybe millions died, millions more were made homeless and the Japanese advanced anyway. The resulting 1938 Yellow River flood was a man-made flood and has been called the 'largest act of environmental warfare in history'.

Yangtze Floods in 1998 – From 7 to 25 September 1998, the Yangtze River experienced its worst floods in the recent history. Three Gorges dam was not completed at that time. More than 4,100 people were killed, more than 5.8 million houses were destroyed and 13.8 million were left homeless. About 240 million people (a number equal to the entire population of the United States) were affected directly by the rising waters. The floods submerged 8 million hectares of land, affected 21 million hectares, and destroyed 4 million hectares of crops. Dikes were blown up in Jianli County to save Wuhan, a city of 7 million people 240 km upstream. Even then waters reached waist level in downtown Wuhan.

Yangtze Floods in 2020 - In early June 2020, heavy rains caused by the regional rainy season led to floods severely affecting large areas of southern China including the Yangtze basin and its tributaries. Three Gorges dam was completed before these floods. Rains and floods extended to central and eastern China during July and were described as the worst since at least 1998. According to the Ministry of Emergency Management, by the end of June flooding had displaced 0.74 million people across 26 provinces. As up to 13 August 2020, the floods have affected about 63 million people and caused a direct economic loss of 179 billion CNY. 219 people were found dead or missing, and 54,000 houses collapsed. There was some moderation of floods due to the completed Three Gorges Dam on the Yangtze River, which had reduced the damage of property.

**Conclusion** – Droughts and floods are the natural events on which we do not have much control. What we can do is to take possible structural measures to reduce intensity of both these events and to minimise their adverse impacts. We can also do advance planning and preparations to deal with these natural calamities so that the affected people would face the situation effectively and would not suffer much. Intensity of natural floods was reduced due to construction of several storage dams in most of the river basins. Effective moderation of floods was also done by systematic operation of spillway gates of major dams constructed on rivers in the basins. Because of the rainfall data from self-recording rain gauge stations, it was possible to know magnitude of floods in advance and forewarn the people from vulnerable areas so that they could face the floods to minimise loss of lives and property. Influence of floods is in the form of damage to property & crops and is confined only in the flood prone area on the banks of rivers and the period is limited to certain number of days or weeks in each such event.

However, influence of droughts is spread over vast area from one or more river basins/states and the period may be about a year or even more. It hence affects large section of the population of the state or the country over a long period of time. Famines in India during the period prior to 1944 had claimed lives of millions of people. But by increasing irrigation facilities provided by the construction of several dam-canal structures of varying sizes, much relief was provided to the drought prone area in the country. Providing of labour-intensive productive water storage/conservation works to the drought affected people and providing them with adequate food grains at subsidised rates had resulted in no casualties during droughts after the independence. Due to increase in the irrigation facilities and providing supporting activities in the agriculture sector, 'Green Revolution' became a reality within about two decades after the independence. Country could hence achieve sustainable food and water security from then onwards till today.

# Chapter 12
# Artificial Rain

*Rainfall and snowfall are the primary sources of water resource. Its total magnitude varies from year to year, place to place and from basin to basin. We have seen so far as to how we can make optimum and equitable use of the finite water resource in the river basins, by constructing suitable infrastructure to achieve intra-basin and inter-basin transfer of water. But there are limitations on such measures because man has no control on the rainfall magnitude or the rainfall pattern at any place or in any river basin. This situation challenged ingenuity of the human mind to explore some measures which would enable him to exercise some control on the natural rainfall. Aim was to create such conditions artificially in the natural clouds which would culminate in occurrence of rainfall at the desired location where there is acute water shortage in a year. If it could be implemented successfully, it would provide some relief to the population from such locations. Artificial rain technique could also be adopted to serve some other purposes such as hailstone suppression, fog/smog dispersal, reduction in the particulate matter in the polluted air above cities etc. The chapter covers technical details of the logic behind 'cloud seeding' as a means to cause artificial rain, and its detailed procedure including scope & limitations of efficacy of the technique of causing artificial rain.*

All the terrestrial ecosystems (rain forests, deciduous forests, savanna etc.) at any place on the earth, have been evolved and developed, by always remaining compatible to the climate and availability of rainwater & groundwater. When it rains, part of it percolates and gets temporarily stored in the ground as groundwater. Rest of it flows through rivers to the sea, but some of it gets stored on way in the natural lakes and man-made reservoirs constructed in the river basin. These water bodies and the water flowing through rivers support the freshwater aquatic ecosystems. Rainwater also meets needs of the man-made ecosystems (farms, pastures etc.). Freshwater bodies, river water and the groundwater also meet various water needs of the humans. Even though magnitude of rainfall varies from year to year, place to place and from basin to basin, over the years, its quantum on an average is finite at a given place. Rainfall pattern, its magnitude and so the water resource at any place depends on its location, topography of the region and climatic conditions. Available water resource in a river basin can be shared equitably by the co-basin countries of the international rivers and co-basin states of the interstate rivers. But the groundwater cannot be shared in a manner similar to the surface water and is exploited freely by the countries and the states within their boundaries. In short, man does not have any control on the process of cloud formation, their conveyance through atmosphere, and finally its condensation & conversion into precipitation. We can only manage the available water resource to meet our water needs as best as is possible.

Let us now see the mechanism of formation of clouds and their condensation into rainfall or snowfall. When lifting of the air takes place due to rise in temperature, the air expands travels upwards and gradually cools adiabatically. As this cooling takes place, the absolute amount of water in vapor form remains the same, but the capacity of the air to hold the water in vapor form decreases. Cool air cannot hold as much water vapor as warm air, so some of the vapor condenses onto tiny pieces of dust that are floating in the air and forms a tiny droplet around each dust particle. When billions of these droplets come together, they become a visible cloud. Any further lifting and cooling results in temperatures at which the available water is greater than can be contained in vapor form in the air parcel, and the excess water is condensed out, generally, in the form of cloud droplets, but, on occasion, directly as ice crystals. It follows then that the amount of cloud water is controlled by the amount of water in an air mass being lifted. If all of this water ends up as precipitation, the precipitation efficiency is 100% at that location. If none of it ends up as precipitation, the precipitation efficiency is 0% at that location.

Clouds which contain water vapour is the primary source of rain, but it cannot be shared by the countries or by the states, over which the clouds float and travel upwards or laterally. This situation challenged the human mind to evolve suitable measures to artificially stimulate the clouds to cause rain at the desired locations. 'Cloud seeding' evolved as a weather modification technique stands as a testament to the human ingenuity in manipulating weather patterns for the greater good (for man). The process involves introduction of substances into the clouds that serve as cloud condensation or ice nuclei, promoting the formation and growth of larger water droplets within the clouds that eventually fall as rain. Clouds are essentially composed of tiny water droplets or ice crystals. Cloud seeding leverages the fact that these droplets need a surface to condense upon, forming larger water droplets. The introduction of seeding agents provides this surface, initiating the coalescence process. Silver iodide, a common cloud seeding agent, has a crystalline structure similar to that of the ice. Other cloud seeding agents are potassium iodide and dry ice (solid carbon dioxide). Use of hygroscopic materials, such as table salt, has also become more popular.

In the year 1891, Louis Gathmann suggested shooting liquid carbon dioxide into rain clouds to cause them to rain. During the 1930s, the Bergeron–Findeisen process theorized that supercooled water droplets present, while ice crystals are released into rain clouds, would cause rain. In July 1946, Schaefer discovered the principle of cloud seeding through a series of serendipitous events. He created a way of experimenting with supercooled clouds using a deep freeze unit of potential agents to stimulate ice crystal growth, i.e., table salt, talcum powder, soils, dust, and various chemical agents with minor effect. While experimenting with 'dry ice' as stimulating agent, he realized that it was more effective to change super-cooled water into ice crystals. At the same time, Dr. Bernard Vonnegut, discovered another method for 'seeding' super-cooled cloud water with the help of 'silver iodide'. Schaefer's method altered a cloud's heat budget, whereas Vonnegut's method altered formative crystal structure. Dry ice and silver iodide agents are effective in changing the physical chemistry of super-cooled clouds, thus useful in augmentation of winter snowfall over mountains. While hygroscopic seeding material most commonly used is table salt for the enhancement of rainfall in warm clouds. In the late 1940s, Langmuir and his colleagues at the General Electric Research Laboratory discovered that dry ice, when dropped into a supercooled cloud deck from an airplane, caused a rapid conversion of water to ice, leading quickly the production of snowflakes and dissipation of cloud in the region seeded. Soon they discovered that silver iodide had same nucleating property. Another method for stimulating the precipitation had been found by injecting salt particles near the base of the cloud to provide centres for droplet formations. After these discoveries, many experiments have been carried out all over the world. The first attempt to modify natural clouds in the field through 'cloud seeding' was experimented by spreading 2.5 kg of dry ice into the target cloud from a plane, near western Massachusetts USA on 13 November 1946.

For over five decades, the study of clouds, rain and the atmosphere has been the work of the Commonwealth Scientific and Industrial Research Organisation (CSIRO) Division of Cloud Physics, now known as Marine and Atmospheric Research. Realising potential importance of above experiments in USA, Taffy Bowen and his staff at the Division of Radio physics, Australia had carried out a trial in eastern New South Wales using RAAF aircraft on the 5th of February 1947. A plane dumped dry ice into one cloud and shortly rain started to fall while the cloud-top mushroomed explosively. This is believed to be the first documented case anywhere in the world of an appreciable man-made rainfall reaching the ground. This striking result held such promise that a systematic program of cloud seeding continued for the next twenty-four years. It was observed that, besides adding dry ice to cold clouds, spraying water into warm clouds was also effective for rainfall in the warmer parts of Australia. The principle of spreading dry ice having a temperature of -80 °C or colder seemed to work best with continental cumulus cloud masses where the air was dirty so that lots of small droplets were formed which were unlikely to coalesce on their own accord. The difficulty with the method of stimulating rainfall was that only a few clouds could be treated on any one day and large amounts of dry ice were required.

This limitation was overcome by the discovery, again in the USA, that tiny quantities of silver iodide smoke could be used as a seeding agent for seeding large areas from the air using silver iodide burners mounted on an aircraft. Silver iodide smoke particles provide 'kernels' on which ice crystals can grow in a supercooled cloud. Theoretically, grams of silver iodide will do much the same job as kilograms of dry ice, so that smaller and cheaper aircraft could be used. Silver iodide seemed to work best in layer clouds formed in air coming in from the sea. From 1955 to 1963 four intensive experiments over South Australia, in the Snowy Mountains were carried out. For each experiment target area of 2 000 to 8 000 sqkm was selected and a neighbouring control area of the same size was not seeded. The first two years were successful, with an estimated rainfall increase of 25%, but in many subsequent years all areas showed a gradual decay of the induced rainfall with time. Subsequent experiments for cloud-seeding trials carried out in 1971 in Tasmania were successful.

During the later part of the decade 1980-1990, the scientific activity of cloud seeding remained subdued mainly because of lack of any new findings. The early decade of 1990-2000, witnessed many advances in the airborne instrumentation, radars, flares and various software packages. The South African cloud seeding experiment was carried out during 1991-1995 with the new technology. The results showed statistical increase in rainfall in all types of clouds (i.e., small to large). This gave impetus to cloud seeding research in different parts of the Globe. Some of the important programmes carried out and in the process were: Mexican experiment: 1996-1998;

United Arab Emirates experiment: 2001-2004; Italy experiment: 2004-2005; Indonesian experiment: 2005; Wyoming experiment: 2005-2010; Southeast Queensland Cloud seeding experiment: 2008-2010.

Such experiments were carried out in many countries of the world subsequently. The largest cloud seeding system was in the People's Republic of China. They had tried it by firing silver iodide rockets into the sky when rain was desired in arid regions, including its capital city, Beijing. However, there were instances when neighbouring regions accused each other of 'stealing rain' by using cloud seeding method. Despite the mixed scientific results, cloud seeding was attempted during the 2008 Summer Olympics in Beijing to coax rain showers out of clouds before they reached the Olympic city in order to prevent rain during the opening and closing ceremonies. In February 2009, China blasted iodide sticks over Beijing to artificially induce snowfall after four months of drought and had blasted iodide sticks over other areas of northern China to increase snowfall. The snowfall in Beijing then lasted for approximately three days. The process of precipitation effectively acts as a natural air purifier, clearing the atmosphere of pollutants. As raindrops form and fall, they capture particulate matter and pollutants present in the air, thereby effectively cleansing the environment. Chinese government used cloud-seeding technique to force rainfall for the evening before the July 1, 2021, celebration event. This rainfall lowered the amount of PM 2.5 pollution by more than two-thirds which helped improve the air quality from "moderate" to "good". The process of precipitation effectively acts as a natural air purifier, clearing the atmosphere of the pollutants. Cloud seeding in the United Arab Emirates (UAE) is a strategy used by the government to address water challenges in the country. Forecasters and scientists have estimated that cloud seeding operations there could enhance rainfall by as much as 30-35% percent in a clear atmosphere, and up to 10-15% in a more humid atmosphere. Since 2021, the UAE has been using a new technology: drones equipped with a payload of electric-charge emission instruments and customised sensors fly at low altitudes and deliver an electric charge to air molecules. In Southeast Asia, open-burning haze pollutes the regional environment. Cloud seeding has been used to improve the air quality by encouraging rainfall. From 1988 onwards, cloud seeding technique was used there for three purposes: filling up dams, lessening the effects of haze, and fighting forest and bush fires.

In some European countries like Slovenia, Germany etc., aircrafts (Cessna 205, 206, 207 & 210) were used since 1983, to fire silver iodide as a cloud seeding reagent. Three crew members work in the operation, two are the pilots in the plane and the third is the radar operator on the ground. The purpose is to prevent damage to farmland and cities in the areas by achieving hail suppression. The activity was financed by local communities and the Ministry of Agriculture had great support among people and farmers from all over the countryside. In Germany, civic engagement societies organized use of aircraft for cloud seeding at regional level to protect agricultural areas from hailstones. Cloud seeding was also used in some federal states particularly known for its winegrowing culture, by organising a program to prevent the formation of hailstones there. Bulgaria operated a national network of hail protection, by planning to fire silver iodide rockets for 7–10 minutes in its entire process with a view to seeding the formation of much smaller hailstones, high in the atmosphere that would melt before reaching ground level. Data collated since the 1960s suggests that huge agricultural sector losses were avoided yearly with this protection system.

In India, pioneering attempts in the field of rainmaking were made by the Tata Firm in 1951 over Western Ghats in the Maharashtra state by using ground-based silver iodide generators. Cloud seeding was also tried later with salt and silver iodide by means of hydrogen filled balloons released from the ground. The committee on the Atmospheric Research of the Council for Scientific and Industrial Research (CSIR) recommended in 1953 that a Rain and Cloud Physics Research (RCPR) unit be set up for undertaking extensive scientific studies on cloud physics and rainmaking. RCPR conducted long term cloud seeding programme over North India using ground-based salt generators during the period 1957-1966, when the results showed an increase in rainfall by 20%. RCPR later became part of Indian Institute of Tropical Meteorology (IITM) and conducted similar experiments Tamil Nadu state during 1973, 1975-1977 and over Mumbai in 1973-74. IITM carried out cloud seeding operations over Rihand dam catchment (Uttar Pradesh state) in 1974 and, over Linganamakki dam catchment (Karnataka state) in 1975. IITM carried out cloud seeding experiments over Baramati region of the Maharashtra state during the period 1973-74, 1976, and 1979-86. The results showed 24% increase in the rainfall. Cloud seeding experiments were caried out in 2003, aimed to benefit 73 Talukas (sub districts) from 8 Districts of drought affected Maharashtra state. Additional rainfall was said to be received in about 286 villages.

Pollution is a year-round problem in Delhi due to factors including high vehicular and industrial emissions and dust. But the city's air turns especially toxic in winter as farmers in neighbouring states burn rice/wheat stubble and crop remnants and the prevailing low wind speeds lead to higher concentration of these pollutants. New Delhi's Air Quality Index (AQI) - which measures the level of PM 2.5 or fine particulate matter in the air - has consistently crossed the 450-mark nearly 10 times the acceptable limit in November 2023. The cloud seeding technology has been planned to be tested in Delhi, but its implementation relied on precise meteorological prerequisites, including the presence of moisture-laden clouds and favourable wind conditions.

From the use of cloud seeding technique in different countries in the world as above, it would be realised that it has served following different objectives:

1. To induce man-made rainfall to meet occasional needs of water in water-short areas.
2. To organise large scale operations of artificial rain in the catchment of a reservoir to increase its storage during acute drought years.
3. To prevent damage to farmlands, grapevines and cities in the areas having temperate climate by achieving hailstone suppression.
4. To lessen the effects of haze and fighting forest and bush fires.
5. Fog/smog dispersal around major airports.
6. To lower down percentage of particulate matter in the polluted air above a city when it is excessive or just before any important celebration/event.

Effectiveness of the cloud seeding technique - While cloud seeding holds promise, it is not without its challenges and controversies. Additionally, the effectiveness of cloud seeding is influenced by a myriad of factors, including cloud type, altitude, wind velocity & direction and atmospheric conditions. Whether cloud seeding is effective in producing a statistically significant increase in precipitation is still a matter of academic debate, with contrasting results depending on the study in question, and contrasting opinion among experts. Following are the opinions expressed by some institutions and experts who have worked extensively in the cloud seeding experiments. "You can squeeze out a little more snow or rain in some places under some conditions, but that's quite different from a program claiming to reliably increase precipitation". "It is difficult to show clearly that cloud seeding has a very large effect". "Cloud seeding could augment the snowpack by a maximum of 3% over an entire season". "Science is unable to say with assurance which, if any, seeding techniques produce positive effects. In the 55 years following the first cloud-seeding demonstrations, substantial progress has been made in understanding the natural processes that account for our daily weather. Yet scientifically acceptable proof for significant seeding effects has not been achieved". "Precipitation from supercooled orographic clouds (clouds that develop over mountains) has been seasonally increased by about 10%". "We cannot make clouds or chase clouds away." From all these observations it would be seen that causing artificial rain by cloud seeding is not a fully dependable or reliable measure but is effective in some cases as below. In Europe where expenses of achieving hail suppression in the cities, farmlands and grapevines by cloud seeding were borne by the beneficiaries, it must be an economically viable and effective measure in such cases. Experiments to lower down percentage of particulate matter and pollutants present in the air, and effectively cleansing the heavily polluted air environment above cities by cloud seeding is worth attempting, duly considering importance of the planned important event. In acute scarcity conditions when the cost of providing water to the people by other alternative measures is costlier than the cloud seeding, it would be worth going for it.

In the case of Australia, there was sufficient precipitation for agriculture and growing pastures in the coastal areas along Eastern, Southern and Northern coast. Central Australia is having very low rainfall and is mostly having arid region. If inducing artificial rain in the coastal areas is successful, naturally there would be corresponding reduction in precipitation in the central arid region. Unfortunately, the terrestrial ecosystems there would not raise any protest for such reduction in their water availability caused by the actions of man but would adjust to live with it. Same is the condition in some areas in America where natural ecosystems would be suffering because of such experiments of artificial rains. But in countries like India, China, and other populous countries of the world, causing artificial rain to benefit certain area would certainly be at the cost of reduction in corresponding rainfall in some nearby area. It would then be like 'Robbing Peter to pay Paul', which would not be acceptable to the sufferers.

Practical limitations in cloud seeding experiments – In the Maharashtra state, cloud seeding was done with the help of airplanes. Detailed procedure of the cloud seeding was as below:

The clouds in which seeding has to be done should have certain percentage of super cooled water. It is desirable to have warm air below which would lift the cloud upwards, and the lateral wind velocity should be moderate. At the same time, in the control room on the ground, equipment such as Radar, Global Positioning System, navigation and tracking system needs to be kept ready. Airplane which can travel at a speed of 300 to 400 km per hour and equipped with arrangements to fire cloud seeding agents from burners are to be kept ready at the nearest airport. In the airplane, instruments which keep constant contact with the control room must be always functional. When the radio waves transmitted from the ground radar get reflected from the prospective cloud cover, they are analysed with the help of computer to know about its coordinates (distance, altitude, and direction), shape, density, water content, velocity, and direction of the cloud travel. This information about the prospective clouds located from a distance of about 250 km can be seen on the screen of the computer after every 6 minutes. If the clouds are suitable for cloud seeding and the direction of wind & its velocity is likely to convey the clouds over the area over which artificial rainfall is needed, further steps have to be taken immediately. Plan of proposed movement of the airplane i.e., longitude, latitude, time, direction, speed of travel, and altitude of the cloud has to be transmitted to the Air Traffic Control Authority of the Govt. and to all the nearest airports located within a radius of 500 km. If the altitude of the clouds is more than 9 to 10 km, it is likely to cause interference in the international flights and hence permission needs to be obtained from that Authority. Only after getting necessary permissions from all these Authorities, the airplane is ready for take-off. Actual time of take-off is then to be decided as per location of the cloud at that time, its distance from the area planned for rainfall, time required between cloud seeding & actual rainfall, and speed of the airplane. If there is delay on account of any reason to get permission from the authorities, the cloud seeding programme needs to be cancelled and postponed. These are the practical limitations which also affect effectiveness of this technique.

Conclusion - During the last 78 years, cloud seeding technique has been adopted in different countries of the world to serve as a source of artificial rain for attaining different purposes. It would be realised from all these experiments that its effectiveness varies from about 5 to 25 percent. It is also very difficult to isolate artificial rainfall from natural rainfall (which would or would not have occurred) to estimate its real effectiveness. Even then this technique could be useful and economically viable to serve some specific purposes such as hail suppression to prevent damage to farmlands, reduction in particulate matter in the polluted air above a city, fog/smog dispersal around major airports etc. Cloud seeding to cause artificial rainfall to meet water needs of drought affected areas is worth giving a try where alternative sources of acquiring water are costly and inadequate to meet water needs of the affected people.

# Chapter 13
# Virtual Water

*'Virtual Water' is quite a new concept which has come before the world at the end of the twentieth century. Certain amount of water is required for producing any organic product which is part of our diet, such as food grains, pulses, oil seeds, vegetables etc., even if we don't see any water in them outwardly. Such water can be said as 'embodied water' or 'virtual water'. We do not realise it because our mindset is not tuned to think that way even though appreciable quantity of water is required for producing them. Even if it is a reality, prima facie it is difficult to visualise it and hence the term 'Virtual Water' was very aptly coined to describe it. Compared with the quantity of water required by us for drinking and domestic use, much more virtual water is required for producing the food that we consume daily. Hence virtual water forms a very significant part which needs to be considered in the planning of our water needs. In all river basins in the world, availability of water resource though variable from year to year, is finite on an average. As against that, human population is increasing in most of the river basins and so the demand of water for them. It is imposing stress on the available water in some of the river basins. Time has now come to think if we can reduce the consumption of produce which needs very high quantity of water per kilogram to produce it. Even if the logic would be easily understood by us, it would be very difficult to change our food habits just to reduce total consumption of water. The term 'Carbon Footprint' for all activities which cause carbon emissions is now accepted by all the countries while planning for reduction in the carbon emissions. On the same lines if 'Water footprint' is printed on every pack of major consumable products, in due course of time it would increase awareness among the consumers to reduce the virtual water consumption. The chapter covers all the related issues.*

The 'virtual water' concept, also known as 'embodied or embedded water', was coined in the year 1993 by John Anthony Allan, who was a British geographer, who had been a long-time water analyst with emphasis on the Middle East. He researched the trade figures of Middle Eastern states to conclude that this water-scarce region was only able to survive through large quantities of food imports in grain, livestock etc. He inferred that, the region was not dependent on its own scarce water resources but could purchase water already embedded in the agricultural produce, imported from water surplus countries. It took nearly a decade to get global recognition of the importance of the concept for achieving regional and global water security. The first international meeting on the subject was held in December 2002 in Delft, Netherlands. A special session was devoted to the issue of virtual water trade at the Third World Water Forum held in Japan, in March 2003. A significant contribution has been the emergence of the concept of benefit-sharing as opposed to water-sharing, or the management of transboundary waters as a public good. In March 2008, Allan was announced to receive the 'Stockholm Water Prize' of US dollars 1,50,000, which is the equivalent to an environmental Nobel Prize. It was awarded due to *'his unique, pioneering and long-lasting work in education and raising the awareness internationally of the interdisciplinary relationships between agricultural production, water use, economies and political processes'.* He has authored or edited seven books and published more than 100 research papers.

The virtual water trade is the hidden flow of water in food or other commodities that are traded from one place to another. The virtual water trade is the idea that when goods and services are exchanged, so is the virtual water. The concept of virtual water trade was introduced to refer to the idea that countries can save domestic water consumption by importing food. Imported food, however, comes from somewhere. Principally two different approaches have been proposed to explain the concept of virtual water. In one approach, the virtual water content is defined as the volume of water that was in reality used to produce the product. In the second approach, one takes a user rather than a producer perspective and defines the virtual water content of a product as the amount of water that would have been required to produce the product at the place where the product was needed. In 2002, Arjen Y. Hoekstra, while working for UNESCO-IHE, introduced the concept of 'Water footprint'. The water footprint shows the link between consumer goods, or a consumption pattern and water use & pollution. Virtual water trade and water footprint can be seen as part of a bigger story, the globalization of water. Hoekstra has defined the virtual-water content of a product (a commodity, good or service) as *"the volume of freshwater used to produce the product, measured at the place where the product was actually produced"*. It refers to the sum of the water use in the various steps of the production chain. Cereal grains have been major carriers of virtual water in countries where water resources are scarce. Therefore, cereal imports can play a crucial role in compensating local water deficit.

Let us now see which are the needs of water for sustenance of life. Food and water are essential for survival of life of all species in the animal kingdom, including humans. Even if water is provided by the nature in the form of rainfall, food is produced only by the plants with the help of water, minerals & nutrients absorbed from soil, and carbon dioxide from the atmosphere, through the process of photosynthesis. The plant food, which is consumed provides nutrients and energy required for our survival, growth, and development. They are conveyed to all parts of the body through the medium of blood. Oxygen is inhaled which is infused in the blood through lungs to purify it and carbon dioxide is exhaled. Hence food, water, solar energy, and oxygen are all essential for survival of all species in the animal world. Besides the water required for drinking, we need water for domestic use such as cooking, washing utensils & clothes and for sanitation & bathing etc. Urban population needs about 100 to 140 litres of water per capita per day for all the above needs. If we ask any educated urbanite as to how much water is required for him every day, he will say about 100 to 120 litres. If we ask him about the water required to produce the food consumed by him every day, he will get confused because he must never have thought about it. If pressed to make a guess, he may say as additional of about 100 to 150 litres, thus making his total water consumption as about 200 to 300 litres per day per person. Reader of this chapter should also make his best guess about the total consumption of water per day per person before reading further.

The following table shows the average virtual water content of some selected products in the farms or other places where they are produced, in India and the world average, in litres per Kilogram (kg).

**Table 1 – Average water consumption to produce organic products.**

| Product | Water required in litres per kg. | |
| --- | --- | --- |
| | **In India** | **World** |
| Rice | 3,000 | 2,300 |
| Wheat | 1,700 | 1,400 |
| Sorghum | 4,100 | 2,900 |
| Sugar cane | 160 | 180 |
| Coffee roasted | 15,000 | 21,000 |
| Tea | 7,000 | 9,200 |
| Milk | 1,400 | 1,000 |
| Beef | 16,500 | 15,500 |
| Pork | 4,500 | 4,900 |
| Goat/Sheep meat | 6,000 | 5,100 |
| Chicken meat | 7,800 | 4,000 |

Source – Wikipedia. (Figures are rounded).

In countries like America, Australia, Canada, Brazil, Russia, South Africa and some European countries, large percentage of irrigated area is under sprinkler irrigation. In countries like Spain Slovak Republic & Israel, percentage of irrigated area under drip irrigation is very high. Crop productivity per hectare in most of these countries is also very high when compared with India. Hence virtual water requirement for the world average figures to produce one kilogram of food grains, milk, and meat, as shown in the Table above are somewhat less than in India.

Let us now see how much water is actually required to produce food grains and other components of our food. Food grains are produced by practicing rain-fed cultivation where use of rainwater is made for growth of the crop. In the case of irrigated agriculture, additional water is applied to the crop as per its needs from sowing to maturity. In both the cases water is directly consumed by the crop. But there are many operations such as levelling, ploughing the field, sowing, removing of weeds, applying fertilisers and insecticides, harvesting, and finally processing to get the food grains. Lot of animal power and manpower is required for all these operations. Water required/consumed by animals and cultivator/labours during the crop growth period should also be charged to produce food grains. On similar lines, water required for all operations such as transporting from field, storing, conveying the food grains up to the consumer should also be added to it, if the total water requirement is measured at the consumer level. Dividing the quantity of total direct and indirect water requirement to produce & supply food grains in one hectare computed as above, by the average production of food grains per hectare in kilograms, we would get following modified figures for some cereals. These are the average requirements of virtual water for producing these food grains and delivering them to the user in India.

| | |
|---|---|
| Rice | 4,500 litres per kg |
| Wheat | 3,500 litres per kg |
| Sorghum | 3,000 litres per kg |

Weighted average for food grains under Indian conditions can be taken as about 4,000 litres per kg.

Average food consumption per capita per day in the year 2000 in India, China and USA was about 550, 980 and 2,850 grams respectively. Annual food need of India was then about 200 million Tonnes (MT). Due to increase in the standard of living of the people during 25 years since then, it is expected to rise to about 750 grams per capita per day in 2025, with total annual food grain demand of about 375 MT in India. If we consider that about 4,000 litres of water are required to produce one kilogram of food (weighted average of cereals, pulses, oil seeds and vegetables), we consume about 3,000 litres (4,000 X 0.75 kg = 3,000) of water through food consumption per day in India. In the developed countries water requirement to produce and deliver up to the user 1 kg of food as above may be less but daily consumption per person is much higher than in India. Hence total water requirement for food per vegetarian person in the developed country may be about 4,000 to 4,500 litres per day. Would you believe that every man consumes about 15 to 22 barrels (oil barrels each of capacity 200 litres) of water through food consumption every day?

Let us now consider water requirement for growing sugar cane and manufacturing refined sugar from it as in the Maharashtra state, India, which produces about 40 to 45% of the sugar produced in India. Sugar cane is a 12 to 14-month duration crop. Firstly, we must consider the rainwater and irrigation water applied to the sugar cane crop from sowing to harvesting. Indirect water required for operations such as cultivating, cutting, and transporting it to sugar factory are to be considered for refined sugar. In addition to it, water requirement for processing the sugar cane in the sugar factory up to the stage of final product of refined sugar cane, as well as for storing and conveying it up to the customer should be added to it. Because irrigation water to sugar cane in the Maharashtra state is mostly delivered by flood irrigation method, it is estimated that, about 20 to 25 million litres of water are required to produce average of about 80 tons of sugar cane per hectare. On an average, ratio of weight of refined sugar to the weight of sugarcane processed is about 10% in the State. It means that to produce 1 kg of sugar, about 2,500 litres of water is required in India. As per figure in the above Table, in India it requires 1,600 litres of water to produce sugar, with a ratio of 10% for sugar to sugarcane weight. For one cup of tea or coffee, about 1 to 1.5 spoonful of sugar (10 to 15 grams) is desirable, which requires about 25 to 35 litres of water to produce. Adding for the water required for milk, tea leaves/coffee powder, total requirement for one cup would be about 35 to 45 litres i.e., more than two bucketsful of water. Would you realise that for two cups of tea or coffee in a day, one consumes about 70 to 90 litres of virtual water every day? Those who do not consume sugar due to diabetes or for health reasons would feel elated to know that they are saving about 60 to 80 litres of precious water every day.

So far, we have seen the water requirement for the vegetarian diet. Now let us see the water requirement for the nonvegetarian diet. In most of the developed countries, in addition to the green or dry fodder from the pastures, supplementary organic food prepared from corn, milo etc. is also fed to cows, sheep, goats and pigs. Such nutritional organic food is invariably given to chicken in their enclosed sheds. After consuming about 10-15 kg of such food by the cattle and about 5 to 7 kg by the chicken, about 1 kg of flesh would be gained by them. Even if it is assumed that only about 1,000 to 1,200 litres of water are required to produce one kg of food & fodder, about 14,000 to 15,000 litres of water would be required to produce one kg of beef and 8,000 to 10,000 litres for goat meat. Whereas about 7,000 litres of water would be required to produce one kg of pork and 5,000 to 6,000 litres to produce one kg of chicken. If we assume that daily food consumption in developed countries is about 1 to 1.5 kg per day per person and 20% of it is beef, pork, and chicken, daily virtual water consumption on an average for food per person may be about 6,000 to 7,500 litres.

In India few decades before, goats, sheep used to consume naturally available food in open fallow areas which were kept reserved in the villages for them. Fodder was also available as biproduct from agriculture. Chickens used to consume household food waste and some low-quality grains. That time virtual water requirement for meat and chicken was much less. But now cows, sheep & goats feed in pastures or on green or dry fodder and some supplementary nutritious food, hence virtual water consumption has increased to about 8,000 to 10,000 litres per kg of meat. Chickens are grown in closed sheds, and they are fed on organic food made from corns, millets etc. and hence virtual water consumption may be about 5,000 to 6,000 litres per kg of chicken meat. Hence meat consumers in India might be consuming about 4,000 to 4,500 litres of virtual water per person per day.

For the aquatic life such as fishes, crabs, prawns etc. which grow in sea water or in the sweet water of lakes and rivers, they require least quantity of water to survive and thrive. They feed on Phyto plankton, Zoo plankton, algae, aquatic plants, and microorganisms etc. Big size fishes consume small size fishes & other aquatic creatures to thrive. One more notable point about fishes and aquatic creatures (excluding water living mammals) is that they are cold blooded creatures. Their body temperature varies as per temperature of the ambient water and does not remain nearly constant like that of the warm-blooded animals. Hence their energy needs to grow and gain flesh are less than the warm-blooded creatures living on land or in water. Compared with cows, goat, sheep, and pigs for their meat, fishes and prawns grow fast to gain flesh with much less food consumption. Prawn farms and fish farms are ideal for growing them in small size sweet-water ponds or saltwater ponds. There are some large size fish farms along coastline of some islands in the Philippines. But fish farming in sea water is not common so far in other countries. In view of this it can be said that consumers of sea food require least virtual water in their food consumption.

Countries which have suitable climate and sufficient water to grow cereals, oil seeds, fruits, vegetables, and flowers firstly produce them to meet their indigenous requirements. But when they produce them on large scale and export them to other rich countries such as petrodollar earning countries in the middle East, Japan, or some European countries, they are actually exporting virtual water. Food producing countries would in turn generate more employment for labourers in the rural area in that process, which is beneficial for the populous developing and underdeveloped countries. By importing cereals, fruits, and meat etc., from such countries, rich countries would actually be importing about 4,000 to 10,000 litres of water (food grains to meat) for every kg of imported product and save their water to that extent. It is hence a mutually beneficial export-import trade. However, low-income countries in the sub-Saharan part of the African continent and other least developed countries may not have the financial resources and knowledge about the green revolution technology for producing adequate food grains to meet food needs of their rising population. They should be provided with financial assistance from the Financial Institutions like World Bank to create water resource development infrastructure on a large scale. If technical guidance is given to them to follow best water management practices and to adopt 'Green Revolution' technology, they can achieve sustainable food security as explained in the earlier chapters. Because of the availability of cheap labour in these underdeveloped countries, they can grow high value crops and export them (virtual water trade) to needy rich countries to support country's economy.

The term 'Carbon footprint' serves as an indicator to compare the total amount of greenhouse gas emissions ($CO_2$-equivalent) from an activity, product, company, or country. For any food product, for the benefit of its consumer, it is customary to print details of contents of its components such as sugar, fat, vitamins etc. on its packing. On similar lines, for cereals, edible oils, tea & coffee powder, beef, meat, chicken etc., 'water footprint' i.e., virtual water in litres per kg required to produce that product should be printed on its package. It would create some awareness among the consumers by realising that how much virtual water they are consuming with it. During the next 2-3 decades, total water demand in the developing countries would increase, till their population stabilises. For the underdeveloped countries, it may stabilise in the last quarter of the 21$^{st}$ century. It is bound to impose stress on the total usable water resource in those countries. Hence all possible efforts should be taken to reduce consumption of actual water and virtual water.

Conclusion – Virtual water is a new concept, and common man would normally may not be aware of it. It is difficult to visualise as to how much water is embodied in an organic food material such as food grains, edible oil, milk, meat etc. When any developing country exports food grains or meat to a developed country it could be visualised as exporting water to that country. Besides that, producing them generates employment in many ways in the developing country, which is beneficial for their economy, provided they have enough assured water to produce those grains and other export products. Concept of 'water footprint' should be started now, because it may gain importance in the future when the water resource would be scarce in comparison with its ever-rising needs.

# Chapter 14
# If the River Could Speak – Autobiography of a River

*Terrestrial ecosystems on the earth have the first charge on the rainwater, next being that of the groundwater and the balance water flowing over the earth surface is conveyed by the rivers to the sea while supporting freshwater aquatic ecosystems. In the initial mountainous reaches, rivers erode their bed & banks, pulverise that material on their way and carry it along with silt conveyed by rainwater towards downstream to deposit along their banks to form fertile lands in the plains right up to formation of delta region in the estuaries. This activity of the rivers had been going on uninterrupted for over many millions of years in the past. Very recently, entry of 'Modern Man' on the earth started to intervene in this natural process. To start with, he destroyed terrestrial ecosystems to grow pastures and food grain crops on land to meet his food needs. He then exploited groundwater for agriculture and harnessed river water by constructing various types of infrastructure on the rivers. Because of that, many perennially flowing rivers started to run dry during summer months. Polluted effluent generated after urban and industrial use of water was released untreated in the rivers to pollute them, thereby degenerating the riverine aquatic ecosystem completely. Rivers which had acted as a lifeline for the 'Living world' for millions of years before, were throttled, strangled, and were degraded due to such actions by the man. How a River would react to such actions by the self-centred and so called 'wise man', if river could speak out her feelings, has been narrated in this chapter.*

**"I remember, I remember, the house where I was born, the little window where the sun came peeping in at morn; He never came a wink too soon, nor brought too long a day, But now, I often wish the night had borne my breath away!"** (Poem by Thomas Hood 1799-1845).

I heard the above poem about 70-80 years before, when school children used to recite it loudly in the school classes. Its first two lines have now been modified by me as follows:

**"I remember, I remember the place where I was born, High up in the mountains covered by trees, from where the sun came peeping in at morn."**

These two lines as above elicit the start of my life. However, the next two lines are as per the original poem, which very aptly describe how I feel at present about my life today, and in reality, it is the miserable story of my life as narrated hereafter.

I was born, just a trickle, high up in the mountains. When it rained, I fully enjoyed trundling down the valley, having trees overhanging along both sides forming an umbriferous canopy through which sunlight filtered here and there. In my childhood I fully enjoyed my downward journey through the picturesque valley overshadowed by clouds & trees and reached the plains beyond the hill ranges. Now I was mature and was flowing steadily downstream when my cousin sisters joined me from left side and right side. We all were flowing together happily through the plains along with the aquatic life supported by us. But who was 'me' in reality? I was constantly on the move and what was there in this moment changed in the very next moment. Some philosopher has said that *'No man ever steps in the same river twice, for it's not the same river and he's not the same man'*. It is my true description because constantly to be on the move is my nature. What was relatively stationary was the channel starting from the mountains up to the sea, which I had carved out and created during last millions of years, through which I was flowing now. Men staying along my banks had given me a name, myself being elder among all my cousin sisters, as a river flowing through the riverbed starting from mountains and ending up to the sea.

I was born in mountains of the Peninsular southern India in high rainfall zone and after traversing tract of rain shadow area finally met sea in the eastern coast. During rainy season, many times I used to flow full when it rained and was very proud of it. It was the clouds who really were my 'Creators' and I was only conveying the water supplied by them during four months of the rainy season. Earlier I had a feeling that it is because of me that the forests were thriving and were green. But after the rainy season I used to get weak day by day but still the forest land was green with trees and bushes. Then I realised that, my creator – the clouds – was firstly satisfying water needs of all the terrestrial ecosystems and was then feeding me with the surplus water. Land which was densely covered with rain forests and deciduous forests was storing good amount of rainwater in the ground which would provide them with water all the year round for their sustenance and growth. The stored groundwater would also feed me during winter and summer season when it rarely rained. Hence in reality, the terrestrial ecosystems and the sub strata below which supported them, in reality were my 'Mentors' after the rainy season. Even then, when at the end of the summer season, when I used to get very weak, I would request my creator to do me a favour by resuming the rain showers. He would then fulfil my demand and that of all my sisters demand as well. I learnt that some of my sisters in the North India rose from snow covered Himalaya mountains. They would have floods during rainy season like me and would also have enough flow in them during the summer season due to snowmelt. Hence unlike me they were perennial rivers. I had some flow even during summer months in my lower reach.

I was happy and proud that I could support several types of water living plants and algae which was food for fishes, frogs, prawns and other aquatic creatures. Many types of birds and animals would also depend on them for their survival. Many four-legged animals used to quench their thirst by drinking my water. Everything was going fine and there was not much change in that routine for the last millions of years. One day a strange looking two-legged animal came near me and quenched his thirst. He used to come then for drinking and bathing in my water. One day some 8-10 similar looking animals came and started living in small huts built up by them on my bank. I was happy to live in their lively company. Then on one day they started cutting trees in a patch of forest land located along my bank and burnt all the cut trees & bushes. With the onset of next rainy season, I could see some grass like plants growing on that patch of land. Later I learnt that he was also tending domesticated animals such as cows and goats on the grass land that was developed by him as pasture on the disforested forest land. He was consuming milk of the cattle and treated other domesticated animals as source of meat for his survival.

After some years, he continued the practice of disforestation over more and more area, but started growing different type of plants which would slowly grow and remain in the field for quite some time till end of the rainy season. I then realised that the produce from those plants was a source of food for him. I then realised that he was very resourceful and quite different from the other four-legged animals living in the forest. I was happy that the fertile land created by the silt which I had carried during last millions of years was of some use to him to grow crops. But to meet his rising food needs, when he started cutting and burning trees and bushes at many places in the forest on my banks, I realised that he was damaging my 'mentor' permanently. Most of the rainwater from such disforested land would flow to the river unobstructed and less would percolate below to recharge the groundwater which was the source of my survival after the rainy season. Such actions were slowly weakening me more and more after the rainy season. But I was helpless and could do nothing to stop him. Earlier even during floods in the rainy season, water carried by me was not much muddy because the grass and bushes growing on the forest land were preventing erosion of the topsoil with the rainwater. But when he started practicing agriculture on several patches of the forest land, soil from the bare land was getting eroded by the rainwater which would make my water very muddy during the entire rainy season. Even if he destructed the forest land for practicing cultivation and caused to erode the soil, I carried that silt with me and deposited it further downstream along my banks to create some fertile land for him. Even if he was selfish, why should I change my nature?

Sometimes the clouds provided by my creator used to do more favour on me to cause my flooding which destroyed the cluster of huts built by the two-legged men to stay and even carried some of them with me. Some land under cultivation along my banks would also get damaged due to floods. Even if I had no control on my floods, still he blamed and cursed me for the damage caused on account of my floods. After some years he started constructing earthen embankment across small streams on my tributaries to store rainwater to create small water ponds which would meet his drinking water needs and that of the cattle after the rainy season. Subsequently, some such small ponds were also constructed to irrigate paddy crop as well. Land under forests which was my mentor, had nearly lost its capacity to hold and provide groundwater for my survival during winter and summer season. In addition to that, he started exploiting groundwater to irrigate the crops which he was growing as rainfed crops. So, I used to go further weak in the winter season and was getting completely dry in the summer months in some years. While meeting his needs of water he did not care that his actions were throttling me to death in some years.

Then he started diverting my water in the lower reaches and that of some of my perennial sisters to convey it to his fields along their banks to irrigate food crops for him. Some years later he constructed a high masonry wall across me to join two small hillocks located near my both banks. My water coming from the high rainfall zone was getting stored against that wall and excess incoming flood water was then conveyed on downstream from over the wall in the central portion. The stored water was then conveyed by means of channels to the fields in the low rainfall zone to irrigate crops during winter and summer season. I was very happy then because of two reasons. First reason was that my water flowing during rainy season which otherwise would simply flow unused to the sea, was getting stored in the lake created by the masonry wall and was of good use to him. Second reason was that, because of the irrigation facilities provided to the dry land, land productivity increased many times, and that much forest land elsewhere was saved from being brought under cultivation by destroying the forest. It prevented destruction of my mentor – the forest land – to provide me some more water during fair weather season.

Still at some locations, instead of spending money on creating reservoirs created by constructing earthen embankments or masonry walls, he preferred the soft option of destroying the forest to bring that land under cultivation to grow crops. Rain forest, deciduous forest, savannah, grassland etc., were all different types of terrestrial ecosystems. Trees, bushes, creepers, and grass growing in these forests had supported different types of insects, birds, herbivore and carnivores. Population of every type of living creature in these forests had acquired a balance based on the principle of survival of the fittest, which formed a relatively stable terrestrial ecosystem. When some part of the forest was destroyed by him, it was the death warrant for the plant life and also for the animal life supported by that part of the forest. Was the wise man not aware of it when he recklessly destroyed the forest land to meet food needs of his ever-increasing population? Could he not control his rising population within reasonable limits, the way in which the nature maintains the balance between plants and animals to suit the availability of natural resources?

When his population increased further and he started industrial development and resulting consequent urbanisation, urban & industrial water demand appreciably increased. To meet rising demand of food grains, it became necessary to provide irrigation facilities on a large scale to the rainfed crops. Unlike irrigated agriculture, lot of water from more dependable sources was required for cities and industries. Hence, he constructed very large infrastructure of earth dams, masonry dams, and concrete dams to meet all those water demands. These large reservoirs submerged some forest land, some villages and occasionally some small towns. In respect of submergence of forest land, it was indirectly compensated because the increased irrigation facilities increased the land productivity and indirectly saved destruction of appreciable area under forests for cultivation. As regards submergence of villages and rehabilitation of affected people to new locations, it was the most difficult social problem for him to handle. I had seen these villages established along both of my banks wherein the villagers were happily staying there for many generations. They had psychological attachment me as their mentor, to the land cultivated by them and to their houses where they and their forefathers had lived happily for many generations. Shifting to a new location and adjusting to the living conditions there was also a psychological problem, and adjusting to the new location would require duration of even one generation. It was very painful for me to see the plight of those project affected people. But fortunately, some social activists united all of them and raised their voice of protest by making demands before the policy makers for providing them all the necessary facilities in the rehabilitated villages at the project cost. It took some time to take necessary policy decisions and to implement them, but ultimately the activists succeeded in their goal. Affected people were allotted land for land and were also provided with irrigation facilities. I was then very happy to see them well settled in their well planned new resettled villages along fringe of the reservoir created by my water. All the social activists should certainly be complimented for this commendable work done by them.

On the same lines, some environmentalists raised their voice against submergence of forest land under these large reservoirs. I learnt that, in practice submergence of reserved forest and National sanctuaries was always avoided during planning of dams. But since dams are preferably located in hilly areas to reduce submergence under reservoirs, acquisition of some forest land was unavoidable. Clearance to construction of such projects was exceptional and was given only after carrying out environmental impact study. For all the developmental activities in the country, I learnt that about 2 to 3% of the total forest land was acquired. I appreciate the concern shown by the environmentalists due to destruction of forest in such cases. But I always wondered where these environmentalists had gone when nearly 13 to 15% forest land in the country had vanished during last 60-70 years after independence? It was firstly because of the gradual but sustained encroachments on the forest land to bring it under cultivation. Secondly there was large scale unauthorised cutting of trees by the forest contractors for the wood required for building construction, woodwork, and furniture business. It has degraded the quality of rich forests at many places. This practice is still continuing in some states in India. If you raise your voice for non-acquisition of forest land for developmental activities such as reservoirs, roads, and railways, it gets good publicity. But for the slow but sustained destruction of forest by the land encroachers and forest contractors, no environmentalists had come forward during last 60-70 years, with the exception of movements initiated by some dedicated enlightened individuals in the Himalayan ranges in the North India. Due to such unauthorised disforestation, degradation of forest land had taken place and many of my sisters were deprived of their fair-weather regeneration flow which was earlier received by them from that forest land.

Sewage generated after urban use of water and effluent generated after industrial use of water was supposed to be treated fully prior to its release in the rivers. Industrial effluent was partially treated but it still contained some toxic chemicals. Most of the urban sewage containing faecal matter, pathogens, nitrates, and phosphates was released in me and my sisters untreated. It provided food for the most aggressive fresh waterweed like 'Water Hyacinth', which had caused to cover most of the rivers completely after rainy season during the fair-weather season. It prevented contact of river water below with the air, to reduce percentage of oxygen in the river water to practically nil, so that no other aquatic plants and creatures could survive in the polluted river water. Even then, my polluted water was being lifted to irrigate fields from the small weirs which were constructed on me and some of my sisters. Where such weirs were not there, cultivators along both banks also lifted river water to irrigate their fields. Such use of polluted water contaminated the agricultural produce grown and polluted groundwater in that area, which then could not be used from wells in the villages for drinking purposes. My polluted water also entered in the reservoirs constructed on me on downstream and polluted them too. I had conveyed most of the rainwater and provided the man with clean fresh water to meet his needs, but what he has given me in return was the polluted water which suffocated me during fair weather season. If presence of pathogens in the polluted water would cause pandemics such as cholera or gastroenteritis, he would still blame me for that. Immediate measures to control the pandemic would be taken by him, but actions to treat entire sewage prior to its release in rivers to remove the root cause of river water pollution would still not be taken by him.

Overuse of groundwater and surface water reduced the flow of fresh water in me and all my sisters. All flow in rivers in the fair-weather season was only that of the untreated or partially treated effluent. Hence environmentalists suggested that environmental flow in the rivers should be maintained during fair weather season even by releasing water from the existing reservoirs. If it was done so, it would only result in dilution of the heavily polluted flow in the rivers. Cultivators on both the banks would then get more water to lift it for irrigation. Hence it was not a practical solution to ensure environmental flow by releasing water from reservoirs. But if the entire urban sewage and industrial effluent would be fully treated and then only released in rivers, there would be environmental flow of treated water in the fair-weather season. It would then support the aquatic life in me as before and I would enjoy their company. However, it would be the responsibility of the implementing agencies and the environmentalists to ensure that only specified quantity would then be lifted for irrigation and balance would be the environmental flow. But it is next to impossible to achieve it in practice because of the pressure from the several needy small cultivators located on both banks of the rivers.

Due to construction of large dams on major rivers, there was lot of moderation in the magnitude of floods on their downstream, which provided great relief for the population of the cities located on my banks. I was happy on that account. However, sustained reduction in the flood magnitude provided very good opportunity for the city slums of poor people to unauthorisedly construct their cluster of huts along my banks and reside there. Since that was the prime location in the cities, influential builders persuaded/pressurised slum dwellers to relocate and constructed multi-storeyed buildings along banks by encroaching permanently in my flow path. Municipal Corporations also constructed more bridges across me which also obstructed in my flow path. Such irresponsible actions by the man used to worry me a lot but what could I do? In some years when my creator was very generous by causing cloud bursts or sustained intense rain spells over long period, I was getting heavily flooded to expose ill effects of such encroachments in my waterway. Even if flooding in cities was caused because of such obstructions, city dwellers would still blame me and the reservoirs on upstream for the damage which the floods had caused. People would clamour for stopping all such constrictions in my waterway thereafter due to encroachments by the multistorey buildings. But within the next 3-4 years people would forget about it and further encroachments on my waterway by the influential builders would continue. Farmers from rural area would also encroach on my waterway by terracing along my banks to grow crops there. If crops on such encroached land got damaged due to my occasional flooding, farmers would still blame me for that and demand compensation for the loss.

Population of man on the earth was increasing during last century and I learnt that it is still increasing very fast in some countries of the world. To meet needs of such uncontrolled increase in the population, lot of natural resources would be snatched by the humans from the ecosystems for their survival and wellbeing. It has already resulted in extinction of many species of plants, insects, animals, and birds from the earth, and it would continue unabated hereafter. Is the 'Wise man' not aware of it? Why cannot the so-called wise man keep check/control on his uncontrolled rising population? Even if he has throttled me and polluted me by his self-centred actions, I cannot change my nature to help the natural ecosystems and to him. When he makes use of my water by storing it in structures constructed by him, which otherwise would flow unused to the sea, I was happy that it could meet his food and water needs. But when he snatched groundwater to weaken me and also polluted my water, I considered it as an ingratitude on his part. What else could I do? That is why I had said in the beginning that, *'But now, I often wish the night had borne my breath away!'*. But that is not in my hand. Water would evaporate from water bodies to form clouds up in the sky and they would eventually shower rain i.e., life for the living world year after year as before. I have no choice but would have to convey the rainwater as before and be of whatever use to him. I only wish that somebody should tell the 'Wise man' that he should take following two actions immediately. First would be to take immediate strict measures to control his rate of rise of population, which would limit his uncontrolled destruction of forest land and snatching of water resource from the terrestrial and aquatic ecosystems. Second would be to treat all the urban sewage and industrial effluent fully prior to its release in the rivers. If both these measures are taken by him, I would live happily thereafter along with him and be his lifeline in the true sense forever. Would somebody apprise that man of my grief and educate him to redress my grievances? I only hope for the best for him and for me!

# Chapter 15
# How the Water Sector can Adapt to the Adverse Effects of Global Warming and Climate Change

*Increase in the emission of Green House Gases because of the various developmental activities undertaken by the humans during last two centuries, happens to be the main cause of Global Warming and consequential Climate Change. These developmental activities such as tending of domestic animals, agriculture, water resource development, industrialisation and urbanisation have accelerated the rate of emission of Green House Gases such as, carbon dioxide, methane, nitrous oxide, etc. Increase in the percentage of these gases in the atmosphere had trapped the heat energy that was getting reflected unobstructed into the outer space earlier. It slowly increased temperature of atmosphere around the Globe, which is known as 'Global Warming', which in turn has caused some adverse impacts on the Climate, which is known as 'Climate Change'. Reduction in concentration of these greenhouse gases in the atmosphere is essential if we want to limit the hazardous effects of climate change. But it needs coordinated efforts primarily by the developed countries and the countries with emerging economy. It must be understood that it is a ground reality that GW & CC have come to stay on the earth. After lot of persuasions and negotiations at the world level, it appears possible to make some headway to reduce the pace of GHG emissions. Under the circumstances, the only course available before all countries of the world would be to gradually stop GHG emissions totally by 2050 or so, if we have to limit the rise in temperature up to about 1.5 degree Celsius. Secondly, they have to take appropriate measures in all the affected developmental sectors to mitigate adverse impacts of the climate change. The Chapter covers full details of the causes of GW & CC, possible measures to reduce their concentration in the atmosphere and about the desirable actions to be taken to adapt to its adverse impacts on the vital Water Sector.*

At the peak of the most recent ice age, around 18,000 years ago, sea level was about 130 meters lower than what it is now. As the ice age receded, average temperature of the globe increased, and substantial part of the earth became habitable from about 12,000 years before. Rise in global temperature resulted in snow melt, receding of glaciers, and rise in the sea level nearly close to its present level. Deforestation by the 'Slash and Burn' process for growing pastures and growing food grain crops on the land, which was practiced by the humans from about 12,000 years before, has caused to increase in the emission of carbon dioxide ($CO_2$). Presence of $CO_2$ in the atmosphere is, however, essential for the plants to produce food by the process of photosynthesis. Methane is produced from the decaying organic matter from the natural wetlands & from the agricultural operations related to the ponded paddy crop. It is also released from the digestion process of flatulent animals (ruminating animals like cow, sheep, goats etc.). Methane is more potent than the $CO_2$ as a Green House Gas (GHG). Use of fossil fuels (coal, oil, and natural gas) as a source of thermal energy and prime mover for the industrial revolution had appreciably accelerated the rate of emission of $CO_2$ in the atmosphere. Growth of industries has caused to release some gases in the atmosphere such as Nitrous Oxide ($N_2O$) and Hydrofluorocarbons (HFC) etc., which also are more potent than the $CO_2$. All these gases are known as Greenhouse Gases (GHG). Before industrialisation, presence of GHG in the atmosphere was not much and most of the solar heat energy falling on the earth was getting reflected in the space. Because of the increased percentage of GHG in the atmosphere, the reflected solar heat energy was getting trapped like a green house. Rapidly increasing percentage (parts per million) of GHG in the atmosphere during the last two centuries has slowly caused to increase temperature of the atmosphere. The first person to spot the connection between atmospheric temperature and the human activities was a 19th century scientist called Swante Arrhenius. In the year 1938, a British Engineer Guy Calendar claimed to have inferred from the analysis of the record of temperatures of sea water extended over many years that, it has been rising consistently and so the world was gradually warming.

Global Warming - Solar energy transmitted from the sun is received on the earth in the form of light and heat waves. Because of the very high temperature of the Sun, frequency of incoming waves is very high, and the wavelength is short. Presence of GHG like $CO_2$, water vapour, methane etc., in the earth's atmosphere does not obstruct the high frequency solar energy while falling on the earth. Some of the light energy is absorbed by the plants to produce food by the process of photosynthesis and some of the solar heat energy is absorbed by the land as well as in oceans and water bodies on the earth. The part of the earth which is covered by ice reflects most of the solar energy received from the sun. The rest of it gets reflected in space from the surface of the earth, again in the form of waves. When the solar energy gets reflected, because of the low temperature of the earth, frequency of heat waves gets shortened, and the wavelength lengthens. Due to that change, transmission of those reflected heat waves into outer space is obstructed by the high presence of GHG in the atmosphere and the heat energy so trapped then contributes to increase in the atmospheric temperature. Hence it is called as 'Global Warming' (GW).

Deforestation caused by adopting 'slash and burn' technique, besides causing carbon emissions, had stopped the sequestration (storing) of carbon that was continuously taking place in the trunks and branches of trees in the forests. Due to rapid growth of industries, the transport sector, and the thermal power generation plants set up in the developed countries during the nineteenth and twentieth century, use of fossil fuels increased appreciably. Hence percentage of GHG emissions in the atmosphere started increasing at a fast rate. At present USA is the world's biggest producer of GHG, though not for long. Since beginning of the last quarter of the 20th century, developing countries like China, India and Brazil have started contributing significantly to GHG emissions. China would shortly overtake America, and India would not be far behind. Levels of GHG (carbon emission equivalent) in the atmosphere have increased from about 280 parts per million (ppm) before the industrial revolution, to about 400 ppm by 2020, and it is rising at the rate of about 2 ppm/year at present. Because of the greenhouse effect caused by the presence of GHG in the atmosphere, global temperature has been rising at a faster rate. It has been estimated to have risen by about 0.6 degree Celsius during the last century. Objectives declared in the World Conferences on this subject is to limit carbon emissions to a conservative figure of 450 ppm and with a permissible rise in global temperature by about 1 to 2 degrees Celsius, but preferably not more than 1.5 degrees Celsius. GW is causing the snow from snow caps and glaciers to melt at a faster rate, resulting in very slow rise in the sea level. Sea level also rises because the water expands as it warms. Over the past 100 years, it seems to have risen, on an average by about 10-20 cm, but measuring that accurately has proved to be a surprisingly hard task. Because most of the ice in the Arctic is 'sea ice', level of the sea would not change much even if it melted. But because ice in Antarctica and Greenland is on land, sea level would rise appreciably when it melts.

Climate Change – Global warming is expected to have impacts on the climate of the world in many ways. Global temperature is expected to rise at an increased pace due to substantial and unabated increase in the quantum of carbon emissions since middle of the twentieth century. It is expected to influence and change the climate of many parts of the world in the near future, and hence is termed as 'Climate Change' (CC). How much the average temperature of the globe would increase in the near and the distant future, would depend primarily on the amount of GHG emissions by the developed and the developing countries, at the global level. Consequently, how it would affect the climate & the precipitation pattern in different countries of the world, and how much would the sea level is likely to rise due to resultant accelerated snowmelt by the year 2050 and 2100, has become a contentious and debatable issue.

Rise in sea level would cause submergence of low-lying agricultural lands along the shallow coastlines (e.g., Bangladesh, Male etc.) and would affect functioning of many major ports in the world. Snow melt from the ice caps would change salinity level of the sea water near it, would reduce temperature of the sea around and would affect the present course and quantum of flow of the Gulf stream and some other sea currents. It would gradually change atmospheric conditions of nearby countries which are at present benefitted by these sea currents. Rise in the temperature of the sea would reduce capacity of the sea to absorb and retain carbon emissions. However, because of the reduction in temperature of the sea water due to snowmelt, water would sink to lower levels and fresh water from there would come to the surface and would absorb more carbon emissions. This is likely to be a favourable issue for storing carbon in the sea water. Rise in sea level would increase ingress of sea water on the land and affect availability of fresh groundwater in the coastal areas. Snow-fed Himalayan rivers would receive increased runoff due to snow melt for some years. CC would affect local climate and the precipitation pattern in the countries influenced by them. But almost all climatologists and weather experts in the world agree on one effect of CC viz., frequency of occurrence of extreme climatic events and their intensity would gradually increase in the future. In simple terms, it would mean that there would be increase in the number of events and the intensity of floods, cyclones, hurricanes, and that of droughts in most of the river basins of the world.

Following coordinated actions were taken so far at the world level to face man-made calamities on the globe –

Ozone layer depletion - Ozone layer exists in the stratosphere between 15 km and 30 km above the earth and it shields us and other living creatures from the sun's harmful Ultraviolet (UV) radiation. Systematic observations of actual concentration of ozone in this layer were started in the seventies of the last century. It was observed that concentration of ozone (in parts per million) in this layer was reducing at some locations in the stratosphere above the earth, which was then termed as ozone depletion. From 1970 to 1984 there was reduction of about 33 percent in the concentration of ozone over Antarctica. Based on these observations, a paper was written by Jo Foreman, Brian Gardiner and Jonathan Shanklin and was published in 1985. Such gradual thinning of earth's protective ozone layer in the upper atmosphere was caused by the release of chemical compounds containing gaseous chlorine or bromine from industries and other human activities. The largest decrease of ozone in the layer took place in the high latitudes (toward the poles), and the smallest decrease occurred in the lower latitudes (the tropics). The thinning was most pronounced in the polar regions, especially over Antarctica. Ozone depletion was a major environmental problem because it increased the amount of UV radiation that reached earth's surface, which increased the rate of skin cancer, eye cataracts, and genetic and immune system damage. In the seventies it was realized that human-produced Chlorofluorocarbons (CFCs) and Bromine monoxide (BrO), were the major sources of chlorine and bromine in the stratosphere. Free chlorine atoms & chlorine-containing gases, such as chlorine monoxide (ClO), and bromine could then break ozone molecules apart by stripping away one of the three oxygen atoms. Worst part in it was that the same atom of chlorine and bromine still remained intact and would continue to convert more and more ozone into oxygen then onwards. Halocarbons produced by industry for a variety of uses, such as refrigerants (in refrigerators, air conditioners, and large chillers), propellants for aerosol cans, blowing agents for making plastic foams etc., were also splitting ozone into oxygen.

These concerns led to organising the world level Conference at Montreal, Canada, in 1987 to discuss these issues and to take possible corrective measures. All the participating nations agreed to adopt the 1987 United Nations Environment Programme (UNEP) Montreal Protocol, which banned the production of CFCs, halocarbons, and other ozone-depleting chemicals. These chemicals were to be replaced by other chemicals which were effective in their purpose but were not producing free chlorine and bromine, which was causing splitting of ozone into oxygen. Following the ban on ozone-depleting chemicals, the concentration of ozone in the layer above the poles started reducing gradually. The ban came into effect in 1989 and very gradually the ozone levels started stabilizing by the mid-1990s. **The Montreal Protocol has been considered the most successful international environmental agreement to date.** All countries of the world acted promptly by replacing the chemicals by their safe alternatives. They were not required to do much extra expenditure for this change and that is the main reason for its prompt implementation by all countries of the world. UN projected that under the current regulations, the ozone layer will completely regenerate by 2045, thirty years earlier than previously predicted.

Reduction in the intensity of Global Warming & Climate Change – Global warming and resulting climate change can be said as an irreversible process. However, some amelioration in its undesirable effects was possible, if GHG emissions could be controlled/reduced by coordinated efforts of all the countries at the global level. Need to take necessary coordinated action was much felt at the world level. The World Meteorological Organization (WMO) and the United Nations Environment Programme (UNEP) established the Intergovernmental Panel on Climate Change

(IPCC) in 1988. IPCC is an intergovernmental body of the United Nations, and its job is to advance scientific knowledge about climate change caused by the human activities. Hence it is an internationally accepted authority on climate change. The United Nations endorsed the creation of the IPCC later that year. First Assessment Report (FAR) was published by the IPCC in 1990.

In 1992, in all 166 nations including the United States, met in Rio de Janeiro to open the UN Framework Convention on Climate Change for signatures. Under the convention, nations agreed to non-binding reductions in emissions of greenhouse gases to 1990 levels by 2000. The agreement also established a framework for continuing negotiations by means of a Conference of Parties (COP) that would meet periodically and whose resolutions would be subject to ratification by parties to the Framework Convention. Spurred by concerns that countries were not achieving the Framework's reduction goals, the COP convened the First Conference on Climate Change in Berlin In 1995. The conference agreed to a uniform approach to emissions reporting and to pursue a binding commitment on emissions reduction goals. This agreement was known as the 'Berlin Mandate'. Since then, the United Nations Climate Change Conferences are yearly conferences held in the framework of the United Nations Framework Convention on Climate Change (UNFCCC), to assess progress in dealing with the issues related to the climate change.

In December 1997, in all 151 nations met in Kyoto, Japan, to finalize the agreement by the nations to regulate the carbon emissions. The greenhouse gases covered by the Kyoto agreement were carbon dioxide ($CO_2$), methane ($CH_4$), nitrous oxide ($NO_2$), hydrofluorocarbons (HFCs), perfluorocarbons (PFCs), and sulphur hexafluoride ($SF_6$). The Kyoto Protocol divided nations into two basic groups viz., economically developed countries and economically developing countries. It noted that the largest share of historical and current emissions originated in the developed countries. Its first basic principle was that these countries should take the lead role in combating climate change and in minimising its adverse impacts. Developed countries were to reduce GHG emissions by an average of 6 to 8% below 1990 levels between 2008 to 2012. The protocol recognized that developing countries had a right to economic development and noted that GHG emissions would grow as these countries expanded their industries to improve social and economic conditions for their citizens. These countries did not have any reduction targets or deadlines, but some must take "meaningful" climate control measures. In addition, developed countries must support climate change activities and technology in the developing countries by providing financial support above what they would otherwise provide. Finally, 'Kyoto Protocol' was initiated in 1997, but it was to be effective from the year 2005. America and Australia did not accept provisions of the protocol (Australia accepted them in 2007)

In the Conference held in 2011 in Durban, South Africa, it was agreed to start negotiations on a legally binding deal comprising all countries, to be adopted in 2015, governing the period post 2020. There was also progress regarding the creation of a Green Climate Fund (GCF) for which a management framework was adopted. The fund was to distribute US$100 billion per year to help poor countries to adapt to the climate impacts. In the conference held in 2012 in Doha, Qatar, the Doha Amendment to the Kyoto Protocol featuring a second commitment period running from 2012 until 2020, limited in scope to 15% of the global carbon dioxide emissions due to the lack of commitments of Japan, Russia, Belarus, Ukraine, New Zealand, United States and Canada and due to the fact that developing countries like China (the world's largest emitter), India and Brazil were not subject to emissions reductions under the Kyoto Protocol. Next COP29 would be held in Baku in Azerbaijan in November 2024 to review actual performance of all countries in respect of their commitments to reduce GHG emissions. Discussions would be held about future course of action in agreeing to specific time bound commitments by the developed countries to reduce their GHG emissions. Most important issue of review of progress regarding the creation of a Green Climate Fund (GCF), would also be discussed. Such financial assistance provided to the underdeveloped and developing countries is most essential for their contribution in reduction of GHG, without jeopardizing their progress in their developmental activities hereafter.

After the First Assessment Report published by the IPCC in 1990, next FARs were published in the years 1995, 2001, 2007 and 2013. The IPCC's most recent report was the Sixth Assessment Report, the final synthesis of which was completed in March 2023. It confirmed that the climate was already changing in every region. Strong reductions in GHG emissions would limit climate change, but it could take 20-30 years for the climate to stabilize. Climate change due to human activities was already affecting the lives of billions of people and it was of a disrupting nature. The world faced unavoidable hazards over the next two decades even with global warming of 1.5°C. It would be impossible to limit warming to 1.5°C without immediate and deep cuts in the greenhouse gas emissions.

Efficacy of actions in the above World Level Conferences –

I have purposefully cited the case of depletion of ozone layer as above in which, all nations in the world agreed to the recommendations of the 1987 Montreal Protocol and acted accordingly and hence the intensity and ill effects of ozone depletion could be controlled and contained. This was possible because there was not much financial liability while replacing the chemicals which were then used as refrigerants, propellants for aerosol cans, blowing agents for making plastic foams etc. by the chemicals which were not causing ozone depletion. Such was not the case with achieving reduction in the emission of GHG which contributed to the hazardous effects of GW & CC. Developed countries were reluctant to bind themselves to a time-bound programme of drastic reductions in their carbon emissions those were presently released because of the extensive use of fossil fuels. Discarding infrastructure already created for those energy sources and replacing them by the non-conventional sources (solar, wind power, atomic energy etc.) was going to involve substantial additional expenses. On the other hand, the developing & underdeveloped countries were blaming the developed countries because contribution of about 70% in the total carbon emissions effected so far was by the developed countries. They felt that they had already enjoyed benefits of their development achieved so far and hence it was the prime responsibility of the developed countries to stop their carbon emissions altogether hereafter. Carbon emissions by the countries with emerging economy have been increasing presently at a very fast rate and hence they should also take actions to make use of non-conventional alternative energy sources. The underdeveloped countries were unwilling to accept any reduction in carbon emissions unless adequate financial assistance was provided to them for making necessary structural changes, so that it would not affect their future developmental plans. Because of such conflicting interests, there has been a stalemate at present in achieving desirable reduction in GHG emissions by means of a time bound commitment by all countries of the world.

Possible adverse impacts of GW & CC in different parts of the world –

General Circulation Models (GCM) are the most credible tools designed to simulate a time series of climate variables globally, accounting for the effects of GHG emissions in the atmosphere. Results of GCM are subject to a number of uncertainties due to incomplete knowledge about the underlying geophysical processes of global change and dynamics of uncertain future scenarios. However, IPCC has made following broad regional projections; **Africa is one of the continents, most vulnerable to increased water stress and low food productivity along the margin of arid and semi-arid areas.** Many countries in Asia are likely to be affected due to flooding and droughts, associated with accelerated glacial melt in the Himalayas. South, East and South-East Asia will be at great risk from sea level rise. Australia would suffer due to reduced precipitation and increased evapotranspiration, resulting in decline in agriculture, forest produce and biodiversity. In Latin America, decrease in soil moisture (green water) may replace tropical forests by savannas and reduce biodiversity in the eastern part of the rain forest. Glaciers on the continent may disappear. North America may suffer due to winter flooding and reduced summer flows, thereby straining the over-allocated water resources. Intensity of tropical storms may also increase. Europe may suffer due to retreating glaciers and longer growing seasons. Reduced runoff would affect water availability, hydropower potential and crop productivity. In general, rise in the global temperature would bring more area under agriculture in the northern parts of Europe and North America.

Impacts of GW & CC on the Indian sub-continent – South-West monsoon is India's predominant source of water. As a result of Global Warming, rate of temperature rise is much higher over the land-covered Northern hemisphere, compared to the predominantly oceanic Southern hemisphere. It provides an increased land-sea thermal contrast, which can be considered as being favourable for strengthening of the S-W monsoon in future. Climate models also indicate possibility of extending of the monsoon season. However, search for an ideal climate model is still on. As regards Himalayan rivers, possible linkage of retreat of glaciers with rise in average annual surface temperature of the country is yet to be confirmed. Even if runoff increases due to enhanced snow melt, its effect on the magnitude of total runoff available would depend on the percentage contribution of snow melt at any given place on these rivers. Enhanced snow melt would, however, have higher potential of flood hazards in the Northern plains. Central and Southern India is likely to be subjected to severe and more frequent droughts as a result of GW & CC, even though average precipitation may be on the higher side.

However, since GW & CC appears to be a ground reality and has come to stay, we must take proactive steps to mitigate or counter its effects on the sectors which are more vulnerable and sensitive to it. 'Water Sector' is the important sector, which would be subjected to some adverse impacts of the GW & CC. Since water is a very potent agent in ensuring socio-economic development of the society, it would be prudent to study these undesirable impacts on the Water

Resource Development (WRD) infrastructure and to take appropriate measures right now to brace the water sector, to face these challenges for a more secured and desirable future. 'Agriculture Sector' is the other sector which would also have serious impact because of probable reduction in productivity of many staple crops due to effects of GW & CC.

Measures to mitigate effects of GW & CC – Atmospheric warming speeded up the water cycle, increasing precipitation & generating glacier melting, altered water availability & seasonality, and influenced both human livelihoods & natural ecosystems. The CC foreseen in the IPCC's Report has major implications for the water sector. Many of the CC impacts on economy, human health, hunger, and diseases are transferred to human livelihoods by temperature-driven alterations of the water cycle. Paragraphs herein below explain the mechanism and current scientific understanding of GW & CC and its impacts on natural & man-made ecosystems, including their vulnerability and their capacity to adapt. Most importantly, it covers the possible measures which could be taken in the WRD infrastructure, to cope up with the adverse effects of GW and CC. For ensuring sustainable food and water security to any country, development of water resource to increase irrigation facilities and the need to take suitable measures in the agriculture sector to increase crop productivity are essential. Hence scope of desirable activities in these two important sectors to ameliorate the adverse effects of GW & CC has been elaborated below.

Water Sector - Firstly, we would have to assess how the existing WRD Infrastructure (Dams and canals) would respond to the contingency of increased frequency and magnitude of floods and droughts, while continuing to meet with expected rise in various competing and conflicting demands on water hereafter till the population stabilises. Secondly, we would have to explore the nature of modifications/improvements those would have to be made in the existing dams and river diversion structures, to cope up with such changes in the precipitation & runoff pattern, causing more frequent and intense floods and droughts. Thirdly, we would have to review and revise the standards and norms for design of dams and canals in the future, to take care of these inevitable ill effects of GW & CC. It could be achieved by taking recourse to appropriate scientific and technological measures, while continuing to effectively meet the ever increasing and changing demands of water.

Following are some of the measures which would fortify the WRD infrastructure to face these future challenges.

1) Major and medium projects in India are at present designed for 75% dependability (reservoirs planned to fill to capacity in 3 out of 4 years), as per Central Water Commission (CWC), New Delhi, guidelines. With the expected increased variability in the precipitation and hence the runoff pattern in future, it is obligatory to design all storages (including the existing storages wherever possible), for 50% dependability (reservoir filling in 2 out of 4 years), or on the basis of average annual runoff (which is usually about the same as 50% dependable runoff). At present such relaxation is permissible for the major & medium projects if they benefit drought prone area. Capacity of reservoirs would thereby increase, to accommodate the excess water available during high-rainfall years, to meet water requirements during low-rainfall years. Incidentally, in view of the Krishna River Water Dispute Tribunal Award recently declared in

December 2010, water availability in the Krishna basin has been estimated on the basis of 65% dependability, for its allocation amongst the co-basin states. Allocation of water amongst co-basin states in the water-short Cauvery River basin in the South India has been based on 50% dependability as per the Award declared some years before. Proposals should hence be made to the CWC before it is too late, for relaxation in the standards of water planning of all the major and medium projects in all the river basins in India, for adopting dependability of 50% or on the basis of average annual runoff.

2) Adequate provision for carryover capacity should be an essential feature while designing storage capacity of all major projects here after, where water is planned to be used for perennial crops and/or for urban/industrial use. Wherever possible, adequate carryover capacity shall be provided for completed/in progress projects. It would take care of the situation of late outbreak of monsoon season and would improve dependability of the supply side.

3) Interstate River Basin Organizations (IRBO) should be set up for Interstate rivers such as Krishna, Godavari, Tapi, Narmada etc. in the Peninsular India, to serve following objectives:

   i) To evolve a policy to decide spillway gate operation schedules and then to regulate/control releases of water from all storages in the basin during drought years in such a manner that, stored water in all the dams in the basin is shared more equitably amongst all co-basin states. Aim would be to share the distress of water shortage experienced during water-short years as much as is practical.

   ii) To evolve a comprehensive computerized model for control, regulation, mitigation, and monitoring of floods, by planning synchronized regulation and control of all gated spillways in the basin. It would then be possible operate the spillway gates to cause moderation of incoming floods. With the installation of self-recording rain gauge stations and tele transmission of that data, real time estimation of probable flood magnitude at vulnerable locations would be known in advance. This information would enable forewarning the affected people, to reduce loss of life and property during high floods.

4) Live storage of all the existing reservoirs in the Maharashtra state gets continuously reduced at the rate of about 0.3 to 1 percent each year because of the siltation, resulting in continuous impairment in its utility to serve the planned design objectives. To make good this loss of live storage, wherever possible, capacity of existing reservoirs should be increased by raising full reservoir level by providing flaps on spillway radial gates, by increasing length of spillway & reducing flood lift to raise Full Reservoir Level, increasing flood discharging capacity of un-gated spillways by providing Labyrinth weir instead of a straight wall and by installing automatic gates on the un-gated spillways. For the reservoirs where rate of siltation is high, Catchment Area Treatment measures should be implemented in the catchments to reduce the rate of siltation and to increase useful life of reservoirs.

5) To meet food grain needs of the projected population of 1700 to 1800 million of our country before 2050, annual food grain production of 290-330 MT in 2020 would have to be increased to about 500-590 MT, in the next 25-30 years. Since the total area under cultivation is not

likely to increase in the next 25-30 years, irrigated agriculture would naturally have to bear the brunt of this onerous task, besides adoption of modern technologies in agriculture sector to increase land productivity. This could be achieved by the soft option of modernizing/upgrading the existing infrastructure and increasing water use efficiency & crop productivity through involvement of beneficiaries in the irrigation management of surface irrigation schemes. Introducing conveyance of water by closed pipe system for new canals and distribution system would appreciably reduce the conveyance losses. Resorting to water saving technologies such as introducing Micro Irrigation (drip & sprinkler systems) even on surface irrigation schemes etc., would also be essential. It should be complemented by promoting use of GW and by augmenting the GW recharge by resorting to soil and water conservation measures through Watershed Development works, wherever there is scope to do so. This would be in addition to the hard option of completing all ongoing water-storage/river diversion schemes and taking up all possible new schemes, by making PAPs as the first beneficiaries of such schemes. As per the present policy, all new WR development structures would have minimum adverse impact on the environment and the natural terrestrial and aquatic ecosystems.

6) With the increasing rate of urbanization and industrialization, non-consumptive use of water would be steadily on the increase, inevitably at the cost of lesser availability of water for irrigation purposes. Lack of any treatment, or grossly inadequate treatment of the effluent generated after such non irrigation use of water has been causing pollution, not only of the rivers, but also of the man-made reservoirs into which these rivers drain. Where polluted river water is presently lifted and used for providing irrigation to land on both the banks, it is causing pollution of the groundwater in such areas. Besides that, the agriculture produce would contain harmful toxic chemicals and carcinogens in it. Removal of pollutants from the GW is a very difficult job. Hence full treatment of all effluent prior to its release in rivers would avoid degradation of all natural and man-made aquatic ecosystems. Only after providing adequate treatment to the entire effluent generated after urban use, reuse of the treated water shall be made for irrigated agriculture. Only then present water allocation for irrigated agriculture would be restored at least partly, which is very vital to achieve sustainable self-sufficiency in food grains till 2050, when the population of the country is expected to stabilise. For the people who use river or reservoir water for drinking purposes, it would also avoid possibility of outbreak of epidemics and would eradicate possibility of incidence of water-borne diseases. Full recycling of water used by industries (use-treat-reuse, and ideally the zero effluent) shall be aimed at and effluent left if any shall be fully treated prior to its release into rivers.

7) With the adoption of Micro Irrigation technology and GW development, there would be increased consumption of electricity, resulting in rise in GHG emissions in case the power is generated by means of thermal power stations. However, it could be more than compensated by generating hydropower, for which sizeable potential exists in the country in the North India. There is good scope for generating electricity by unconventional measures such as atomic power, wind power and solar power, which is free from GHG emissions. Solar power-driven pumps would be a very good alternative for introducing MIS on well irrigation in most of the states in India because of availability good sunlight during winter and summer season.

8) One important viable measure to augment water availability in the country would be, to implement right earnestly, the Inter Basin Water Transfer Project (Interlinking of Rivers - ILR) at the national level. It would meet many of the challenges posed by the CC, in the following manner:

   i) It would mitigate flood hazards (more necessary with the increased intensity and frequency because of CC) in the river basins of snow-fed Himalayan rivers in the North India because construction of some major dams on the northern tributaries of the Brahmaputra River has been planned in the Inter Linking of Rivers.

   ii) It would generate about 34,000 MW of environment-friendly hydropower to reduce GHG emissions to that extent and to get corresponding Carbon Credits.

   iii) It would mitigate drought situation in the peninsular river basins and in the totally water scarce river basins in the North-West, because of water transfers to these river basins from water-surplus river basins in the Central and the North India respectively.

   iv) It would augment utilizable surface water availability of the country by about 25 percent of the present ultimate availability, to provide irrigation facilities to additional 34 million hectares of land, to increase food grain production. It would also provide water security to large sections of the population.

   v) It would provide water transport facilities through some of the link canals and some sections of the rivers, to enable cheap and lesser GHG emission alternative, when compared with other means of transport.

9) With the increased frequency of occurrence of droughts because of CC, WR development planning should be aimed to achieve equity in water distribution at the national level and to ensure availability of water to the more needy sections of the society. At the intra-basin level, it could be achieved by promoting minor irrigation schemes, GW development and watershed development schemes. At the national level it could be achieved by Inter basin water transfer.

In short, if the challenges posed by GW & CC on the water sector are to be effectively countered, we would have to chalk out an adaptive strategy. It should ensure minimum loss in utility of the existing WRD infrastructure and should achieve implementation of plans of development in the future by taking appropriate actions as above, and as summarized below:

- Design all dams for a lower dependability to have larger size storages.
- Provide carryover storage capacity in dams at the planning stage.
- Set up the River Basin Organizations to enable coordinated operation of all reservoirs in the basin to mitigate flood hazards and to share water distress during drought years.
- Increase live storages of completed dams wherever possible, to make good actual loss in their live storage on account of siltation of the reservoirs.
- Adopt soft options of improving water-use efficiency of completed projects and hard option of completing all the ongoing schemes and taking up all possible new storages/river diversion schemes.

- Ensure adequate treatment to all the effluent generated from urban and industrial use, for its reuse in irrigated agriculture, to restore the curtailed irrigation to increase food productivity and to prevent pollution of rivers and reservoirs.

- Take up all the environment-friendly hydropower projects on priority, including pumped storage schemes.

- Implement Interlinking of Rivers at the national and the state level, to ensure optimum exploitation and equitable allocation of water.

Agriculture Sector – Due to rise in the average temperature of the atmosphere, present production of staple food grain crops such as wheat, maize, rice etc., is expected to reduce in the future. It would be necessary to do field experiments through Agriculture Universities to evolve new strains of these crops which would thrive even with the rise in temperature and under drought conditions. Suitability of the present food grain strains would slowly shift northwards in the northern hemisphere and southwards in the southern hemisphere. It would also mean that some additional area in both the hemispheres would be brought under cultivation due to rise in the global temperature. Effects of rise in temperature for all other crops would have to be studied and attempts should be made to evolve new strains of crops which would be compatible to the effects of climate change. There is substantial emission of methane gas from the ponded paddy crop which is cultivated on very extensive scale in the Asian region. Some experiments carried out indicate that, by modifying the present method of ponded paddy it is possible to reduce methane emissions. If that practice is promoted on a large scale in Asia, it is possible to reduce carbon emissions by about 3 to 4 giga tonnes. Agriculture Universities and other institutions should carry out more experiments to refine such techniques.

Conclusion – Global Warming is the adverse side effect of the developmental activities initiated by humans during the last two centuries and has come to stay on the globe. Concerted efforts are being taken by all the developed countries and countries with emerging economies to keep the GHG emissions within pre decided safe limit. But still there are some uncertainties about the expected rate of GHG emissions in the near and the distant future, and its adverse effects on the global climate, and more importantly on the precipitation pattern in different regions of the world. Since 'Water' is a very effective potent agent in meeting basic needs of sustenance of life on the earth and in ensuring socio-economic development of the humans, it is vital to study effects of GW & CC on the possible changes in the availability of WR in different parts of the world. Since there are limitations on what we can do to control and regulate climate and the precipitation, best approach would be to prognosticate it on a scientific basis and prepare ourselves to face the situation as best as is possible. This is possible to a certain extent by implementing optimum development of water resource, making appropriate modifications in the WR development infrastructure, managing the water more efficiently and by making necessary modifications in the agriculture sector so that they are responsive in moderating undesirable impacts of the climate change.

# Chapter 16
# Actions at the World level on Water, Environment and Climate Change

*United Nations took initiative to organise discussions at the global level on issues related to Environment, Water and Climate Change. Several conferences were organised in which these issues were discussed with experts from many countries in the world, to evolve good guidelines for all the countries to follow. It increased awareness amongst the countries about the need to change their outlook while dealing with complexities of the problems in achieving sustainable development. Issue of ozone layer depletion could be resolved only because of discussions in one such conference and the coordinated actions taken by all countries of the world. Some Institutions were established at the world level for detailed study of certain aspects of water resource. Some world water weeks were celebrated in some developed countries to spread awareness about water and environment related issues. Based on experience in their country, many experts presented technical papers, and representatives of the countries were exposed during deliberations, to the latest technology being practiced in those countries. Issue of climate change was discussed in the world level annual conferences and some positive actions were taken by some developed countries to mitigate its adverse impacts. However, much needs to be done hereafter to reduce carbon emissions during the next two-three decades. The chapter covers details of such conferences, issues discussed therein, and effectiveness of the actions taken by all countries in the world.*

During second quarter of the twentieth century, activities in most of the countries in the world were overshadowed by the 'Second World War'. League of Nations established after the first world war was not seen to be much effective. Hence issue of establishing a new organisation of countries of the world was discussed even during the world war time. Finally, The United Nations officially succeeded in existence on 24th October 1945, when the UN Charter had been ratified by a majority of the original 51 Member states. The purpose of the United Nations was to bring all nations of the world together to work for peace and development, based on the principles of justice, human dignity, and well-being of all the people. It allowed countries to balance global interdependence and national interests when addressing international problems. The United Nations has four purposes: to maintain international peace and security; to develop friendly relations among nations; to cooperate in solving international problems & in promoting respect for human rights; and to be a centre for harmonizing the actions of nations. Cooperating in this effort there are more than 30 affiliated organizations, known together as the UN system. United Nations Organisation took initiative in organising many international conferences to discuss important issues such as Water, Environment, Climate Change etc. Many vital issues on these topics were discussed in these conferences whereas the concerned institutions ensured implementation of the enabling policies to achieve the desired goals. Experience gained by different countries was shared in the 'world week festivals' for their mutual benefits. This is how coordinated efforts were taken by all countries of the world to respond to the various challenges before them. Following are the brief details of all these activities taken at the world level.

A) <u>**Actions at the World level through various Conferences**</u> -

1) <u>**Conferences on the Human Environment** -</u>

**1.10 United Nations Conference on the Human Environment, 5-16 June 1972, Stockholm, Sweden** – It is said to be the birth of the United Nations Environment Programme (UNEP). It was the first world conference to make the environment a major issue. In all 122 countries participated in the conference, of which 70 were the developing countries. The roots of the Stockholm conference lie in a 1968 proposal from Sweden that the UN should hold an international conference to examine environmental problems and identify those issues which required international cooperation to solve. The participants adopted a series of principles for sound management of the environment including the Stockholm Declaration and Action Plan for the Human Environment and several resolutions. The Stockholm Declaration, which contained 26 principles, placed environmental issues at the forefront of international concerns and marked the start of a dialogue between industrialized and developing countries on the link between economic growth, pollution of the air, water, & oceans and well-being of the people around the world. The resolutions called for a ban on nuclear weapon tests that may lead to radioactive fallout, an international databank on environmental data, the need to address actions linked to development and environment, international organizational changes, and the creation of an environmental fund. The final declaration was a statement of human rights as well as an acknowledgment of the need for environmental protection. The first principle began *"Man has the fundamental right to freedom, equality and adequate conditions of life, in an environment of a quality that permits a life of dignity and well-being."* Developing nations supported the creation of the UNEP, which was created as a result of this conference. It was the first UN agency to be based in Nairobi, Kenya, a developing country.

**1.20 Brundtland Commission Report 1983** - The Brundtland Commission, formerly the World Commission on Environment and Development, was a sub-organization of the United Nations that aimed to unite countries in pursuit of sustainable development. It was founded in 1983 with Gro Harlem Brundtland, former Prime Minister of Norway, as chairperson of the commission, because of her strong background in the sciences and public health. The Brundtland Commission's mandate was to re-examine the critical issues of environment and development and to formulate innovative, concrete, and realistic action proposals to deal with them.

The Commission focused its attention on the areas of population, food security, the loss of species and genetic resources, energy, industry, and human settlements - realizing that all of these are connected and cannot be treated in isolation one from another. The commission suggested that while the 'environment' was previously perceived as a sphere separate from human emotion or action, and 'development' was a term habitually used to describe political goals or economic progress, it is more comprehensive to understand the two terms in relation to each other. It stated that, the environment is where we live; and development is what we all do in attempting to improve our lot within that abode. The two are inseparable. The Brundtland Report elaborated the conflict between globalized economic growth and accelerating ecological degradation by redefining economic development in terms of sustainable development. It is credited with crafting the most prevalent definition of sustainability: *"Sustainable development is development that meets the needs of the present without compromising the ability of future generations to meet their own needs."*

The Brundtland Commission was officially dissolved in 1987 after releasing 'Our Common Future', also known as the 'Brundtland Report'. The document popularized the term "sustainable development" and won the Grawemeyer Award in 1991.

**1.30 United Nations Conference on Environment and Development, Rio de Janeiro, Brazil, 3-14 June 1992 -** The Stockholm conference motivated countries around the world to monitor environmental conditions as well as to create environmental ministries & agencies. Despite these institutional accomplishments, including the establishment of UNEP, the failure to implement most of its action programme prompted the UN to have follow-up conferences. Hence The United Nations Conference on Environment and Development (UNCED), also known as the 'Rio Conference' or the 'Earth Summit', was held in Rio de Janeiro, Brazil, from 3-14 June 1992. This global conference brought together political leaders, diplomats, scientists, representatives of the media and Non-Governmental Organizations (NGOs) from 179 countries for a massive effort to focus on the impact of human socio-economic activities on the environment. The primary objective of the 'Earth Summit' was to produce a broad agenda and a new blueprint for international action on environmental and developmental issues that would help guide international cooperation and development policy in the twenty-first century. One of the major results of the UNCED conference was Agenda 21, a daring program of action calling for new strategies to invest in the future to achieve overall sustainable development in the 21st century. The 'Earth Summit' concluded that the concept of sustainable development was an attainable goal for all people of the world, regardless of whether they were at the local, national, regional, or international level.

Important issues such as alternative sources of energy to replace the use of fossil fuels, new reliance on public transportation systems in order to reduce vehicle emissions, the growing usage and limited supply of water etc., were discussed in the conference. The Rio Declaration on Environment and Development consisted of 27 principles intended to guide countries in future sustainable development. It was signed by over 175 countries. Agenda 21 is a non-binding action plan of the United Nations with regard to sustainable development. It is an action agenda for the UN, other multilateral organizations, and individual governments around the world that can be executed at local, national, and global levels. One major objective of the 'Agenda 21' initiative is that every local government should draw its own local Agenda 21. The full text of Agenda 21 was made public, where 178 governments voted to adopt the program.

**1.40 Earth Summit II or Rio +10 Conference held in Johannesburg, South Africa, from 26 August to 4 September 2002 -** The alarming deterioration in the earth's ecosystems compelled the global leaders to organise the Summit II to pursue new initiatives on the implementation of sustainable development and the building of a prosperous and secure future for their citizens. The Summit gives a political statement in the form of a 'Johannesburg Declaration', to be agreed by world leaders, reaffirming their commitment to work towards sustainable development. The Summit set the priorities for the detailing of the implementation plan and actions for the countries on way of sustainability. It was one of the largest and important global meetings ever held on the integration of economic, environmental, and social decision-making. It focussed on building a commitment at the highest levels of government and society to implement Agenda 21, the roadmap for achieving sustainable development. The declaration concludes that, *'From the African continent, the cradle of humankind, we solemnly pledge to the people of the world and the generations that will surely inherit this Earth that we are determined to ensure that our collective hope for sustainable development is realized'*.

## 2) Conferences on Water –

### 2.10 The World Water Congress held in Chicago, USA in 1973 -

The World Water Congress is a global event held every two years in different cities around the world under the auspices of the International Water Resources Association (IWRA). Its objective is to provide a unique meeting place to share experiences, promote discussion, and present new knowledge, research results and developments in the fields of water sciences, policy, and practice, globally. For five decades, the World Water Congresses have become one of the most respected and anticipated events for the identification of major global themes concerning the water agenda, and for bringing together large cross-sections of between 1,000 to 2,000 stakeholders for the development and implementation of decisions in the field of water. The first Congress was held in 1973 on the theme of the 'Importance and Problems of Water in the Human Environment in Modern Times' and formed part of the international water community's first earnest attempts to address global water issues (e.g., the ground-breaking Stockholm Declaration of 1972 and the Mar del Plata Conference of 1977). Since then, the Congress has been held in various countries, each time attracting high profile international attention and bringing together major water stakeholders. Last conference was held in Beijing, China in 2023.

The 1994, World Water Congress in Cairo passed a Resolution which created the 'World Water Council', an international think tank, which aimed to mobilize action on critical water issues at the highest political decision-making level. The World Water Council (WWC) was founded in 1996, with its headquarters in Marseille, France. It has 358 members which encompass organizations from the UN and intergovernmental organizations, the private sector, governments and ministries, academic institutions, international organizations, local governments, and civil society groups. Founders and constituent members are ICID, IUCN, IWA, AquaFed, UNDP, UNESCO, and WB. Its mission is *'to promote awareness, build political commitment and trigger action on critical water issues at all levels, including the highest decision-making level, to facilitate the efficient conservation, protection, development, planning, management, and use of water in all its dimensions on an environmentally sustainable basis for the benefit of all life on earth.'* Starting from 1997, every third year the WWC organized the World Water Forum in close collaboration with the authorities of the hosting country.

Under the WWC, Global Water Partnership (GWP) having its secretariat in Stockholm, Sweden, was founded in 1996, with the support of the World Bank, the United Nations Development Programme (UNDP) and the Swedish International Development Cooperation Agency (Sida). It is an international network created to foster an approach to Integrated Water Resources Management (IWRM) and provide practical advice for sustainably managing water resource. The GWP network currently comprises 13 Regional Water Partnerships, 68 accredited Country Water Partnerships and includes more than 3,000 institutional partners located in over 170 countries. Most important tasks of GWP are capacity building and knowledge sharing. This is done through publications, workshops, training courses, meetings and through ground level actions by the 13 Regional Water Partnerships & 170 Country Water Partnerships. Each country has prepared a 'Vision document' which highlighted their vision for the development, management, and use of the water resource in their country. They have also prepared 'Framework for Action document' which outlined the actions necessary and the procedure of implementation to bring the 'Vision' into practice. During the conferences held at the regional level and at the country level discussions are done to review actual progress of implementation of the framework for action.

**2.20 The United Nations Water Conference on March 14, 1977, in Mar Del Plata, Argentina** - The United Nations Water Conference was held on March 14, 1977, in Mar Del Plata, Argentina. It was the first intergovernmental meeting on problems ensuring adequate water supply for the future. Delegates from 105 countries, as well as intergovernmental and non-governmental organizations, were also present. Its purpose was to avoid a water crisis at the end of the century. There was need for extensive improvements in food grains and crop yields. A set of ten resolutions were made directed at United Nations agencies, governments, and the international community overall. These ten resolutions included: assessment of water resources, community water supply, agricultural water use, research and development of industrial technologies, the role of water in combating desertification, technical co-operation among developing countries, river commissions in international river basins, institutional arrangements for international co-operation in the water sector, financing arrangements for international co-operation in the water sector, and water policies in the occupied territories.

Common problems in water scarce countries were identified as below: The amount of water available to an area is dependent on its climate and position in the global water cycle. The tropical climate makes countries more vulnerable to floods, droughts, and land degradation (desertification). High water stress is a serious problem, growing season is short and recurrent droughts make irrigation necessary for food supply to be attained. **The increasing threat of famine and drought in Africa is cause for global concern.** Climate issues in different climates are much more far reaching to be more of a global concern.

**2.30 International Conference on Water and the Environment (ICWE), Dublin, Ireland, 26–31 January 1992.**

International Conference on Water and the Environment (ICWE), Dublin, Ireland, was organised on 26–31 January 1992. It was also the most significant global conference on water since the United Nations Water Conference held in Mar del Plata, Argentina, In 1977. The Dublin Statement on Water and Sustainable Development, also known as the 'Dublin Principles' recognises the increasing scarcity of water as a result of the different conflicting uses and overuses of water.

The declaration sets out recommendations for action at local, national, and international levels to reduce the scarcity, through the following four guiding principles:

1. Fresh water is a finite and vulnerable resource, essential to sustain life, development and the environment.
2. Water development and management should be based on a participatory approach, involving users, planners, and policymakers at all levels.
3. Women play a central part in the provision, management, and safeguarding of water.
4. Water has an economic value in all its competing uses and should be recognized as an economic good.

(although the full text of principle 4 does state *'it is vital to recognize first the basic right of all human beings to have access to clean water and sanitation at an affordable price'*).

Based on these four guiding principles, the conference participants developed recommendations which would enable countries to tackle their water resources problems on a wide range of fronts. The major benefits to come from implementation of the Dublin recommendations would be; alleviation of poverty and disease, protection against natural disasters, water conservation and reuse, sustainable urban development, agricultural production and rural water supply, protecting aquatic ecosystems and resolving water conflicts. Implementation of action programmes for water and sustainable development will require a substantial investment, not only in the capital-intensive projects concerned, but, crucially, in building the capacity of people and institutions to plan and implement those projects.

In November 2002, however, the UN Committee on Economic, Social and Cultural Rights adopted General Comment No.15 as, *'water is recognised not only as a limited natural resource and a public good but also as a human right'*. On 30 September 2010, the 15th Session of the UN Human Rights Council passed Resolution which recognized the right to safe and clean drinking water and sanitation as a human right that is essential for the full enjoyment of life and all human rights. It clarifies that the human right to safe drinking water and sanitation is derived from the right to an adequate standard of living and inextricably related to the right to the highest attainable standard of physical and mental health, as well as the right to life and human dignity.

**2.40 The United Nations Water Conference in New York on 22-24 March 2023** – The UN Water Conference was organized in New York from 22 to 24 March 2023, to get the world back on track for reaching the targets of Sustainable Development Goal 6 (SDG 6), to ensure access to water and sanitation for all by 2030. Nearly 6,500 delegates from over 185 countries participated in the conference. Since the first UN Water Conference held in Mar Del Plata, Argentina in 1977, the Earth's population has doubled to about 8 billion people and demand for water has been skyrocketing. The conference coincided with the Midterm Comprehensive Review of the International Decade for Action (2018–2028), 'Water for Sustainable Development'. Some of the salient observations were as below: Governments will need to work four times faster, on average, to meet their SDG6 targets by 2030. However, they cannot solve this conundrum on their own. Water affects everyone, so everyone needs to take action. There are still too many gaps in our knowledge of the water cycle and the impact of competing water uses – domestic, agricultural, industrial, for energy generation, etc - on this cycle. That is why we need a regular science-based global assessment of water resources to generate a comprehensive knowledge base and integrate fragmented data and information to support policy, regulation, and decision-making. This assessment would be undertaken by national entities and validated through a specific intergovernmental process. Groundwater is fundamental to life on earth, but many aquifers are becoming overexploited or polluted.

### 3) **Conferences on Climate Change -**

**3.10 The Montreal Protocol 1987 -** The Montreal Protocol is an international treaty designed to protect the ozone layer by phasing out the production of numerous substances that are responsible for Ozone depletion. It was agreed on 16 September 1987 and entered into force on 1 January 1989. Since then, it has undergone nine revisions, in 1990 (London), 1991 (Nairobi), 1992 (Copenhagen), 1993 (Bangkok), 1995 (Vienna), 1997 (Montreal), 1998 (Australia), 1999 (Beijing) and 2016 (Kigali). As a result of the international agreement, the ozone hole in Antarctica is slowly recovering. Climate projections indicate that the ozone layer will return to 1980 levels between 2040 (across much of the world) and 2066 (over Antarctica). **Due to its widespread adoption and implementation, it has been hailed as an example of successful international co-operation. Former UN Secretary-General Kofi Annan stated that "***perhaps the single most successful international agreement to date has been the Montreal Protocol***".** The two ozone treaties have been ratified by 198 parties (197 states and the European Union), making them the first universally ratified treaties in United Nations history. These truly universal treaties have also been remarkable in the expedience of the policy-making process at the global scale, where only 14 years lapsed between a basic scientific research discovery (1973) and the international agreement signed (1985 and 1987). The treaty is structured around several groups of halogenated hydrocarbons that deplete stratospheric ozone. All the ozone depleting substances controlled by the Montreal Protocol contain either chlorine or bromine (substances containing only fluorine do not harm the ozone layer). Some Ozone-Depleting Substances (ODS) are not yet controlled by the Montreal Protocol, including nitrous oxide ($N_2O$). To enable the developing countries to switch over to non-ODS, special fund was created. The main objective of the Multilateral Fund for implementation of the Montreal Protocol was to assist developing country parties to the Montreal Protocol whose annual per capita consumption and production of ODS was less than 0.3 kg to comply with the control measures of the Protocol. Currently, 147 of the 196 Parties to the Montreal Protocol meet these criteria.

**3.20 The United Nations Climate Change Conference held in Berlin, Germany from 28 March to 7 April 1995 (COP1)** – Another key achievement of the 1992 Rio conference was the establishment of the United Nations Framework Convention on Climate Change (UNFCCC). It is the first of the yearly conferences held in the framework of the UNFCCC. They serve as the formal meeting of the UNFCCC parties, Conference of the Parties (COP) to assess progress in dealing with climate change. At the first COP in Berlin in 1995, it became obvious that most of the industrialised countries had not taken adequate measures to achieve the objectives of the Convention. Hence at COP1 the 'Berlin Mandate' was adopted, which required the parties to initiate talks to reduce emissions beyond 2000 by means of quantitative objectives and specific deadlines. At the first conference, the signatories agreed to meet annually to maintain control over global warming and see the need to reduce emissions of polluting gases. Two years of negotiations eventually led to the signing of the Kyoto Protocol in Japan at COP3, and beginning in the mid-1990s, to negotiate the Kyoto Protocol to establish legally binding obligations for developed countries to reduce their greenhouse gas emissions.

**3.30 Kyoto Protocol, 11 December 1997 (COP3)** - Kyoto Protocol was adopted in Kyoto, Japan, on 11 December 1997 and entered into force on 16 February 2005. There were 192 parties (Canada withdrew from the protocol, effective December 2012) to the Protocol in 2020. The Kyoto Protocol was an international treaty which extended the 1992 UNFCCC that commits state parties to reduce greenhouse gas emissions, based on the scientific consensus that global warming is occurring and that human-made $CO_2$ emissions are driving it. The Kyoto Protocol applied to the seven greenhouse gases viz.: carbon dioxide ($CO_2$), methane ($CH_4$), nitrous oxide ($N_2O$), hydrofluorocarbons (HFCs), perfluorocarbons (PFCs), sulphur hexafluoride ($SF_6$), nitrogen trifluoride ($NF_3$).

The Protocol acknowledged that individual countries have different capabilities in combating climate change, owing to economic development, and therefore placed the obligation to reduce current emissions on developed countries on the basis that they are historically responsible for the current levels of greenhouse gases in the atmosphere. The Kyoto Protocol sets binding emission reduction targets for 37 industrialized countries and economies in transition and the European Union. Overall, these targets add up to an average 5 percent emission reduction compared to 1990 levels over the five-year period 2008–2012 (the first commitment period). The United States was the only country not to ratify the Kyoto Protocol. In Doha, Qatar, on 8 December 2012, the Doha Amendment to the Kyoto Protocol was adopted for a second commitment period, starting in 2013 and lasting until 2020. During the second commitment period, Parties committed to reduce GHG emissions by at least 18 percent below 1990 levels in the eight-year period from 2013 to 2020. The Adaptation Fund was also established to finance adaptation projects and programmes in developing countries that are parties to the Kyoto Protocol. Perhaps because of its lack of worldwide support, the Kyoto Protocol has been limited in its success: greenhouse gas output has increased since 1997, not decreased. Despite not meeting its goals, Kyoto has been significant as a symbol. It was the first step in the process to combat global warming.

**3.40 The Paris Agreement, 12 December 2015 (COP21)** - The Paris Agreement was adopted on 12 December 2015 and came into force less than a year later, on 4 November 2016. Although the 1997 Kyoto Protocol also technically remained in force, the Paris Agreement has, in effect, superseded the Kyoto Protocol as the principal regulatory instrument governing the global response to climate change. The Paris Agreement is the first global pact to call for emissions pledges from both developed and developing countries, who were asked to pledge Nationally Determined Contributions (NDCs), with increasing ambition every five years. Signatories promise to try to keep global warming within 1.5 degrees Celsius of the preindustrial average. The Paris Agreement takes a bottom-up approach to the substance of climate change policy, allowing parties to nationally determine their contributions to address climate change, in contrast to the Kyoto Protocol, which prescribed emissions limitation targets from the top-down, through international negotiations. After years of often contentious negotiations, the consensus adoption of the Paris Agreement represented a considerable achievement. Nevertheless, the initial round of NDCs submitted by parties pursuant to the Paris Agreement do not put the world on a pathway to limiting global warming to well below 2°C, much less 1.5°C.

The 27th session of the Conference of the Parties of the UNFCCC (COP27) was held in Sharm El-Sheikh in Egypt from 6 to 20 November 2022. Delegates from 197 countries, civil society and other institutions participated, discussed, and negotiated the further implementation of the Paris Agreement and the UNFCCC.

### 3.50 IPCC Special Report on Global Warming of 1.5°C, October 2018 –

The IPCC is an intergovernmental body of the United Nations. Its job is to advance scientific knowledge about climate change caused by human activities. The World Meteorological Organization (WMO) and the United Nations Environment Programme (UNEP) established the IPCC in 1988. The Special Report on Global Warming of 1.5°C was approved by the IPCC on 8$^{th}$ October 2018 in Incheon, Republic of Korea. As part of the decision to adopt the Paris Agreement, the IPCC was invited to produce, in 2018, a Special Report on global warming of 1.5°C above pre-industrial levels and related global GHG emission pathways. The Report's full name is *'Global Warming of 1.5°C, an IPCC special report on the impacts of global warming of 1.5°C above pre-industrial levels and related global greenhouse gas emission pathways, in the context of strengthening the global response to the threat of climate change, sustainable development, and efforts to eradicate poverty'*. With more than 6,000 scientific references cited and the dedicated contribution of thousands of expert and government reviewers worldwide, this important report testifies to the breadth and policy relevance of the IPCC. Ninety-one authors and review editors from 40 countries prepared the IPCC report in response to an invitation from the UNFCCC when it adopted the Paris Agreement in 2015.

One of the key messages that comes out very strongly from this report is that we are already seeing the consequences of 1°C of global warming through more extreme weather, rising sea levels and diminishing Arctic Sea ice, among other changes. The Report highlights a number of climate change impacts that could be avoided by limiting global warming to 1.5°C compared to 2°C, or more. Every extra bit of warming matters, especially since warming of 1.5°C or higher increases the risk associated with long-lasting or irreversible changes, such as the loss of some ecosystems. The Report finds that limiting global warming to 1.5°C would require *'rapid and far-reaching'* transitions in land, energy, industry, buildings, transport, and cities. Global net human-caused emissions of Carbon dioxide ($CO_2$) would need to fall by about 45 percent from 2010 levels by 2030, reaching 'net zero' around 2050.

## 4) World level Institutions established for Water Resource Development & Management –

**4.10 The International Commission on Large Dams – ICOLD -** The International Commission on Large Dams - ICOLD, is an international non-governmental organization dedicated to the sharing of professional information and knowledge of the design, construction, maintenance, and impact of large dams. It was founded in 1928 and has its central office in Paris, France. It consists of 100-member national committees which have a total membership of about 10,000 individuals. It is a non-governmental International Organization which provides a forum for the exchange of knowledge and experience in dam engineering. The organization leads the profession in ensuring that dams are built safely, efficiently, economically, and without detrimental effects on the environment. Its original aim was to encourage advances in the planning, design, construction, operation, and maintenance of large dams and their associated civil works, by collecting and disseminating relevant information and by studying related technical questions. Since the late sixties, focus was put on subjects of current concern such as dam safety, monitoring of performance, reanalysis of older dams and spillways, effects of ageing and environmental impact. More recently, new subjects include cost studies at the planning and construction stages, harnessing international rivers, information for the public at large, and financing.

For inclusion in the World Register of Dams, a large dam is defined as any dam above 15 metres in height (measured from the lowest point of foundation to top of dam) or any dam between 10 and 15 metres in height which meets at least one of the following conditions:

a) the crest length is not less than 500 metres.

b) the capacity of the reservoir formed by the dam is not less than one million cubic metres.

c) the maximum flood discharge dealt with by the dam is not less than 2 000 cubic metres per second.

d) the dam had especially difficult foundation problems.

e) the dam is of unusual design.

**4.20 The International Commission on Irrigation and Drainage (ICID)-**

Central Board of Irrigation and Power (CBIP), New Delhi, India in 1946 took initiative by requesting GoI to invite other countries of the world to cooperate with them in setting up of a non-governmental international organization for development of the science and technique of irrigation all over the world. Consequently, the 'International Commission on Irrigation and Canals' was formed by eleven countries as founder members, on the 24 June 1950, with its Secretariat in New Delhi, India. During the First International Executive Council meeting of the Commission, held in New Delhi in January 1951, name of the Commission was changed to 'International Commission on Irrigation and Drainage (ICID)'. However, in April 1957 scope of the Commission was widened by including in its function the subject of flood control and river training. In recognition of its significant contribution to the programs and objectives of International Year of Peace proclaimed by the UN General Assembly, on 15 September 1987 ICID was designated as a Peace Messenger by the UN Secretary General.

ICID has a 'Vision' to have *'A water secure world free of poverty and hunger through sustainable rural development'*. Its 'Mission' is *'Working together towards sustainable agriculture water management through inter-disciplinary approaches to economically viable, socially acceptable and environmentally sound irrigation, drainage and flood management'*. ICID has more than seventy years of experience in the transfer of water management technology and in the handling of related issues. Building on its past experience, accomplishments, and the comprehensive water management framework, ICID strives to promote programs to enhance sustainable development of irrigated agriculture. ICID has been involved in the global discussions leading to Agenda 21, World Water Vision, and World Water Forum etc., which have become the focal point of several of its technical activities.

**4.30 The International Water Management Institute (IWMI), Colombo, Sri Lanka –** It is a non-profit international water management research organisation under the CGIAR with its headquarters in Colombo, Sri Lanka, and offices across Africa and Asia. It was founded as 'International Irrigation Management Institute (IIMI)' in 1985 by the Ford Foundation and the Government of Sri Lanka, supported by the Consultative Group on International Agricultural Research and the World Bank. Research at the Institute focuses on improving how water and land resources are managed, with the aim of underpinning food security and reducing poverty while safeguarding the environment. The Green Revolution of the 1940s to 1970s, was achieved by the use of new fertilizers, pesticides and high-yielding varieties of seeds, which helped many countries to produce greater quantities of food crops. By the mid-1980s, however, these irrigation systems were no longer performing efficiently; IIMI's job was to find out why. It advocated 'Participatory Irrigation Management' (PIM) as the solution, an approach that sought to involve farmers in water management decisions. In 1998, its name changed to 'International Water Management Institute (IWMI)', reflecting this new wider approach. In 2012, IWMI was awarded the prestigious Stockholm Water Prize Laureate by Stockholm International Water Institute (SIWI) for its pioneering research, which has helped to improve agricultural water management, enhance food security, protect environmental health, and alleviate poverty in developing countries.

**4.40 The International Water Association (IWA) -** It is a nonprofit organization and knowledge hub for the water sector, connecting water professionals and companies to find solutions to the world's water challenges. IWA has a global secretariat in London, UK, and a regional office in Chennai, India. The IWA has its roots in the International Water Supply Association (IWSA), established in June 1947, which finally formed the present IWA on 7 September 1999. IWA works across a wide range of issues covering the full water cycle, with four programmes viz. Digital Water, Basins of the Future, Cities of the Future, Water and Sanitation Services, that work towards achieving the SDGs and addressing the threat to sustainable water supplies posed by climate change. IWA annually hosts more than 40 specialist conferences and workshops on various aspects of water management. At present there are following programs at the IWA: Basins and cities of the future, Water, and sanitation services (wastewater management) and Water policy & regulation. Since 2000, in every alternate year IWA, World Water Congress & Exhibition is held in different countries of the world.

**4.50 International Lake Environment Committee (ILEC) -** ILEC was founded in 1986 with its office in Kusatsu, Shiga, Japan. Its objective is to promote sustainable lake management and conservation of sound lakes and their ecosystems through cooperation among government agencies, scientists, and local stakeholders for lakes in various environments worldwide and values the connection between people and nature. It works to ensure international cooperation for conservation of lake environments and to promote environmentally sound management of world lakes. It is achieved through encouraging investigations and research on rational and suitable methods for harmony between environmental management & sustainable development, and scientific knowledge on lake environments internationally.

Some other Associations and Committees are also functioning and working to promote improvements in different aspects of development and management of water resource.

**B) Books which have changed our concepts about the living world and the environment –**

**On the Origin of Species** - The Theory of Evolution by natural selection was first formulated in the Charles Darwin's book *'On the Origin of Species by Means of Natural Selection, or the Preservation of Favoured Races in the Struggle for Life'*, published on 24th November 1859. It revolutionised the concepts of evolution of life on the earth which were prevailing till then. In his book, Darwin described how organisms evolve over generations through the inheritance of physical or behavioural traits. According to the theory, all species of organisms arise and develop through the natural selection of small, inherited variations that increase the individual's ability to compete, survive, and reproduce. Individuals with traits that enable them to adapt to their environments will help them survive and have more offspring, which will inherit those traits. Individuals with less adaptive traits will less frequently survive to pass them on to the next generation. The exhaustive field study carried out by him during his sea voyage on HMS Beagle ship from 1831 to 1836, and further search for corroborative evidence during the next 22 years, crystalised his ideas about evolution and culminated in his book published in 1859. Darwin did not know the mechanism by which traits were passed on, or about genetics, the mechanism by which genes encode for certain traits and those traits are passed from one generation to the next. He also did not know about genetic mutation, which is the source of natural variation. But future research by geneticists provided the mechanism and additional evidence for evolution by natural selection. Even then it is surprising that many educated people still do not believe in his theory of evolution. Presumably, they do not have any alternative theory of evolution based on logic, reasoning, and supportive evidence but still, they do not believe the theory of evolution by natural selection. More details about the book are given in Chapter No.2.

**Silent spring** - Book that has contributed significantly to protect the 'Environment' from degradation due to some actions by the humans, is titled as 'Silent Spring', an environmental science book written by Rachel Carson and published on September 27, 1962. It documented the environmental harm caused by the indiscriminate use of pesticides and insecticides, mainly the DDT. The overarching theme of Silent Spring is the powerful - and often negative - effect humans have on the natural world. Chemical pesticides & insecticides in use since 1950 affected many useful insects and some bird species. Carson predicted that, increased consequences in the future, especially since targeted pests may develop resistance to pesticides and weakened ecosystems would fall prey to unanticipated invasive species. Silent Spring is considered the book that started the global grassroots environmental movement. It turned out to be a milestone in raising global awareness of environmental issues. The book closes with a call for a biotic approach to pest control as an alternative to chemical pesticides. Silent Spring has been featured in many lists of the best non-fiction books of the twentieth century. It was fifth in the Modern Library List of Best 20th-Century Non-fiction books. In 2006, Silent Spring was named as one of the 25 greatest science books of all time by the editors of Discover Magazine.

**On Climate Change** – Unfortunately, to the best of my knowledge, no such comprehensive book on global warming and climate change has been written and published so far for the benefit of educated people in the world. Such book should cover causes of global warming due to emission of greenhouse gases, adverse effects of the resulting climate change on our lives, urgency for taking immediate reduction in the greenhouse gases and other different measures which would make it possible. Such book should then be translated in all major languages in the world. It would then help in building up public opinion for taking immediate actions to reduce carbon emissions and other greenhouse gases, for a safe and sustainable future.

## C) World Water Festivals celebrated on Topics Water and Environment –

Water festivals are celebrated in some cities of the world to discuss on a common platform about various water related issues and to deliberate on workable solutions evolved in different countries. Papers and posters based on results of on-field experiments are presented on a specific water or environment related subject and are discussed in such festivals held every year. Such interaction amongst experts, policy makers and NGOs educate them for adoption of solutions which are appropriate in their countries. Following are the details of some such festivals.

**World Water Week, Stockholm, Sweden** - World Water Week in Stockholm is a week-long global water conference held each year in late August or early September. Initially it was part of a public water festival in the Swedish capital, Stockholm. The World Water Week in Stockholm originally began as the Stockholm Water Symposium in 1991 and has been convened annually ever since. In 2001, the official name became 'World Water Week in Stockholm'. This event is now the leading annual conference on global water issues, which is organized and led by the Stockholm International Water Institute (SIWI). Events and conference sessions address a wide range of the world's water, development and sustainability issues and related concerns of international development. Now it has become the meeting place for everyone who wants to understand how water can help us address the world's greatest challenges. SIWI identifies a conference theme to place a specific focus on one aspect of the world's escalating water crisis. Initially, one theme was promoted for 4–5 years. Since 2008, a different theme has been selected for each year. Water and Food Security, Energy and Water, Water for Development, Water for Sustainable Growth, Water, Ecosystems and Human Development, Water and Wastewater: Reduce and Reuse, Responding to Global Climate Change: Water in an Urbanising World etc., were some of the themes discussed in the World Water Week festivals.

'Stockholm Water Prize' is an award that recognizes outstanding achievements in water related activities. It is presented annually since 1991 and over the past more than three decades. Stockholm Water Prize Laureates have come from across the world and represented a wide range of professions, disciplines and activities in the field of water. Any activity which contributes broadly to the conservation and protection of the world's water resources, and to improved water conditions which contribute to the health and welfare of the planet's inhabitants and our ecosystems, is eligible to be nominated for the Stockholm Water Prize. The Stockholm Water Prize includes a US$150,000 award and an Orrefors crystal sculpture. It is awarded to the recipient during the World Water Week in Stockholm, from H.M. King Carl XVI Gustaf of Sweden, who is the patron of the Stockholm Water Prize.

The U.S. Stockholm Junior Water Prize (SJWP) was founded in 1997 by SIWI to complement the Stockholm Water Prize. The SJWP is the world's most prestigious award presented to a high school student for a water-research project. The winner receives a cash prize of $10,000, a crystal trophy, and represents the U.S. at the international competition each August held at World Water Week in Sweden. The 'Stockholm Industry Water Award' recognises impressive contributions made by businesses and industries to improve the world water situation. The honorary prize has been awarded annually since 2000, with an aim to encourage and reward improved business performance, production, and innovation to reduce industrial water consumption and pollution.

**International River*symposium*, Brisbane, Australia –**

Brisbane Festival was one of Australia's leading international arts festivals, and is held each September in Brisbane, Australia. From 1998, the Brisbane City Council decided to celebrate International River*symposium* along with it to increase awareness about rivers and environment amongst the participants. Australia had carried out systematic development and management of water resource in the Murray-Darling River basin and engineers from all over the world used to visit it for studying the same. The International River Foundation (IRF) was hence established in Brisbane, Australia in 2003, to support the sustainable management of river basins to achieve improved health, ecological, economic, and social outcomes. It is a no-profit organisation helping to revive and protect the world's rivers and the communities who depend on them. It is done through recognising, rewarding, and applying best practice river management and restoration world-wide. In the International River*symposium*, participants from all over the world present papers on the theme. There are many presentations by experts in the field of water sector.

IRF is also well known for awarding the most prestigious global river management award 'The Thiess International River*prize*'. In association with the IRF, Thiess awards a biennial International Riverprize, recognising organisations who have achieved remarkable outcomes for their local rivers and communities. To date, 16 international prizes and 14 Australian River*prizes* have been awarded. After awarding these prizes, IRF helps to establish twinning projects between River*prize* winners and communities in need across the globe. This highly successful peer-to-peer knowledge exchange program connects 35 countries. IRF also has a growing portfolio of on-ground river restoration projects which apply holistic Integrated River Basin Management practices, driven by local stakeholders.

**International Yellow River Forum, Zeng Zhou, China** - The Yellow River basin in the People's Republic of China (PRC) is one of the longest, most unique, and fragile rivers in the world. The basin covers nine provinces in the PRC, has a total population of 420 million people and is a global biodiversity hotspot to preserve. It is the birthplace of origin of civilisation in China. For the last 3-4 millennia, lives of people in the North China depended on the Yellow River or *Hwang Ho* River. Because of the severe floods to the river and droughts in the basin which caused many casualties in the past, it used to be called as 'River of Sorrow'. Between 1950 and 2000, China constructed thousands of large dams in the basin to meet different needs of water for the people to mitigate the drought situation and to ameliorate magnitude of floods to the river. Due to phenomenal increase in the use of water for several cities and industries in the basin but inadequate treatment to the effluent generated river water was getting heavily polluted. Due to increased water use in the basin, since nineties of the last century, about 80% of the 5464 km length of lower reach of the river started getting dry for 3-4 months each year. Hence PRC took following actions to improve and restore the status of the heavily polluted river.

The 'Yellow River Conservancy Commission (YRCC)' is a government agency of Ministry of Water Resources of the PRC, with head quarter in Zeng Zhou. The YRCC was empowered by the Central government of China in 1999 to manage and integrate water allocation in the entire Yellow River basin. It takes responsibility of water administration of the Yellow River basin and the inland river basins in such provinces as Xinjiang, Qinghai, Gansu, and Inner Mongolia. YRCC then acted on all fronts by taking stern actions to ensure that all the effluent generated after every type of use of water, gets treated prior to its release in the river. After more than a decade of coordinated efforts, the quality of river water improved. During the Singapore International Water Week held in 2010, the YRCC was awarded the 'Lee Kuan Yew Water Prize' for its outstanding accomplishments in integrated river basin management that was unrivalled in scale. YRCC's innovative policies and solutions have brought about widespread and sustainable social, economic, and environmental benefits in just 10 years. Learning from this experience, China felt the need to bring all such river related issues before all countries of the world to share their experience to increase their awareness in taking similar actions. The YRCC hence organised 1st International Yellow River Forum in Zeng Zhou, China in 2003. Participants from several countries of the world presented papers in the sessions and shared their experience. Such sessions were organised in every alternate year since then.

In addition to above, such 'water weeks' are being celebrated in some cities of the world, to bring experts together to share their experiences and to initiate actions for achieving better management of the water resource and the environment.

**Conclusion** - During 20th century, population of the world increased by about 3 times, but the water use increased by about 7 times. It was primarily due to increase in the area under irrigated agriculture to ensure food security to the ever-rising population of the world. Rain-fed agriculture being practiced during last ten millennia before that period had caused extensive destruction of terrestrial ecosystems – rich forests. Since average productivity of irrigated land is about 2.75 times that of the rain-fed land, irrigated agriculture which started about 5,000 years before, had substantially stalled the destruction of forest land to a considerable extent in many countries. Activity of construction of large dams increased appreciably after 1950 to meet rapidly rising needs of water for irrigation, urban & industrial use. However, it has caused stress on the finite availability of water resource in some water-scarce river basins in the world. Patent lack of or only partial treatment of effluent generated after urban and industrial use of water caused degradation of most of the riverine aquatic ecosystems. Increase in carbon emissions from industries, thermal power stations & the transport sector together with methane generated from ponded paddy cultivation & tending of flatulent animals had caused global warming which resulted in the climate change. With the result, optimum development and management of water resource, protection of environment, and limiting adverse effects of climate change, became the critical issues at present imminent before most of the countries of the world.

United Nations took a lead role in bringing all countries of the world on one platform to discuss these problems and find out viable solutions for their implementation by all the countries. Scope of the deliberations in the periodical conferences on these three subjects would be clear from the details given above. Many institutions and organisations were also set up in some countries as listed above, to take up these subjects before the professionals and to initiate necessary actions at the ground level. To bring these three issues at the global level, some water festivals were organised by some institutions. In these festivals, solutions evolved in different countries in dealing with these three issues were discussed and were shared by experts from many countries in the respective fields. Benefits of efficient handling of water and environment related issues would be gained primarily by the respective countries. However, problem of achieving food security to the underdeveloped and least developed countries would have to be settled by providing them necessary financial assistance by the World Bank and by providing technical guidance by the developed and developing countries. However, all countries of the world and notably the developed countries, will have to contribute to the reduction in their carbon emissions, if its adverse impacts on the climate are to be limited within the pre decided safe limits. Next two-three decades are very critical for taking time bound actions primarily by the developed and developing countries if these targets are to be achieved. **It is hence essential that these three critical issues are discussed in the International Conferences held hereafter and monitoring of the actions taken by the concerned countries shall also be done.**

# Chapter 17
# Way Forward

Sustainable development has been very aptly defined as *"Sustainable development is development that meets the needs of the present without compromising the ability of future generations to meet their own needs."* It calls for introspection of the human development policies adopted at present by all countries of the world and make suitable changes in their policies to achieve sustainable development. Primary responsibility of achieving sustainable development rests on the policy makers of today, by taking long term approach while adopting the development policies and to refrain from adopting policies aimed at achieving short term gains. As seen in the earlier chapters of the book, issues such as food and water security, development and environment, degradation of terrestrial and aquatic ecosystems, global warming and climate change etc., have been discussed in many world level conferences during the last more than five decades. On the first three of the above issues, necessary actions are to be taken by the respective countries to achieve the desired objectives and they would be benefitted by such actions. In respect of mitigation of adverse impacts of the climate change, actions shall have to be taken in a coordinated time bound programme, primarily by the developed countries and by the countries with emerging economies and all countries of the world would be benefitted by these actions.

Main problem before the underdeveloped and least developed countries is to achieve sustainable food & water security and to achieve their development by causing minimum degradation of the environment. It is necessary for them to construct water resource development infrastructure on a large scale to increase the area under irrigation and adopt latest practices in agriculture technology to increase crop productivity per hectare of the land and their total food grain production. Secondly, it is absolutely essential for all these countries to take immediate measures to lower down their present rate of increase in their population. However, on their own they are not in a position to achieve these targets, and they would need immediate financial assistance from International Financing Agencies like World Bank/Asian Development Bank and also need technical guidance from the developed countries. They would also have to take some measures to limit their carbon emissions for which financial assistance (subsidies/funds) would have to be given by the developed countries. Detailed guidelines for all countries of the world which they should follow in this respect, should be discussed, and finalised in the relevant international conferences. With the initiative of the United Nations, respective annual conferences should continuously monitor actual implementation of these guidelines by the developed, developing, and underdeveloped countries. Necessity of some changes if any in these guidelines shall be reviewed and discussed in the annual international conferences and revised guidelines shall be issued from time to time.

Problem before the developing and underdeveloped countries is about pollution and degradation of all aquatic ecosystems due to release of untreated urban sewage and industrial effluent into rivers. Some of them would need some financial support from International Financing Agencies for setting up several sewage treatment plants in all cities and towns. Whereas serious problem before all countries of the world is to carry out drastic reduction in the carbon emissions within the next two-three decades to reduce carbon emissions to nil by 2050, so as to restrict adverse impacts of the climate change within the pre-decided safe limits of rise in global temperature of 1.5 degrees Celsius. Developed countries would have to play major role in achieving these targets and followed by the countries with emerging economy & developing countries.

All the above issues have been discussed in detail in the relevant chapters. It is now proposed to sum up them as below by highlighting the necessity to take coordinated actions by the developed, developing, and underdeveloped countries of the world to achieve the goal of sustainable development. Developed and developing countries of the world should act like elder brothers in a joint family, to help the underdeveloped and least developed countries as their younger brothers, till they become self-supporting in their life. Following are the three pressing problems before all countries of the world.

**Food and water security** – It would be seen from the population projection graph (Chapter 5) that population of all the developed and developing countries is either declining or is reaching climax and likely to decline within the next two-three decades. However, population of the underdeveloped and the least developed countries is increasing at a faster rate and may possibly stabilise only after 2100. Population of Africa for example is likely to increase from about 1.3 billion in 2020 to about 4.3 billion (231% increase in 80 years) which would be about 40% of the world population then.

If we see the World Map as below, it will make us to see the World in a new way! This map is informative and can elucidate much about phenomenal increase in the population of some underdeveloped countries of the world. It would be seen that in almost all the sub-Saharan countries, except South Africa, there are about 4 to 7 children per family. This is the reason for rapid increase in their population. Unless strict measures are taken to control it, there is no possibility of stabilising their population as indicated below.

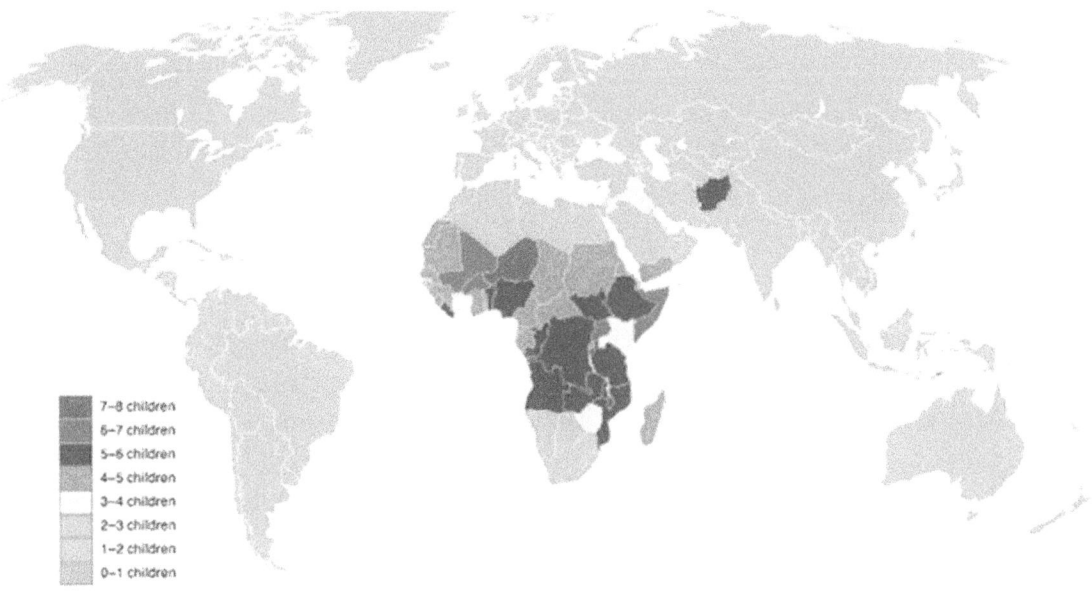

**How many children per family.**

(**Source** - https://www.ba-bamail.com/baba-recommends/these-world-maps-made-me-see-the-world-in-a-new-way/)

World Population Prospects 2022 indicate that, population of Sub-Saharan Africa and Least developed countries would increase from 1.15 & 1.11 billion (total 2.26 billion) in 2022 to 2.09 & 1.91 billion (total 4 billion) respectively in 2050. Projections about population rise as up to 2100 as shown in the graph should hence be reviewed by the world level demographists and graph of revised projections should be prepared. Based on that information, workable targets should be set before the above underdeveloped countries of the world for limiting their population. It is essential that sub-Saharan countries in Africa and the least developed countries, must take necessary measures immediately to reduce the present rate of increase in their population. If such actions are taken from right now, its intended effects would be seen only after two-three decades. **Ultimate objective before these countries should be to achieve stabilisation of their population before 2075. Then only their natural resources of land and water would not be over strained while meeting their basic needs of food and water.**

At present these countries are practicing rainfed cultivation over most of their cultivable land, because of lack of facilities to harness ground water and due to inadequate infrastructure for water resource development to support surface irrigated agriculture. Study carried out by Stockholm International Water Institute (SIWI) indicates that about 60% of the world's cultivable but unused land lies in Sub Saharan Africa. African farmers value rainwater (green water) like none other, as 80% of all small-holder farming activity relies on it for dry farming. Because of its uncertainty and variation in magnitude, average productivity of cultivated land per hectare and the total food grain production in these countries is barely adequate at present to meet their food needs. Every dollar that is invested in enhanced practices for rainfed agriculture gives six times more return, according to a preliminary study led by SIWI. A relatively small investment per year per hectare can lead to a doubling of yields and reduces risk of crops withering during dry spells. Hence emphasis would have to be given on increase in productivity of land under rainfed cultivation. Firstly, it can be by adopting improved strains of crops which would be more compatible to the rainfall pattern and by following improved cultural practices. Next step would be to promote ground water development by providing subsidies for digging/drilling wells and installing electric or solar operated motor-pumps for irrigation. In due course of time drip irrigation system can also be introduced on well irrigation to increase crop productivity with same quantity of water use.

At present these countries do not have buffer stock of food grains to support during drought years. As per broad regional projections made by the Intergovernmental Panel on Climate Change (IPCC), Africa is one of the Continents, most vulnerable to increased water stress and low food productivity along the margin of arid and semi-arid areas. In view of this, any major drought occurring in some of these countries would create serious problem of food shortage, resulting in heavy casualties due to starvation, unless food grains are supplied by other countries having surplus buffer stock of food grains. To meet food needs of the rising population, at present these countries are bringing more area under cultivation by disforestation of land under forests to cause degradation of terrestrial ecosystems. Besides increase in the carbon emissions on that account, it is putting a stop to the carbon sequestration that is naturally taking place through those trees in the forest. Hence better way would be to increase surface irrigation facilities and increase land productivity by two to three folds from the same land when provided with irrigation facilities.

**Poverty alleviation** – Many of the countries of the world in the African Continent have very low GDP per Capita. Notably, countries in sub-Saharan Africa encounter significant challenges that hinder their economic growth. South Sudan, the world's youngest country, attained independence in 2011 and confronts enormous economic issues, political instability, recurrent wars, and poor infrastructure to impede its growth. The majority reliant on traditional agriculture, warfare, and harsh weather occurrences that frequently disrupt crops and prolong poverty in this landlocked country of over 11 million people, makes it the world's poorest country in 2024. These smaller and less powerful nations struggle with limited resources, underdeveloped financial sectors, and unfavourable tax regimes, all of which deter foreign investment and stifle economic development. The same applies to even larger African nations like the Democratic Republic of the Congo and Mozambique, which grapple with poverty due to internal conflicts, political instability, and inadequate infrastructure, hindering their economic progress. Present status of poverty would be clear from the figures given in the Table below:

**Top 10 Poorest Countries Worldwide by GDP per capita in 2024:**

| Rank | Country name | GDP per Capita | Continent |
|---|---|---|---|
| 1 | South Sudan | $455.16 | Africa |
| 2 | Burundi | $915.88 | Africa |
| 3 | Central African Republic | $1,200 | Africa |
| 4 | Democratic Republic | $1,550 | Africa |

|   | of the Congo (DRC) |         |        |
|---|--------------------|---------|--------|
| 5 | Mozambique         | $1,650  | Africa |
| 6 | Niger              | $1,670  | Africa |
| 7 | Malawi             | $1,710  | Africa |
| 8 | Liberia            | $1,880  | Africa |
| 9 | Madagascar         | $1,980  | Africa |
| 10| Yemen              | $2,000  | Asia   |

Source: International Monetary Fund (IMF), as of September 2024.

Creating water resource development infrastructure is a very capital-intensive work and these countries would not have enough financial resources to construct them so as to increase irrigation facilities. Hence International Financing Agencies like World Bank (WB), Asian Development Bank (ADB), United States Aid for International Development (USAID), Japan International Cooperation Agency (JICA) etc., should provide them necessary financial support and technical guidance to create such facilities. Since gestation period of such dam-canal irrigation projects is long one, this activity should be taken up immediately so that area under irrigation would start increasing rapidly at least after a decade. Groundwater harnessing is also not significant in these countries due to lack of necessary electricity network in the rural area. Because water-use efficiency for irrigation by harnessing GW is very high compared with dam-canal projects, and they provide irrigation benefits to the land in upper reaches of river basins, priority should be given to it on equity considerations. Financial assistance (subsidies) should also be given for digging/drilling wells and technical guidance should be given to them for making use of solar panel driven electric pumps for lifting water from wells for irrigation. Wherever possible, network of supplying electricity in the rural area should be created and electricity should be provided at subsidised rates. Well irrigation is done entirely in the private sector and Govts. have to invest only by way of various subsidies as above. Secondly, gestation period of GW development from investment to commissioning irrigation is not much. Hence top priority should be given to the activity of GW irrigation in all these countries. **However, taking necessary measures to reduce the present rate of increase in their population as indicated above should be a precondition for providing all such financial assistance.**

Technical assistance and guidance should also be extended in the agriculture sector for use of high yielding strains of major food grain crops and for judicious use of chemical fertilisers and pesticides. Aim should be to bring green revolution in the country, the way in which India and China had achieved it in the sixth and seventh decade of the last century. Such assistance would enable them to bring green revolution into practice, to increase crop productivity and achieve sustainable food security. Increase in irrigated agriculture would result in 'More crop, cash, and jobs per drop of water'. It would create more employment opportunities to the landless labourers and increase the standard of living of the people in the rural area. Increase in agriculture produce would promote development of industries in semi-urban areas for processing the agriculture produce. By taking all such measures, it would be possible to attain sustainable food and water security to these underdeveloped countries within the next two-three decades. Because of the adverse effects of the climate change, frequency and intensity of droughts and floods (Two extreme climatic events) is certain to increase in the future. To effectively face the contingency of frequent occurrence of droughts, achieving sustainable food and water security has become a top priority target before sub-Saharan African countries and the least developed countries in the world.

It is suggested that the World Bank should take initiative immediately by taking following actions. Committees of experts having members in the water resource development sector, agriculture sector and economists in the rural development sector should be formed for every country in the sub-Saharan Africa and least developed countries in Asia & elsewhere. Those committees shall visit these countries and take review of status of water resource development and their scope of ultimate potential in the future. They should also assess the GW potential, its present status of development and possible measures to increase its use on priority. Rough estimation of financial investment necessary to achieve surface water resource development shall then be made. Committee should explore present technology in the irrigated agriculture and prepare a plan for adoption of latest technology to achieve 'Green Revolution' through irrigated agriculture. Economist should review the present status of their economy, other natural resources available for their development and estimate scope & possibilities of improvements in the future. Review of present rate of rise of population and need to introduce measures to control it within desired limits should be elaborated by experts in that field. Such comprehensive reports of the committees for all the countries, should preferably be received within six months. These Reports would form the basis for preparing time bound programmes of reducing the rate of rise of population and implementation of surface & ground water resource development, supplemented by improvements in the agriculture sector etc. for taking further actions on all the fronts.

From these reports, prioritisation of the countries shall be done according to the criticality of their food and water security situation. Teams of experts shall then by deployed by the various International Financing Agencies to prepare plans of development of water resource in those more vulnerable countries to start with. Agriculture experts shall ensure that new strains of high yielding/Hybrid food grain crops shall be introduced, and green revolution technology is adopted in the irrigated agriculture and also in dry land cultivation. Measures to lower down the rate of rise of their population should be suggested and mechanism to introduce them strictly and to monitor it continuously shall be formulated. After every year then onwards, review of the actual achievement of each country shall be taken by teams of experts and improvements shall be suggested where necessary. Similar action shall be taken in respect of all the remaining countries as per priority of their criticality. It is going to be a programme extending over the next more than two decades. It would then be possible to achieve sustainable food and water security within about two decades.

**Degradation of Environment** – Any developmental activity benefitting the people is certain to have some adverse impacts on the environment. Such impact is firstly on the terrestrial ecosystems viz., forest land. Out of the alternatives available to achieve the same objective, the one which is having minimum adverse impact on the environment should be chosen for implementation, even if it is somewhat costly. Unavoidable destruction of terrestrial ecosystems (forests) would be in the form of acquisition of forest land required for roads, railways, industries, canal-distributaries, and due to submergence under man-made reservoirs. In such cases, afforestation on twice the area of acquired forest land, shall be carried out on degraded forest land or fallow land and full cost of the same shall be borne by the respective developmental project. Such action would partly restore the degradation of forest in due course of time. Strict measures should be taken on the practice of illegal encroachments on forests for agriculture and on degradation due to unauthorised cutting of trees for firewood, for building material and for making wooden furniture. Afforestation schemes should also be taken up on degraded forest land, fallow land, and roadsides for long term carbon sequestration, thereby reducing carbon emissions sustainably in the future.

Other adverse impact because of use of water for the people takes place on the aquatic ecosystems in the developing and underdeveloped countries is by way of pollution of rivers as well as reservoirs into which the polluted rivers drain. Consumption of water for drinking and domestic purposes in the rural and semiurban area is generally not much and usually the effluent generated after such use does not create problem of pollution of rivers, provided human excreta is treated locally by means of septic tanks or other suitable measures as suggested in Chapter 8. But in urban areas (cities and towns) per capita consumption of water for drinking and domestic use is substantial. Adequate treatment is usually not provided to the sewage generated after such use and untreated sewage in large quantities gets released in rivers directly without adequate treatment. Release of it in the rivers has caused severe pollution of almost all rivers in India and so in most of the developing and underdeveloped countries. Presence of organic matter in the pollutants has promoted growth of aggressive water hyacinth plant in most of the rivers in India. Within two-three months after the monsoon season, the water hyacinth forms a floating green carpet, decorated with violet-coloured flowers on the river water. Such layer prevents oxidation of organic matter and their part stabilisation that takes place naturally in the rivers. Due to lack of oxygen in the river water, no aquatic life survives in such polluted rivers. Presence of pathogens in the pollutants occasionally give rise to pandemics like Cholera and Gastro enteritis. As the pace of development increases in the developing and underdeveloped countries, there is continuous migration of rural population to the cities in search of jobs and for getting the benefit of higher education for students. Such migration increases the urban population and the urban water use. It then increases gravity of the problem of pollution of rivers further. Percentage of urban population in the total population of the developing and underdeveloped countries all over the world has always increased on that account. Most of the developed countries have gone through that phase of river pollution during the last century. Their urban population and urban use of water was stabilised long back. All cities and towns had underground drainage system and almost all the sewage generated was fully treated prior to its release in the rivers. Hence degradation of riverine ecosystems no longer remained a serious problem there.

To improve this situation in the developing countries, actions such as fixing statutory responsibility of sewage treatment on the Municipal Corporations and Municipalities, levying 'Pollution tax' on urban citizens on the principle 'Polluter pays', must be taken to resolve the problem of river pollution. Time bound programme for setting up required number of Sewage Treatment Plants (STP) should be prepared for every city and town and shall be implemented accordingly so that within the next two decades, all the sewage generated in the cities, would be fully treated prior to its release in rivers. Introducing underground drainage system and treatment of sewage is a very capital-intensive work and also has a high recurring annual cost for its operation, maintenance, depreciation, and modernisation/replacement. But the time bound programme must be implemented by providing necessary funds by the above public bodies and mainly by the countries/state Govts. Entire recurring expenses for the STPs shall be borne by the Municipal Corporations and Municipalities. For cities in the developing countries, financial assistance/soft loans and technical guidance should be provided by the International Financing Agencies like the World Bank for establishing underground drainage system and setting up of STPs. Fully treated sewage, which may be about 80% of the urban water use, should then be pumped back into canal of the irrigation project from where water stored in the reservoirs was diverted for such urban use. It would partly restore the irrigation which had to be curtailed due to diversion of water for urban use. For small towns and villages, individual and common septic tanks shall be constructed and operated. Two-pit latrines shall be provided in small villages. Continuous monitoring of their performance in the treatment of human excreta shall be done as suggested in Chapter No. 8.

Another source of pollution of rivers is due to release of inadequately treated industrial effluent into rivers. Because it contains toxic chemicals, compounds of heavy metals and carcinogens, such untreated effluent is more harmful to the aquatic life and for the users located on downstream who use river water as a source for drinking purposes. One way to reduce the quantity of industrial effluent is by levying high rates per unit of water, as an economic instrument to reduce the industrial use of water. With such high rates, industries would benefit by adopting, use-treat-reuse-recycle for the water, instead of using more fresh water. It is possible only if water is used as a coolant or as a catalyst in the manufacturing process. When water is used as a part of the final product such as soft drinks, wines, liquors, beer etc., high consumption of fresh water is unavoidable. But effluent generated in the process of manufacturing in all the industries must be fully treated and reused again & again prior to its release in rivers. If the industries are located close to the urban growth centres, urban sewage should be directly delivered to them for its treatment and use by the industries themselves instead of using fresh water. Ultimate target for the industrial use of water should be 'Zero effluent' to be achieved in the next two decades. It would minimise the quantity of water for industrial use and also solve the problem of river pollution on that account.

Pollution of river water also takes place when regenerated water from the irrigated agriculture containing residues of chemical fertilisers and chemical insecticides & pesticides percolates below into soil and flows as groundwater back into the rivers. It has created serious problem in the states of Punjab, Haryana, and Uttar Pradesh in India because of the presence of toxic chemicals and carcinogens from pesticides, in the regenerated water from the irrigated tracts. Hence use of only less harmful chemical pesticides shall be permitted for use in irrigated agriculture. More research shall be promoted for evolving effective bio measures in lieu of harmful chemical pesticides. More use of organic fertilisers, though it is difficult to implement in practice, would reduce the use of chemical fertilisers. Use of bio-measures in lieu of chemical pesticides should be encouraged. In most of the rivers in India at present, polluted river water is lifted from rivers and used to irrigate lands on either bank of the rivers. Besides affecting contamination of the agriculture produce on that account, it has resulted in pollution of groundwater in such areas. Once polluted, restoration of quality of groundwater to its earlier status is the most difficult job to implement in practice.

Even if the problem of river pollution due to above reasons has been controlled in most of the developed countries because of the measures taken in the last century, it has become a serious problem at present before most of the developing countries. Underdeveloped countries having lower percentage of urban population and having less irrigation facilities would also not be far behind the developing countries in that respect. Hence action to take immediate measures to control pollution of rivers has become a serious problem before majority of the developing and underdeveloped countries in the world.

**Global warming and climate change** – Phenomenal increase in the carbon emissions and its accumulation in the atmosphere has been the result of setting up of several industries and thermal power plants in the presently developed countries during the last two centuries. Developing countries have also contributed to it during last 5 - 6 decades. Fossil fuels viz. coal, oil and natural gas have been the traditional sources of energy for all the industries. It was also the source for generating electric energy by means of thermal power plants. If these carbon emissions are to be reduced to limit the adverse impacts of the climate change, all countries should now gradually switch over to the non-conventional sources of energy such as wind power, solar power, atomic energy etc. Research in generating atomic power by the process of 'fusion' instead of 'fission', which is being done at present, should be expedited. It would permanently solve the problem of generation of electrical energy, because it would be free from harmful radiation, which has been the potential risk associated with generation of atomic power by 'fission' as at present (Chernobyl in Russia and Fukushima in Japan). Wherever possible more hydroelectric projects should be taken up on priority to generate hydropower, which is environment friendly, being free from carbon emissions. Secondly their power generation can be started and closed at short notice to meet high demand of electricity during morning and evening hours.

Appreciable quantity of methane gas ($CH_4$), which is more potent than the carbon dioxide, is released annually in the atmosphere through man-made activities (351 MT – Million Tons) and through natural processes (233 MT). Out of the total methane emissions, natural wetlands contribute 194 MT whereas ponded paddy fields & from the digestion process of flatulent animals together contribute 152 MT. Wetland emissions have been declining due to their gradual draining for agricultural and building areas. An additional 100 MT of methane gas is flared each year from oil wells. A ton of methane gas emitted into the atmosphere creates approximately 85 times the atmospheric warming as a ton of $CO_2$ over a period of 20 years. On a 100-year timescale, it is in the range of 28–34. Hence it is more beneficial to introduce measures which would reduce methane gas released especially from the man-made sources. Methanotrophs, or methane-oxidizing bacteria oxidizes methane, thereby reducing its concentration in the atmosphere. These bacteria thrive in environments where both methane and oxygen are present, such as wetlands, rice fields, ponds, and other water bodies. This bacterium is larger than most other bacteria, comparable in size to small yeast, and has a strict mesophilic nature, unable to grow above 37°C. This unique and potentially endemic methanotroph is crucial for future research in culture conditions and large-scale cultivation for reducing atmospheric methane levels. More research and experiments in the field should be done to promote such technologies. Ponded paddy is extensively grown in most of the countries in the Asian continent. Large scale application of this technology in paddy fields would appreciably reduce the methane emissions.

Estimated global anthropogenic methane emissions by source in 2020 were 27% from ruminant enteric emissions. Hence lot of research has been done to reduce methane emission from flatulent domesticated animals such as cows and sheep. Changes in the type of fodder such as shredded maize stem, lemon grass etc. reduce methane emissions to some extent. Asparagopsis seaweed as a livestock feed additive has reduced methane emissions by more than 80%. Development of 3-nitrooxyypropanol (3-NOP), now a commercial product - a feed additive, specifically interferes with the final step of methanogenesis. It exemplified the application of microbiological knowledge to mitigation of the methane gas emissions from domesticated ruminants. Recently some face masks for cows have been found to convert methane during eructation or belching from their mouth (which is about 93-95% of the total emissions) into carbon dioxide and water vapour. Some food supplements to the domestic animals mixed in the fodder are also seen to be effective in the reduction of methane gas during their digestion process.

Since methane is much more potent than carbon dioxide as explained above, more research should be initiated to find out activities and measures which would help in reducing methane emissions released from the ponded paddy fields and from the domesticated flatulent animals. These activities would be less capital intensive and could be easily adopted by all the developed, developing and underdeveloped countries of the world. The 2025 UN Climate Change Conference (UNFCCC COP30) would be convened in Brazil. **This important issue should be discussed in that conference. Research papers on the same should be invited for presentation and discussions in that conference. Ultimate aim should be to promote large scale adoption of all such possible measures to reduce methane emissions at the field level during this and the next decades.**

Increased percentage of these greenhouse gases (GHG) in the atmosphere obstructs the passage of heat energy of the solar rays which gets reflected into space from the earth surface. Gradually, during the last two-three centuries, concentration of GHG in the atmosphere had increased and it acted like a greenhouse to cause gradual rise in the temperature of the atmosphere close to earth. Hence this effect is called as 'Global warming'. It has caused changes in the climate of the earth to cause some adverse impacts on the Globe, which is called as 'Climate Change'. Climate change is causing adverse impacts on many development sectors and more so on the water sector and the agriculture sector. These two sectors are vital for achieving sustainable food and water security to the people now onwards. Intensity of such adverse impacts would further increase with the rise in global temperature.

Levels of GHG emissions (carbon emission equivalent) in the atmosphere have increased from about 280 ppm before the industrial revolution, to about 400 ppm by 2020, and it is rising at the rate of about 2 ppm/year at present. Global temperature has been estimated to have risen by about 0.6 degree Celsius during the last century. Global Warming is causing the snow from snow caps and the glaciers to melt at a faster rate, resulting in very slow rise in the sea level. Over the past 100 years, it seems to have risen by about 10 - 20 cm. Sea level would rise at a faster rate when ice in Antarctica and Greenland would melt due to global warming. It would submerge low lying land from Bangladesh, Maldives & some other countries and would affect functioning of some major ports in the world. Objective declared in the international conferences on Climate Change is to limit final carbon emissions to a conservative figure of 450 ppm and with a permissible rise in Global temperature by about 1 to 2 degrees Celsius, but preferably maximum up to 1.5 degrees Celsius.

Developing and underdeveloped countries argue that about 70% of the total carbon emissions as at present have been released by the developed countries and only because of that, they have reached their present state of development. Hence it is their primary responsibility to reduce rate of carbon emissions hereafter to zero as early as possible by deploying only non-conventional sources of energy from now onwards. Underdeveloped countries expect the same response from countries with emerging economies such as China, India, Brazil etc. They expect that the developed and developing countries should provide them the necessary financial and technical assistance to implement necessary changes which are capital intensive. It would then enable them to adopt measures which would have less carbon emissions and still would meet their rising energy demands, without jeopardising the rate of achieving their development hereafter. Due to such complexities in this respect, it has become a very contentious issue which has been deliberated in many international conferences on the climate change. All countries would have to commit to reduce the rate of carbon emissions to zero before the end of a specific year but in any case, before 2050. Their actual performance would have to be closely monitored through the international conferences. Then only there is a possibility to achieve the planned targets of reducing total carbon emissions.

Our earth and the living world have faced disastrous effects of some mass extinctions and ice ages in the past, which were the result of natural events including the last catastrophic mass extinction which occurred about 66 million years before. Resilience of the natural world had enabled it to restore it to the 'New normal' after every such mass extinction, though during next some millions of years after every such occasion. But 'Modern man' entered on the scene only about 12,000 years ago and commenced destruction of terrestrial ecosystems to meet food needs of his rising population. Then came the industrial revolution about 250 years before, followed by several activities associated with his modern living. All such actions have caused to increase 'Green House Gas' emissions on large scale to lead to 'Global Warming and Climate Change'. It is still possible to take coordinated actions by all countries of the world to confine adverse impacts of these actions within safe limits. Looking to these several actions of the 'modern man' during last twelve millennia, and inadequate actions on his part to mitigate the situation on a sustainable basis, a thought comes to mind whether we are heading very fast towards the last future man-made

'Holocene Extinction' or which can be more aptly called as the 'Anthropocene Extinction' of our 'Living World'.

**Conclusion -** Dark clouds of the catastrophic calamities as above are looming large on the horizon. All countries of the world would have to come together and act in unison like a family, to disperse them before they overshadow our living world. Lack of sustainable food and water security is threatening the underdeveloped countries, whereas adverse effects of degradation of aquatic ecosystems like rivers and reservoirs are being faced by most of the underdeveloped and developing countries. Developed countries should provide them the necessary financial assistance and technical guidance to enable them to mitigate those problems. However, in the near future all countries of the world cannot escape from the inevitable severe adverse impacts of the climate change, especially on the water sector and the agriculture sector. All countries should immediately take suitable measures to adapt to the situation to minimise their adverse impacts. All countries can certainly confine the rise in global temperature within the pre-decided acceptable safe limits, provided they all strictly reduce greenhouse gas emissions as planned, within the next two-three decades. Role of developed countries and countries with emerging economies is the most vital in this respect. If all countries of the world treat themselves as a part of the 'World Family' in helping their weak younger brothers to gain strength, all problems before the family would be solved. Let us hope that wisdom would prevail, and we would save our 'Living World' from leading to a man-made mass extinction.

**Vidyanand Ranade.**

# About the Author

Vidyanand Mahadeo Ranade, born in November 1937, graduated in civil engineering in 1960 in first class and stood 2nd in Pune University, India. He ranked first in the competitive examination and was selected for direct Class I post in the Irrigation Department, Govt. of Maharashtra. During service, he has looked after surveying, planning, design, construction, and operation of several Major, Medium, and Minor irrigation projects in the Maharashtra State (India). Completed 3-month course on 'Water Resource System Analysis, in USA in 1988. After 34 years of service, he retired as Secretary Irrigation Department, in November 1995. During service, he was involved in preparation of feasibility reports of ten major irrigation projects in the Maharashtra, Madhya Pradesh, Odisha, and West Bengal states for securing financial assistance from the World Bank. He has worked as a senior Consultant to National Irrigation Administration, Manila, Philippines for one and quarter year in 1981-82 & as a short-term Consultant to the World Bank, in India and Indonesia in 1993 & 1995.

After retirement, worked as Chairman & member of several committees appointed by the Govt. of Maharashtra and has worked as an Arbitrator/Adjudicator for settlement of 8 contractual disputes. Working as Chairman Upper Bhima Water Partnership since 2001, he had prepared a document viz., 'Vision for the development of Upper Bhima basin by 2025', which was presented in the first South Asia Water Forum 2002 in Kathmandu Nepal. Worked as a consulting engineer in Ethiopia for planning and design of an irrigation project for 6 months in 2006. Worked for 9 years (2005 to 2014) as member of Dam Safety Review Panel Maharashtra and for 13 years (2006 to 2019) as Member/Chairman Dam Safety Panel for Goa state Govt. in India. He has worked as a Consulting Engineer for Jain Irrigation Systems Ltd. Jalgaon, Maharashtra, for more than 20 years and learnt fully about Micro Irrigation systems. For them he had visited and studied 'Modern Irrigation Systems' in Italy & Spain, and reviewed irrigation projects in Kenya, Mozambique, Uganda & Bhutan.

He has participated and presented more than 10 papers/posters in the International Conferences /Symposia held in Brazil, Kenya, Pakistan(twice), Nepal, Sweden(twice), Russia, Australia(twice), China and Austria. Presented about 20 papers in National/State Conferences in

India. Delivered more than 400 lectures on technical subjects including Inter-Linking of Rivers in India, at various places in the country. Written a 152-page book titled 'Reservoirs and Environment' in 1992, based on study of environmental impacts of two major reservoirs in the Maharashtra state. Book on 'Watershed Development Technique and Technology' was written in 2004. A 345-page Book explaining 'All facets of Water as a Resource for Development', written in 'Marathi' (language of the state) was written and published in March 2021. It received an Award in the 'Environment Sector' from the Govt. of Maharashtra in 2022 and received two more awards from other Institutions.

Ph +91 20 24336076   Cell +91 98227 92798   Email vranade2003@yahoo.com

**Note** – *The Book has been printed in Black and White, including all Maps in the different chapters. However, it is felt that the 'Reader' would appreciate the contents of the maps better if they were in colour. Please send email to the author at the email-id vranade2003@yahoo.com, to get soft copies of the maps in colour.*

# Protect the Living World on Our Mother Earth
# References

| Sr.No. Report, Book, Article Reference | Name | Year |
|---|---|---|

## A) **Various Committee Reports** -

**1** Integrated State Water Plan for Godavari Basin in Maharashtra. Committee of Experts
Volume I – Executive Summary — Ch.- K.P.Bakshi
Volume II – Integrated Plan–Part I & II — Mem -V. M. Ranade — **6/2017**

**2** Report on Working of Irrigation Dev. Corporations and their conversion into River Basin Agencies — Study Group, Ch.-Suresh Kumar, Mem-V.M. Ranade — **6/2016**

**3** Report on recommended remedial measures for Temghar dam, near Pune — Expert Committee, Ch.-V.M. Ranade — **6/2016**

**4** Report on Special Investigations about Irrigation Sector, Maharashtra — Special Investigation Team
Vol.1 – Main Report — Ch.- Dr. M.A. Chitale
Vol.2 – Appendices, Maps — Mem – V.M. Ranade — **2/2014**

**5** Optimum & Equitable use of Water Resource in Maharashtra State, Committee — Ch.V.M. Ranade — **10/2010**

**6** Irrigation backlog of Drought Prone Talukas in Maharashtra State, Committee — Ch. Ranganathan, Mem - V.M. Ranade — **11/2009**

**7** Report on causes & remedial measures for Landslide at Ghatghar pumped storage scheme — Expert Committee, Ch.- A.K. Shenolikar, Mem -V.M. Ranade — **5/2006**

**8** Maharashtra Water & Irrigation Commission Vol. 1-3 – Sub-basin-wise Planning, Management & Supporting information — Ch. Dr. M.A. Chitale, V.M. Ranade contributed to many chapters. — **9/1999**

(Ch. - Chairman, Mem. - Member)

## B) Books written by Vidyanand Ranade –

1 Written a 345-page Book on 'Multifaceted Water Resource'
in 'Marathi' - my mother tongue -     'पाण्या तुझा रंग कसा?'     **3/2021**

2 *"सुभाषित-रत्न मंजुषा"* संकलन केलेल्या 211 संस्कृत सुभाषितांचा

अंतर्भाव असलेले व स्वतः प्रकाशित केलेले पुस्तक

(Book is a collection of 211 traditional age old 'verses of wisdom'
in Sanskrit language)     **5/2012**

3 Written 50 articles (1000-1200 words each) on the subject
*'Water'* in 'Marathi' In the magazine 'Uttishtat Jagrat', Pune     **6/2004 to 1/2009**

4 Written a book on *'Watershed Development - Technique
and Technology'* in Marathi     **8/2004**

5 *"Vision for the development of Upper Bhima Basin by 2025"*
Report based on study of UBB, in the Krishna basin, Maharashtra.
Presented in the First South Asia Water Forum, Kathmandu, Nepal     **2/2002**

6 *"Reservoirs and Environment"* – 153-page Book based on
field study of environmental impacts on account of
Majalgaon & Terna Dam-Canal projects in Maharashtra State     **1-1992**

7 *"Manual on Design of Canals and Canal Structures"*
– 4 volumes, 500 pages, for National Irrigation Administration,
Manila, Philippines.     **11/1981 to 3/1983**

## C) Papers, Posters presented in the international - National Conferences/Water Week Festivals. and Articles, written by Vidyanand Ranade –

1 *'Computer applications in Water Resources Development'*,
Paper presented in the 16th Annual Convention of
Computer Society of India - CSI-81in New Delhi     **3/1981**

2 *"Resettlement and Rehabilitation policy in the
Maharashtra State (India), Case study of Majalgaon Irrigation
Project"* - Paper in the 15-day Workshop on 'Resettlement

on account of Power Projects' in Florianopolis, Brazil **5/1992**

**3** *"Jayakwadi Lake – A case study of improving habitat for Birds & Environment near the Dam"*, Paper accepted for National conference held in Trivendrum, Kerala, India. **1993**

**4** *'Flow Irrigation to Micro Irrigation – A journey on the path of Prosperity and equity, through optimum use of scarce Water Resource',* Paper read in the International Conference on Micro and Sprinkler Irrigation Systems at Jalgaon, India. **2-2000**

**5** *"Environmental effects of dams"* paper presented in the International Workshop on 'Ecosystem Impacts of Large dams' by the United Nations Environment Programme, Nairobi–Kenya. **12- 2000**

**6** Keynote address on "*Watershed Development in Hard Rock Area"* in the XIX Annual Convention & Seminar on National Watershed Development, by the Association of Hydrologists of India, Vishakhapatnam, at Aurangabad, India. **12-2000**

**7** *"Genesis & performance evaluation of Watershed Development works in India- with specific reference to Peninsular Drought Prone Area",* Paper presented in the Second South Asia Water Forum, Islamabad, Pakistan. **12-2002**

**8** Article, *"Future trends in Water Resource Development in India to strengthen Rural Economy through development of Irrigated Agriculture"* published in the 'Artha Vijnana' Vol XLV, Journal of Gokhale Institute of Politics & Economics, Pune, India. **3/6-2003**

**9** Poster presentation on *"Modern management in the Upper Bhima Basin in rain-shadow area of the Peninsular India"* in the 13th Stockholm Water Symposium held in Stockholm, Sweden. **8-2003**

**10** Poster presentation on *"Watershed Development approach - A sustainable development alternative for rain-fed cultivators"* in the 14th Stockholm Water Symposium held in Stockholm, Sweden. **8-2004**

**11** *"Integrated Water Resource Management – A case study of*

*an Interstate River Basin from Peninsular India"* Paper accepted,
for MTERM International Conference, Bangkok AIT, Thailand. **6-2005**

**12** Poster presentation on *"Urban-Rural conflict in sharing Water Resources and possible solutions for water-scarce Upper Bhima Basin in Peninsular India"* in the 8th International River Symposium, Brisbane, Australia. **9-2005**

**13** *"Interlinking of Rivers in India"* Paper presented in the 2nd International Yellow River Forum held in Zhengzhou, China. **10-2005**

**14** *"Integrated Management of Droughts and Floods"*, Paper for National Seminar on Integrated Management Issues, New Delhi, India. **12-2005**

**15** *"Environmental flows in water-scarce River basins in Peninsular India"* – Paper read in the 9th International River Symposium 2006, Brisbane, Australia. **9-2006**

**16** *"Lake Management – Issues and Challenges, A case study of Ujjani Reservoir in Maharashtra (India)"*, Paper published in 'World Lake Vision, Action Report' Kusatsu city Shiga, Japan **2-2007**

**17** *"Integrated Lake Basin management (ILBM) – A case study of Yeshwantsagar (Ujjani), Maharashtra, India"* – Joint Paper for International Conference on Integrated Lake Basin Management. **Year 2008**

**18** *"Ensuring social progress through water resource Development in Maharashtra State"* Article in 'Marathi' published, in the Book titled as 'Water – Trends and Actions for desirable future. **7-2013**

**20** *"Adaptation of Water Sector to Global Warming and Climate Change"*, Paper accepted for National Seminar (NSCCIWRS) held in Ahmedabad, India. **11-2013**

**21** *"जलसंपदेचे संवर्धन"* हा लेख महाराष्ट्र प्रदूषण नियंत्रण मंडळ आणि लोकसत्ता यांनी संपादित केलेल्या 'ग्लोबल वॉर्मिंग – व्याप्ती, आव्हान व मार्ग' या पुस्तकात अंतर्भूत (Article on *'Development of Water Resource'* Published in Book 'Global Warming – Scope, Challenges, and ways', Edited by 'Loksatta' Daily Newspaper in Marathi, in Maharashtra. **Year 2013**

**22** *"Vision for the development of Upper Bhima Basin through Upper Bhima Water Partnership"* Paper presented in the All India Conference on JAL-PATHIK, at Aurangabad, India.   **8-2015**

**23** *"Governance in the Water Sector"* Article published in *The Journal of Governance*, IC Center for Governance, New Delhi, India.   **1-2017**

**24** *"Governance in the Water Sector"* Article published in the Book series Springer Water, in the Book titled as 'W*ater Governance: Challenges and Prospects'*   **Year 2019**

**25** *"Intra-Regional Development Disparities: Strategy for Development of Water-stressed Regions in Maharashtra"* Presentation in the National Conference on Intra-Regional Development Disparities: by GIPE, IDF, MSEPP & PIC, Pune, India.   **12-2021**

**26** *"Surface and Ground Water Resources of Maharashtra: Status, Management, Governance Issues, and Future Policy"* Article Published in Special Publication of the Geological Society of India No. 12   **Year 2022**

**27** *"Intra-Regional Development Disparities: Virtual Regions Strategy for Development of Tribal Communities and Water-stressed Regions in Maharashtra, Andhra Pradesh, and Telangana"* coauthor (Sheela Bhide, Vidyanand Ranade and Kiran Kulkarni) of the Article published in 'Review of Market Integration, Development Foundation, SAGE Publications.   **5-2022**

# Shortforms used in the Book

| | |
|---|---|
| AQI | - Air Quality Index |
| BC | - Before Christ |
| bcm | - billion cubic meters, equal to - cubic kilo meter |
| BOD | - Bio-chemical Oxygen Demand |
| BOOT | - Build-Own-Operate-Transfer |
| CBIP | - Central Board of Irrigation and Power |
| CC | - Climate Change |
| CFCs | - Chlorofluorocarbons |
| CGWA | - Central Ground Water Authority |
| CGWB | - Central Ground Water Board |
| COD | - Chemical Oxygen Demand |
| COP | - Conference of Parties |
| CSIR | - Council for Scientific and Industrial Research |
| cukm | - cubic kilo meters, equal to - bcm |
| cumecs | - cubic meters per second |
| cusecs | - cubic feet per second |
| CWPC | - Central Water and Power Commission |
| CWR | - Crop Water Requirement |
| ETP | - Effluent Treatment Plant |
| FAR | - First Assessment Report |
| GCM | - General Circulation Model |
| GHG | - Green House Gases |
| GoI | - Govt. of India |
| GoM | - Govt. of Maharashtra |
| GSDA | - Groundwater Surveys & Development Agency |
| GTS | - Great Trigonometrical Survey |
| GW | - Global Warming |

| | |
|---|---|
| GW | - Ground Water |
| GW & CC | – Global Warming and Climate Change |
| GWP | - Global Water Partnership |
| GWT | - Ground Water Table |
| IBWT | - Inter Basin Water Transfer |
| ICID | - International Commission on Irrigation and Drainage |
| ICOLD | - International Commission on Large Dams |
| ICRISAT | - International Crops Research Institute for Semi-Arid Tropics |
| ICWE | - International Conference on Water and the Environment |
| IITM | - Indian Institute of Tropical Meteorology |
| ILEC | - International Lake Environment Committee |
| ILR | - Interlinking of Rivers (in India) |
| IPCC | - Intergovernmental Panel on Climate Change |
| IRBO | - Interstate River Basin Organizations |
| IRF | - International River Foundation |
| ISWP | - Integrated State Water Plan |
| IWA | - International Water Association |
| IWMI | - International Water Management Institute |
| IWRA | - International Water Resources Association |
| IWRM | - Integrated Water Resources Management |
| mcum | - million cubic meters |
| mcumecs | - million cubic meters per second |
| MIDC | - Maharashtra Industrial Development Corporation |
| MIS | - Micro Irrigation System |
| MoU | - Memorandum of Understanding |
| MMISF Act | - Maharashtra Management of Irrigation Systems by Farmers Act |
| MWRRA | - Maharashtra Water Resource Regulatory Authority |
| mya | - million years ago |
| NDCs | - Nationally Determined Contributions |
| NGO | - Non-Govt. Organisation |

| | |
|---|---|
| NIDM | - National Institute of Disaster Management |
| NRLD | - National Register of Large Dams |
| NWDA | - National Water Development Agency |
| ODS | - Ozone-Depleting Substances |
| PAP | - Project Affected People |
| PIL | - Public Interest Litigation |
| ppm | - parts per million |
| PRC | - People's Republic of China |
| RCC | - Reinforced Cement Concrete |
| RCPR | - Rain and Cloud Physics Research |
| RWDT | - River Water Disputes Tribunal |
| SIWI | - Stockholm International Water Institute |
| sqkm | - square kilo meter |
| STP | - Sewage Treatment Plant |
| SWC | - State Water Council |
| UN | - United Nations |
| UNCED | - United Nations Conference on Environment and Development |
| UNDP | - United Nations Development Programme |
| UNEP | - United Nations Environment Programme |
| UNFCCC | - United Nations Framework Convention on Climate Change |
| UNO | - United Nations Organisation |
| USAID | - United States Agency for International Development |
| UV rays | - Ultraviolet rays |
| WALMI | - Water and Land Management Institute |
| WB | - World Bank |
| WCD | - World Commission on Dams |
| WMO | - World Meteorological Organization |
| WRD | - Water Resource Department |
| WRD | - Water Resource Development |

WUA       - Water User's Association
WWC       - World Water Council
YRCC      - Yellow River Conservancy Commission

www.ingramcontent.com/pod-product-compliance
Ingram Content Group UK Ltd.
Pitfield, Milton Keynes, MK11 3LW, UK
UKHW060214240426
12048UKWH00031BB/1723